THE DIRECTORY OF
British Tram Depots

Keith Turner, Shirley Smith & Paul Smith

Open car No.50 of 1901 outside the Kinver Light Railway's **Hyde Depot** in the early 1900s. The car, like the depot, was normally only operational during the summer months. The building was later removed and utilized as a cattle shed.
Len Dunn Kinver Photographic Archive. (See Page 54)

OPC
Oxford Publishing Co

CONTENTS

Artwork & Design by **Paul Smith**

All tram shed maps reproduced by kind permission
of
The Syndics of Cambridge University

This book is dedicated to Carol Smith

First published 2001

ISBN 0 86093 557 4

All rights reserved. No part of this book may be reproduced or transmitted in any form or by any means, electronic or mechanical, including photocopying, recording or by any information storage and retrieval system, without permission from the Publisher in writing.

© Keith Turner, Shirley Smith & Paul Smith 2001

Published by Oxford Publishing Co

an imprint of Ian Allan Publishing Ltd, Hersham, Surrey KT12 4RG.
Printed by Ian Allan Printing Ltd, Hersham, Surrey KT12 4RG.

Code: 0107/A1

Front cover, top: Inside Blackpool's Blundell Street depot with cars awaiting scrapping or rebuilding; the rear of the shed has been screened off for use as an ambulance garage. November 1979. R. J. Buckley

Front cover, bottom: Inside the preserved section of the Pacific Road car shed, Birkenhead, 1999. Jan Dobrzynski

Back cover, top: The derelict Johnstown depot of the Wrexham & District system, 2000. Nick Pigott

Back cover, bottom: Aberdeen's former Constitution Street combined tram and omnibus depot, 2000. M. Donnison

CORRIGENDA & ADDITIONAL INFORMATION

Since finalising the artwork, the following corrections and additional information have come to light regarding the London tram system.

Fulwell: Became trolleybus depot in 1935.

Hanwell: First trolleybuses operated on 15th November 1936. Closed 12th December 1936.

Stonebridge Park: Closed 5th July 1936. Closed as trolleybus depot 2nd January 1962.

Sutton: Closed as omnibus garage 28th January 1964.

Chiswick Depot: Used as bus depot in 1935/6 and trolleybus depot in 1937.

Clapham High Street: Rebuilt depot building used as Museum of British Transport 1961-1973.

Hendon Depot: In 1909, it was the site of the first trial of trolleybus equipment in Britain. Was used as tram repair works after closing as running shed, finally closed 5th July 1936. After service as tram and trolleybus depots, was used for dismantling both types of vehicle.

Cressy Road: Tram storage ceased by 1950 when it passed to BRS as a lorry depot.

Holloway Car Shed: Trolleybuses housed from 6th March 1938. Closed to trolleybuses 25th April 1961.

Finchley Depot: Trolleybuses first operated on 2nd August 1936.

Camberwell Depots: Omnibuses first operated in 1950.

Telford Avenue Depot: Buses first operated on 7th January 1951.

Poplar Car Shed: Closed 1st June 1940

Hackney Depot: Closed to trams on 10th September 1939. At one stage used as Go-kart circuit but now again an omnibus garage (as Clapton Garage).

Edmonton: First trolleybuses operated on 16th October 1938, First buses operated on 25th April 1961 and fully became omnibus garage on 19th July 1961. Closed on 1st February 1986.

Wood Green Depot: Buses first operated on 26th April 1961 and fully became omnibus garage on 20th November 1961.

Plumstead: Some tram track remained in the entrance from Lakedale Road at least until the 1980s.

The **Club House Depot** on the Murcar Tramway with the Murcar Golf Club House visible beyond.

Courtesy RA Griffiths (See Page 156)

• THE DIRECTORY OF •
BRITISH TRAM DEPOTS

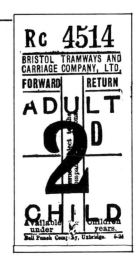

PREFACE

*"What is that, my dear Mama
that looks like Strawberry Jam?"
"Hush Hush dear child, that's poor Papa ...
.... run over by a tram!"*

Although the tramway depots of Britain have been truly astonishing in their diversity, all had but one primary purpose: to protect the tramway's rolling stock, both when not in service and whilst undergoing repair or repainting. The very first urban tramways, dating from the 1860s, used single- or double-deck horse-drawn tramcars and, whilst a short line or small system could manage with just one depot, it was often judged a better use of resources to provide depots at the ends of long routes in order to cut down on time wasted in moving men and cars around the system at the beginning and end of each working day.

In its simplest form, a horsecar depot could be just a small yard, covered or uncovered, located off the main highway and with an associated stable block. Quite often, for reasons of ready availability, these were existing hostelry or omnibus yards with stables shared or adapted to house tramcars. Occasionally, to cut costs to a minimum, an access track was not even bothered with, the lightweight cars being drawn or manhandled off the tramway and into their yard at the end of the day! Other depots were purpose-built, especially on the larger systems, and housed the tramway's own granaries, smithies, workshops, offices and the like.

With the advent of steam and cable tramways in the 1880s and 1890s, their special requirements meant that purpose-built structures were definitely the order of the day: steam tramways usually needed both locomotive and carriage sheds, whilst cable tramways had to have a depot to house the winding gear. The same was true for the electric tramways which arrived in ever-increasing numbers from the 1880s onwards whilst, at the same time, economies of scale and the faster speed of the cars meant that all but the largest systems could make do with just one central depot. In turn, the sheer size of the larger networks meant that one depot, the "works", could often be devoted to the assembly and repair of the tramcar fleet and not be utilized as a running shed. (Such dedicated works have not been included in this Directory.)

As might be expected, the smallest and most basic systems tended to cut costs by roofing existing yards, or by erecting cheap timber or corrugated iron sheds. (Many operators were also reluctant to invest large amounts of money in buildings since, under the provisions of the 1870 Tramways Act, local authorities were given the option of purchasing tramways within their boundaries at a later date.) In common though with many late-Victorian and Edwardian institutions, the larger tramway companies and local authority operators took a great deal of pride in themselves and their works, and their buildings reflected this. Ornate stone and brickwork structures were the norm, with their ownership legends writ large above the entrance for all to see, which is one reason why so many have survived half a century or more after the closure of the tramways they served: many were pressed into use as motor omnibus or trolleybus garages, whilst others were sold off for a range of commercial uses (a new life as a car showroom being a common fate!). It is hoped now that readers will, through the use of this Directory, help to keep on record the continuing story of those still standing. A word of warning: if a date is displayed prominently above the doorway, this is usually the year that construction began, not necessarily the date that the depot opened.

A depot's internal track layout was influenced by a number of factors, the three principal ones being the size of the car fleet (existing or envisaged), the size and shape of the available site and the ease of accessibility. In practice, the result was a depot of one of three types: a dead-ended shed (with access at one end only), a through-road shed (with access from both ends) or a combination of both. Additional features to be found in, or by, a typical depot included offices, staff rest room, passengers' waiting room, smithy, paint shop, machine shop, yard storage sidings and stores of all kinds.

After World War I, when the large city systems were still expanding, a certain degree of rationalization was the order of the day with some smaller, older depots being closed down and larger, newer ones taking their place. These were often built of concrete and steel with provision for those two afore-mentioned modes of public transport that put paid to the tramcar almost everywhere in the years either side of World War II: the trolleybus and motor omnibus.

Today the wheel has come full circle and the tramway is experiencing something of a revival with major, state-of-the-art systems constructed during the 1980s and 1990s in Sheffield, Manchester, the West Midlands and Croydon, and with more to come! Brief details of the storage sidings utilized by these systems can be found in the Appendix.

The aim of *The Directory of British Tram Depots* is to record the location and basic details of every tramway depot, temporary as well as permanent, that has existed in Great Britain. It is hoped that all such sites have been listed, though the authors are only too well aware from similar research endeavours in the past that one or two may have escaped their notice. (In this respect, Glasgow has proved especially problematical.) If this is the case, any information regarding those overlooked, as well as further information regarding those recorded, would be gratefully received. To date, over 600 have been identified, ranging from tiny open yards tucked away behind public houses for storing a couple of horse trams overnight to massive, purpose-built structures capable of housing and maintaining a whole fleet of electric double-deckers. No similar listing has, to the best of the authors' knowledge, been compiled before and it is hoped that this *Directory* will fill a major gap in the historical account of Britain's tramways.

Keith Turner, Kidderminster

Shirley Smith
&
Paul Smith
Kings Heath, Birmingham

NOTES ON THE USE OF THIS BOOK

The three countries have been divided into pre-war counties and conurbations, each containing details of those depots located within the boundaries. (As the Greater London section encompasses a large conurbation and contains a considerable number of sites, a further method of sub-division is employed and consists of sectioning the area into National Grid 10km [6.214 miles] squares.) An Index to the counties and conurbations can be found on Page 1 and to the Tram Depots between Pages v and xiv.

The basic information given for each depot is:

Name of Depot: Usually the depot's official working name.

Location: A general description of the location with, where known, an 8-digit National Grid reference for the building.

Opened: The opening date, operator, and any subsequent changes of ownership during the depot's existence. (*The date given is assumed to be that on which the system, or part of the system, opened for public service.*)

Traction System: Methods employed on the tramway, or part of the system, during the depot's existence.

Gauge: Gauge(s) utilized during the depot's existence.

Description: A general description of the building(s) and track layout, where known, and any alterations made to the depot. The abbreviation "TS" indicates "track straighthouse".

Closed: Closure date and subsequent use of the building(s). (*Some dates are those when routes served by the depot ceased operating public services. Further updated information regarding the site may be found in the Tram Depot Index.*)

Each entry is also accompanied by a 25in/1 mile Ordnance Survey map, where possible contemporary to the existence of the depot but otherwise showing the location of the site. Where the tramway was also considered to be a light railway the depots are also covered and coded in *"The Directory of British Engine Sheds and Principal Locomotive Servicing Points"* Volumes 1 (0 86093 542 2) and 2 (0 86093 548 5) by Roger Griffiths and Paul Smith [OPC 1999 & 2000].

Although preferable, it has not been possible to arrange each depot in alphabetical order within each section. In order to accommodate all the sites within an economically viable book a "best-fit" approach has had to be undertaken in order to conserve space, and the Tram Depot Index should be consulted if difficulty is encountered.

ACKNOWLEDGEMENTS

Amongst the individuals who have given invaluable assistance in the accumulation of information for this volume, may we thank:

Stan Berry, RJ Buckley, Chris Bush, Margaret Connolly at the Mitchell Library in Glasgow, Peter Davey, Jan Dobrzynski, Michael and Yvonne Donnison, Len Dunn, Andrew Farthing of Southport Library, Noel Hanson, Paul Jackson of South Yorkshire PTE, Margaret, Neil DG Mackenzie, Peter Turner, David Voice, John Williams and Douglas Yelland.

We would also particularly like to thank Tony Rawlings, Anne Taylor, Karen Amies, Andrew Alexander and Ian Walker at the Cambridge University Map Library for their enthusiastic assistance in helping us to compile a full set of maps of the depots.

A debt of gratitude is, as always, owed to those recorders and historians of the tramway scene, past and present, without whose earlier diligence a book such as this would have been impossible to produce.

The former Dunfermline & District Tramways **St Leonard's Depot** (*far left*) with the later omnibus garage extension, still in use.
Neil DG Mackenzie (See Page 154)

THE DIRECTORY OF
BRITISH TRAM DEPOTS

A 1930s view of the terminus at **Mill Street Station**, Wantage. A coal wagon stands on the shed road to **Depot No.2** and, immediately to the right, a petrol railcar can be seen parked in front of **Depot No.1** which by now had been sheeted-in with corrugated iron and employed as a set of lock up garages.

Courtesy RA Griffiths (See Page 13)

INDEX TO COUNTIES & CONURBATIONS

Track Diagrams are Scaled at 25in/1 mile

0 FEET 100 200 300 400 500 600

Birmingham Corporation tramcars Nos 438 and 450, built in 1912-13, passing **Moseley Road Depot**, the building on the far right immediately behind the office block.

Courtesy Andrew Maxam (See Page 55)

The southern end of Birmingham's **Kyotts Lake Road Depot & Works** after the closure of the tramway system. The single-track entrance was behind the railings.

Courtesy Andrew Maxam (See Page 56)

The most recent loss from the dwindling list of Britain's surviving tram sheds is Birmingham's **Kyotts Lake Road Depot & Works**, here being demolished after the disastrous fire of February 9th, 2001. *K Turner (See Page 56)*

The grandly-named Victoria Tramways Station in Bristol, formerly **Victoria Street** horse tramway depot, it was refurbished following electrification of the system.
Courtesy Peter Davey Photograph Collection
(See Page 47)

The impressive **Swadlincote Depot** and power station on the Burton & Ashby Light Railways system. *Courtesy Lens of Sutton (See Page 75)*

Inside Blackburn Corporation's electric car depot at **Intack.** *Courtesy Lens of Sutton (See Page 79)*

Blundell Street Depot in Blackpool originated on the north side of Rigby Road with later extensions being built on the south side of this road. As the original shed went out of use these extensions became known as **Rigby Road Depot**. The utilitarian, but commodious, building is seen here in the 1970s, by then a still functioning relic of another age. *K Turner (See Page 90)*

Rutland Street [1st] **Depot** at sometime in the 1920s with a small saddle tank locomotive parked on the shed road.
Courtesy RA Griffiths (See Page 134)

A general view of the station, with a steam train awaiting departure, and the depot at **Glynceiriog GVT Station**. *Courtesy RA Griffiths (See Page 137)*

The Great Orme Tramway's **Victoria Station** train shed at Llandudno in 1974 (when it was entitled a railway). Between 1902, when the line opened, and 1904 when the train shed was built, the section's lower car was stored in the open in the Victoria Hotel pub yard immediately above the shed. *K Turner (See Page 140)*

The **Halfway (Lower) Depot** tram shed at the top of the Lower Section of the Great Orme Tramway in 1974. The track remnant in the foreground once connected the two sections of line. *K Turner (See Page 140)*

The **Summit Station Depot** and station building at the top of the Upper Section of the Great Orme Tramway in 1974. *K Turner (See Page 140)*

The Llandudno & Colwyn Bay Electric Railway's depot in **Tramway Avenue**, Colwyn with No.9 (ex-Bournemouth No.108 of 1921) in service and two ex-Accrington single-deckers on shed.
Author's Collection (See Page 138)

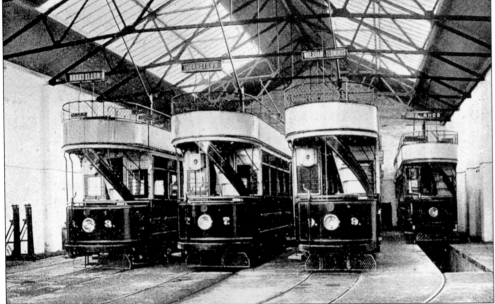

Inside the Wrexham & District's electric car depot at **Johnstown**. *Author's Collection (See Page 138)*

The tiny terminal **Crossgates Depot** tram shed built on to a row of cottages at Inchture Village Station, converted after closure of the branch into a cottage itself. *Neil DG Mackenzie (See Page 155)*

THE DIRECTORY OF
BRITISH TRAM DEPOTS

PART ONE
ENGLAND

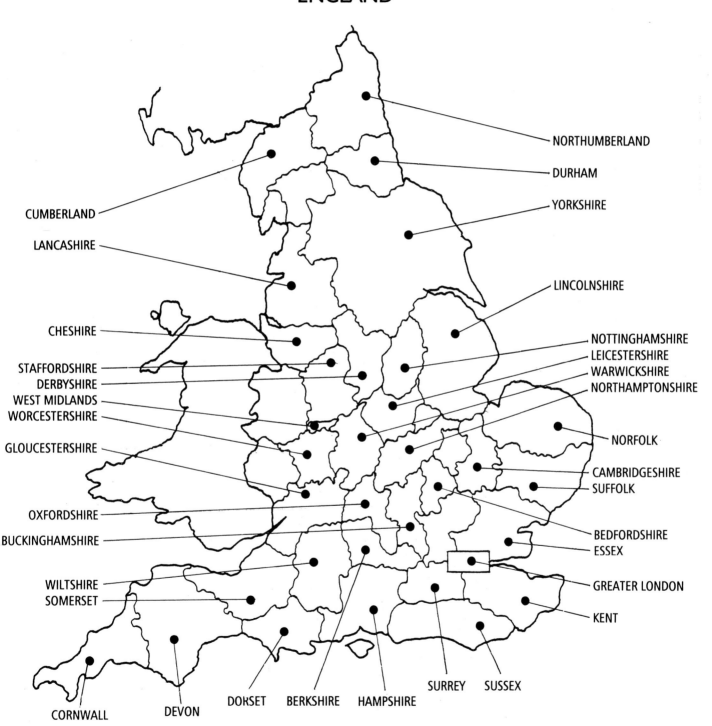

NORTHUMBERLAND

DURHAM

YORKSHIRE

CUMBERLAND

LANCASHIRE

LINCOLNSHIRE

CHESHIRE

NOTTINGHAMSHIRE
LEICESTERSHIRE
STAFFORDSHIRE
WARWICKSHIRE
DERBYSHIRE
NORTHAMPTONSHIRE
WEST MIDLANDS
WORCESTERSHIRE

NORFOLK

GLOUCESTERSHIRE

CAMBRIDGESHIRE
SUFFOLK

OXFORDSHIRE

BUCKINGHAMSHIRE

BEDFORDSHIRE
ESSEX

WILTSHIRE
GREATER LONDON
SOMERSET

KENT

CORNWALL   DEVON   DORSET   BERKSHIRE   HAMPSHIRE   SURREY   SUSSEX

ALL OTHER COUNTIES: NO DEPOTS

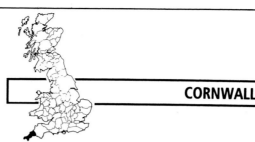

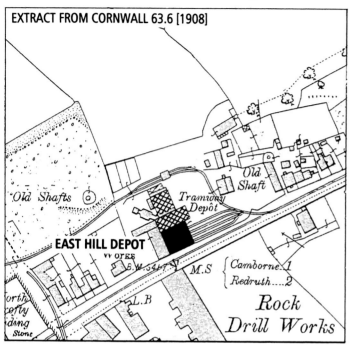

EXTRACT FROM CORNWALL 63.6 [1908]

EAST HILL DEPOT

CARN BREA

East Hill

Location: At SW66394133, on the north side of Trevenson Road, west of Pool and between Camborne & Redruth.
Opened: November 7th, 1902 by the Camborne & Redruth Tramway.
Traction System: Overhead Electric.
Gauge: 3ft 6in.
Description: A stone built 4TS dead ended tram shed.
Closed: Following the withdrawal of passenger services on September 29th, 1927 the depot remained open for the tramway's two freight locomotives, which were housed in a small wooden extension shed on the northernmost shed road. This service ceased in August 1934 and by 1972 the building was being utilized by the South Western Electricity Board, successor to the tramway's parent company, the Urban Electric Supply Co. Ltd.

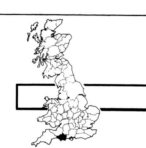

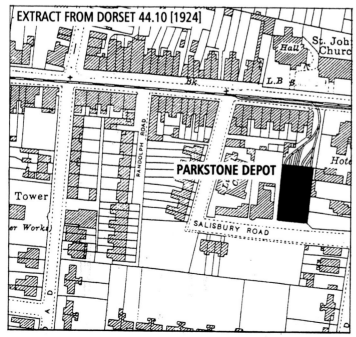

EXTRACT FROM DORSET 44.10 [1924]

PARKSTONE DEPOT

POOLE

Parkstone Depot

Location: At SZ04359208 on the south side of Ashley Road, west of Bournemouth.
Opened: April 6th, 1901 by the Poole & District Electric Traction Co. Ltd, purchased by Poole Corporation in 1905 and leased to Bournemouth Corporation. It was taken over by the Hants & Dorset Motor Services Ltd in 1935.
Traction System: Overhead Electric.
Gauge: 3ft 6in.
Description: A 7TS dead ended tram shed.
Closed: June 7th, 1935 and further utilized as an omnibus garage.

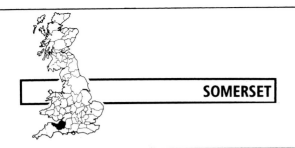

BATH

Fosse Way

Location: At ST97576588, behind the Porter Butt Hotel on the London Road Section of the Fosse Way in Kensington.

Opened: December 24th, 1880 by the Bath Tramways Co. Ltd and purchased by Bath Corporation in 1902.

Traction System: Horse.

Gauge: 4ft.

Description: A 1TS dead ended tram shed and stables.

Closed: July 25th, 1902 and demolished in the 1970s.

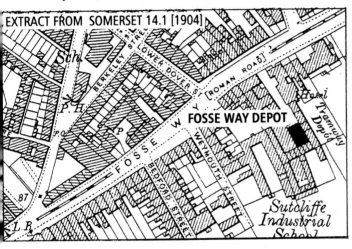

EXTRACT FROM SOMERSET 14.1 [1904]

Walcot Street

Location: At ST75136524 on the east side of Walcot Street, north of Bath city centre.

Opened: January 2nd, 1904 by Bath Electric Tramways and taken over by the Bristol Tramways & Carriage Co. Ltd in 1936.

Traction System: Overhead Electric.

Gauge: 4ft 8.5in.

Description: A brick built 8TS dead ended tram shed sited adjacent to the company's generating station.

Closed: May 6th, 1939. By 1960 it had been gutted to become a factory and, later, a storage garage for cars. In 1992 it was utilized as a Saturdays Antiques Market.

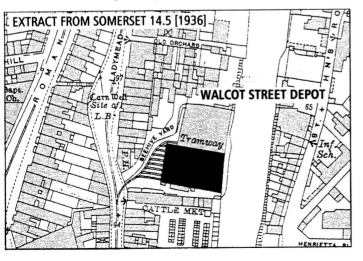

EXTRACT FROM SOMERSET 14.5 [1936]

TAUNTON

East Reach

Location: At ST23752483 on the north side of East Reach, east of Taunton town centre.

Opened: August 21st, 1901 by The Taunton & West Somerset Electric Railways & Tramways Co. Ltd (later the Taunton Electric Traction Co. Ltd).

Traction System: Overhead Electric.

Gauge: 3ft 6in.

Description: A brick and corrugated iron built 3TS dead ended tram shed.

Closed: May 28th, 1921 and subsequently utilized as a bus garage. By 1975 it was in use as a warehouse.

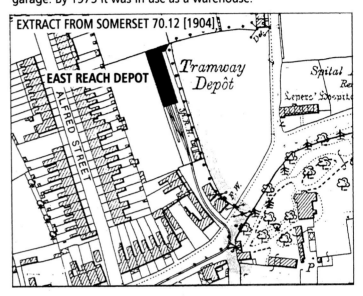

EXTRACT FROM SOMERSET 70.12 [1904]

WESTON SUPER MARE

Locking Road

Location: At ST33506162, on the south side of Locking Road, east of Weston super Mare town centre.

Opened: May 13th, 1902 by the Weston super Mare & District Electric Supply Co. Ltd.

Traction System: Overhead Electric.

Gauge: 4ft 8.5in.

Description: Constructed in corrugated iron on concrete base walls, it was originally a 6TS dead ended tram shed. Two tracks were removed after the car fleet was reduced in 1902 and one was re-instated in 1927.

Closed: April 17th, 1937 and by 1960 it had been incorporated into the adjacent electricity works.

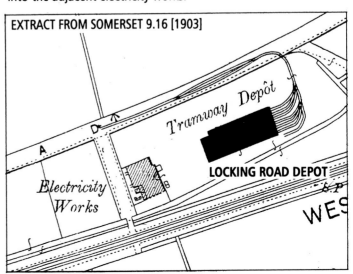

EXTRACT FROM SOMERSET 9.16 [1903]

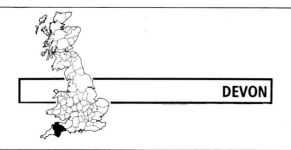

DEVON

PLYMOUTH

Camel's Head Depot

Location: At SX45185750, on the east side of Wolseley Road, in Camel's Head.

Opened: June 26th, 1901 by the Devonport & District Tramways Co. Ltd.

Traction System: Overhead Electric.

Gauge: 3ft 6in.

Description: A 2TS dead ended tram shed built in corrugated iron.

Closed: In 1903 and utilized, until 1927, as a store for defective tramcars. Subsequently used as garage but later demolished and the site re-developed.

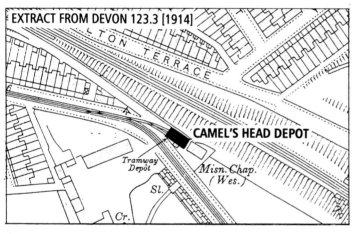

EXTRACT FROM DEVON 123.3 [1914]

CAMEL'S HEAD DEPOT

Compton Depot

Location: At SX48875654, on the north side of Lower Compton Road, Compton.

Opened: April 3rd, 1893 by Plymouth Corporation.

Traction System: Horse (until April 4th, 1901) and then Overhead Electric.

Gauge: 3ft 6in.

Description: A brick built 4TS dead ended tram shed. It was converted to electric working by raising the height of the roof.

Closed: Officially on April 10th, 1932 by which time it was in use to store tramcars awaiting scrapping and for working football specials. It was sold to the Plymouth Transport Company in March 1933 and utilized as a lorry garage until 1968. It was subsequently demolished and the site is now occupied by flats.

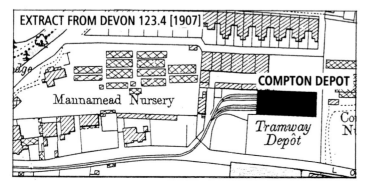

EXTRACT FROM DEVON 123.4 [1907]

COMPTON DEPOT

Manor Lane Depot

Location: At SX46875449, on the west side of Manor Street, north of Union Street, in Stonehouse.

Opened: March 18th, 1872 by the Plymouth, Stonehouse & Devonport Tramways Co. Ltd.

Traction System: Horse.

Gauge: 4ft 8.5in.

Description: A medium sized tram shed with one access road.

Closed: In 1901 for reconstruction of the system and never re-opened as a depot. In 1960 it was being utilized as a garage and, by 1990, as a car repair depot.

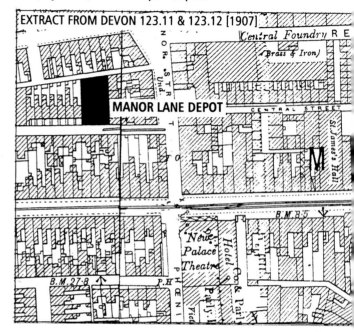

EXTRACT FROM DEVON 123.11 & 123.12 [1907]

MANOR LANE DEPOT

Millbay Depot

Location: At SX47135403, on the east side of West Hoe Road, in Millbay.

Opened: November 4th, 1884 by the Plymouth, Devonport & District Tramways Co. Ltd. The company went into liquidation in 1885 and was taken over by the Plymouth Tramways Co. Ltd in 1886 with horse working. Taken over by Plymouth Corporation in 1892.

Traction System: Steam (until 1884) and then Horse.

Gauge: 3ft 6in.

Description: A 4TS dead ended tram shed with 2 access roads radiating from a small turntable.

Closed: Temporarily in 1884 when the Plymouth, Devonport & District Tramways Co, Ltd ceased operations and re-opened in 1886. Finally closed on June 22nd, 1907 and then utilized as Tuckett's Sweet Factory until destroyed in the blitz in 1941. Site now occupied by flats.

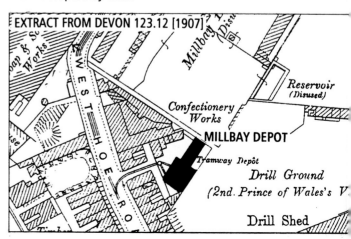

EXTRACT FROM DEVON 123.12 [1907]

MILLBAY DEPOT

Market Street Depot

Location: At SX46405444, on the east side of Market Street, north of Edgcumbe Street, Stonehouse.

Opened: November 18th, 1901 by the Plymouth, Stonehouse & Devonport Tramways Co. Ltd and taken over by Plymouth Corporation on July 1st, 1922.

Traction System: Overhead Electric.

Gauge: 3ft 6in.

Description: A 6TS dead ended tram shed with a single access road leading onto a traverser.

Closed: Following the takeover the cars were gradually transferred to Milehouse Depot with the tram shed finally closing in 1923. In 1990 it was in use as a tyre warehouse.

EXTRACT FROM DEVON 123.11 [1914]

Milehouse Depot

Location: At SX46655607, on the south east side of Tavistock Road, in Devonport.

Opened: June 26th, 1901 by the Devonport & District Tramways Co. Ltd and taken over by Plymouth Corporation on October 20th, 1915.

Traction System: Overhead Electric.

Gauge: 3ft 6in.

Description: The main depot and works, it originally consisted of a brick built 3TS running shed with one through road. A 3TS dead ended shed was added on the south side in 1923 and this was further extended in 1927.

Closed: September 29th, 1945 and further utilized as an omnibus garage.

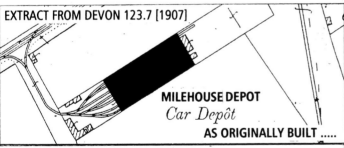

EXTRACT FROM DEVON 123.7 [1907]

MILEHOUSE DEPOT
Car Depôt
AS ORIGINALLY BUILT .....

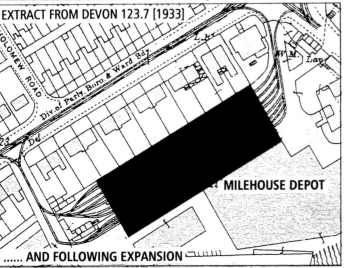

EXTRACT FROM DEVON 123.7 [1933]

MILEHOUSE DEPOT

...... AND FOLLOWING EXPANSION

Prince Rock Depot

Location: At SX49545435, on the east side of Elliott Road, at the south end of Harvey Avenue, south of Laira Bridge Road, in Prince Rock.

Opened: September 22nd, 1899 by Plymouth Corporation.

Traction System: Overhead Electric.

Gauge: 3ft 6in.

Description: Originally a 2TS dead ended tram shed, it was later extended to a 4TS building.

Closed: February 22nd, 1936, sold in May 1937 and later demolished. The site has since been re-developed.

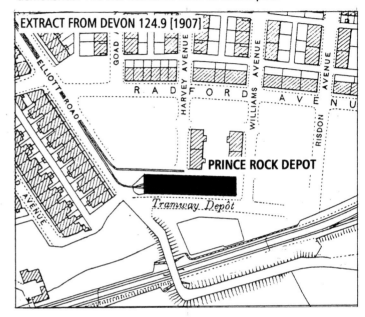

EXTRACT FROM DEVON 124.9 [1907]

PRINCE ROCK DEPOT

Tramway Depot

SEATON

Riverside Depot

Location: At SY25219028, on the east side of the line, north of Seaton terminus.

Opened: August 28th, 1970 by the Seaton & District Tramway.

Traction System: Battery (until June 7th, 1970) and then Overhead Electric.

Gauge: 2ft 9in.

Description: A 4TS dead ended tram shed built in brick and concrete blocks with asbestos sheeting on a steel frame. It was extended by one car's length in 1997.

The depot was still operational in 2000.

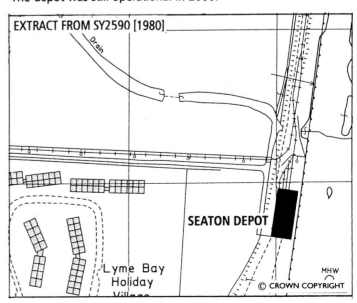

EXTRACT FROM SY2590 [1980]

SEATON DEPOT

Lyme Bay
Holiday
Village

EXETER

New North Road

Location: At SX92229304, on the east side of New North Road.
Opened: April 6th, 1882 by the Exeter Tramway Company and taken over by Exeter Corporation on February 1st, 1904.
Traction System: Horse.
Gauge: 3ft 6in.
Description: A 3TS dead ended tram shed with a single access road.
Closed: April 4th, 1905.

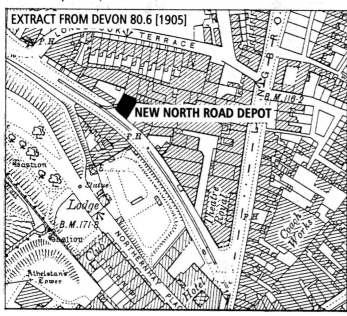

Heavitree Road

Location: At SX92229304, on the south side of Heavitree Rd, east of its junction with Paris Street.
Opened: April 4th, 1905 by Exeter Corporation Tramways.
Traction System: Overhead Electric.
Gauge: 3ft 6in.
Description: A brick built 7TS dead ended tram shed.
Closed: August 19th, 1931 and further utilized as an omnibus depot until 1970. It was subsequently demolished.

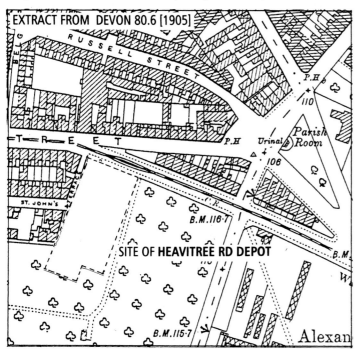

PAIGNTON

Preston Depot

Location: At SX89546202, on the south side of Orient Road on the corner with Torquay Road.
Opened: July 17th, 1911 by the Torquay Tramways Co. Ltd .
Traction System: Overhead Electric
Gauge: 3ft 6in.
Description: A brick built 4TS dead ended tram shed.
Closed: January 14th, 1934. In 1960 it was in use as a garage.

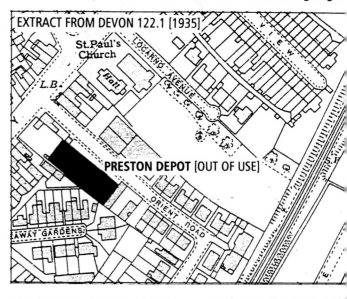

TORQUAY

Westhill Avenue

Location: At SX91736537, on the east side of Westhill Avenue just north of its junction with St.Marychurch Rd.
Opened: April 4th, 1907 by the Torquay Tramway Construction Co. Ltd (later the Torquay Tramways Co. Ltd).
Traction System: Stud (Until 1911) and then Overhead Electric
Gauge: 3ft 6in.
Description: A brick built 6TS dead ended tram shed. Power was supplied to tramcars within the shed by means of long leads until the system was converted to Overhead Electric. bus garage was added on the side in 1920 and much of the depot was destroyed on June 3rd, 1921 when a petrol storage tank exploded. The depot was subsequently rebuilt.
Closed: January 31st, 1934. Prior to demolition, in the 1990s, had been utilized to house corporation dustcarts

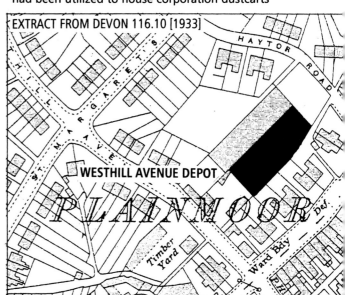

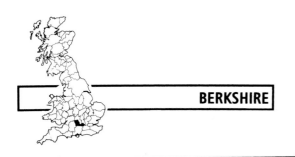

WANTAGE

Mill Street Station

Location: On the north side of Mill Street, in Wantage town centre.
Gauge: 4ft 8.5in.

DEPOT No.1
Opened: October 11th, 1875 by the Wantage Tramway.
Traction System: Horse/steam.
Description: The 1TS dead ended train shed at the station which was open along one side and located at SU39798801, was utilized as covered accommodation for rolling stock.
Closed: July 31st, 1925. It was sheeted-in with corrugated iron and converted to lock-up garages in 1927.

DEPOT No.2*
Opened: c1877 by the Wantage Tramway.
Traction System: Steam.
Description: A timber built 1TS dead ended shed, known as the "Large" shed and located at SU39818803. It was also utilized as the repair shop.
Closed: December 21st, 1946 and subsequently demolished.

DEPOT No.3*
Opened: 1894 by the Wantage Tramway.
Traction System: Steam.
Description: A timber built 1TS through road shed, known as the "Small" shed and located at SU39848807.
Closed: December 21st, 1946.

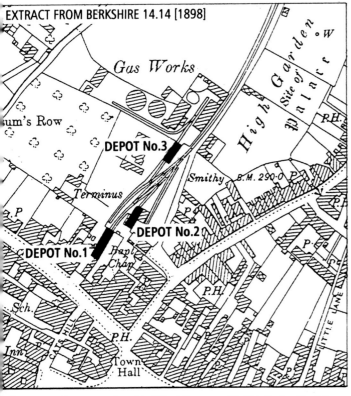

EXTRACT FROM BERKSHIRE 14.14 [1898]

*These two depots are listed in "The Directory of British Engine Sheds" as SU3988.2/1A and SU3988.1/1A respectively.

Oxford Road

Location: At SU70307338, on the south side of Oxford Road, west of Reading town centre.
Opened: April 5th, 1879 by Reading Tramways and taken over by Reading Corporation on November 1st. 1901.
Traction System: Horse.
Gauge: 4ft.
Description: A 1TS dead ended tram shed.
Closed: July 21st, 1903 and subsequently utilized as a school. Demolished prior to World War 1 and the site was used for terraced housing.

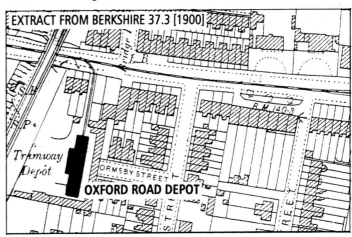

EXTRACT FROM BERKSHIRE 37.3 [1900]

OXFORD ROAD DEPOT

Mill Lane

Location: On the north side of Mill Lane, south of Reading town centre.
Opened: July 22nd, 1903 by Reading Corporation,
Traction System: Overhead Electric.
Gauge: 4ft.
Description: Originally constructed as a brick built 10TS dead ended tram shed (located at SU71627326) it was extended by 2 roads on the east side following the enlargement of the car fleet in 1904. A 4TS dead ended shed, located at SU71687320 and accessed via a turntable, was utilized as a repair shop. In 1923 a bus depot, 2TS body shop and 1TS paint shop were constructed on the eastern side of the site.
Closed; The tram shed was demolished in 1936 and a trolleybus depot built on the site. It is believed that the trams were housed on temporary tracks in the bus depot and workshops until the system was closed on May 20th, 1939. The whole site, which had been utilized as a depot and maintenance facility for Reading Buses, was cleared in May 1998 to make way for a shopping and leisure complex.

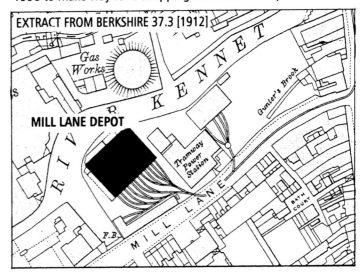

EXTRACT FROM BERKSHIRE 37.3 [1912]

MILL LANE DEPOT

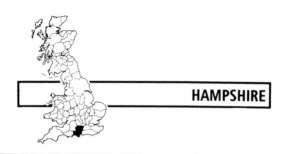

HAMPSHIRE

Southcote Road

Location: At SZ10449198, on the north side of Southcote Road, east of Bournemouth town centre.
Opened: July 23rd, 1902 by Bournemouth Corporation.
Traction System: Overhead Electric and Conduit.
Gauge: 3ft 6in.
Description: A brick built tram shed with 2 through roads, each dividing into three tracks. A 2TS workshop was constructed alongside and, in 1920 a 5TS dead ended workshop was added.
Closed: April 8th, 1936. It was subsequently utilized as an omnibus depot until final closure came in 1965.

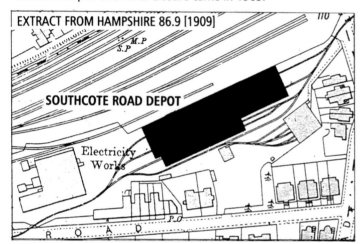

EXTRACT FROM HAMPSHIRE 86.9 [1909]
SOUTHCOTE ROAD DEPOT

Christchurch Road

Location: At SZ12439233, on the south side of Christchurch Road, Pokesdown.
Opened: October 17th, 1905 by Bournemouth Corporation.
Traction System: Overhead Electric and Conduit.
Gauge: 3ft 6in.
Description: A 5TS dead ended tram shed with 2 access tracks.
Closed: April 8th, 1936 and subsequently utilized as a trolleybus and omnibus depot until final closure came in 1967.

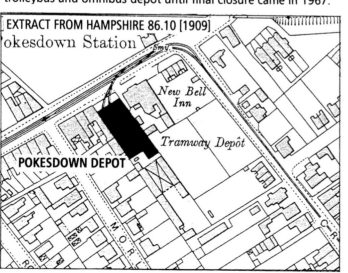

EXTRACT FROM HAMPSHIRE 86.10 [1909]
Pokesdown Station
New Bell Inn
Tramway Depôt
POKESDOWN DEPOT

Wimborne Road

Location: At SZ08999403, on the east side of Wimborne Road, Moordown.
Opened: June 1906 by Bournemouth Corporation.
Traction System: Overhead Electric and Conduit.
Gauge: 3ft 6in.
Description: A 6TS dead ended tram shed with 4 access tracks. The building incorporated a paint shop and a 4TS extension was added in 1919.
Closed: June 6th, 1935. It was subsequently utilized as an omnibus depot until final closure came in 1953.

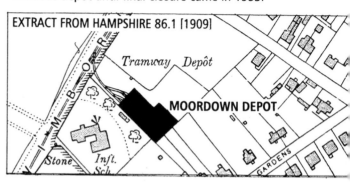

EXTRACT FROM HAMPSHIRE 86.1 [1909]
Tramway Depôt
MOORDOWN DEPOT
Stone
Inft. Sch.
GARDENS

Pier Gates

Location: Approximately at SZ59399394, on the east side of Pier Gates Station.
Opened: November 1871 by the Ryde Pier Company.
Traction System: Horse, until 1886 (when the line was partially electrified or 1889 when the scheme was completed), and Steam from February 1881 until October 1884.
Gauge: 4ft 8.5in.
Description: A tram car shed, it also housed the two steam cars.
Closed: 1886, or 1889 upon total electrification.

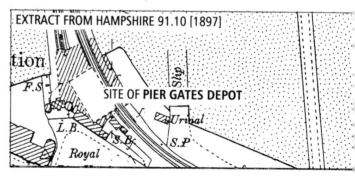

EXTRACT FROM HAMPSHIRE 91.10 [1897]
...tion
F.S
SITE OF **PIER GATES DEPOT**
L.B.
Royal
Slip
Urinal
S.P

St.John's Road

Location: At SZ59759207, on the east side of the tramway, north of the Isle of Wight Railway Station.
Opened: August 7th, 1871 by the Ryde Pier Company.
Traction System: Horse.
Gauge: 4ft 8.5in.
Description: A 2TS dead ended tram car shed.
Closed: April 5th, 1880 upon the opening of the railway extension to the pier.

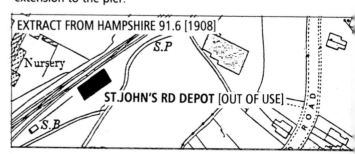

EXTRACT FROM HAMPSHIRE 91.6 [1908]
S.P
Nursery
ST.JOHN'S RD DEPOT [OUT OF USE]
S.B

Broad Street

Location: At SZ62939941, on the north east corner of Tower Street and Tower Alley, to the west off Broad Street, at The Point.

Opened: 1874 by the Portsmouth Street Tramways Co. and taken over by Portsmouth Corporation on January 1st, 1901.

Traction System: Horse.

Gauge: 4ft 7.75in.

Description: A 1TS dead ended tram shed.

Closed: 1901.

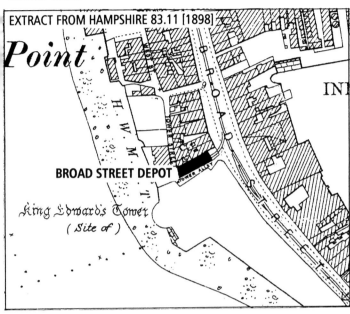

Eastney Depot

Location: At SZ66509905, on the west side of Highland Road, Eastney.

Opened: January 21st, 1932 by Portsmouth Corporation.

Traction System: Overhead Electric.

Gauge: 4ft 7.75in.

Description: A 6TS dead ended tram shed incorporating workshops and accommodation for omnibuses.

Closed: November 10th, 1936 and further utilized as a trolley-bus and omnibus depot.

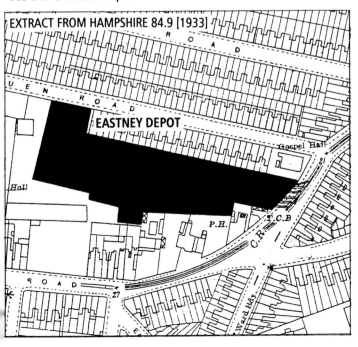

Fratton Road

Location: At SU65130100, on the west side of Fratton Road, opposite Cardigan Road, Fratton.

Opened: February 22nd, 1886 by the Portsmouth Street Tramways Co. and taken over by Portsmouth Corporation on January 1st, 1901.

Traction System: Horse.

Gauge: 4ft 7.75in.

Description: A 1TS dead ended tram shed.

Closed: 1901 and subsequently demolished. The site was later utilized for a Police Station.

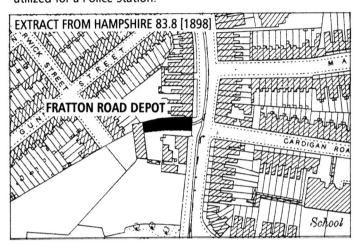

Gladys Avenue [North End] Depot

Location: At SU64860242, on the west side of Gladys Avenue, just north of the junction of Angerstein Road and London Road, North End.

Opened: 1874 by the Portsmouth Street Tramways Co. and taken over by Portsmouth Corporation on January 1st, 1901.

Traction System: Horse (until 1901) and then Overhead Electric. A steam railcar was also in operation between 1896 and 1901.

Gauge: 4ft 7.75in.

Description: Originally a 2TS dead ended horsecar shed it was reconstructed and re-opened for electric traction as a brick built 16TS dead ended tram shed with two access tracks.

Closed: November 10th, 1936 and further utilized as an omnibus depot.

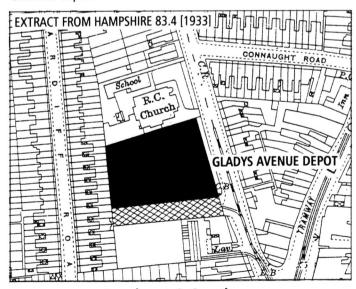

Landport & Southsea

The Landport & Southsea Tramway Company may have had a depot somewhere along its route between Clarence Pier and Portsmouth Town Station (1865-1873).

Ordnance Row

Location: At SU63120012, on the west side of Ordnance Row in Portsea.

Opened: June 17th, 1878 by the Portsmouth Street Tramways Co. and taken over by Portsmouth Corporation on January 1st, 1901

Traction System: Horse.

Gauge: 4ft 7.75in.

Description: A 2TS dead ended tram shed.

Closed: 1901 and later demolished. The site was utilized in 1954 for a signal box.

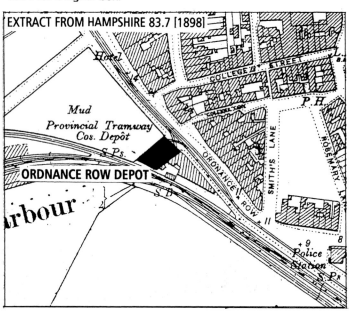

Powerscourt Road

Location: At SU64980181, on the north side of Powerscourt Road, east of Buckland Road, Buckland.

Opened: April 19th, 1886 by the Portsmouth (Borough), Kingston, Fratton & Southsea Street Tramways Co. and taken over by the Portsmouth Street Tramways Co. in 1892.

Traction System: Horse.

Gauge: 4ft 7.75in.

Description: A small, possibly 1TS dead ended, tram shed.

Closed: 1892.

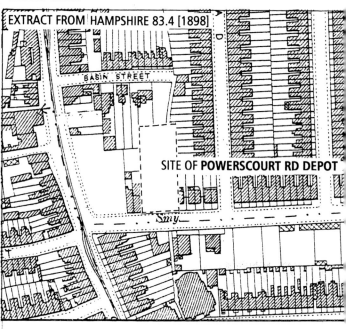

Park Lane Depot

Location: At SU69011089, on the west side of London Road, Cowplain.

Opened: March 3rd, 1903 by the Hampshire Light Railways (Electric) Co. Ltd for the Portsdown & Horndean Light Railway.

Traction System: Overhead Electric.

Gauge: 4ft 7.75in.

Description: A brick built 3TS dead ended tram shed and work-shop.

Closed: January 9th, 1935 and later utilized as a Fodens diesel lorry service station until at least 1954. It was subsequently demolished and a supermarket built on the site.

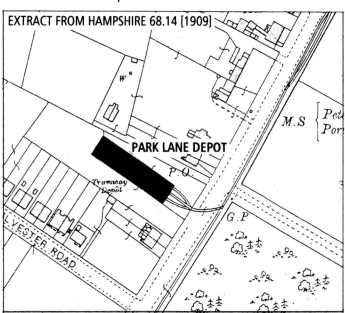

Rudmore Row

Location: At SU64370191, on the north side of Rudmore Road, to the west of the junction of Commercial Road and Kingston Crescent, Stamshaw.

Opened: 1874 by the Portsmouth Street Tramways Co. and taken over by Portsmouth Corporation on January 1st, 1901.

Traction System: Horse

Gauge: 4ft 7.75in.

Description: A medium sized dead ended tram shed with a single access track.

Closed: 1901 and, by 1951, was in use as a mattress factory.

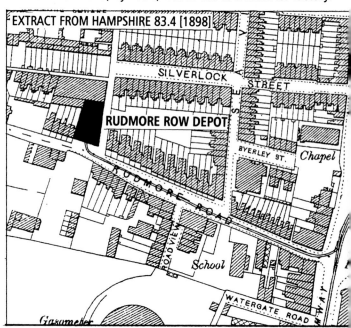

High Street

Location: At SZ62139980, on the south side of High Street, behind the India Arms Hotel, in Gosport town centre.

Opened: 1882 by the Gosport Street Tramways Co. and taken over by the Portsmouth Street Tramways Co. in August 1883.

Traction System: Horse.

Gauge: 3ft.

Description: A 3TS dead ended tram shed accessed via an archway under the hotel.

Closed: 1905. The building still stood in 1960, as premises for the Southern Electricity Board.

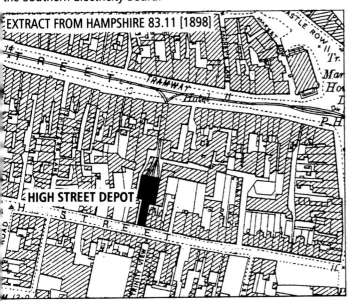

EXTRACT FROM HAMPSHIRE 83.11 [1898]

HIGH STREET DEPOT

Gosport Road

Location: At SU57930468, on the east side of Gosport Road, Hoeford.

Opened: December 20th, 1905 by the Portsmouth Street Tramways Co. trading as Gosport & Fareham Tramways.

Traction System: Overhead Electric.

Gauge: 4ft 7.75in.

Description: A 6TS dead ended tram shed with a 2TS workshop

Closed: December 31st, 1929 and further utilized as part of an omnibus depot.

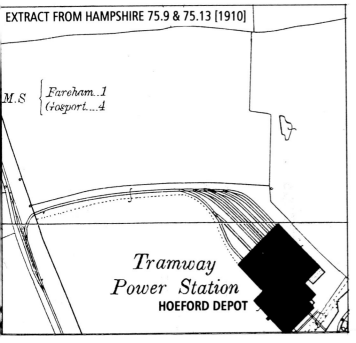

EXTRACT FROM HAMPSHIRE 75.9 & 75.13 [1910]

Tramway Power Station
HOEFORD DEPOT

Shirley Depot

Location: At SU39721385, on the south west side of Carlisle Road, Shirley.

Opened: June 9th, 1879 by the Southampton Tramways Co. and taken over by Southampton Corporation on June 30th, 1898.

Traction System: Horse (Until June 21st, 1900) and then Overhead Electric.

Gauge: 4ft 8.5in.

Description: Originally a 2TS dead ended horse car shed, works and stables it was rebuilt and re-opened on June 22nd, 1900 as a brick built 15TS tram shed for electric cars.

Closed: December 31st, 1949 and then further utilized as an omnibus depot.

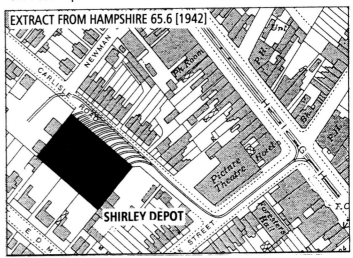

EXTRACT FROM HAMPSHIRE 65.6 [1942]

SHIRLEY DEPOT

Portswood Depot

Location: At SU42931432, on the east side of Portswood Road, Portswood.

Opened: May 5th, 1879 by the Southampton Tramways Co. and taken over by Southampton Corporation on June 30th, 1898.

Traction System: Horse (Until 1900) and then Overhead Electric.

Gauge: 4ft 8.5in.

Description: Originally a brick built 2TS dead ended horse car shed, works and stables it was rebuilt and re-opened on October 4th, 1900 as a brick built 8TS tram shed with adjoining workshop tracks.

Closed: March 5th, 1949 for service cars but remained in use as a storage depot for withdrawn cars until 1950. It was then further utilized as an omnibus depot.

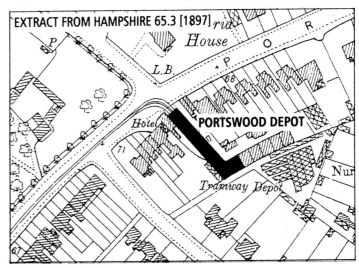

EXTRACT FROM HAMPSHIRE 65.3 [1897]

PORTSWOOD DEPOT

Tramway Depot

FARNBOROUGH

Farnborough Road

Location: At SU87005593, on the corner of Workhouse Lane and Farnborough Road, Farnborough.
Opened: c1881by the Aldershot & Farnborough Tramways Co.
Traction System: Horse.
Gauge: 4ft 8.5in.
Description: A 1TS dead ended tram shed.
Closed: 1906.

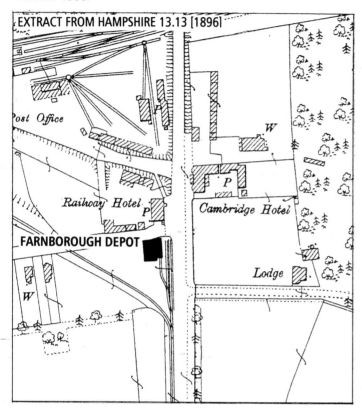

EXTRACT FROM HAMPSHIRE 13.13 [1896]

FARNBOROUGH DEPOT

WILTSHIRE

SWINDON

Mill Street

Location: At SU15208504, on the south side of the junction of Mill Street and Carlton Street, north east of Swindon town centre.
Opened: September 22nd, 1904 by Swindon Corporation.
Traction System: Overhead Electric
Gauge: 3ft 6in.
Description: Originally a brick built 3TS dead ended tram shed, it was extended to 4-roads in 1906 by the addition of a second hand lean-to extension obtained from Bristol.
Closed: July 11th, 1929. By 1960 it had become the workshops for the Corporation's adjacent omnibus garage.

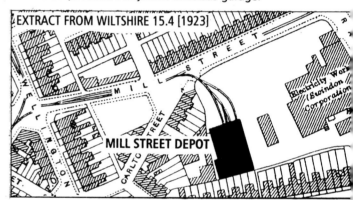

EXTRACT FROM WILTSHIRE 15.4 [1923]

MILL STREET DEPOT

OXFORDSHIRE

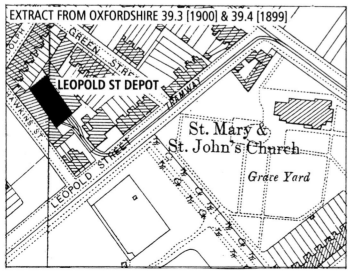

EXTRACT FROM OXFORDSHIRE 39.3 [1900] & 39.4 [1899]

LEOPOLD ST DEPOT

St. Mary & St. John's Church

Grave Yard

OXFORD

Leopold Street

Location: At SP53010546, on the north side of Leopold Street, west of Cowley Road.
Opened: December 1st, 1881 by the City of Oxford & District Tramways Co. Ltd.
Traction System: Horse.
Gauge: 4ft
Description: A 4TS dead ended tram shed.
Closed: August 7th, 1914 (or shortly after) and subsequently utilized as an omnibus depot. In 1990 it was in use as a laundry.

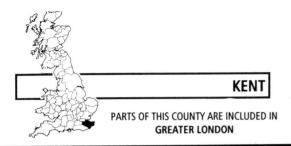

KENT

PARTS OF THIS COUNTY ARE INCLUDED IN
GREATER LONDON

HERNE BAY

Herne Bay Pier

Location: At TR17246847, at the shore end of the Pier.
Opened: During 1934 by the Herne Bay UDC.
Traction System: Petrol-Electric/Battery.
Gauge: 3ft 4.5in.
Description: A corrugated iron built 1TS dead ended train shed.
Closed: November 3rd, 1939 and subsequently dismantled.

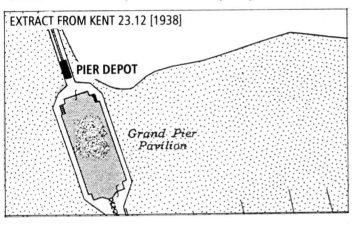

EXTRACT FROM KENT 23.12 [1938]

BEXLEY HEATH

Broadway

Location: At TQ49467407, on the south side of Broadway, just east of Market Place.
Opened: October 3rd, 1903 by Bexley Urban District Council and taken over by London Transport on July 1st, 1933.
Traction System: Overhead Electric.
Gauge: 4ft 8.5in.
Description: A brick built 6TS dead ended tram shed.
Closed: November 23rd, 1935 and utilized by the Council's Engineering Department until at least 1962.

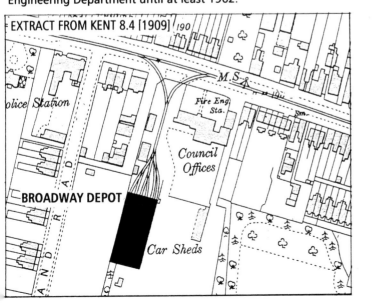

EXTRACT FROM KENT 8.4 [1909]

BROADSTAIRS

Northdown Hill

Location: At TR38076899, on the west side of Northdown Hill.
Opened: April 4th, 1901 by the Isle of Thanet Electric Tramways & Lighting Co, Ltd.
Traction System: Overhead Electric.
Gauge: 3ft 6in.
Description: Originally a corrugated iron built 8TS dead ended tram shed, a 2TS extension was added on the west side in 1901.
Closed: March 27th, 1937 and subsequently utilized as an omnibus depot. It still stood in 1972.

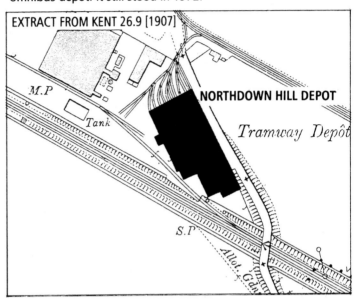

EXTRACT FROM KENT 26.9 [1907]

CHATHAM

Luton Road

Location: At TQ77266652 on the south west side of Luton Road.
Opened: June 17th, 1902 by the Chatham & District Light Railways. Co.
Traction System: Overhead Electric.
Gauge: 3ft 6in.
Description: A brick built 8TS dead ended tram shed.
Closed: September 30th, 1930 and subsequently utilized as an omnibus depot. It was completely rebuilt in 1970.

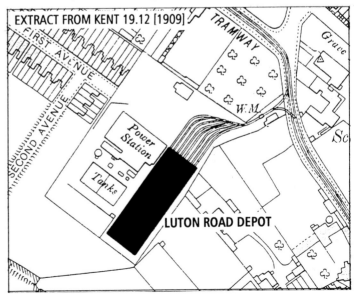

EXTRACT FROM KENT 19.12 [1909]

Buckland Bridge

Location: At TR30634281 on the corner of Whitfield Avenue and London Road, Buckland.
Opened: September 6th, 1897 by Dover Corporation.
Traction System: Overhead Electric.
Gauge: 3ft 6in.
Description: A brick built 4TS dead ended tram shed.
Closed: December 31st, 1936. Later utilized as a toy factory and still stood, in commercial use, in 1992.

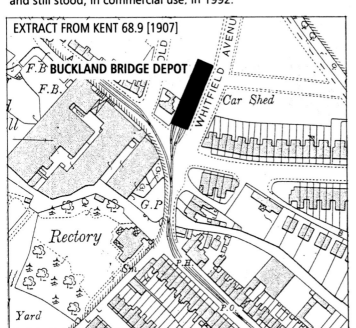

EXTRACT FROM KENT 68.9 [1907]

Folkestone Road

Location: At TR30394088 on the corner of Folkestone Road and Maxton Road.
Opened: December 1897 by Dover Corporation.
Traction System: Overhead Electric.
Gauge: 3ft 6in.
Description: A brick built 2TS dead ended tram shed.
Closed: December 31st, 1936 and subsequently utilized as an omnibus depot. It still stood in 1992, in use as a Corporation Highways Department lorry garage.

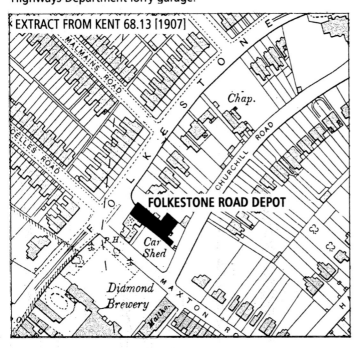

EXTRACT FROM KENT 68.13 [1907]

Walnut Tree Road

Location: At TQ51277809 in the Council Yard on the west side of Walnut Tree Road.
Opened: August 26th, 1905 by Erith Urban District Council and taken over by London Transport on July 1st, 1933.
Traction System: Overhead Electric.
Gauge: 4ft 8.5in.
Description: A brick built 4TS dead ended tram shed.
Closed: December 28th, 1935, and later utilized as a Council Highways Department vehicle depot.

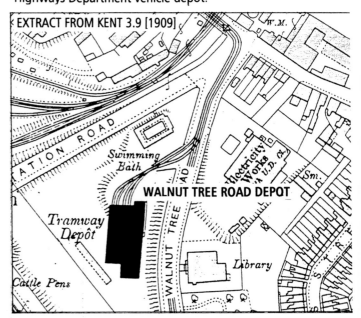

EXTRACT FROM KENT 3.9 [1909]

Red Lion Square

Location: At TR15923468 on the corner of Rampart Road and Red Lion Square.
Opened: June 6th, 1894 by the South Eastern Railway for its Folkestone, Hythe & Sandgate Tramways.
Traction System: Horse.
Gauge: 4ft 8.5in.
Description: A timber built 2TS dead ended tram shed in front of a brick built office building. Stables were added in 1898.
Closed: September 30th, 1921 and subsequently utilized as a furniture and antique warehouse, furniture repository and a restaurant. It still stood in 1987.

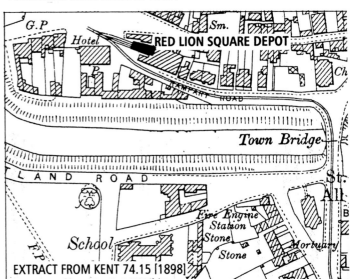

EXTRACT FROM KENT 74.15 [1898]

Victoria Road

Location: At TQ53847470, on the south side of Burnham Road at the west end of Victoria Road.

Opened: February 14th, 1906 by Dartford Urban District Council.

Traction System: Overhead Electric.

Gauge: 4ft 8.5in.

Description: A brick built 4TS dead ended tram shed.

Closed: The depot, along with the trams contained within it, was destroyed by a fire on August 7th, 1917. The system was subsequently operated from Bexley Heath Depot.

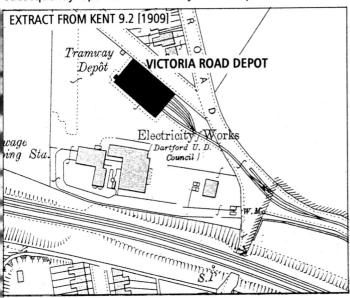

EXTRACT FROM KENT 9.2 [1909]

The Hill

Location: At TQ62487409, on the west side of The Hill, Northfleet.

Opened: June 15th, 1883 by the Gravesend, Rosherville & Northfleet Tramways Co. Ltd. The company became the National Electric Traction Co. Ltd in 1889 and was taken over by the British Electric Traction Co. on June 1st, 1901.

Traction System: Horse and Conduit Electric (Electric Cars were housed in 1889-1890).

Gauge: 3ft 6in.

Description: Originally a 2TS dead ended tram shed, a 1TS extension, built in corrugated iron, was added to accommodate the electric cars.

Closed: June 30th, 1901. Site of Catholic Church of Our Lady.

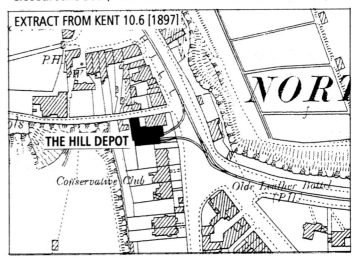

EXTRACT FROM KENT 10.6 [1897]

Canterbury Road [Westbrook] Depot

Location: At TR33827005, on the north side of Canterbury Road, west of Margate.

Opened: During 1902 by the Isle of Thanet Electric Tramways & Lighting Co. Ltd.

Traction System: Overhead Electric.

Gauge: 3ft 6in.

Description: A brick and corrugated iron built 2TS dead ended tram shed.

Closed: March 27th, 1937. Further utilized as an electricity sub-station and still stood in 1972.

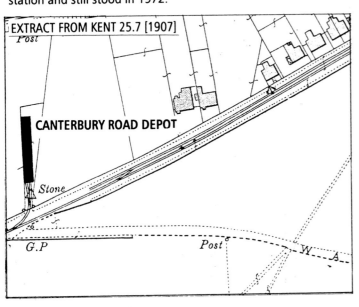

EXTRACT FROM KENT 25.7 [1907]

Dover Road

Location: At TQ63527359, on the north east side of the Dover Road and Dover Road East junction.

Opened: August 2nd, 1902 by Gravesend & Northfleet Electric Tramways Ltd.

Traction System: Overhead Electric.

Gauge: 4ft 8.5in.

Description: A brick built 5TS dead ended tram shed.

Closed: February 28th, 1929, and subsequently utilized as an omnibus garage until 1935. It was later in use as an engineering works and still stood in 1999.

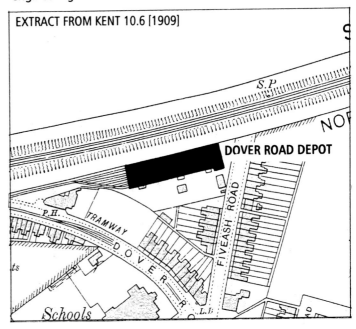

EXTRACT FROM KENT 10.6 [1909]

MAIDSTONE

Tonbridge Road

Location: At TQ73735502 on the north side of Tonbridge Road, just east of Queen's Road, Barming.
Opened: July 14th, 1904 by Maidstone Corporation.
Traction System: Overhead Electric.
Gauge: 3ft 6in.
Description: Originally a 2TS tram shed with an adjoining 1TS workshop, it was extended with two more roads in 1907/8. From 1928 the building also accommodated trolleybuses.
Closed: To trams on February 11th, 1930 and to trolleybuses in 1967.

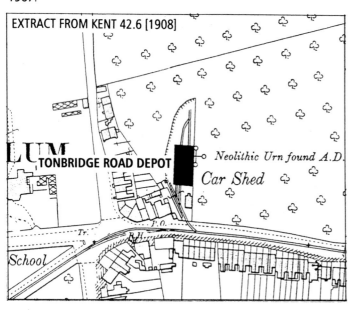

EXTRACT FROM KENT 42.6 [1908]

Loose Road

Location: At TQ76405268, on the east side of Loose Road, north of Pickering Street, Loose.
Opened: October 16th, 1907 by Maidstone Corporation.
Traction System: Overhead Electric.
Gauge: 3ft 6in.
Description: A 2TS dead ended tram shed.
Closed: February 11th, 1930 and subsequently demolished.

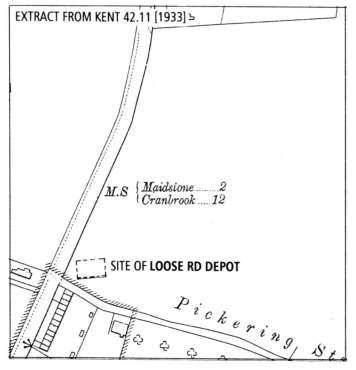

EXTRACT FROM KENT 42.11 [1933]

SHEERNESS

Power Station Road

Location: At TQ93167348 on the north side of Sheerness East Station, on the east side of Power House Road.
Opened: April 9th, 1903 by the Sheerness & District Electrical Power & Traction Co. Ltd.
Traction System: Overhead Electric.
Gauge: 3ft 6in.
Description: A 5TS dead ended tram shed.
Closed: July 7th, 1917 and rebuilt as an omnibus garage in 1932.

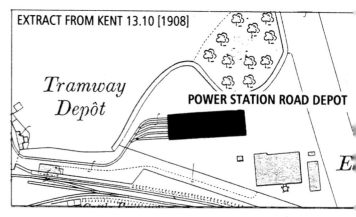

EXTRACT FROM KENT 13.10 [1908]

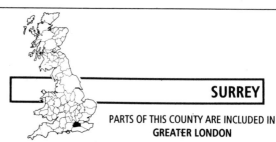

SURREY

PARTS OF THIS COUNTY ARE INCLUDED IN **GREATER LONDON**

PURLEY

Brighton Road

Location: At TQ32026225, on the corner of Brighton Road and Purley Downs Road.
Opened: September 26th, 1901 by Croydon Corporation and taken over by London Transport on July 1st, 1933.
Traction System: Overhead Electric.
Gauge: 4ft 8.5in.
Description: A brick built 8TS dead ended tram depot.
Closed: April 7th, 1951. Later utilized as a mineral water store and still standing in 1983.

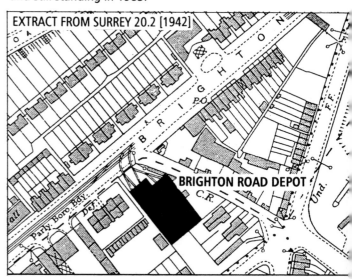

EXTRACT FROM SURREY 20.2 [1942]

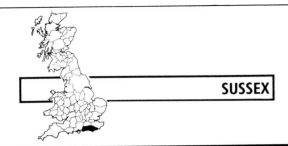

SUSSEX

BRIGHTON

Lewes Road

Location: *At TQ32280603, on the east side of Lewes Road, north of Hollingdean Road.*
Opened: November 25th, 1901 by Brighton Corporation.
Traction System: Overhead Electric.
Gauge: 3ft 6in.
Description: A brick built 6TS dead ended tram shed adjoined by a paint shop and workshops.
Closed: August 31st, 1939 and subsequently utilized as an omnibus depot.

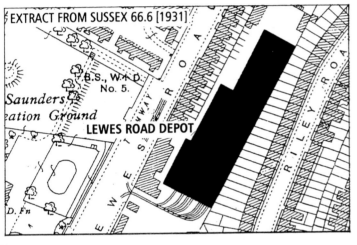

EXTRACT FROM SUSSEX 66.6 [1931]

LEWES ROAD DEPOT

HASTINGS

Beaufort Road [Silver Hill] Depot

Location: *At TQ80171068, on the north side of Beaufort Road, east of Battle Road, Silverhill.*
Opened: July 31st, 1905 by the Hastings & District Electric Tramways Co.
Traction System: Overhead Electric.
Gauge: 3ft 6in.
Description: A 7TS dead ended tram shed.
Closed: May 15th, 1929 and utilized as a trolleybus depot until 1959 and subsequently as an omnibus depot.

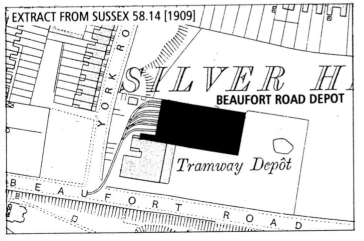

EXTRACT FROM SUSSEX 58.14 [1909]

SILVER H

BEAUFORT ROAD DEPOT

Tramway Depôt

ST LEONARDS

Bulverhythe

Location: *At TQ78150880, on the south side of Bexhill Road.*
Opened: April 9th, 1906 by the Hastings & District Electric Tramways Co.
Traction System: Overhead & Stud Electric and Petrol-Electric.
Gauge: 3ft 6in.
Description: A 6TS dead ended tram shed.
Closed: September 8th, 1928 and utilized as a trolleybus depot until 1959 and subsequently as an omnibus depot.

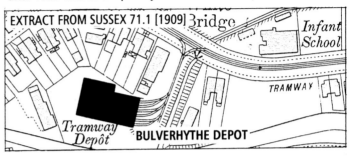

EXTRACT FROM SUSSEX 71.1 [1909] Bridge   Infant School

TRAMWAY

Tramway Depôt   **BULVERHYTHE DEPOT**

SHOREHAM

Albion Street

Location: *At TQ24280497, on the north side of Albion Street, west of Station Road.*
Opened: July 3rd, 1884 by the Brighton District Tramways Co., taken over by the Brighton & Shoreham Tramways Co. in November 1889 and bought by the British Electric Traction Co. in 1896. (For electrification but this not undertaken)
Traction System: Steam between 1884 & 1893, and Horse from May 23rd, 1885 until closure of the system.
Gauge: 3ft 6in.
Description: Originally built as a 2TS dead ended steam loco and carriage shed, it was also used for horse trams from 1885.
Closed: June 6th, 1913.

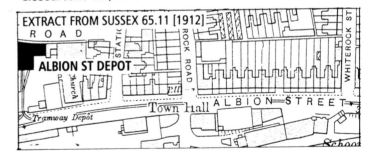

EXTRACT FROM SUSSEX 65.11 [1912]
ROAD   ROCK ROAD   WHITEROCK ST.

ALBION ST DEPOT

Tramway Depôt   Town Hall   ALBION STREET   School

EASTBOURNE

The Crumbles

Location: *At TQ63110063, at the eastern end of Princes Park, The Crumbles.*
Opened: July 4th, 1954 by Modern Electric Tramways Ltd.
Traction System: Overhead Electric.
Gauge: 2ft.
Description: A concrete block built 3TS dead ended tram shed.
Closed: September 14th, 1969 and demolished to make way for a road.

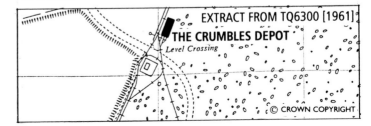

EXTRACT FROM TQ6300 [1961]
THE CRUMBLES DEPOT
Level Crossing
© CROWN COPYRIGHT

GREATER LONDON

INCLUDING **MIDDLESEX** AND PARTS OF **SURREY, KENT & ESSEX**

TQ08

Hillingdon Depot

Location: *At TQ08198220, on the north side of Uxbridge Rd, Hillingdon.*

Opened: June 1st, 1904 by the London United Tramways Co. Ltd.

Traction System: Overhead Electric.

Gauge: 4ft 8.5in.

Description: A 4TS dead ended tram shed.

Closed: c1909 and subsequently utilized to store and scrap withdrawn tram cars. It was leased for commercial purposes on June 7th, 1923, sold in 1950 and still in business use in 1998.

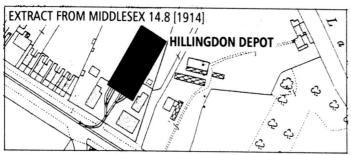

TQ17

Fulwell Depot

Location: *At TQ14827190, between Stanley Rd and Wellington Rd, Fulwell.*

Opened: April 2nd, 1903 by the London United Tramways Co. Ltd and became part of London Transport from July 1st, 1933.

Traction System: Overhead Electric.

Gauge: 4ft 8.5in.

Description: A brick built 15TS through road tram shed with a 3TS dead ended repair shop on the south side. From May 16th, 1931, the ten northernmost roads were taken over for trolley buses and the depot was also utilized for the scrapping of tram cars.

Closed: To trams on October 27th, 1935 and subsequently used as an omnibus garage.

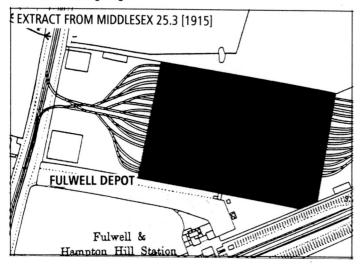

Hounslow Depot

Location: *At TQ14907627, on the north side of London Ro east of Star Rd, Isleworth.*

Opened: July 6th, 1901 by the London United Tramways Co Ltd and became part of London Transport from July 1st, 1933.

Traction System: Overhead Electric.

Gauge: 4ft 8.5in.

Description: A brick built 10TS dead ended tram shed.

Closed: It was loaned to the London General Omnibus Co during WWI for military training and closed on October 27th 1935 when trolley buses took over. The building was sold to the Post Office in 1968.

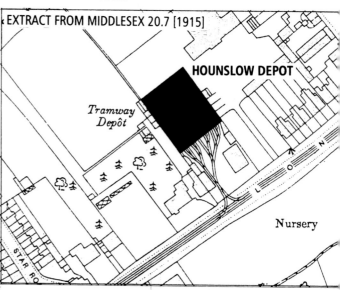

Richmond Depot

Location: *At TQ18227546, on the west side of Kew Rd (at No.125), Richmond.*

Opened: April 17th, 1883 by the West Metropolitan Tramways Co. Ltd and taken over by the London United Tramways Ltd on July 19th, 1894.

Traction System: Horse.

Gauge: 4ft 8.5in.

Description: A 2TS dead ended covered yard and brick built stables.

Closed: April 20th, 1912 and utilized as commercial premises prior to conversion to a Fire Station in 1932.

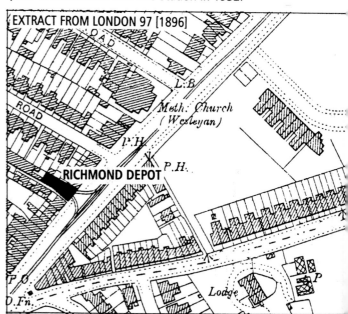

Hanwell Depot

Location: At TQ15608012, east of Boston Rd and on the south side of Hanwell Broadway.

Opened: July 10th, 1901 by the London United Tramways Co. Ltd and became part of London Transport from July 1st, 1933.

Traction System: Overhead Electric.

Gauge: 4ft 8.5in.

Description: Originally a brick built 10TS dead ended tram shed it was enlarged in 1929/30 with steel framed asbestos sheeted extensions at the front and a 2TS dead ended shed on the south side.

Closed: December 5th, 1936 and subsequently utilized as a trolley bus depot.

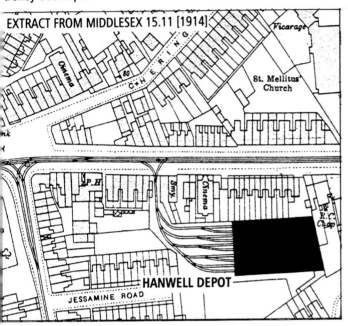

EXTRACT FROM MIDDLESEX 15.11 [1914]

Acton Depot

Location: At TQ19588018, on the south side of Acton High St., Acton Hill.

Opened: March 1896 by the London United Tramways Co. Ltd and became part of London Transport from July 1st, 1933.

Traction System: Horse, until 1901, and then Overhead Electric.

Gauge: 4ft 8.5in.

Description: A brick built 7TS dead ended tram shed. The depot also housed trolley buses from April 5th, 1936.

Closed: To trams and trolley buses on March 3rd, 1937 and subsequently utilized as an omnibus garage and workshops.

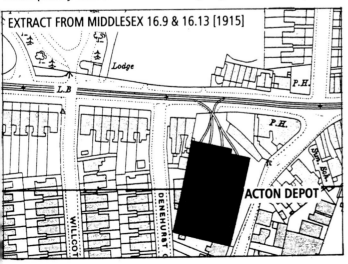

EXTRACT FROM MIDDLESEX 16.9 & 16.13 [1915]

Stonebridge Park

Location: At TQ19948410, on the south side of Harrow Rd, Wembley.

Opened: October 10th, 1906 by the Metropolitan Electric Tramways Ltd and became part of London Transport from July 1st, 1933.

Traction System: Overhead Electric.

Gauge: 4ft 8.5in.

Description: Originally a 12TS dead ended tram shed constructed in brick and corrugated iron, it was extended in 1912 and a motor tower wagon building was added in 1922.

Closed: August 22nd, 1936 and utilized as a trolley bus depot from the following day. It was later used as an omnibus garage and closed in 1981.

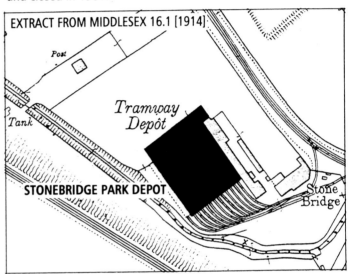

EXTRACT FROM MIDDLESEX 16.1 [1914]

Sutton Depot

Location: At TQ26786466, on the north side of Westmead Rd, between Harold Rd and Byron Avenue.

Opened: November 11th, 1906 by the South Metropolitan Electric Tramways & Lighting Co. Ltd. Became part of London Transport on July 1st, 1933.

Traction System: Overhead Electric.

Gauge: 4ft 8.5in.

Description: A brick built 8TS dead ended tram shed.

Closed: December 7th, 1935 and utilized as a trolley bus depot from the following day. Became an omnibus garage on March 4th, 1959 and was sold for commercial use in 1981.

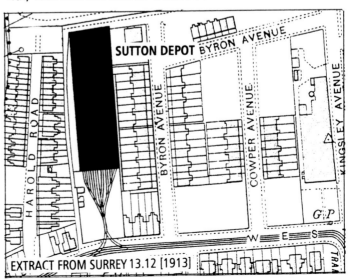

EXTRACT FROM SURREY 13.12 [1913]

Chiswick Depot

Location: At TQ21587970 on the north side of Chiswick High Rd between Merton Avenue and Ennismore Avenue.

Opened: 1883/4 by the West Metropolitan Tramways Co. Ltd, taken over by the London United Tramways Co. Ltd on July 19th, 1894 and taken over again by London County Council Tramways on October 12th, 1922.

Traction System: Horse, until April 3rd, 1901, and then Overhead Electric.

Gauge: 4ft 8.5in.

Description: Originally a 2TS dead ended tram shed and stables, at electrification it was converted to a 4TS works and a brick built 11TS dead ended tram shed accessed via a traverser was constructed on the west side.

Closed: As a running shed on May 5th, 1932 by which time it was utilized as a store for withdrawn tram cars. In 1935 it was in use as a trolley bus depot and later saw use as an omnibus works and store. In 1963 it was leased out as commercial premises and in 1966 was converted to a garage for airport coaches.

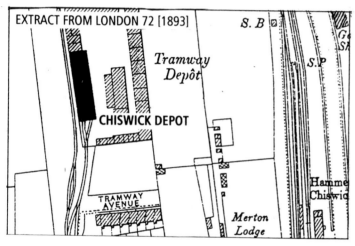

EXTRACT FROM LONDON 72 [1893]

Goldhawk Road Yard

Location: At TQ23267966 on the south side of Goldhawk Road, (at 43a), east of Wells Road.

Opened: August/September 1892 by the West Metropolitan Tramways Co. Ltd and taken over by the London United Tramways Co. Ltd on July 19th, 1894.

Traction System: Horse.

Gauge: 4ft 8.5in.

Description: A rented yard with 2 dead ended roads.

Closed: September 1902, upon expiry of the lease.

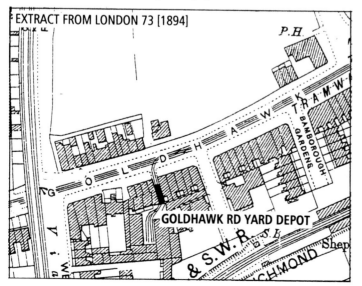

EXTRACT FROM LONDON 73 [1894]

Clapham Junction

Location: At TQ27337548 on the north side of St.John's Hill, west of Falcon Rd and behind The Falcon pub.

Opened: June 13th or 14th, 1882 by the South London Tramways Co. and taken over on November 22nd, 1902 by London County Council Tramways.

Traction System: Horse.

Gauge: 4ft 8.5in.

Description: A 4TS dead ended tram shed.

Closed: 1909.

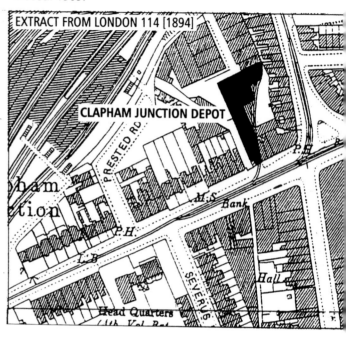

EXTRACT FROM LONDON 114 [1894]

Queen's Road Depot

Location: At TQ28897668 on the east side of Queen's Road, Battersea.

Opened: January 1st, 1881 by the South London Tramways Co. and taken over on November 22nd, 1902 by London County Council Tramways.

Traction System: Horse.

Gauge: 4ft 8.5in.

Description: A timber built 5TS dead ended tram shed accessed via two turntables, stables and workshops.

Closed: December 22nd, 1906 and sold for use as commercial premises.

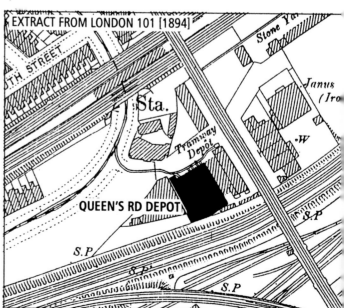

EXTRACT FROM LONDON 101 [1894]

Jews Row, Wandsworth

Location: At TQ25967533, in Jews Row, on the north side of York Rd.

Opened: May 6th, 1883 by the South London Tramways Co. and taken over on November 22nd, 1902 by London County Council. Became part of London Transport on July 1st, 1933.

Traction System: Horse, until 1906, and then Conduit Electric.

Gauge: 4ft 8.5in.

Description: Originally a dead ended tram shed, it was demolished in 1906 and replaced by a brick built 16TS dead ended tram shed with access via two traversers for electric working. Trolley buses were also accommodated from September 12th, 1937.

Closed: To trams and trolley buses on September 30th, 1950 and subsequently utilized as an omnibus garage.

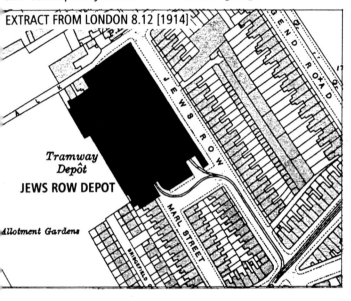

EXTRACT FROM LONDON 8.12 [1914]

Tramway Depôt
JEWS ROW DEPOT

Allotment Gardens

Shepherds Bush

Location: At TQ23277995, on the south side of Uxbridge Rd, between The Lawn and the Hammersmith & City Line.

Opened: June 1st, 1874 by the Southall, Ealing & Shepherds Bush Tram Railway Co. Ltd, taken over on January 25th, 1878 by the tramway's contractors, Reid Brothers of City Road, and taken over again by the West Metropolitan Tramways Co. Ltd on March 6th, 1882.

Traction System: Horse.

Gauge: 4ft 8.5in.

Description: A dead ended tram shed, probably of 2 roads, and stables.

Closed: Summer of 1892 and the site was later partially utilized in 1896 as a Public Library.

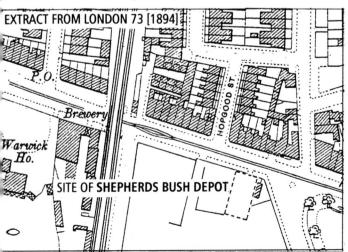

EXTRACT FROM LONDON 73 [1894]

P.O.

Brewery

Warwick Ho.

SITE OF **SHEPHERDS BUSH DEPOT**

Marius Road [Balham] Depot

Location: At TQ28177278, on the corner of Marius Rd and Balham High Rd.

Opened:December 15th, 1888 by the London Tramways Co. Ltd and taken over by London County Council on January 1st, 1899.

Traction System: Horse, and then Conduit Electric from May 15th, 1903.

Gauge: 4ft 8.5in.

Description: Originally a brick built 6TS dead ended tram shed, upon electrification it was utilized as a temporary depot with a traverser being installed outside the entrance.

Closed: As a running shed on August 28th, 1904. The access road was removed and the depot then used as a store and for the scrapping of horse cars. It re-opened on September 1st, 1915 as a running shed for trailer cars before finally closing on November 18th, 1922. The building was subsequently sold for commercial use and became a garage prior to demolition and redevelopment as a housing estate.

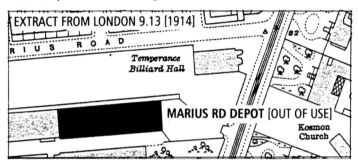

EXTRACT FROM LONDON 9.13 [1914]

RIUS ROAD

Temperance Billiard Hall

MARIUS RD DEPOT [OUT OF USE]

Kosmon Church

Hammersmith Car Shed

Location: At TQ23507855, at 243-245 Hammersmith Rd.

Opened: May 30th, 1908 by London County Council and became part of London Transport from July 1st, 1933.

Traction System: Conduit Electric.

Gauge: 4ft 8.5in.

Description: A brick built 8TS dead ended car shed accessed via a traverser and constructed in stages between October 1907 and April 1911. Part of the depot was used as a paint and repair shop between 1909 and 1915.

Closed: September 12th, 1937 and subsequently utilized as a trolley bus depot.

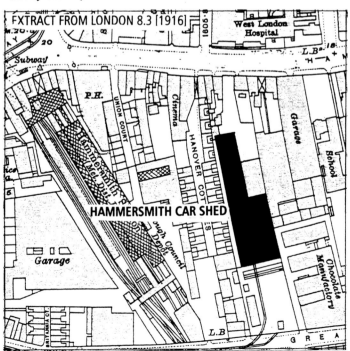

EXTRACT FROM LONDON 8.3 [1916]

West London Hospital

P.H.

Cinema

HAMMERSMITH CAR SHED

Garage

Victoria Depot

Location: At TQ29777839, on the south west side of the junction of Vauxhall Bridge Rd and Bessborough Gardens.
Opened: October 20th, 1873 by the London Tramways Co. Ltd and taken over by London County Council on January 1st, 1899.
Traction System: Horse.
Gauge: 4ft 8.5in.
Description: A tram shed and stables.
Closed: Not known, but probably shortly before the line re-opened with electric working on August 5th, 1906.

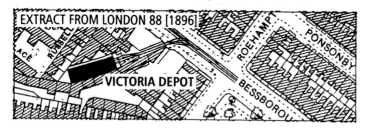

Clapham Plough Depot

Location: At TQ29417536, on the north side of High St.
Opened: May 1st, 1871 by the Metropolitan Street Tramways Co. and became part of London Tramways Co. Ltd in 1873.
Traction System: Horse.
Gauge: 4ft 8.5in.
Description: A 2TS dead ended tram shed on the west side of the hotel and a 1TS dead ended tram shed and stables on the east.
Closed: Not known, but shortly prior to electric working on May 5th, 1903.

Clapham High Street

Location: At TQ29607530, on the corner of Clapham Park Rd and High St.
Opened: July 28th, 1888 by London Tramways Co. Ltd and taken over by London County Council on January 1st, 1899. Became part of London Transport on July 1st, 1933.
Traction System: Horse, until 1903, and Conduit Electric from May 15th, 1903.
Gauge: 4ft 8.5in.
Description: Originally a, probably 4TS, dead ended tram shed and stables it was rebuilt in two stages, 1903 on the west side and 1904 on the site of the original depot and stables. In its final form it was a brick built 25TS through road shed with two central traversers and also housed the Motor School for staff training. It was rebuilt following bomb damage during Word War II and also housed omnibuses from October 1st, 1950.
Closed: To trams on January 7th, 1951.

Park Road

Location: At TQ27638537, on the west side of Park Rd, south off Fleet Rd, Hampstead.
Opened: May 10th, 1880 by the London Street Tramways Co. and taken over by London County Council on October 13th 1897.
Gauge: 4ft 8.5in.
Description: A dead ended tram shed and stables.
Closed: Exact date unknown but by November 30th, 190 when the route re-opened following electrification.

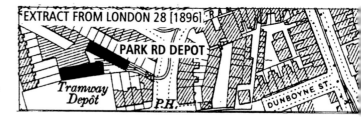

Trenmar Gardens

Location: At TQ22708280, on the east side of Trenmar Gardens, south of Harrow Rd, College Park.
Opened: July 7th, 1888 by the Harrow Road & Paddington Tramways Co. and taken over on August 16th, 1906 by the Metropolitan Electric Tramways Ltd .
Traction System: Horse.
Gauge: 4ft 8.5in.
Description: A 3TS tram shed with two through roads accessing a turntable at the rear, and stables.
Closed: At the end of horse working on September 1st, 1906. Sold for use as a cinema and still in industrial use in 1984.

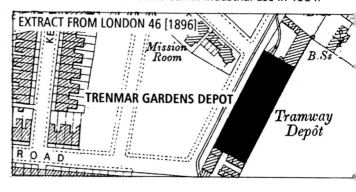

Kentish Town Rd

Location: At TQ29008405, on the east side of Kentish Town Rd, between Nos 36 and 42, just south of Regents Canal.
Opened: November 27th, 1871 by the London Street Tramways Co.
Traction System: Horse.
Gauge: 4ft 8.5in.
Description: A temporary depot.
Closed: October 1st, 1872 upon the opening of Parkhurst Rd Depot.

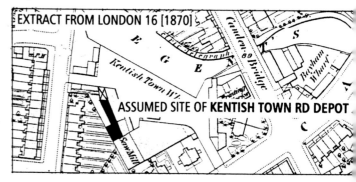

Hendon Depot

Location: At TQ20728981, on the corner of Edgware Rd and Annesley Avenue.

Opened: December 3rd, 1904, by the Metropolitan Electric Tramways Ltd and became part of London Transport from July 1st, 1933.

Traction System: Overhead Electric.

Gauge: 4ft 8.5in.

Description: A brick built, 8TS dead ended tram shed. Four roads were later utilized as a paint shop and, between 1905 and 1920, various works buildings and facilities were added. In 1912 an omnibus garage was constructed on the south side, but this was sold in 1914 for use in aircraft manufacture.

Closed: As a running shed in 1930/31, re-opening in the autumn of 1935 before finally closing on August 1st, 1936. The works had been converted for trolley bus maintenance in May 1936 and the remainder of the depot was re-opened as a trolley bus depot on August 2nd, 1936.

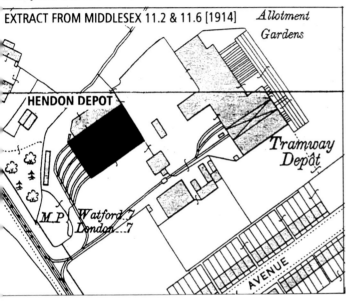

EXTRACT FROM MIDDLESEX 11.2 & 11.6 [1914]

Junction Road

Location: At TQ29168637, on the west side of Junction Rd, Kentish Town.

Opened: May 1874 by the London Street Tramways Co. and taken over by London County Council on October 13th, 1897.

Traction System: Horse.

Gauge: 4ft 8.5in.

Description: Probably a 4TS dead ended tram shed and stables.

Closed: Exact date unknown but by July 22nd, 1909 when the route re-opened following electrification.

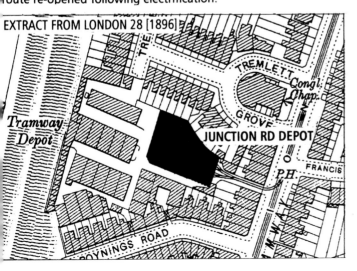

EXTRACT FROM LONDON 28 [1896]

Cressy Rd [Hampstead Car Shed]

Location: At TQ27518551, on the west side of Cressy Rd, north off Fleet Rd, Hampstead.

Opened: c1890 by the London Street Tramways Co. and taken over by London County Council on October 13th, 1897. Became part of London Transport from July 1st, 1933.

Traction System: Horse, until November 1909, and then Conduit Electric.

Gauge: 4ft 8.5in.

Description: Originally a 6TS dead ended tram shed, 2TS repair shop, 2TS paint shop and stables, it was reconstructed for electric working as a brick built 18TS car shed accessed via traversers. A corrugated iron paint shop was removed from Holloway Depot and re-erected here in 1924.

Closed: The depot was requisitioned for use as a military garage between 1915 and 1922 and the additional paint shop was closed in 1926. The depot closed on July 9th, 1938 and was utilized for storing withdrawn tramcars.

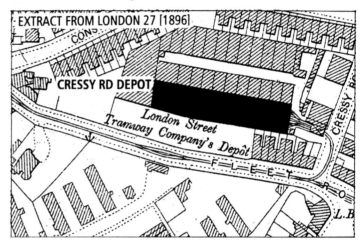

EXTRACT FROM LONDON 27 [1896]

Highgate Hill

Location: At TQ28638739, on the north side of Highgate High St., east of Southwood Lane.

Opened: May 29th, 1884 by the Highgate Hill Tramways Co. and taken over by Highgate Hill Tramways Ltd on August 14th, 1896.

Traction System: Cable.

Gauge: 3ft 6in.

Description: A brick built dead ended tram shed, probably 3 or 4TS, with a traverser at the front and a winding house.

Closed: August 23rd, 1909 prior to re-gauging and overhead electrification.

EXTRACT FROM LONDON 19 [1896]

Holloway Car Shed

Location: At TQ29458639, between Pemberton Rd and Monnery Rd, Holloway.

Opened: November 28th, 1907 (east side) and November 30th, 1909 (west side) by London County Council and became part of London Transport from July 1st, 1933.

Traction System: Conduit Electric.

Gauge: 4ft 8.5in.

Description: A brick built depot consisting of 22TS and 26TS dead ended sections accessed via a central traverser, and a workshop. Three roads were used as a paint shop until the facility moved to Hampstead Car Shed. Trolley buses were also housed from July 10th, 1938. It was re-named as Highgate Depot in 1950.

Closed: To trams and trolley buses on April 6th, 1952 and then utilized as an omnibus garage.

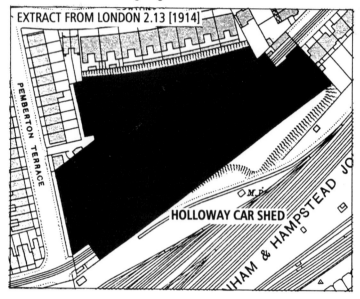

Highgate Depot

Location: At TQ29548684, at the "Archway Tavern" on the north side of Holloway Road, Highgate.

Opened: 1873 by the North Metropolitan Tramways Co. and taken over by London County Council on April 1st, 1906.

Traction System: Horse.

Gauge: 4ft 8.5in.

Description: A dead ended tram shed and stables.

Closed: Exact date unknown but by November 28th, 1907 when the route re-opened following electrification.

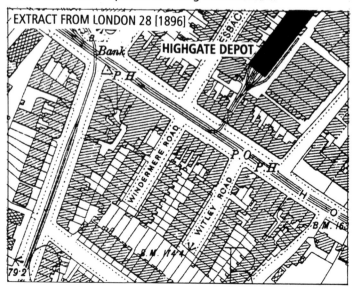

Finchley Depot

Location: At TQ26309181, on the east side of Woodberry Grove, between Rosemont Avenue and Christchurch Avenue.

Opened: June 7th, 1905 by the Metropolitan Electric Tramways Ltd and became part of London Transport from July 1st, 1933.

Traction System: Overhead Electric.

Gauge: 4ft 8.5in.

Description: Originally a 15TS dead ended tram shed constructed in brick and corrugated iron, it was extended at the rear in 1912 and again in 1930 when a 14TS maintenance depot, with access via a traverser, was added.

Closed: March 5th, 1938 and utilized as a trolley bus depot from the following day. By 2000 it was in use as an omnibus garage.

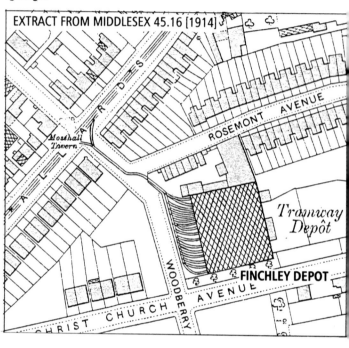

Alexandra Palace

Location: At TQ29709016 in Alexandra Park opposite the north east end of Alexandra Palace.

Opened: May 13th, 1898 by the Elektrizitäts-gesellschaft Wandruska of Berlin.

Traction System: Overhead Electric.

Gauge: 4ft 8.5in.

Description: A 2TS dead ended tram shed, constructed in corrugated iron, and generating station.

Closed: With the tramway on September 30th, 1899 and later removed.

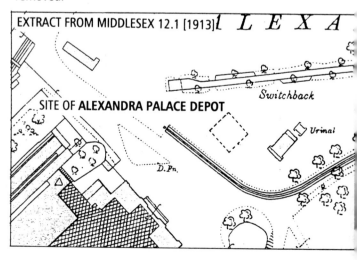

Aurelia Road Depot

Location: At TQ30526716, on the east side of Aurelia Rd, on the north side of Mitcham Rd.

Opened: May 26th, 1906 by the South Metropolitan Electric Tramways & Lighting Co. Ltd. Became part of London Transport on July 1st, 1933.

Traction System: Overhead Electric.

Gauge: 4ft 8.5in.

Description: A 4TS dead ended tram shed.

Closed: As a running shed upon the takeover by London Transport and subsequently utilized as a store and for the scrapping of tram cars. Sold in September 1937 and purchased in April 1946 by Surrey County Council. By 1982 it was in use by the Borough Engineer's Department.

EXTRACT FROM SURREY 14.5 [1913]

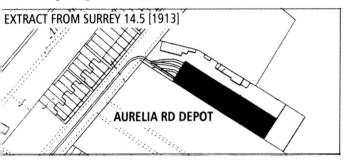

Thornton Heath Depot

Location: At TQ31276765, on the west side of London Rd, opposite Brigstock Rd.

Opened: October 9th, 1879 by the Croydon Tramways Co. (Became Croydon & Norwood Tramways Co. on August 2nd, 1883), taken over by a new Croydon Tramways Co. on January 1st, 1890 and taken over again on January 2nd, 1900 by Croydon Corporation. Became part of London Transport from July 1st, 1933.

Traction System: Horse, until February 1902, and Overhead Electric from September 26th, 1901.

Gauge: 4ft 8.5in.

Description: Originally a brick built dead ended horse tram shed, upon electrification it was converted to a 3TS through road building with the southern two roads turning south at right angles behind the building to enter a new 4TS dead ended tram shed and workshop.

Closed: December 31st, 1949 and subsequently demolished to make way for a new omnibus garage.

EXTRACT FROM SURREY 14.1 [1912] & 14.5 [1913]

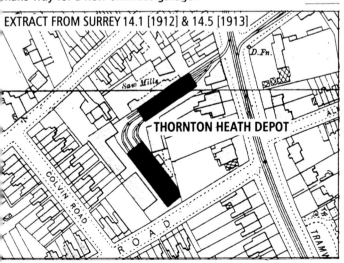

NB. From May 14th, 1880, until a connecting line was opened on June 6th, 1897, cars on the isolated southern portion were stored (off-track) in a yard behind the Swan & Sugar Loaf on the east side of the junction of South End and Brighton Road.

Penge

Location: At TQ35306950, on the north east side of Oak Grove Road, Penge.

Opened: April 12th, 1906 by the South Metropolitan Electric Tramways & Lighting Co. Ltd and became part of London Transport on July 1st 1933.

Traction System: Overhead Electric.

Gauge: 4ft 8.5in.

Description: A brick built 5TS dead ended tram shed.

Closed: December 6th, 1933 and subsequently utilized for the scrapping of tram cars. Leased out as commercial premises from 1936 and still stood, disused, in 1982.

EXTRACT FROM KENT 7.14 [1912]

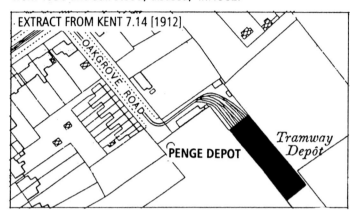

Spring Lane

Location: At TQ34786736, on the east side of the junction of Spring Lane and Portland Rd, Woodside.

Opened: December 15th, 1883 by the Croydon & Norwood Tramways Co.

Traction System: Horse.

Gauge: 4ft 8.5in.

Description: A dead ended tram shed and stables.

Closed: Shortly after October 25th, 1887 when the company went into liquidation. Sold in 1893 for use as commercial premises and demolished in 1972 to make way for housing.

EXTRACT FROM SURREY 14.7 [1898]

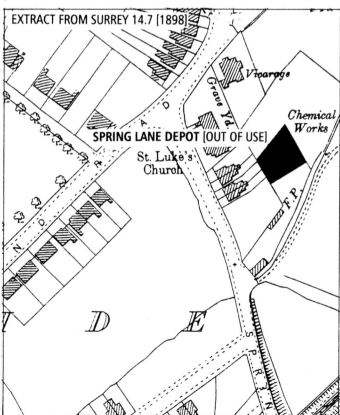

Camberwell Depots

Location: In a triangle formed by Orchard Row (Later Medlar St), Camberwell Rd and Camberwell New Rd on the east side of the railway line.

Opened: September 25th, 1871 [East Shed] and April 15th, 1873 [West Shed] by the Pimlico, Peckham & Greenwich Street Tramways Co. and became part of London Tramways Co. Ltd in 1873. Taken over by London County Council on January 1st, 1899 and became part of London Transport on July 1st, 1933.

Traction System: Horse, until 1903, and Conduit Electric from June 25th, 1903.

Gauge: 4ft 8.5in.

EAST SHED

Description: Originally a 6TS dead ended shed, located at TQ32467689, the final form was as a 9TS dead ended shed at the front and 15TS dead ended tram shed at the rear, linked by a central traverser and accessed by two tracks from Camberwell Road.

WEST SHED

Description: Originally a 3TS dead ended shed, located at TQ32357690, and stables, it was converted for temporary electric working in 1903. The final form was as a 9TS dead ended tram shed and 3TS paint shop accessed from Camberwell New Road and via a traverser at the front.

The depots were first rebuilt in brick and enlarged in 1904/5 as Camberwell Car Sheds, with the first section opening on October 17th, 1905. They were subsequently enlarged again in 1913 and later rebuilt after suffering extensive bomb damage during World War II. It was finally re-named as Walworth Depot in 1950.

Closed: October 7th, 1951 and subsequently utilized as an omnibus garage.

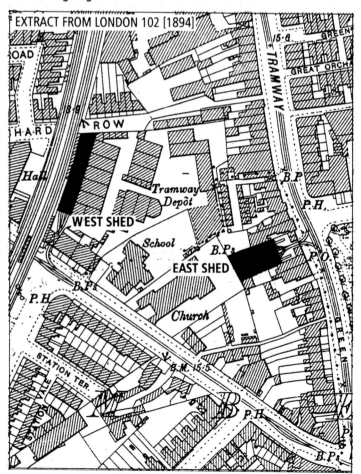

Norwood Car Shed

Location: At TQ31847261, on the east side of Norwood Rd, Tulse Hill.

Opened: October 10th, 1909 by London County Council.

Traction System: Overhead Electric.

Gauge: 4ft 8.5in.

Description: A brick built 15TS dead ended car shed with central traverser. The front entrance was utilized for temporary omnibus accommodation during the 1951 Festival of Britain.

Closed: April 6th, 1952 and subsequently sold for commercial use.

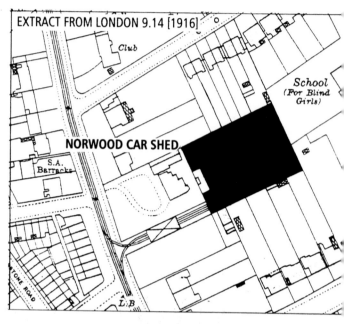

Peckham Rye

Location: At TQ34337552, on the corner of Peckham Rye and East Dulwich Rd, Peckham Rye.

Opened: 1896 by the London, Camberwell & Dulwich Tramways Co.

Traction System: Horse.

Gauge: 4ft 8.5in.

Description: A 2TS dead ended tram shed and stables.

Closed: 1900 after only intermittent operation.

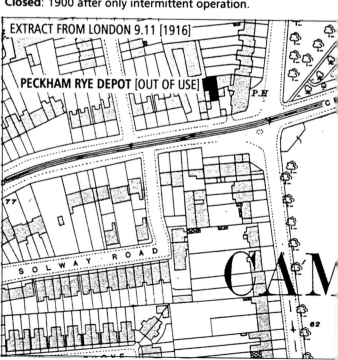

Rye Lane Depot

Location: At TQ34007665, on the west side of Basing Rd, south off Peckham High St.

Opened: January 29th, 1872 by the Pimlico, Peckham & Greenwich Street Tramways Co. and became part of London Tramways Co. Ltd in 1873. Taken over by London County Council on January 1st, 1899 and became part of London Transport from July 1st, 1933.

Traction System: Horse, until 1903/4, and Conduit Electric from January 24th, 1904.

Gauge: 4ft 8.5in.

Description: Originally a 4TS dead ended tram shed and stables, at electrification the stables were converted into workshops, a new 3TS dead ended shed was added across the yard on the east side and six dead ended roads in the yard were covered. All roads into the depot were accessed via a traverser.

Closed: As a running shed in 1906 and converted to tramway workshops with the former horse depot being adapted as a road vehicle garage and workshop. It was commandeered for military use during WWI and part of it was later utilized for tram car assembly. The depot finally closed on June 26th, 1950 and was demolished to make way for an omnibus garage.

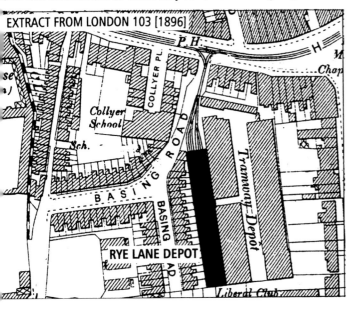

EXTRACT FROM LONDON 103 [1896]

Brixton Depot

Location: Approximately at TQ31437550, under the railway arches on the east side of Canterbury Rd.

Opened: May 2nd, 1870 by the Metropolitan Street Tramways Co. and became part of London Tramways Co. Ltd in 1873.

Traction System: Horse.

Gauge: 4ft 8.5in.

Description: A temporary depot utilizing railway arches as a dead ended shed and stables.

Closed: 1874.

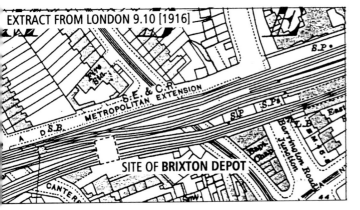

EXTRACT FROM LONDON 9.10 [1916]

SITE OF BRIXTON DEPOT

Penrose Street

Location: At TQ32267819, on the south side of Penrose St., west off Walworth Rd.

Opened: September 25th, 1871 by the Pimlico, Peckham & Greenwich Street Tramways Co. and became part of London Tramways Co. Ltd in 1873. Taken over by London County Council on January 1st, 1899.

Traction System: Horse.

Gauge: 4ft 8.5in.

Description: A dead ended shed and works with the adjacent railway arches utilized for stables. Omnibuses were also housed at the depot.

Closed: As a running shed in 1903 and used for horse tram car maintenance until 1906 when the work was transferred to LCC's Leytonstone Car Works. The building was let out for commercial use in 1907 with part of it being utilized as an omnibus garage.

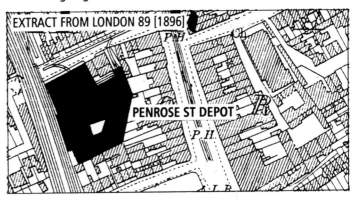

EXTRACT FROM LONDON 89 [1896]

PENROSE ST DEPOT

East Greenwich Depot

Location: At TQ38887810, on the north side of Old Woolwich Rd and west side of Hoskins St.

Opened: March 4th, 1871 by the Pimlico, Peckham & Greenwich Street Tramways Co. and became part of London Tramways Co. Ltd in 1873. Taken over by London County Council on January 1st, 1899.

Traction System: Horse, until 1903, and Conduit Electric from January 17th, 1904.

Gauge: 4ft 8.5in.

Description: A dead ended, probably 4TS, tram shed, and stables. It was converted for temporary electric use in 1903/4.

Closed: June 16th, 1905 and subsequently demolished to make way for a tramway generating station.

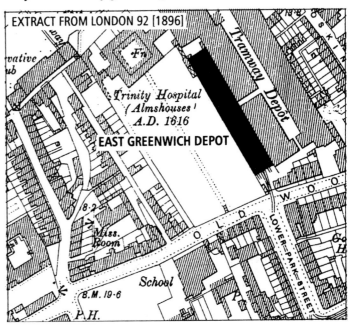

EXTRACT FROM LONDON 92 [1896]

EAST GREENWICH DEPOT

Borough Rd

Location: At TQ31967951 on the north side of Borough Road, west of Southwark Bridge Road.

Opened: May 29th, 1883 by the South London Tramways Co. and taken over on November 22nd, 1902 by London County Council Tramways.

Traction System: Horse.

Gauge: 4ft 8.5in.

Description: A dead ended tram shed with one through road.

Closed: Not known, but probably out of use by 1902.

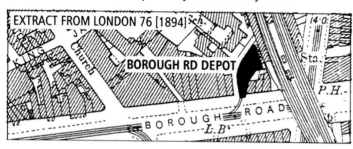

Evelyn Street

Location: At TQ36007846, on the south west side of the Lower Rd & Evelyn St. junction, Rotherhithe.

Opened: October 28th, 1880 by the Southwark & Deptford Tramways Co. (Renamed as the London, Deptford & Greenwich Tramways Co. in 1893) and taken over by London County Council on July 7th, 1904.

Traction System: Horse, probably until February 25th, 1911, and oil-gas from 1892 to 1895/6.

Gauge: 4ft 8.5in.

Description: A 6TS dead ended tram shed and stables.

Closed: At the end of horse working it was utilized as a store and part let for commercial use. It re-opened on August 31st, 1916 to house electric trailer tramcars, until such working was abandoned from April 17th, 1925, and then was used for the sale and scrapping of trailers, after which it was sold.

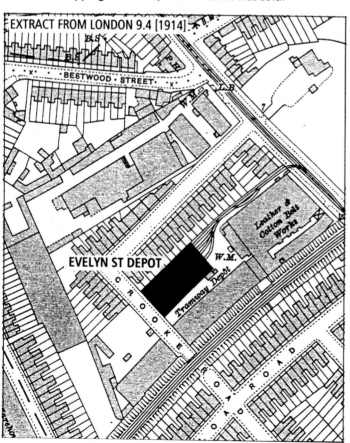

Stockwell Rd

Location: At TQ30907598, on the north east side of Stockwell Rd, west of Brixton Rd and behind the Old Queen's Head Pub.

Opened: December 7th, 1883 by the London Southern Tramways Co. Operated by London County Council from October 2nd, 1906 and taken over by them on December 20th, 1906.

Traction System: Horse.

Gauge: 4ft 8.5in.

Description: A dead ended tram shed, probably of 3 or 4 roads, and stables.

Closed: 1908 and subsequently utilized as commercial premises.

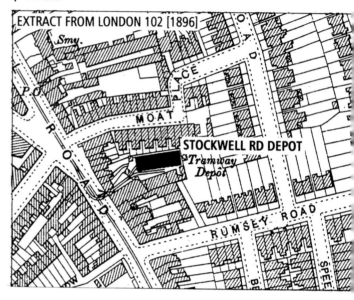

Lansdowne Hill

Location: At TQ31787233, at the rear of Lansdowne Hill off the west side of Norwood Rd (Thurlow Place), West Norwood.

Opened: June 4th, 1885 by the London Southern Tramways Co. Operated by London County Council from October 2nd, 1906 and taken over by them on December 20th, 1906.

Traction System: Horse.

Gauge: 4ft 8.5in.

Description: A dead ended tram shed, probably of 3 or 4 roads, and stables.

Closed: 1909.

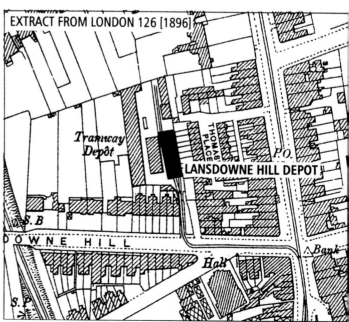

Telford Avenue Depot

Location: At TQ30507314, at the top of Streatham Hill, opposite Telford Avenue.

Opened: Probably on December 7th, 1892 by the London Tramways Co. Ltd and taken over by London County Council on January 1st, 1899. Became part of London Transport from July 1st, 1933.

Traction System: Cable, until April 5th, 1904, and then Conduit Electric from February 3rd, 1906.

Gauge: 4ft 8.5in.

Description: Originally a brick built depot with one entrance road and four storage roads linked by a traverser to six dead ended storage roads, a 1TS repair shop and a winding house. Upon electrification the running shed was rebuilt as a 6TS dead ended depot with traverser and the winding house was rebuilt as a 10TS dead ended tram shed with traverser. A brick built 6TS dead ended tram shed with traverser was constructed on the south side of the site in 1911/12. In 1950 it was re-named as Brixton Depot.

Closed: April 7th, 1951 and then used as an omnibus garage.

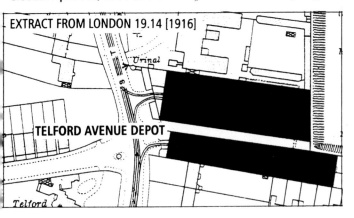

EXTRACT FROM LONDON 19.14 [1916]

TELFORD AVENUE DEPOT

Brixton Hill Car Shed

Location: At TQ30507352, at No.219 on the east side of Brixton Hill.

Opened: March 6th, 1924 by London County Council and became part of London Transport from July 1st, 1933.

Traction System: Overhead & Conduit Electric.

Gauge: 4ft 8.5in.

Description: A brick built 7TS dead ended car shed. Originally constructed as a trailer car running shed it was not utilized as such, but was used as an overhead/conduit running shed and a store for withdrawn trailers awaiting disposal.

Closed: April 7th, 1951 and sold for commercial use.

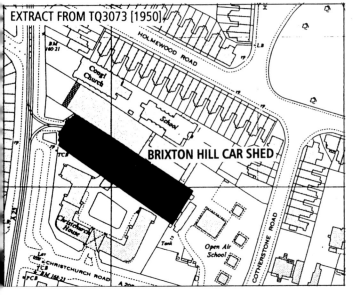

EXTRACT FROM TQ3073 [1950]

BRIXTON HILL CAR SHED

Bowles Road

Location: At TQ34227781, at the end of Bowles Rd, south off Old Kent Rd.

Opened: 1874 by the London Tramways Co. Ltd and taken over by London County Council on January 1st, 1899.

Traction System: Horse, and then Conduit Electric from January 17th, 1904.

Gauge: 4ft 8.5in.

Description: A dead ended tram shed and stables. It was converted for temporary electric use in 1903.

Closed: May 20th, 1905. The lease was surrendered and the building converted to an omnibus garage.

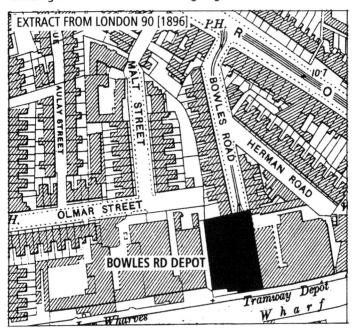

EXTRACT FROM LONDON 90 [1896]

BOWLES RD DEPOT

Leo Street

Location: At TQ35007738, on the south west side of Old Kent Rd, between Leo St. and Gervase St.

Opened: May 1st, 1871 by the Pimlico, Peckham & Greenwich Street Tramways Co. and became part of London Tramways Co. Ltd in 1873. Taken over by London County Council on January 1st, 1899.

Traction System: Horse, until 1903, and Conduit Electric from January 17th, 1904.

Gauge: 4ft 8.5in.

Description: A dead ended, probably 4TS, tram shed, and stables. It was converted for temporary electric use in 1903.

Closed: May 28th, 1905 and utilized by the LCC as a central stores until 1928. The stables were then demolished to make way for a cinema and the remaining southern part of the depot converted for use as a garage.

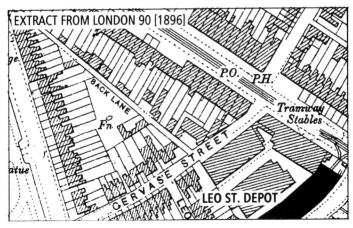

EXTRACT FROM LONDON 90 [1896]

LEO ST. DEPOT

Black Horse Depot

Location: *At TQ37787354, by the Black Horse, on the east side of Rushey Green (Broadway), Catford.*
Opened: October 11th, 1890 by the South Eastern Metropolitan Tramways Co. and taken over by London County Council on April 1st, 1902.
Traction System: Horse.
Gauge: 4ft 8.5in.
Description: A 2TS dead ended tram shed.
Closed: In the summer of 1906 shortly after the start of electric working on June 10th, 1906. It was subsequently demolished and the site utilized for part of a Coach Station.

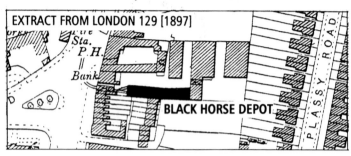

Queen's Road Depot

Location: *At TQ35107691, on the west side of Astbury Rd, north off Queen's Rd.*
Opened: January 29th, 1872, by the Pimlico, Peckham & Greenwich Street Tramways Co. and became part of London Tramways Co. Ltd in 1873. Taken over by London County Council on January 1st, 1899.
Traction System: Horse.
Gauge: 4ft 8.5in.
Description: A 2TS through road shed on the west side of the railway with a turntable at the rear accessing another turntable and 3TS dead ended tram shed and stables on the east side.
Closed: 1903/4 when the route was electrified. The west side of the site was cleared to make way for a footpath.

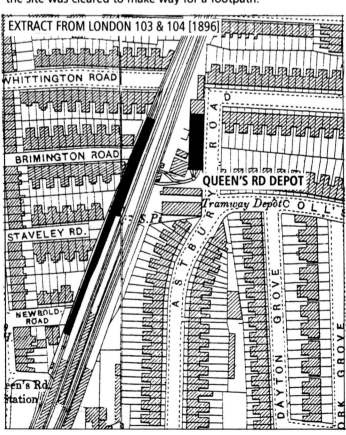

Brixton Road

Location: *At TQ31217740, at No.20 Brixton Rd, Kennington.*
Opened: Probably on December 7th, 1892 by the London Tramways Co. Ltd and taken over by London County Council on January 1st, 1899.
Traction System: Cable.
Gauge: 4ft 8.5in.
Description: A brick built 1TS dead ended tram shed and stables for horses used on connecting horse car services and shunting.
Closed: Not known, but probably shortly before the line re-opened with electric working on August 2nd, 1903. Part of the site was subsequently utilized for a tramway sub-station.

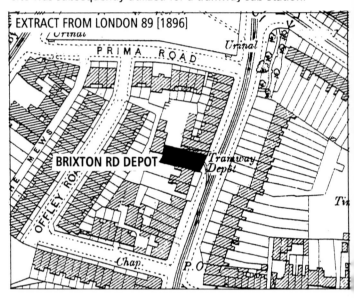

Balls Yard

Location: *At TQ31137830, on the west side of the junction of Kennington Rd and Upper Kennington Lane, south of Sancroft St.*
Opened: 1874 by the London Tramways Co. Ltd and taken over by London County Council on January 1st, 1899.
Traction System: Horse.
Gauge: 4ft 8.5in.
Description: A dead ended tram shed and stables.
Closed: Not known, but probably shortly before the line re-opened with electric working on May 15th, 1903.

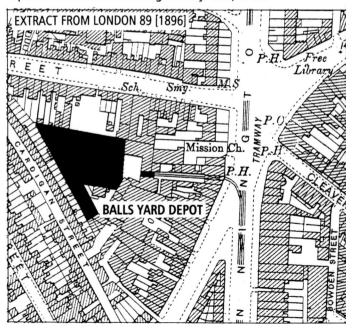

New Cross Car Shed

Location: At TQ35967670, at "Fairlawn" on the south side of New Cross Rd, east of New Cross Gate.
Opened: May 15th, 1905 by London County Council and became part of London Transport from July 1st, 1933.
Traction System: Conduit Electric.
Gauge: 4ft 8.5in.
Description: A brick built tram shed with 29 front roads and 32 rear roads with a central traverser and 7 workshop roads.
Closed: July 6th, 1952 and subsequently utilized as an omnibus garage.

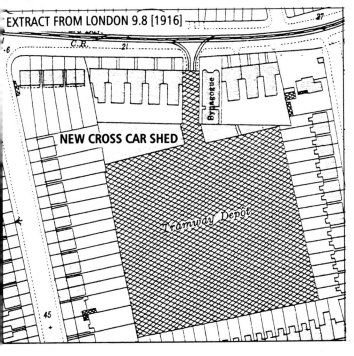

EXTRACT FROM LONDON 9.8 [1916]

NEW CROSS CAR SHED

Greenwich Depot

Location: At TQ37617705, on the north west side of Greenwich Rd, north of the junction with Blackheath Rd, Deptford.
Opened: December 13th, 1870 by the Pimlico, Peckham & Greenwich Street Tramways Co. and became part of London Tramways Co. Ltd in 1873.
Traction System: Horse.
Gauge: 4ft 8.5in.
Description: A dead ended, possibly 6TS, tram shed and stables
Closed: Not known, but as a running shed as outlying depots opened. Became Deptford Wharf PW Depot and Granary and was enlarged by London County Council after their take over on July 1st, 1899. Used by London Transport until the closure of the system on July 5th, 1952.

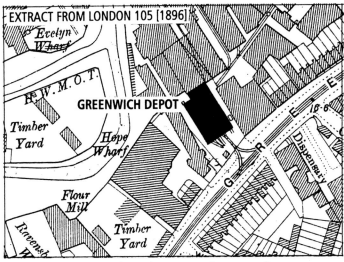

EXTRACT FROM LONDON 105 [1896]

GREENWICH DEPOT

NB. This depot may have been a replacement for temporary premises located nearby.

Bristol Tramways' **Brislington Depot**, with the running shed nearest the camera and the works beyond.
Courtesy Peter Davey Photograph Collection
(See Page 47)

York St

Location: At TQ30688299 on the west side of York (Later Lorenzo) Street.

Opened: December 16th, 1886 by the London Street Tramways Co. and taken over by London County Council on October 13th, 1897.

Traction System: Horse.

Gauge: 4ft 8.5in.

Description: A dead ended tram shed and stables.

Closed: Exact date unknown but by May 29th, 1909 when the route re-opened following electrification.

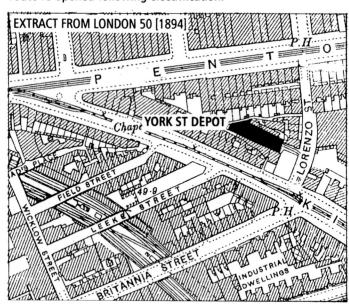

Angel Yard

Location: At TQ31398320, on the west side of The Angel and north side of Pentonville Rd, Islington.

Opened: June 25th, 1883 by the London Street Tramways Co. and taken over by London County Council on October 13th, 1897.

Gauge: 4ft 8.5in.

Description: Probably a covered yard and stables.

Closed: Exact date unknown but by July 29th, 1907 when the route re-opened following electrification.

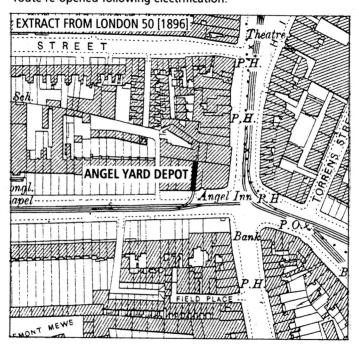

Parkhurst Road

Location: At TQ30308591, on the north side of Parkhurst Rd, Holloway Park.

Opened: October 1st 1872 by the London Street Tramways Co. and taken over by London County Council on October 13th, 1897.

Gauge: 4ft 8.5in.

Description: A 6TS dead ended tram shed and stables.

Closed: Probably in November 1908 when the route conversion to electric working began.

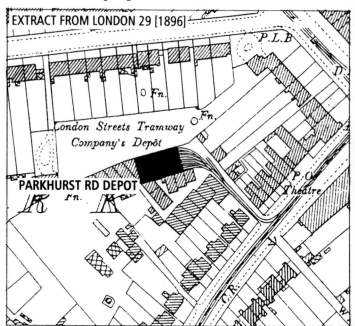

Warlter's Rd

Location: At TQ30538683 on the north side of Camden Road, Holloway Park.

Opened: September 28th, 1878 by the London Street Tramways Co. and taken over by London County Council on October 13th, 1897.

Traction System: Horse.

Gauge: 4ft 8.5in.

Description: A dead ended tram shed, possibly of 1 to 3 roads, and stables.

Closed: Exact date unknown but by August 15th, 1908 when the route re-opened following electrification.

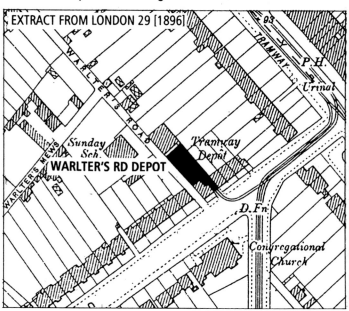

Russell Road

Location: Approximately at TQ37588797, on the corner of Lea Bridge Rd and Russell Rd, Leyton.
Opened: May 12th, 1883 by the Lea Bridge, Leyton & Walthamstow Tramways Co.
Traction System: Horse.
Gauge: 4ft 8.5in.
Description: A horse tram shed. No details are known.
Closed: October 1884 upon closure of the tramway. The company was wound up on December 13th, 1884 and evicted from the depot.

Lea Bridge Road

Location: At TQ37728799, on the south east side of Lea Bridge Rd, between Dunton Rd and Westerham Rd, Leyton.
Opened: May 13th, 1889 by the Lea Bridge, Leyton & Walthamstow Tramways Co. Ltd, taken over by Leyton UDC on June 1st, 1905 and taken over again by London County Council on July 1st, 1921. Became part of London Transport from July 1st, 1933.
Traction System: Horse, until December 9th, 1908. Overhead Electric from December 1st, 1906.
Gauge: 4ft 8.5in.
Description: Originally a dead ended tram shed, probably 1 or 2TS, and stables it was reconstructed in 1906-8 as a brick built 10TS dead ended tram shed and 2TS dead ended works. A central traverser was installed In 1931.
Closed: To trams on June 10th, 1939 and utilized as a trolley bus depot from the following day.

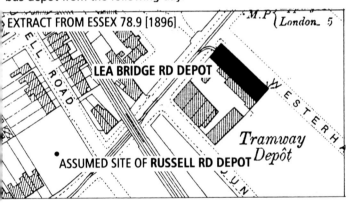

EXTRACT FROM ESSEX 78.9 [1896]
LEA BRIDGE RD DEPOT
ASSUMED SITE OF RUSSELL RD DEPOT
Tramway Depôt

Kingsway Subway

Location: At TQ30648101, at the southern end of Kingsway Subway beneath the western half of Aldwych.
Opened: February 24th, 1906 by London County Council.
Traction System: Conduit Electric.
Gauge: 4ft 8.5in.
Description: The south end of Kingsway Subway was converted to a temporary 2TS dead ended depot whilst the line was being extended to Victoria Embankment.
Closed: Prior to through running to Victoria Embankment on April 10th, 1908.

EXTRACT FROM LONDON 5.10 [1916]
SITE OF KINGSWAY SUBWAY DEPOT

Bow Car Shed

Location: At TQ37408310, on the north east side of Fairfield Rd.
Opened: June 25th, 1908 by London County Council and became part of London Transport from July 1st, 1933.
Traction System: Stud Contact Electric. until July 31st, 1908 and then Overhead Electric from August 14th, 1908.
Gauge: 4ft 8.5in.
Description: A brick built depot constructed in two halves, in 1908 and 1910, with a final configuration of an 18TS dead ended car shed with two central traversers. Part of it was utilized as a workshop.
Closed: November 5th, 1939 and subsequently utilized as a trolley bus depot.

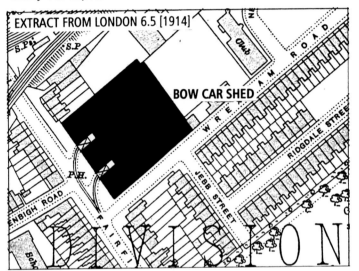

EXTRACT FROM LONDON 6.5 [1914]
BOW CAR SHED

Stamford Hill Car Shed

Location: At TQ34058790, on the east side of Rookwood Rd, opposite the end of Egerton Rd, Stamford Hill.
Opened: February 7th, 1907 by London County Council and became part of London Transport from July 1st, 1933.
Traction System: Overhead & Conduit Electric.
Gauge: 4ft 8.5in.
Description: A brick built 28TS dead ended tram shed with two traversers.
Closed: February 5th, 1939 and subsequently utilized as a trolley bus depot.

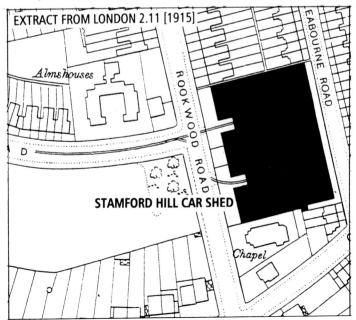

EXTRACT FROM LONDON 2.11 [1915]
Almshouses
STAMFORD HILL CAR SHED
Chapel

Finsbury Park

Location: At TQ32958845, in Kingsford Terrace on the north side of Seven Sisters Road, Finsbury Park.

Opened: October 24th, 1885 by the North London Tramways Co. From August 1st, 1891 it was operated by the North Metropolitan Tramways Co. and taken over by them on April 12th, 1892.

Traction System: Steam, until July 31st, 1891, and then Horse.

Gauge: 4ft 8.5in.

Description: A 2TS dead ended tram shed.

Closed: Not known but probably between 1895 and 1900.

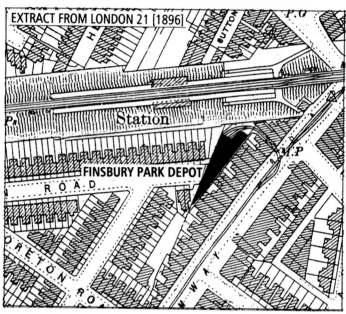

Manor House Depot

Location: At TQ32098758, on the east side of Green Lanes and north side of Seven Sisters Rd, Manor House.

Opened: 1899 by the North Metropolitan Tramways Co. and taken over by Metropolitan Electric Tramways Ltd on November 26th, 1902.

Traction System: Horse.

Gauge: 4ft 8.5in.

Description: A dead ended tram shed and stables.

Closed: Not known but prior to completion of electrification on July 22nd, 1904. It was subsequently rebuilt and utilized as offices and a pw and engineering depot and stores. Taken over by London Transport on April 1st, 1933 and retained as offices.

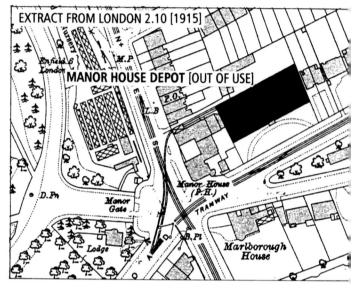

Poplar Car Shed

Location: At TQ38418160, on the north east side of Leven Rd, west of the River Lea.

Opened: December 15th, 1906 by London County Council and became part of London Transport from July 1st, 1933.

Traction System: Conduit Electric.

Gauge: 4ft 8.5in.

Description: Constructed in brick between 1906 and 1912, with a final configuration of 2 access roads to 2 central traversers with 18 dead ended tracks at the front and 20 dead ended tracks at the rear, with four of these in use as a repair shop. The rear part of the site was utilized as a pw depot.

Closed: June 9th, 1940 and subsequently used as a trolley bus depot.

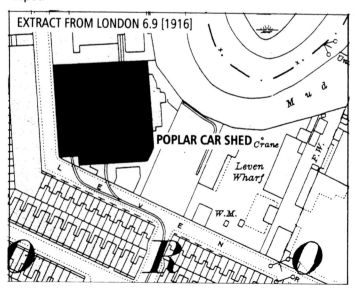

Lea Bridge Depot

Location: At TQ34888633, on the east side of Upper Clapton Rd, north of Prout Rd, Clapton.

Opened: July 12th, 1873 by the North Metropolitan Tramways Co. and taken over by London County Council on April 1st, 1906.

Traction System: Horse.

Gauge: 4ft 8.5in.

Description: A 2TS dead ended tram shed and stables.

Closed: May 17th, 1907.

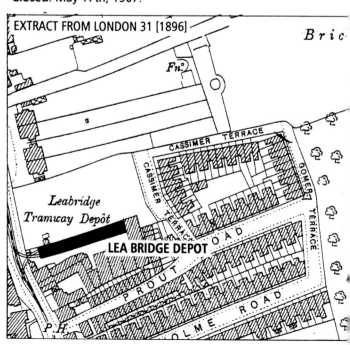

Bow Bridge Wharf

Location: At TQ37928318, in a contractors yard on the east side of Bow Bridge and north side of High St.

Opened: May 9th, 1870 by the North Metropolitan Tramways Co.

Traction System: Horse.

Gauge: 4ft 8.5in.

Description: There was no building. Tram cars were stored on the spur line.

Closed: 1874 and let out for commercial use until 1878 when it was utilized for tramway stabling.

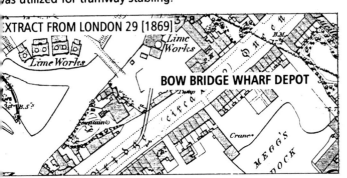

Stratford Depot

Location: At TQ38978431, on the east side of West Ham Lane.

Opened: February 27th, 1904 by West Ham Corporation.

Traction System: Overhead Electric.

Gauge: 4ft 8.5in.

Description: A temporary 8TS dead ended tram shed constructed in corrugated iron.

Closed: 1906. Site subsequently cleared to make way for housing and the Broadway Cinema.

Swan Yard Depot

Location: At TQ39018434, east of West Ham Lane and on the south side of Stratford Broadway.

Opened: March 1st, 1871 by the North Metropolitan Tramways Co. and taken over by London County Council on April 1st, 1906.

Traction System: Horse. Also Battery Electric between July 6th, 1886 and July 8th, 1888.

Gauge: 4ft 8.5in.

Description: A 5TS dead ended tram shed and stables.

Closed: March 31st, 1906 and subsequently utilized as a sweet factory.

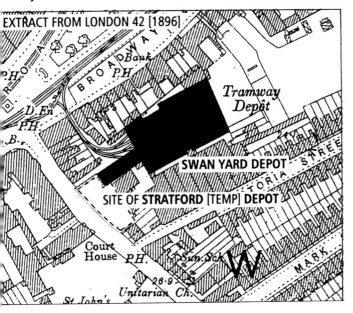

Hackney Depot

Location: At TQ35128499, at the east end of Bohemia Place.

Opened: Summer 1883 by the North Metropolitan Tramways Co., taken over by London County Council on April 1st, 1906 and became part of London Transport on July 1st, 1933.

Traction System: Horse, until May 17th, 1907 and then Conduit Electric from March 31st, 1909.

Gauge: 4ft 8.5in.

Description: Originally a 6TS dead ended tram shed and stables, it was replaced in 1909 by a shed with 13 dead ended storage roads and two access roads at the front, two central traversers and 16 roads at the rear. It also accommodated trolley buses from June 11th, 1939.

Closed: To trams on December 9th, 1940 and subsequently utilized as a trolley bus depot.

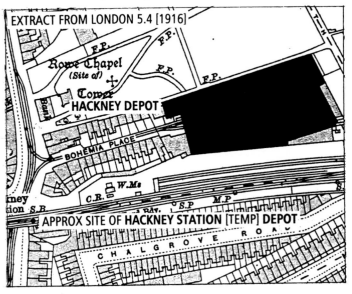

NB. From mid-1873 until mid-1875 temporary horse and tram car accommodation was provided under the railway arches at Hackney Station. Approximately located at TQ35008493, it was utilized until Stamford Hill Depot was completed.

Stamford Hill [Portland Avenue] Depot

Location: At TQ33918750, on the east side of the corner of Portland Ave and Darenth Rd, Stamford Hill.

Opened: April 3rd, 1875 (or shortly after) by the North Metropolitan Tramways Co. and taken over by London County Council on April 1st, 1906.

Traction System: Horse.

Gauge: 4ft 8.5in

Description: An 8TS tram shed, with five through roads, and stables.

Closed: September 23rd, 1909.

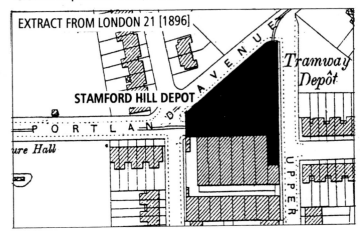

Grove Road

Location: At TQ36188276, on the west side of Grove Rd, Mile End.

Opened: October 5th, 1872 by the North Metropolitan Tramways Co. and taken over by London County Council on April 1st, 1906.

Traction System: Horse.

Gauge: 4ft 8.5in.

Description: A 3TS dead ended tram shed and stables.

Closed: August 11th, 1914 when all the horses were requisitioned by the War Department, thus ending horse working on London's tramways.

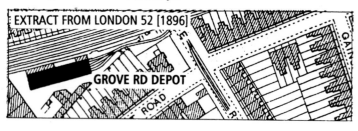

EXTRACT FROM LONDON 52 [1896]
GROVE RD DEPOT

Green Lanes

Location: At TQ32318630, on the west side of Green Lanes and corner of Riversdale Rd and Highbury Quadrant.

Opened: September 4th, 1883 (or shortly after) by the North Metropolitan Tramways Co. and taken over by London County Council on April 1st, 1906.

Traction System: Horse.

Gauge: 4ft 8.5in.

Description: A dead ended tram shed, probably 5TS, and stables.

Closed: Exact date unknown but by August 3rd, 1912 when the route re-opened following electrification.

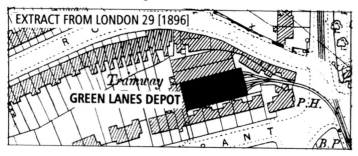

EXTRACT FROM LONDON 29 [1896]
Tramway
GREEN LANES DEPOT

Finsbury Park

Location: At TQ31468691, on the east side of Finsbury Park (GN) Railway Station.

Opened: 1872 by the North Metropolitan Tramways Co. and taken over by London County Council on April 1st, 1906.

Traction System: Horse.

Gauge: 4ft 8.5in.

Description: A dead ended tram shed and stables.

Closed: Exact date unknown but by July 9th, 1908 when the route re-opened following electrification.

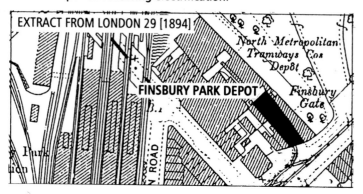

EXTRACT FROM LONDON 29 [1894]
North Metropolitan Tramways Co's Depot
FINSBURY PARK DEPOT
Finsbury Gate

Poplar [Athol St] Depot

Location: At TQ38508119 on the corner of Aberfeldy St. a Athol St., Poplar.

Opened: September 9th, 1872 by the North Metropolit Tramways Co. and taken over by London County Council April 1st, 1906.

Traction System: Horse.

Gauge: 4ft 8.5in.

Description: A 6TS dead ended tram shed and stables.

Closed: July 31st, 1909.

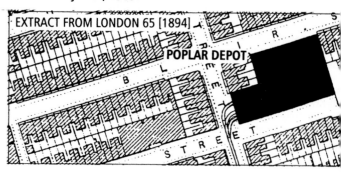

EXTRACT FROM LONDON 65 [1894]
POPLAR DEPOT
STREET

Canonbury [Highbury] Depot

Location: At TQ31798480, on the north side of St Paul's R Highbury.

Opened: March 26th, 1879 by the North Metropolita Tramways Co. and taken over by London County Council April 1st, 1906.

Traction System: Horse. Conduit Electric between Novemb 16th, 1906 until November 28th, 1907 when Holloway C Shed opened.

Gauge: 4ft 8.5in.

Description: A dead ended tram shed, probably 2TS, wit stables above. It was converted to a temporary electric shed 1906.

Closed: June 13th, 1913 and subsequently utilized as a garage

EXTRACT FROM LONDON 39 [1896]
Bank
Tramway Depot
CANONBURY DEPOT
P.O.
P.H.
P.H.

TRAINS TRAMWAYS

In 1861 George Francis Train opened three Horse Tramways the London area. These were;

1. From Marble Arch to Porchester Terrace via Bayswater Rc operating as the Marble Arch Street Rail Co. Ltd. Opened o March 23rd, 1861 and closed by mid-September 1861.

2. From Victoria Station to Parliament Square via Victoria St operating as the Westminster Street Rail Co. Ltd. Opened o April 15th, 1861 and closed on March 6th, 1862.

3. From the east side of Westminster Bridge, past Lambet Palace, to Kennington Gate, operating as the Surrey Side Stree Rail Co. Ltd. Opened on August 15th, 1861 and closed on Jun 21st, 1862.

Neither the gauge of these lines (possibly 4ft 8.5in), nor th existence, or location, of any sheds is known.

Edmonton

Location: At TQ35179468, in Tramway Avenue, on the east side of Hertford Rd.

Opened: April 10th, 1881 by the North London Suburban Tramways Co. Ltd and taken over by the North London Tramways Co. in 1882. From August 1st, 1891 it was operated by the North Metropolitan Tramways Co. and taken over by them on April 12th, 1892. It was finally taken over by the Metropolitan Electric Tramways Ltd on November 26th, 1902 and became part of London Transport on July 1st, 1933.

Traction System: Horse, until May 31st, 1885 and then from August 1st, 1891 until 1905. Steam, from April 1st, 1885 until July 31st, 1891 and Overhead Electric from July 19th, 1905.

Gauge: 4ft 8.5in.

Description: Originally a brick built 12TS dead ended tram shed, it was converted to electric working in 1904 and extended in 1907.

Closed: November 5th, 1938 and utilized as a trolley bus depot from the next day and, later, as an omnibus garage. It closed in 1968.

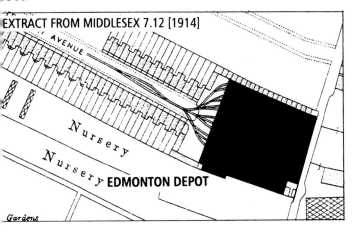

EXTRACT FROM MIDDLESEX 7.12 [1914]

Wood Green Depot

Location: At TQ30889044, on the west side of High Rd, south of Watson's Rd, Wood Green.

Opened: 1895 by the North Metropolitan Tramways & Omnibus Co. and leased to the North Metropolitan Tramways Co. Became the Metropolitan Electric Tramways Ltd on January 15th, 1902 and part of London Transport from July 1st, 1933.

Traction System: Horse, until 1904 and then Overhead Electric from July 24th, 1904.

Gauge: 4ft 8.5in.

Description: Originally a brick built 7TS dead ended tram shed and stables, it was converted to electric working as a 7TS dead ended tram shed and extended at the rear in 1908 and 1912.

Closed: May 7th, 1938 and utilized as a trolley bus depot from the following day. By 2000 it was in use as an omnibus garage.

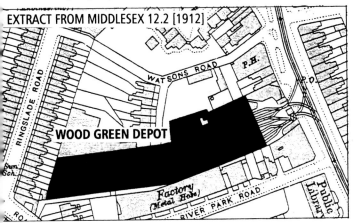

EXTRACT FROM MIDDLESEX 12.2 [1912]

Walthamstow

Location: At TQ37289016, on the west side of Chingford Rd.

Opened: June 3rd, 1905 by Walthamstow UDC (as Walthamstow UDC Light Railways). Became part of London Transport from July 1st, 1933.

Traction System: Overhead Electric.

Gauge: 4ft 8.5in.

Description: Originally a brick built 8TS dead ended tram shed with a 4TS paint and repair shop at the rear, it was extended at the front in 1919/20 and a 2TS extension was constructed on the north west side in 1928. In 1934/5 a siding was added beyond the north west wall to facilitate the scrapping of trams. The depot was also utilized to accommodate trolley buses from October 18th, 1936.

Closed: To trams from June 12th, 1937 and to trolley buses on April 26th, 1960, from which date it was used exclusively for omnibuses until 1993. The site was redeveloped for housing in 1995.

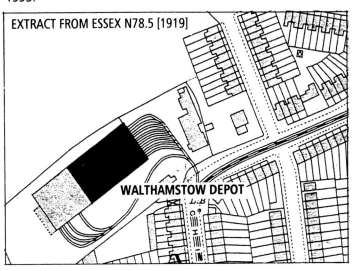

EXTRACT FROM ESSEX N78.5 [1919]

Abbey Wood Car Shed

Location: At TQ47297894, on the north side of Abbey Wood Rd, just south of Abbey Wood Station.

Opened: July 23rd, 1910 by London County Council and became part of London Transport from July 1st, 1933.

Traction System: Overhead Electric.

Gauge: 4ft 8.5in.

Description: Originally a brick built dead ended car shed, an extension was added on the east side on October 1914 and the final configuration was of a 20TS dead ended shed accessed via a central traverser.

Closed: July 6th, 1952 and subsequently utilized as an omnibus garage.

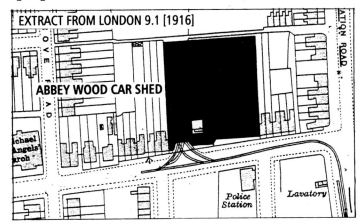

EXTRACT FROM LONDON 9.1 [1916]

Plumstead

Location: At TQ42537851, on the west side of Cage Lane (Lakedale Rd from 1884), south of Plumstead High St.

Opened: 1882 by the Woolwich & South East London Tramways Co. Ltd and taken over by London County Council on June 1st, 1905.

Traction System: Horse, until September 1907 and then again from August 29th, 1910 for shuttle working, and Overhead Electric from April 17th, 1908.

Gauge: 3ft 6in (Horse) & 4ft 8.5in (Overhead Electric).

Description: Originally two adjacent brick built 3TS dead ended tram sheds, a 3TS works and stables; part of it was converted and re-gauged for electric working in 1908.

Closed: Part of the premises were let out for stabling in 1910 and the depot closed on November 24th, 1913 when it was requisitioned for use as stables during World War I.

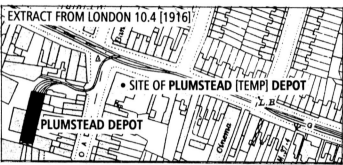

EXTRACT FROM LONDON 10.4 [1916]

NB. A temporary depot, located at TQ45317853, on the east side of the corner of Cage Lane and Plumstead High St. was utilized from June 4th, 1881 until Plumstead Depot opened.

Tunnel Avenue

Location: At TQ40077837, on the west side of Tunnel Avenue.

Opened: September 1907 by London County Council.

Traction System: Horse.

Gauge: 3ft 6in.

Description: A temporary depot consisting of corrugated iron clad stables with tram cars being housed under tarpaulins on two storage roads. Sited on Council land leased as allotments, it was used as the principal storage area for cars utilized on the former Woolwich & South East London Tramways system whilst it was being re-gauged and electrified. Horses were stabled here throughout, but the tram cars were intermittently stored at other locations as the reconstruction work progressed.

Closed: Prior to August 29th, 1910 when the tram cars reverted back to the former W&SELT depot at Plumstead.

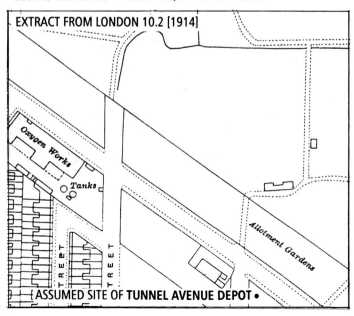

EXTRACT FROM LONDON 10.2 [1914]

ASSUMED SITE OF TUNNEL AVENUE DEPOT •

East Ham

Location: At TQ42758350, on the north side of Nelson St., the corner of Barking Rd and High St.South.

Opened: June 22nd, 1901 by East Ham Corporation. Becam part of London Transport from July 1st, 1933.

Traction System: Overhead Electric.

Gauge: 4ft 8.5in.

Description: Originally a 3TS dead ended tram shed an workshop, it was extended in stages to a brick built 9TS dead ended tram shed.

Closed: As a running shed on August 16th, 1933. It was final closed on September 30th, 1933 and subsequently sold.

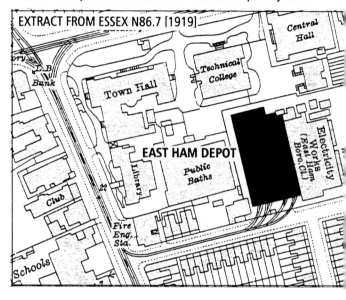

EXTRACT FROM ESSEX N86.7 [1919]

Barking

Location: At TQ44448200, on the east side of Jenkins Lane Beckton.

Opened: December 1st, 1903 by Barking Town UDC (as Barkin Town Urban District Council Light Railways)

Traction System: Overhead Electric.

Gauge: 4ft 8.5in.

Description: A 4TS dead ended tram shed constructed i corrugated iron.

Closed: The shed was dispensed with on February 10th, 192 and immediately demolished to make way for an omnibu stand. The trams were then stored on the neighbourin terminal road until February 16th when this part of the syster closed.

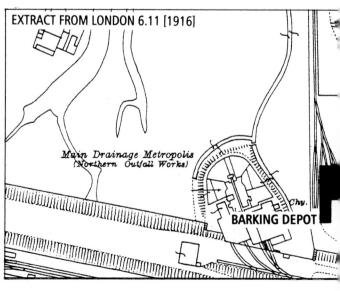

EXTRACT FROM LONDON 6.11 [1916]

Ilford

Location: At TQ44468766, on the west side of Ley St , north of Perth Rd.
Opened: March 14th, 1903 by Ilford UDC and became part of London Transport from July 1st, 1933.
Traction System: Overhead Electric.
Gauge: 4ft 8.5in.
Description: Originally a brick built 6TS dead ended tram shed, it was enlarged in 1909 and a 2TS extension was added to the north side in 1921.
Closed: February 6th, 1938 and subsequently utilized as a trolleybus depot. The building was later used for tram car restoration.

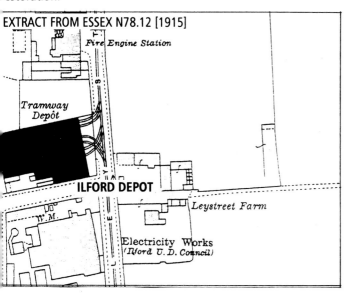
EXTRACT FROM ESSEX N78.12 [1915]

West Ham Depot

Location: At TQ40648290 on the west side of Greengate St , south of The Broadway.
Opened: Officially on October 25th, 1906 by West Ham Corporation and became part of London Transport from July 1st, 1933.
Traction System: Overhead Electric.
Gauge: 4ft 8.5in.
Description: A 16TS tram shed and workshops with 15 through roads constructed in brick and corrugated iron. The depot was also used by trolleybuses from June 6th, 1937.
Closed: To trams on June 8th, 1940 and subsequently utilized as a trolleybus depot.

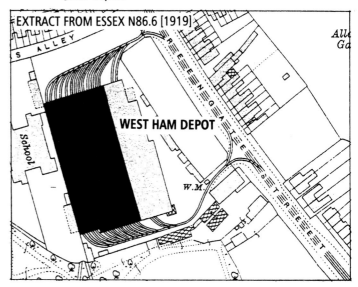
EXTRACT FROM ESSEX N86.6 [1919]

Tunmarsh Lane Depot

Location: At TQ41038283, on the corner of Jedburgh Rd and Tunmarsh Lane, Plaistow.
Opened: September 29th, 1886 by the North Metropolitan Tramways Co.
Traction System: Horse. Also Battery Electric between June 14th, 1889 and July 27th, 1892.
Gauge: 4ft 8.5in.
Description: A 3TS tram shed with 1 through road, and stables. The depot also accommodated horse buses.
Closed: To trams on June 30th, 1903 and horse buses in 1905. The building was later sold.

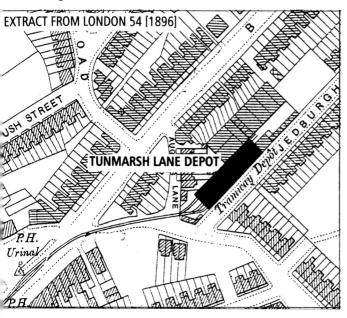
EXTRACT FROM LONDON 54 [1896]

Manor Park Depot

Location: On the south side of Romford Rd, east of Red Post Lane (Later Katherine Rd), Manor Park.
Opened: July 31st, 1886 by the North Metropolitan Tramways Co.
Traction System: Horse.
Gauge: 4ft 8.5in.
Description: Originally a 5TS dead ended and stables located at TQ41358508, a 2TS dead ended tram shed was constructed in 1896/7 to the east of the original shed at TQ41538514
Closed: April 28th, 1908. The whole site was subsequently redeveloped.

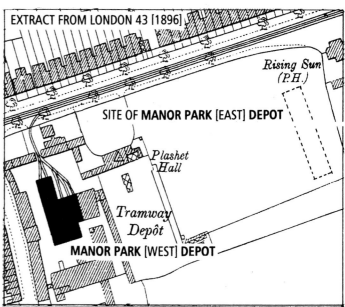
EXTRACT FROM LONDON 43 [1896]

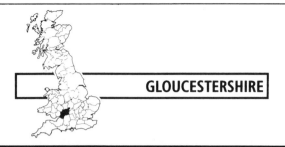

GLOUCESTERSHIRE

Bedminster

Location: At ST58367138, on the east side of West Street, Bedminster.

Opened: November 17th, 1880 by the Bristol Tramways Co. Ltd. (renamed as the Bristol Tramways & Carriage Co. Ltd from October 1st, 1887) and taken over by Bristol Corporation on October 1st, 1937.

Traction System: Horse (until December 1900) and then Overhead Electric.

Gauge: 4ft 8.5in.

Description: Originally a horse car shed, it was rebuilt as a 6TS dead ended tram shed for electric working.

Closed: Forced to close following extensive bomb damage sustained during an air raid on the night of January 3rd/4th, 1941.

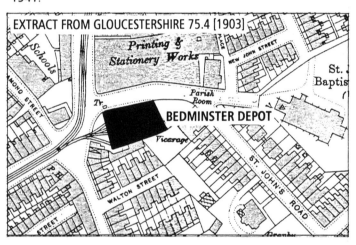

St George's

Location: At ST62307353, on the east side of Beaconsfield Rd.

Opened: October 1886 by the Bristol Tramways Co. Ltd. (renamed as the Bristol Tramways & Carriage Co. Ltd from October 1st, 1887) and taken over by Bristol Corporation on October 1st, 1937.

Traction System: Horse (until October 15th, 1900) and then Overhead Electric.

Gauge: 4ft 8.5in.

Description: Originally a horse car shed, it was rebuilt in brick as a 3TS dead ended shed, with a 1TS body works on the north side, for electric working.

Closed: April 11th, 1941 and taken over by the Fire Service.

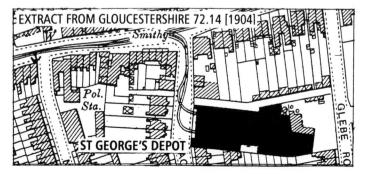

Eastville

Location: At ST61087489, on the north side of Fishpond Road, Eastville.

Opened: June 1876 by the Bristol Tramways Co. Ltd. (renamed as the Bristol Tramways & Carriage Co. Ltd from October 1st 1887) and taken over by Bristol Corporation on October 1st 1937.

Traction System: Horse, until February 1st, 1887, and then Overhead Electric.

Gauge: 4ft 8.5in.

Description: Originally a horse car shed it was rebuilt as a 6TS dead ended tram shed for electric working.

Closed: September 3rd, 1938 and subsequently utilized as an omnibus garage.

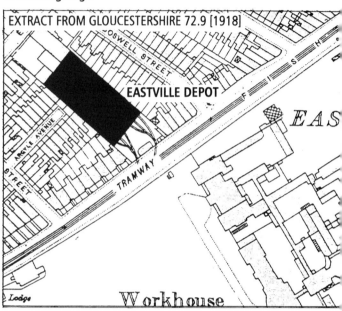

Whitson Street

Location: At ST58877350, on the east side of Whitson Street.

Opened: November 18th, 1880 by the Bristol Tramways Co. Ltd

Traction System: Steam.

Gauge: 4ft 8.5in.

Description: A 2TS steam loco shed.

Closed: By November 4th, 1881 when steam working ceased and subsequently utilized as a permanent way depot and stores. In 1958/9 it was incorporated into the 'bus station.

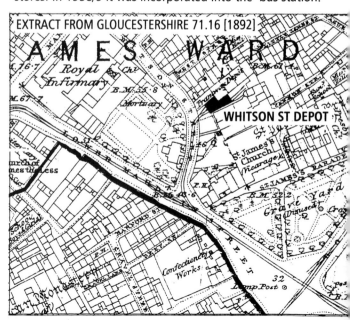

Brislington

Location: At ST61257158, on the east side of Kensington Hill.
Opened: July 13th, 1899 by the Bristol Tramways & Carriage Co. Ltd and taken over by Bristol Corporation on October 1st, 1937.
Traction System: Overhead Electric.
Gauge: 4ft 8.5in.
Description: A brick built 12TS dead ended tram shed with a 12TS works on the north east side.
Closed: September 3rd, 1938 and subsequently utilized as an omnibus depot.

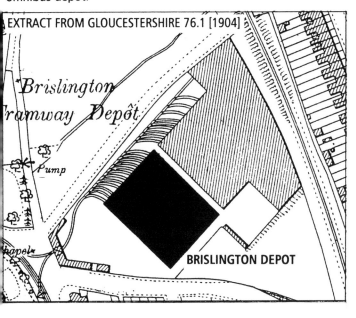

Staple Hill

Location: At ST65297595, on the north side of Broad Street, Staple Hill.
Opened: November 6th, 1897 by the Bristol Tramways & Carriage Co. Ltd and taken over by Bristol Corporation on October 1st, 1937.
Traction System: Overhead Electric.
Gauge: 4ft 8.5in.
Description: A 6TS tram shed with four roads extending into the workshops at the rear.
Closed: September 3rd, 1938 and subsequently utilized as an omnibus depot.

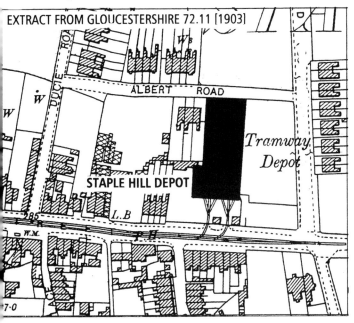

Victoria Street

Location: At ST59567238, on the east side of Victoria Street.
Opened: April 1879 by the Bristol Tramways Co. Ltd (renamed as the Bristol Tramways & Carriage Co. Ltd from October 1st, 1887).
Traction System: Horse.
Gauge: 4ft 8.5in.
Description: A 2TS tram shed.
Closed: July 13th, 1899 and converted to a Tramway Station serving Temple Meads Railway Station. Subsequently utilized as a BR Staff Canteen.

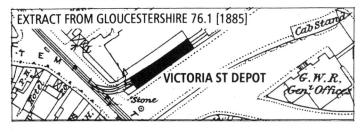

Colston Street

Location: At ST58557320, on the west side of Colston Street.
Opened: August 9th, 1875 by the Bristol Tramways Co. Ltd (renamed as the Bristol Tramways & Carriage Co. Ltd from October 1st, 1887).
Traction System: Horse.
Gauge: 4ft 8.5in.
Description: A 2TS dead ended tram shed.
Closed: December 22nd, 1900 and subsequently utilized as commercial premises.

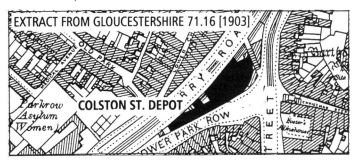

Horfield

Location: At ST59357640, on the west side of Gloucester Road, Horfield.
Opened: 1892 by the Bristol Tramways & Carriage Co. Ltd and taken over by Bristol Corporation on October 1st, 1937.
Traction System: Horse (until December 22nd, 1900) and then Overhead Electric.
Gauge: 4ft 8.5in.
Description: Originally a horse car depot it was rebuilt in brick as a 10TS dead ended shed for electric working.
Closed: July 15th, 1939 and sold for commercial use.

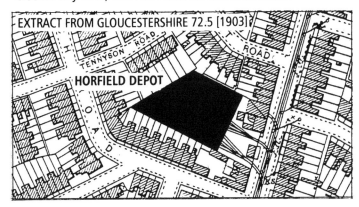

Kingswood

Location: At ST65547383, on the north side of High Street, Kingswood.

Opened: October 15th, 1895 by the Bristol Tramways & Carriage Co. Ltd and taken over by Bristol Corporation on October 1st, 1937.

Traction System: Overhead Electric.

Gauge: 4ft 8.5in.

Description: A brick built 5TS dead ended tram shed. In 1938 the centre track was extended through the back wall to access two new sidings to facilitate the scrapping of the tram fleet.

Closed: April 11th, 1941 and subsequently handed over to the Ministry of Supply. It was in commercial use in 1969.

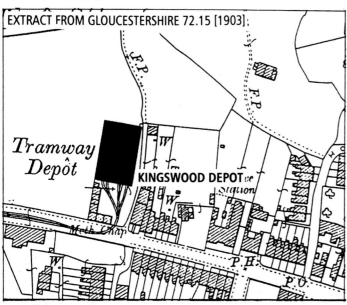

NB The Bristol Tramways & Carriage Co. Ltd continued to operate the system after the take over by Bristol Corporation.

CHELTENHAM

St Mark's

Location: At SO93262236, on the north side of Gloucester Road, adjacent to the west side of the MR Gloucester to Birmingham line.

Opened: Probably on August 17th, 1901 by the Cheltenham & District Light Railway Co.

Traction System: Overhead Electric.

Gauge: 3ft 6in.

Description: A brick built 3TS dead ended tram shed it was also used as the tramway's works.

Closed: December 31st, 1930 and subsequently utilized as an omnibus garage. It was still in use in 1960.

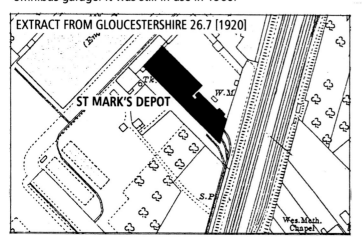

GLOUCESTER

India Road

Location: At SO84141776, on the north side of the India Road and Barton Street junction.

Opened: May 24th, 1879 by the Gloucester Tramways Co. Ltd, purchased by the City of Gloucester Tramways Co. Ltd in July 1881 and taken over by Gloucester Corporation on September 30th, 1902.

Traction System: Horse.

Gauge: 4ft.

Description: A 4TS horse car depot and stables.

Closed: Probably on March 17th, 1904 when horse services ceased and subsequently let out and sold. In use in 1983 as a transport garage.

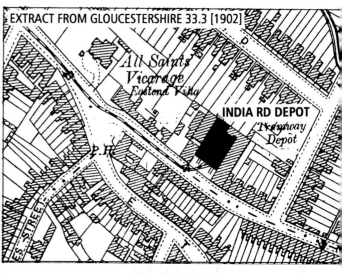

Bristol Road

Location: At SO82541717, on the east side of Bristol Road.

Opened: July 10th, 1897 by the City of Gloucester Tramways Co. Ltd and taken over by Gloucester Corporation on September 30th, 1902.

Traction System: Horse (until March 17th, 1904) and then Overhead Electric.

Gauge: 4ft (until 1904), 3ft 6in.

Description: Originally a 4ft gauge horse car shed, it was rebuilt as a 3ft 6in gauge 6TS dead ended tram shed for electric working. From September 8th, 1929 it was also utilized to accommodate Corporation omnibuses.

Closed: To trams on January 11th, 1933. By 1960 it was in use as a factory.

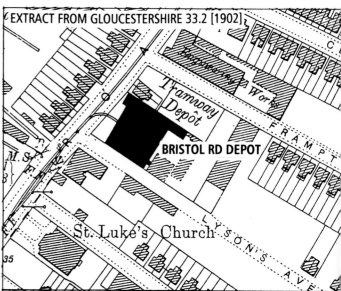

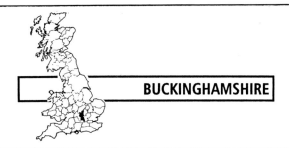

BUCKINGHAMSHIRE

STONY STRATFORD

Wolverton Road

Location: At SP79004053, on the north side of Wolverton Road, east of Russell Street.

Opened: May 27th, 1887 by the Wolverton & Stony Stratford District Light Railways Co. Ltd, taken over by the L&NWR in February 1920 and absorbed into the LMS in 1923.

Traction System: Steam.

Gauge: 3ft 6in.

Description: Originally a 2TS loco shed located between a 2TS carriage shed and a 1TS fitting shop. One of the tracks was removed from the loco shed in 1920.

Closed: May 3rd, 1926 and subsequently utilized as an omnibus depot for Eastern National.

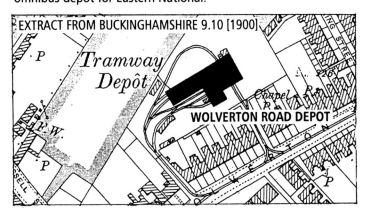

EXTRACT FROM BUCKINGHAMSHIRE 9.10 [1900]

WOLVERTON ROAD DEPOT

Buckingham Road

Location: At SP77914110, on the south side of the junction of Watling Street and Buckingham Road, in Old Stratford.

Opened: In 1888 by the Wolverton & Stony Stratford District Light Railways Co. Ltd to serve the Deanshanger extension.

Traction System: Steam.

Gauge: 3ft 6in.

Description: A 1TS dead ended loco and carriage shed.

Closed: The tramway temporarily closed on December 17th, 1889, but when it re-opened the Deanshanger extension was abandoned and the depot dispensed with.

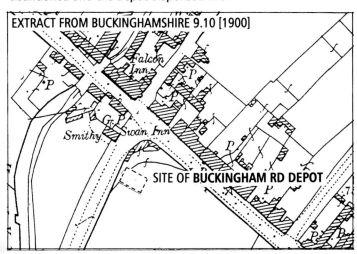

EXTRACT FROM BUCKINGHAMSHIRE 9.10 [1900]

SITE OF BUCKINGHAM RD DEPOT

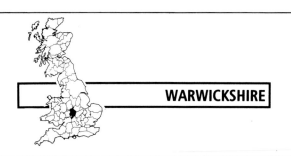

WARWICKSHIRE

WARWICK

Coten End

Location: At SP28916521, on the south side of Coten End.

Opened: January 1882 by the Leamington & Warwick Tramways & Omnibus Co. Ltd. The company name was changed to the Leamington & Warwick Electrical Co. Ltd in 1902.

Traction System: Horse.

Gauge: 4ft 8.5in.

Description: Originally adapted from existing outbuildings, a 2TS dead ended tram shed, possibly constructed in timber, was added at the rear in the same year.

Closed: Probably on May 16th, 1905 when the system was closed for reconstruction. The site was subsequently cleared and redeveloped.

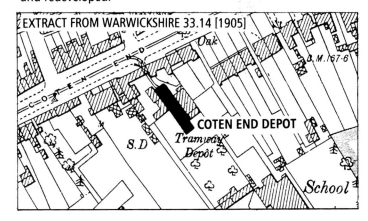

EXTRACT FROM WARWICKSHIRE 33.14 [1905]

COTEN END DEPOT

Emscote Road

Location: At SP29786549, on the south side of Emscote Road.

Opened: July 12th, 1905 by the Leamington & Warwick Electrical Co. Ltd.

Traction System: Overhead Electric.

Gauge: 3ft 6in.

Description: A brick built 4TS dead ended tram shed.

Closed: August 16th, 1930.

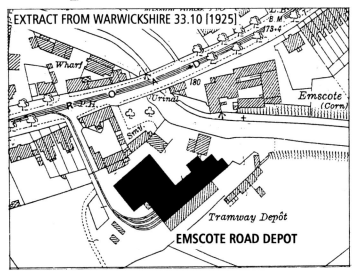

EXTRACT FROM WARWICKSHIRE 33.10 [1925]

EMSCOTE ROAD DEPOT

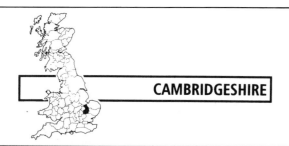

CAMBRIDGESHIRE

WISBECH

Wisbech East Station

Location: On the south side of Wisbech East Station.
Traction System: Steam (Diesel locomotives utilized for freight traffic after 1958).
Gauge: 4ft 8.5in.

LOCO SHED*

Opened: August 20th, 1883 by the Wisbech & Upwell Tramway.
Description: A brick built 1TS dead ended loco shed, located at TL46130893 and rebuilt to a 2TS dead ended building in 1895.
Closed: December 31st, 1927 but utilized for freight traffic until May 20th, 1966.

CARRIAGE SHED

Opened: August 20th, 1883 by the Wisbech & Upwell Tramway.
Description: A timber built 1TS dead ended carriage shed, located at TL46130891.
Closed: December 31st, 1931 and subsequently demolished, the track being utilized as a locomotive siding.

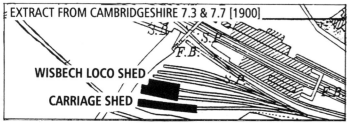

EXTRACT FROM CAMBRIDGESHIRE 7.3 & 7.7 [1900]

WISBECH LOCO SHED

CARRIAGE SHED

*This depot is listed in "The Directory of British Engine Sheds" as TL4608.1/1.

CAMBRIDGE

East Road

Location: At TL45865840, on the corner of East Road and Dover Street.
Opened: January 1881 by the Cambridge Street Tramways Co.*
Traction System: Horse.
Gauge: 4ft.
Description: A brick built 2TS dead ended tramshed.
Closed: February 18th, 1914 and subsequently utilized as a fish market, corn chandlers, motor engineering workshop and, in 1944, a furniture depository before falling into disuse. In the 1980s it was converted into a public house.

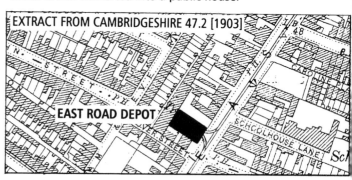

EXTRACT FROM CAMBRIDGESHIRE 47.2 [1903]

EAST ROAD DEPOT

Prior to this, and from the opening of the tramway on October 28th, 1880, tramcars were kept in the GNR Goods Yard beside the Railway Station (at approx TL46025723).

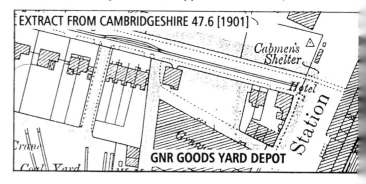

EXTRACT FROM CAMBRIDGESHIRE 47.6 [1901]

GNR GOODS YARD DEPOT

BEDFORDSHIRE

EXTRACT FROM BEDFORDSHIRE 33.5 & 33.6 [1924]

Sewage Works
(Luton Corporation)

PARK STREET DEPOT

Tramway Depôt

LUTON

Park Street

Location: At TL09782077, on the east side of Park Street in Parktown.
Opened: February 21st, 1908 by Luton Corporation.
Traction System: Overhead Electric.
Gauge: 4ft 8.5in.
Description: A brick built 4TS dead ended tram shed.
Closed: From February 1932 the accommodation was shared for a short period of time between trams and omnibuses until the system closed on April 16th, 1932. It was then utilized as an omnibus garage and later extended. Later demolished and site now occupied by a car park.

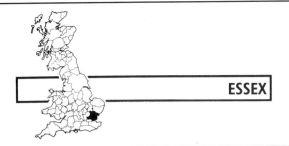

ESSEX

COLCHESTER
Magdalen Street
Location: At TM00152477, on the south side of Magdalen Street.
Opened: July 28th, 1904 by Colchester Corporation. From 1927 it was also utilized for omnibuses.
Traction System: Overhead Electric.
Gauge: 3ft 6in.
Description: A 6TS dead ended tram shed.
Closed: December 8th, 1929 and subsequently utilized as an omnibus depot. It was still in use in 1981.

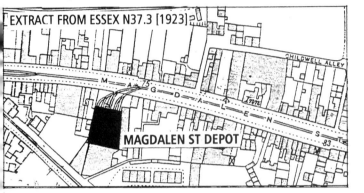

CANVEY ISLAND
Canvey Island
From c1901 to c1904 a horse drawn monorail tramway was operated on Canvey Island between Benfleet and Leigh Beck on the River Thames by Frederick Hester. The existence of a car shed is unconfirmed.

London Road
Location: At TQ87658603, on the north side of London Road, west of Victoria Circus.
Opened: July 19th, 1901 by Southend on Sea Corporation.
Traction System: Overhead Electric
Gauge: 3ft 6in.
Description: A brick built 6TS dead ended tram shed adjoined, on the south side, by the power station. In 1924 a 4TS shed was added on the west side of the power station and in 1931 both sheds were extended and joined. From 1925 it was also utilized to accommodate trolleybuses and, from 1932, omnibuses.
Closed: April 8th, 1942 and utilized for trolleybuses, until 1954, and omnibuses until a new garage was built in 1960.

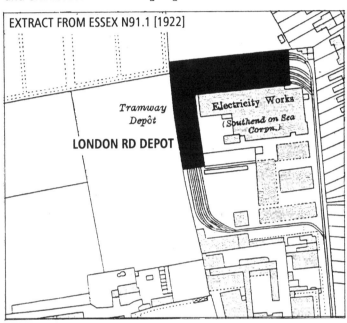

Southend Pier
From 1875 to 1881 a c3ft 6in gauge horse tramway was operated on Southend on Sea Pier by the Southend Local Board The existence of a car shed is unconfirmed.

The shed yard at **Wisbech East Station** in early BR days when it was coded as 31C(s), a sub-shed of King's Lynn. The ex-LNER Tram Loco No.68225, on the left of the picture, stands on the site of the former **Carriage Shed**.
Courtesy RA Griffiths (See Page 50)

SUFFOLK

IPSWICH

Quadling Street

Location: On the north side of Quadling Street.
Opened: October 13th, 1880 by Mr SA Graham, taken over in 1881 by the Ipswich Tramway Co. and purchased by Ipswich Corporation on November 1st, 1901.
Traction System: Horse.
Gauge: 3ft 6in.
Description: Originally a yard with two tracks, sited on the west side of New Cardinal Street at TM15874409, it was replaced at an unknown date by a 2TS dead ended car shed and stables on the east side at TM15924410.
Closed: June 6th, 1903. By 1999 both sites had been cleared to make way for a major commercial redevelopment.

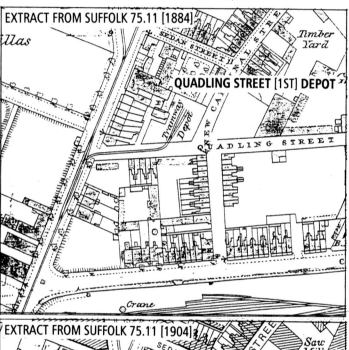

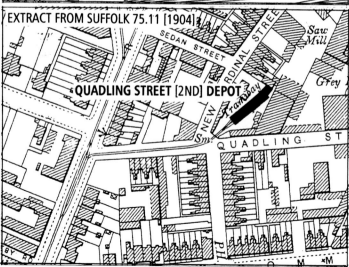

NB. Between the summer of 1883 and June 1884 an isolated section of tramway was worked from a temporary depot and stables behind the Railway Hotel in Foxhall Street.

Constantine Road

Location: At TM15534430, on the corner of Constantine Road and Portmans Walk.
Opened: November 23rd, 1903 by Ipswich Corporation.
Traction System: Overhead Electric.
Gauge: 3ft 6in.
Description: A brick built 8TS dead ended tram shed, with one workshop road.
Closed: July 26th, 1926 and subsequently utilized as an omnibus garage.

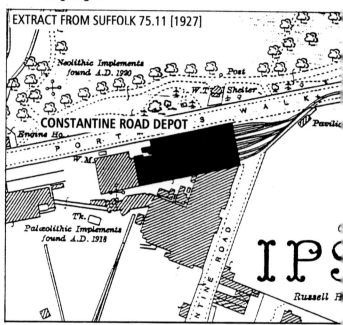

LOWESTOFT

Rotterdam Road

Location: On the east side of Rotterdam Road.
Opened: July 22nd, 1903 by Lowestoft Corporation.
Traction System: Overhead Electric.
Gauge: 3ft 6in.
Description: A brick built 4TS dead ended tram shed, located at TM53899316, and a small 1TS shed which was added later and was located at TM53909312. From 1927 it also accommodated omnibuses.
Closed: May 8th, 1931 and subsequently utilized as an omnibus depot.

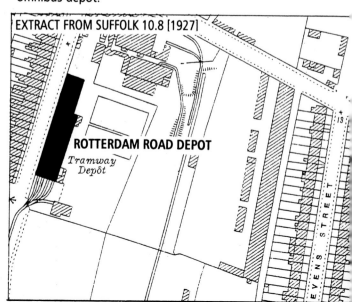

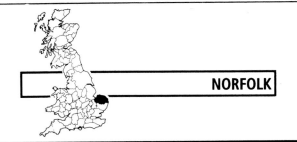

NORFOLK

NORWICH

Silver Road

Location: *On the east side of Silver Road.*
Opened: July 30th, 1900 by the Norwich Electric Tramways Co.
Traction System: Overhead Electric.
Gauge: 3ft 6in.
Description: A brick built 6TS dead ended tram shed, located at TG23541026, and a brick built 6TS dead ended tram shed sited just north at TG23541029. An omnibus garage was later added at the east end of the site.
Closed: December 10th, 1935 and both buildings were still standing in 1999, in commercial use.

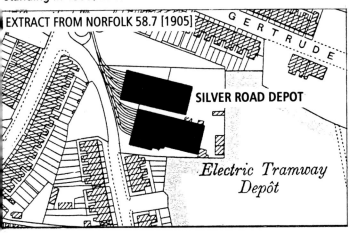

EXTRACT FROM NORFOLK 58.7 [1905]

SILVER ROAD DEPOT

Electric Tramway Depôt

YARMOUTH

Caister Road

Location: *At TG52460909, on the east side of Caister Road.*
Opened: June 19th, 1902 by Great Yarmouth Corporation.
Traction System: Overhead Electric.
Gauge: 3ft 6in.
Description: Originally a brick built 4TS dead ended tram shed, the building was later modified with two tracks passing through the shed and three tracks being fitted with turntables to enable access to workshops later sited at right angles and to the south.
Closed: December 14th, 1933 and subsequently utilized as an omnibus depot.

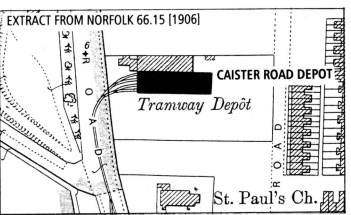

EXTRACT FROM NORFOLK 66.15 [1906]

CAISTER ROAD DEPOT

Tramway Depôt

St. Paul's Ch.

GORLESTON

Southtown Road

Location: *At TG52310607, on the north side of Waveney Rd, west of Southtown Rd.*
Opened: March 25th, 1875 by the East Suffolk Tramway Co. and purchased by the Yarmouth & Gorleston Tramways Co. Ltd in 1878.
Traction System: Horse.
Gauge: 4ft 8in.
Description: A horse car shed.
Closed: 1882.

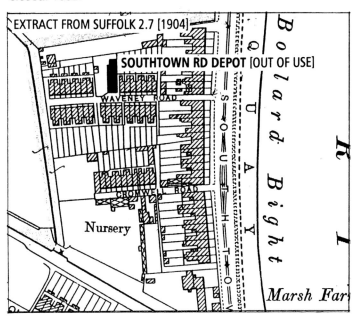

EXTRACT FROM SUFFOLK 2.7 [1904]

SOUTHTOWN RD DEPOT [OUT OF USE]

WAVENEY ROAD

Nursery

Bolard Bight

Marsh Far

Baker Street

Location: *At TG52640427, on the corner of Baker Street and Lowestoft Road.*
Opened: 1882 by the Yarmouth & Gorleston Tramways Co. Ltd and purchased by Great Yarmouth Corporation on March 12th, 1905.
Traction System: Horse, until July 3rd, 1905, and then Overhead Electric.
Gauge: 3ft 6in.
Description: Originally consisting of 2TS and 1TS dead ended tram sheds and stables, a brick built 2TS dead ended tram shed and works were constructed on the east side for electric working. The horse tram shed was demolished in 1907 to make way for a Public Library.
Closed: September 25th, 1930 and utilized as an Enquiry/Ticket Office until March 31st, 1931. The Library was extended into the adjacent portion of the depot later that year and was demolished in 1974 for replacement by a new Library building.

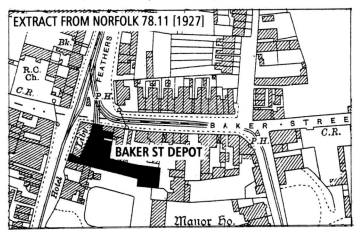

EXTRACT FROM NORFOLK 78.11 [1927]

BAKER ST DEPOT

BAKER STREE

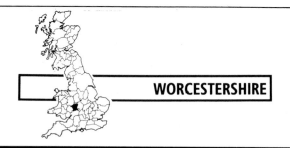

WORCESTERSHIRE

KIDDERMINSTER
New Road

Location: At SO82987670, on the west side of New Road.
Opened: May 25th, 1898 by the Kidderminster & Stourport Electric Tramway and acquired by the Kidderminster & District Electric Lighting & Traction Co. Ltd on December 19th, 1898.
Traction System: Overhead Electric.
Gauge: 3ft 6in.
Description: A brick built 5TS dead ended tram shed.
Closed: Although officially closed on April 2nd, 1929, it had been utilized as a Midland Red omnibus garage from December 1st, 1928 with the trams for the skeleton service, utilized until the closure of the system, being stored outside. The date when it closed as an omnibus garage is not known but by 1999 only the back wall remained standing, the remainder of the tram shed site having been demolished.

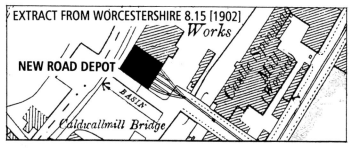

WORCESTER
Bull Ring

Location: At SO84105455, on the west side of the Bull Ring in St Johns.
Opened: February 18th, 1884 by the Tramways Trust Co. Ltd and taken over by the City of Worcester Tramways Co. Ltd in 1890. It was bought by Worcester Tramways Ltd in 1894, acquired by Worcester Electric Traction Co. Ltd in 1902.
Traction System: Horse (until 1903) and then Overhead Electric.
Gauge: 3ft (until 1903), 3ft 6in.
Description: Originally a 3ft gauge brick built 2TS dead ended shed, upon electrification it was converted to 3ft 6in gauge and a 4TS extension constructed on the eastern side.
Closed: June 28th, 1903 and re-opened upon electrification on February 6th, 1904. Finally closed on May 31st, 1928 and utilized as a municipal depot until the 1970s. It was subsequently demolished and a supermarket built on the site.

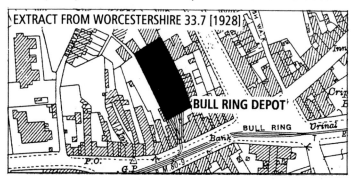

AMBLECOTE
Stourbridge Road

Location: At SO89748556, on the corner of Stourbridge Road and Collis Street, Coalbournbrook.
Opened: October 1905 by the Dudley, Stourbridge & District Electric Traction Co. Ltd. to serve the Kinver Light Railway. The line was bought by them on September 29th, 1902 and from July 1st, 1904 control passed to the Birmingham & Midland Tramways Joint Committee.
Traction System: Overhead Electric.
Gauge: 3ft 6in.
Description: Originally a brick built 4TS dead ended tram shed, a steel framed corrugated iron clad 2TS lean-to was added on the west side in c1908 and this was increased to 3TS in c1914.
Closed: May 12th, 1926 and utilized as a tram store until 1930. The building was then let out for private use with the extension being rebuilt in brick and the original depot being reinforced with breeze blocks. It still stood in 1999, in use as a laser game centre.

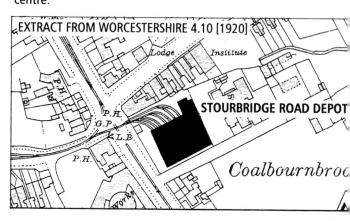

KINVER
The Hyde

Location: At SO85258448 in a small wood, north west of the tramway, by Hyde Meadows north of Kinver village.
Opened: About July 1901 by the British Electric Traction Co. Ltd for the Kinver Light Railway. Operated from the opening of the line on April 5th, 1901 by the Dudley, Stourbridge & District Electric Traction Co. Ltd, the line was bought by them on September 29th, 1902 and from July 1st, 1904 control passed to the Birmingham & Midland Tramways Joint Committee. The depot was only opened between Easter and October each year to cope with the excursion traffic.
Traction System: Overhead Electric.
Gauge: 3ft 6in.
Description: A steel-framed corrugated iron clad 4TS dead ended tram shed.
Closed: 1929. The building was dismantled and re-erected on a farm a few miles away to serve as a cattle shed. It still stood in 1995.

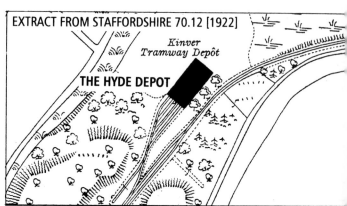

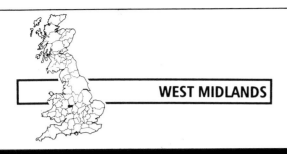

WEST MIDLANDS

BIRMINGHAM

Moseley Road

Location: At SP07868403, on the corner of Moseley Road and Trafalgar Road, Moseley.
Opened: January 1st, 1907 by Birmingham Corporation.
Traction System: Overhead Electric.
Gauge: 3ft 6in.
Description: A brick built 15TS dead ended tram shed with access via an unusual oval track configuration.
Closed: October 1st, 1949 and further utilized as an omnibus depot. Latterly in a variety of commercial uses, including a Go Kart track, but in 1999 was out of use.

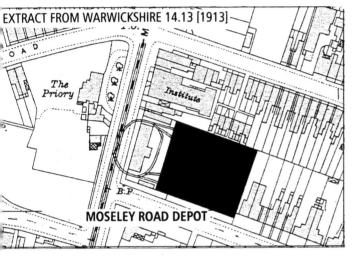

EXTRACT FROM WARWICKSHIRE 14.13 [1913]

MOSELEY ROAD DEPOT

Selly Oak

Location: At SP04008266, on the west side of Harborne Lane, Selly Oak.
Opened: July 12th, 1927 by Birmingham Corporation.
Traction System: Overhead Electric.
Gauge: 3ft 6in.
Description: A brick built 10TS dead ended tram shed with five access roads.
Closed: July 5th, 1952 and further utilized as an omnibus depot. Still standing in 2000, in commercial use.

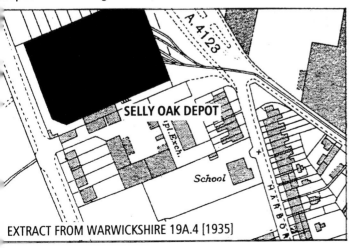

SELLY OAK DEPOT

EXTRACT FROM WARWICKSHIRE 19A.4 [1935]

Malt Shovel Inn

Location: At SP04578317, behind the Malt Shovel Inn, on the north side of Bristol (High) Road (now Bristol Road) and the west side of Grange Road.
Opened: June 17th, 1876 by the Birmingham Tramways. & Omnibus Co. Ltd and taken over by the Birmingham Central Tramway Co. Ltd in January 1886.
Traction System: Horse.
Gauge: 4ft 8.5in.
Description: A horse car depot and stables. The Malt Shovel Inn was demolished in 1877 and replaced by the Bournbrook Hotel (now the Old Varsity Tavern) with the yard being roofed over in 1880.
Closed: October 1889 and later utilized as part of the premises of the Ariel Motorcycle Company.

Bournbrook

Location: At SP04648299, on the west side of Dawlish Road.
Opened: July 24th, 1890 by Birmingham Central Tramway Co. Ltd and taken over by the City of Birmingham Tramways Co. Ltd on September 29th, 1896. On July 1st, 1911 it was rented to Birmingham Corporation and purchased by them on January 1st, 1912.
Traction System: Battery Electric, until May 14th, 1901, and then Overhead Electric.
Gauge: 3ft 6in.
Description: A brick built 3TS dead ended tram shed. It was also utilized for omnibuses from July 19th, 1913.
Closed: July 11th, 1927 and subsequently used as commercial premises.

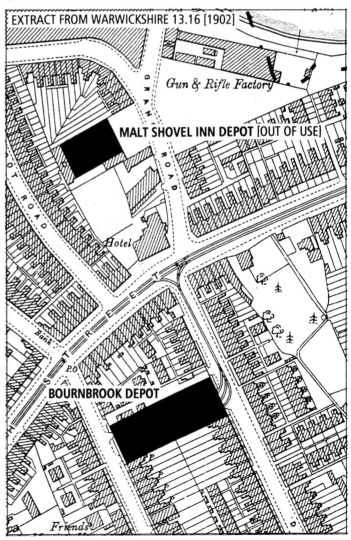

EXTRACT FROM WARWICKSHIRE 13.16 [1902]

Gun & Rifle Factory

MALT SHOVEL INN DEPOT [OUT OF USE]

BOURNBROOK DEPOT

Albion Depot

Location: At SP02799014, on the south side of Holyhead Road, Handsworth, west of Middlemore Road.

Opened: 1885 by the South Staffordshire & Birmingham District Steam Tramways Co. Ltd (renamed as the South Staffordshire Tramways Company in 1889), taken over by the South Staffordshire Tramways (Lessee) Co. Ltd on June 23rd, 1900 and taken over again, by Birmingham Corporation on July 1st, 1911. It was leased again to the South Staffordshire Tramways (Lessee) Co. Ltd between October 7th, 1912 and March 31st, 1924.

Traction System: Steam until June 1904. Overhead Electric had commenced from December 19th, 1902.

Gauge: 3ft 6in.

Description: A brick built 2TS dead ended loco shed adjoined, on the west side, by a brick built 2TS dead ended car shed.

Closed: From April 1st, 1924 to all workings except football specials and totally on April 2nd, 1939.

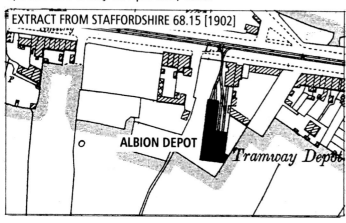

EXTRACT FROM STAFFORDSHIRE 68.15 [1902]
ALBION DEPOT
Tramway Depot

Hockley

Location: At SP05668861, on the north side of Whitmore St, west of Soho Hill, Hockley.

Opened: March 24th, 1888 by the Birmingham Central Tramway Co. Ltd and taken over on September 29th, 1896 by the City of Birmingham Tramways Co. Ltd.

Traction System: Cable, until June 30th, 1911, and then Overhead Electric.

Gauge: 3ft 6in.

Description: Originally a brick built 9TS dead ended tram shed with a 2TS dead ended works, it was rebuilt in brick as a 12TS dead ended shed to accommodate overhead electric trams.

Closed: June 30th, 1911 when cable working ceased, re-opened for electric working on June 12th, 1912 and closed to trams on April 1st, 1939. Still in use in 1999 as an omnibus depot.

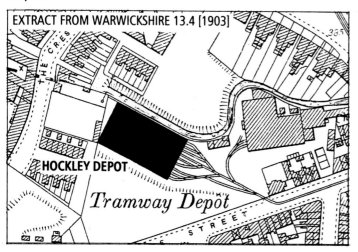

EXTRACT FROM WARWICKSHIRE 13.4 [1903]
HOCKLEY DEPOT
Tramway Depot

Silver Street

Location: On the south side of Silver Street, west side of High Street, Kings Heath.

Opened: February 1st, 1887 by Birmingham Central Tramway Co. Ltd, taken over by the City of Birmingham Tramways Co Ltd and taken over again by Birmingham Corporation on April 1st, 1908.

Traction System: Steam, until December 31st, 1906 and then Overhead Electric.

Gauge: 3ft 6in.

Description: A brick built 6TS dead ended car shed located at SP07328174 adjoined, at the western end, by a brick built 6TS dead ended loco shed located at SP07308171.

Closed: December 31st, 1906 when steam working ceased and re-opened on April 1st, 1908 for overhead electric working. Finally closed on March 31st, 1912, the site was later cleared and utilized for commercial premises.

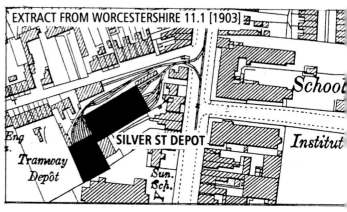

EXTRACT FROM WORCESTERSHIRE 11.1 [1903]
School
SILVER ST DEPOT
Institut
Tramway Depot

Kyotts Lake Road

Location: At SP08558535, on the north side of Kyotts Lake Road, east of Stratford Road, Sparkbrook.

Opened: February 1885 by the Birmingham Central Tramway Co Ltd, taken over by the City of Birmingham Tramways Co Ltd on September 29th, 1896 and purchased on July 1st, 1906 by Birmingham Corporation.

Traction System: Steam, until December 31st, 1906, and then Overhead Electric.

Gauge: 3ft 6in.

Description: Originally a 2TS dead ended loco shed, adjoined by a 6TS dead ended car shed and a 4TS works, it was completely rebuilt and converted for overhead electric working as an electric car overhaul works.

Closed: It effectively closed as a tram depot at the end of steam on December 31st, 1906, but the three westernmost tracks of the new works were utilized for service cars for a short period during 1907.

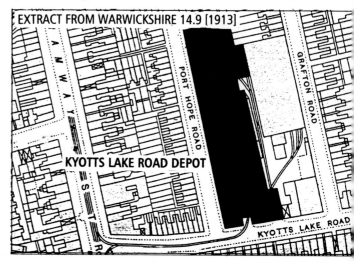

EXTRACT FROM WARWICKSHIRE 14.9 [1913]
KYOTTS LAKE ROAD DEPOT
KYOTTS LAKE ROAD

Washwood Heath Road

Location: At SP10538865, on the south side of Washwood Heath Road, Ward End.
Opened: May 2nd, 1907 by Birmingham Corporation.
Traction System: Overhead Electric.
Gauge: 3ft 6in.
Description: A brick built 9TS dead ended tram shed with six access roads. At some stage it was lengthened at the southern end and also accommodated trolleybuses on the three western roads from November 22nd, 1922 to September 30th, 1940. The depot was also utilized for omnibuses between January 15th, 1923 and October 27th, 1925, October 1st, 1940 and May 3rd, 1941 and from August 19th, 1946 onwards.
Closed: September 30th, 1950 to trams and still in use as an omnibus garage.

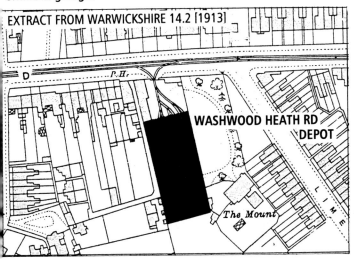

EXTRACT FROM WARWICKSHIRE 14.2 [1913]

WASHWOOD HEATH RD DEPOT

Miller Street

Location: At SP07358833, on the south side of Miller Street and west side of Elkington Street, Newtown.
Opened: January 4th, 1904 by Birmingham Corporation.
Traction System: Overhead Electric.
Gauge: 3ft 6in.
Description: Originally a 4TS dead ended tram shed, a 5TS dead ended shed was added along the west side in 1908. The building was progressively enlarged to a brick built 17TS dead ended structure and was partially rebuilt following bomb damage sustained in 1941.
Closed: July 4th, 1953 and further utilized as an omnibus depot.

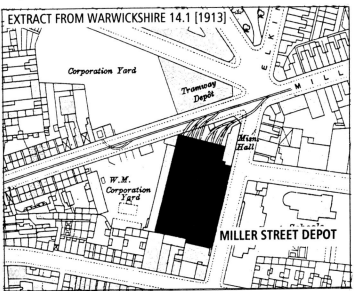

EXTRACT FROM WARWICKSHIRE 14.1 [1913]

MILLER STREET DEPOT

Coventry Road

Location: At SP08938621, on the corner of Arthur Street and Coventry Road, Bordesley.
Opened: November 24th, 1906 by Birmingham Corporation.
Traction System: Overhead Electric.
Gauge: 3ft 6in.
Description: A brick built 19TS dead ended tram shed with six access roads. It was also utilized to accommodate trolleybuses from January 7th, 1934.
Closed: October 2nd, 1948 and further utilized as an omnibus and trolleybus depot.

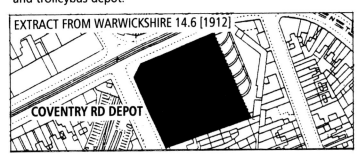

EXTRACT FROM WARWICKSHIRE 14.6 [1912]

COVENTRY RD DEPOT

Highgate Road

Location: At SP08658454, on the south side of Highgate Road, west of Stratford Road, Balsall Heath.
Opened: November 25th, 1913 by Birmingham Corporation.
Traction System: Overhead Electric.
Gauge: 3ft 6in.
Description: A brick built 11TS dead ended tram shed.
Closed: January 5th, 1937 and further utilized as an omnibus depot. It was still standing in 2000, in commercial use.

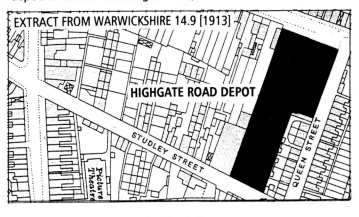

EXTRACT FROM WARWICKSHIRE 14.9 [1913]

HIGHGATE ROAD DEPOT

Cotteridge

Location: At SP04907973, on the south side of Pershore Road, Cotteridge.
Opened: June 23rd, 1904 by the City of Birmingham Tramways Co. Ltd and taken over by Birmingham Corporation on July 1st, 1911.
Traction System: Overhead Electric.
Gauge: 3ft 6in.
Description: Formerly a 4TS dead ended tram shed, in 1919/20 it was enlarged to a brick built 8TS dead ended tram shed.
Closed: July 5th, 1952 and further utilized as an omnibus depot. Since demolished and replaced with housing.

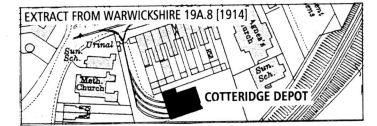

EXTRACT FROM WARWICKSHIRE 19A.8 [1914]

COTTERIDGE DEPOT

Witton Lane

Location: At SP07879041 on the north east side of Witton Lane, north of Station Road.

Opened: December 26th, 1882 by the Birmingham & Aston Tramways Co. Ltd, purchased by Aston Manor UDC on June 30th, 1902, leased to the City of Birmingham Tramways Co. Ltd from October 1st, 1904 and taken over on January 1st, 1912 by Birmingham Corporation.

Traction System: Steam, until October 1st, 1904, and then Overhead Electric.

Gauge: 3ft 6in.

Description: Originally a brick built 1TS dead ended loco shed adjoined by a brick built 7TS dead ended car shed, in 1904 it was converted to an electric tramcar shed with four access roads.

Closed: September 30th, 1950 and utilized for storing and scrapping cars until July 9th, 1953. It was also in use as an outstation for Miller Street between November 10th, 1952 and July 4th, 1953 and, following closure to trams, it became an omnibus depot. Still standing in 2000 in use as *Aston Manor Road Transport Museum*.

EXTRACT FROM WARWICKSHIRE 8.13 [1904]
WITTON LANE DEPOT

Birchfield Road

Location: At SP06709076, on the west side of Birchfield Road, north of Wilmore Road, Perry Barr.

Opened: November 25th, 1884 by the Birmingham Central Tramway Co. Ltd and taken over on September 29th, 1896 by the City of Birmingham Tramways Co. Ltd. It was purchased by Handsworth UDC on December 31st, 1906 and operated by Birmingham Corporation from May 2nd, 1907.

Traction System: Steam, until 1906, and then Overhead Electric.

Gauge: 3ft 6in.

Description: A 6TS dead ended tram shed.

Closed: January 1st, 1909, re-opened c1913-15 and finally closed to trams on October 3rd, 1924. It was utilized as an omnibus depot from January 7th, 1925 until 1966.

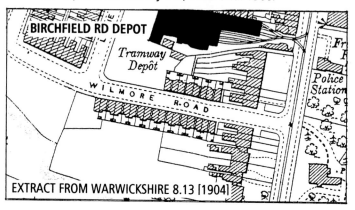

BIRCHFIELD RD DEPOT
EXTRACT FROM WARWICKSHIRE 8.13 [1904]

Yardley

Location: At SP12548486., on the west side of Yardley Road, South Yardley.

Opened: March 29th, 1904 by City of Birmingham Tramways Co. Ltd and taken over by Birmingham Corporation on January 1st, 1912.

Traction System: Overhead Electric.

Gauge: 3ft 6in.

Description: A 3TS dead ended tram shed.

Closed: January 1st, 1912 and sold for commercial use in 1916.

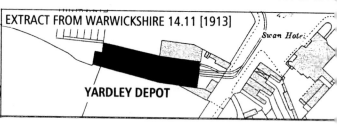

EXTRACT FROM WARWICKSHIRE 14.11 [1913]
YARDLEY DEPOT

Butlin Street

Location: At SP09068919, on the north side of Butlin Street.

Opened: June 6th, 1887 by the Birmingham Central Tramway Co. Ltd and taken over by the City of Birmingham Tramway Co. Ltd on September 29th, 1896.

Traction System: Horse.

Gauge: 3ft 6in.

Description: A 2TS dead ended tram shed.

Closed: September 30th, 1906 and subsequently utilized as a transport yard.

EXTRACT FROM WARWICKSHIRE 8.14 [1902] & 14.2 [1905]
BUTLIN ST DEPOT

Rosebery Street

Location: At SP05238776, on the north side of Rosebery Street, Winson Green.

Opened: April 14th, 1906 by Birmingham Corporation.

Traction System: Overhead Electric.

Gauge: 3ft 6in.

Description: A brick built 16TS dead ended tram shed. It was also utilized to accommodate omnibuses from May 19th, 1947.

Closed: August 30th, 1947 and subsequently utilized as an omnibus depot.

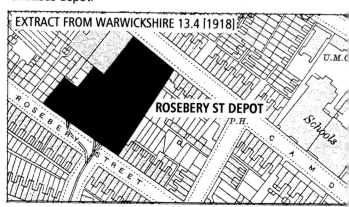

EXTRACT FROM WARWICKSHIRE 13.4 [1918]
ROSEBERY ST DEPOT

Lozells Road

Location: At SP05968952, on the north side of Lozells Road, east of the junction with Villa Road.

Opened; 1878 by the Birmingham Tramways & Omnibus Co. Ltd, taken over by the Birmingham Central Tramway Co. Ltd on December 8th, 1885 and taken over again on September 29th, 1896 by the City of Birmingham Tramways Co. Ltd.

Traction System: Horse, until June 1st, 1887, and then Steam.

Gauge: 4ft 8.5in until June 1st 1887/3ft 6in.

Description: Originally a horse car depot and works, the yard was roofed over in 1880 and subsequently re-gauged and converted for steam working. The depot was also utilized to accommodate horse omnibuses.

Closed: May 7th, 1906 upon electrification of the route.

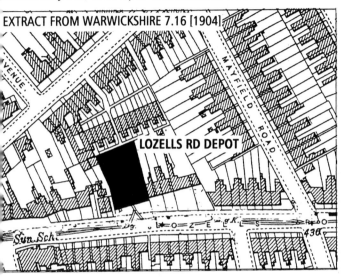

EXTRACT FROM WARWICKSHIRE 7.16 [1904]

New Inns Hotel

Location: At SP03598989, in the yard behind the New Inns Hotel, Handsworth on the north side of Holyhead Road and east side of Sandwell Road.

Opened: 1876 by the Birmingham Tramways & Omnibus Co. Ltd.

Traction System: Horse.

Gauge: 4ft 8.5in.

Description: A horse car depot and stables apparently utilizing the shed buildings which had been previously employed at Tildasley Street Depot, West Bromwich. The yard was roofed over in 1880.

Closed: 1883. The hotel was rebuilt in c1900.

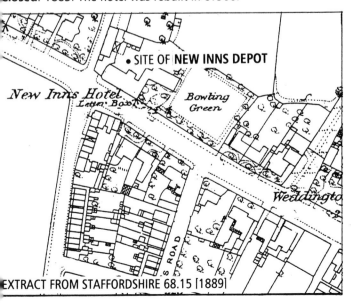

EXTRACT FROM STAFFORDSHIRE 68.15 [1889]

Birchills Depot

Location: At SK00620052, on the west side of Bloxwich Road, Birchills.

Opened: Mid-1885 by the South Staffordshire & Birmingham District Steam Tramways Co. Ltd (renamed the South Staffordshire Tramways Co. in 1889). Leased with the system from June 23rd, 1900 by the South Staffordshire (Lessee) Co. Ltd. Taken over by Walsall Corporation on January 1st, 1901 and leased back. Operated by the Corporation from January 1st, 1904.

Traction System: Steam (until January 1st, 1893) and then Overhead Electric.

Gauge: 3ft 6in.

Description: Originally a brick built 4TS dead ended loco and tram car shed, it was rebuilt in 1892 as a 5TS dead ended tram shed incorporating a 2TS workshop. A 2TS extension was added on the north side in 1912.

Closed: September 30th, 1930.

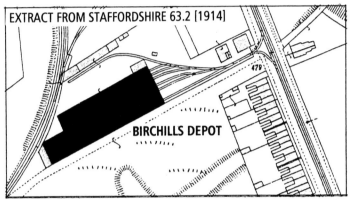

EXTRACT FROM STAFFORDSHIRE 63.2 [1914]

Darlaston Depot

Location: At SO96519801, off the east side of Darlaston Road, Kings Hill.

Opened: July 16th, 1883 by the South Staffordshire & Birmingham District Steam Tramways Co. Ltd (renamed as the South Staffordshire Tramways Company in 1889), taken over by the South Staffordshire Tramways (Lessee) Co. Ltd on June 23rd, 1900 and taken over again, by the Birmingham & Midland Tramways Joint Committee on July 1st, 1904.

Traction System: Steam. Overhead Electric was partially phased in on January 1st, 1893 and totally from June 15th, 1904.

Gauge: 3ft 6in.

Description: A brick built 9TS dead ended tram shed adjoined by a 6TS dead ended works on the south side. The two northernmost roads were wired for electric working in 1892 and an additional shed road added by 1902. The workshop was reduced to two roads following the opening of Tividale Works in 1904.

Closed: March 31st, 1924 and re-opened on September 1st, 1928 by the Dudley, Stourbridge & District Electric Traction Co. Ltd. It finally closed on September 30th, 1930 and the site was cleared and later redeveloped.

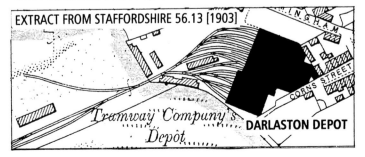

EXTRACT FROM STAFFORDSHIRE 56.13 [1903]

Paradise Street

Location: At SP00439105 on the south side of Paradise Street in Mr B.Crowther's Station Mews.
Opened: 1893 and leased by Crowther from Birmingham & Midland Tramways Ltd.
Traction System: Horse.
Gauge: 3ft 6in.
Description: A 1TS dead ended horse car shed.
Closed: 1903.

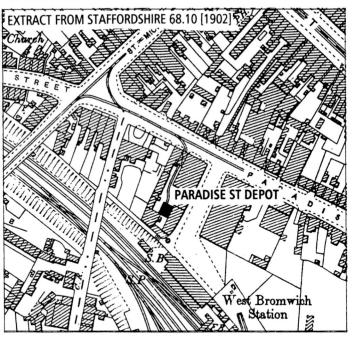

Tildasley Street

Location: At SO99679212, on the south side of the junction of Tildasley Street and Old Meeting Street.
Opened: May 20th, 1872 by Birmingham & District Tramways Co. Ltd and taken over by Birmingham Tramways & Omnibus Co. Ltd on May 1st, 1876.
Traction System: Horse.
Gauge: 4ft 8.5in.
Description: A depot and stables.
Closed: June 1876.

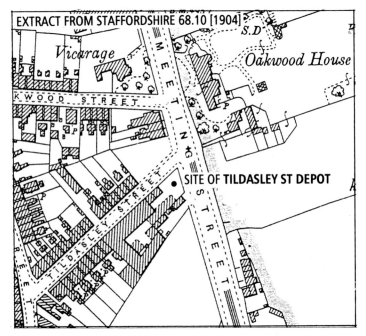

Priestley's Bridge

Location: At SP34308020, on the east side of Stony Stanton Road and west of the Coventry Canal.
Opened: July 22nd, 1899 by the Coventry Electric Tramways Co. Ltd and taken over by Coventry Corporation on January 1st, 1912.
Traction System: Overhead Electric.
Gauge: 3ft 6in.
Description: Originally a brick built 6TS dead ended tram shed, a 6TS dead ended extension was added on the south west side in 1913. The latter portion was then utilized as the running shed with the original building becoming the repair shop. An omnibus garage was constructed on the south east part of the site in 1921.
Closed: The depot closed on December 24th, 1940 when the system was abandoned due to extensive Blitz damage. It was utilized for scrapping trams until 1941, suffered further bomb damage, and then later used for bus repairs. Site now occupied by housing.

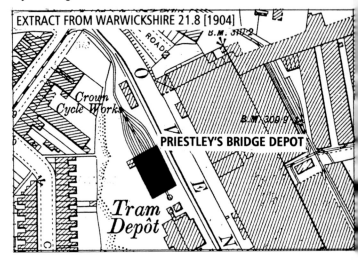

Foleshill Road

Location: At SP34498229, on the west side of Foleshill Road, Foleshill.
Opened: 1884 by the Coventry & District Tramways Co., taken over by the Coventry Electric Tramways Co. Ltd on December 5th, 1895 and taken over again by Coventry Corporation on January 1st, 1912.
Traction System: Steam, until 1893, and then Overhead Electric.
Gauge: 3ft 6in.
Description: Originally a 6TS dead ended loco and car shed accessed via a traverser, it was rebuilt as a brick built 6TS dead ended shed with conventional access to accommodate overhead electric tram cars.
Closed: 1893 and re-opened as an electric car depot on December 5th, 1895. The depot closed on December 24th, 1940 when the system was abandoned due to extensive Blitz damage It was utilized for scrapping trams until 1941 and then became an omnibus garage until September 1954. Site now occupied by industrial units.

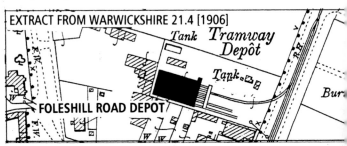

Cleveland Road

Location: At SO91929826 on the north side of Cleveland Road.

Opened: February 6th, 1902 by Wolverhampton Corporation.

Traction System: Stud-Contact Electric until 1921 and then Overhead Electric.

Gauge: 3ft 6in.

Description: Originally a brick built 10TS dead ended tram shed with three access roads, a 4TS dead ended shed was added on the western side in 1909 and further 2TS dead ended extensions were constructed in 1913 and 1921. The depot was converted to overhead working in 1921 and trolleybuses were then accommodated from October 29th, 1923. It was also utilized for motor omnibuses between 1905 and 1909 and from 1911 onwards.

Closed: For trams from August 26th, 1928.

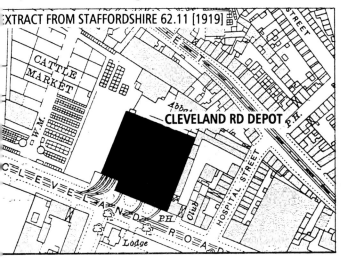

EXTRACT FROM STAFFORDSHIRE 62.11 [1919]

CLEVELAND RD DEPOT

Newbridge Depot

Location: At SO8960996 on the north east side of Tettenhall Road, Newbridge.

Opened: 1878 by the Wolverhampton Tramways Co. Ltd and taken over by Wolverhampton Corporation on May 1st, 1900.

Traction System: Horse/Steam.

Gauge: 4ft 8.5in.

Description: A 2TS through road horse car shed and stables. Two 1TS dead ended sheds were later added on the north side, one of which was probably utilized as the shed/workshop for the steam loco shedded here between May and November in 1881.

Closed: March 8th, 1902 and sold with part of the site going to the Electricity Department.

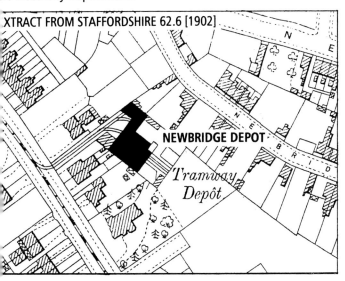

EXTRACT FROM STAFFORDSHIRE 62.6 [1902]

NEWBRIDGE DEPOT

Tramway Depôt

Darlington Street

Location: At SO90979854, behind the Tramway Offices at 45 Darlington Street, on the south side.

Opened: May 1st, 1878 by the Wolverhampton Tramways Co. Ltd and taken over by Wolverhampton Corporation on May 1st, 1900.

Traction System: Horse.

Gauge: 4ft 8.5in.

Description: A 2TS through road horse car depot and stables.

Closed: The offices closed in 1903/4 and the depot closed shortly afterwards when horse services ceased. The building was let to the Water Department in the same year and later sold.

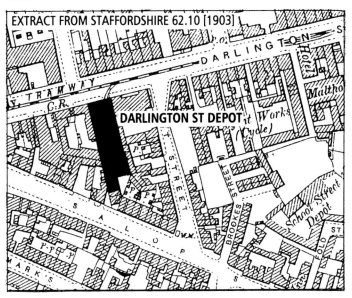

EXTRACT FROM STAFFORDSHIRE 62.10 [1903]

DARLINGTON ST DEPOT

Moxley

Location: At SO96619582, on the south side of High Street, Moxley.

Opened: 1879 by Wolverhampton Tramways Co. Ltd and taken over by Wolverhampton District Electric Tramways Ltd on May 1st, 1900.

Traction System: Horse.

Gauge: 4ft 8.5in.

Description: A 2TS dead ended tram shed.

Closed: 1900.

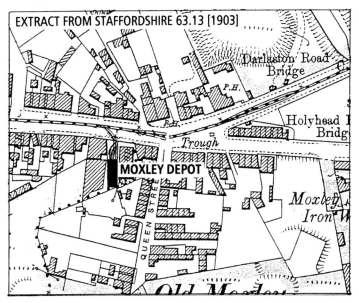

EXTRACT FROM STAFFORDSHIRE 63.13 [1903]

MOXLEY DEPOT

DUDLEY

Tipton Road

Location: At SO95079068 on the corner of Castle Hill and Tipton Road, adjacent to Dudley L&NWR Station.

Opened: May 31st, 1884 by the Dudley & Stourbridge Steam Tramways Co. Ltd (renamed as the Dudley, Stourbridge & District Electric Traction Co. Ltd on April 2nd, 1898) and taken over by the Birmingham & Midland Tramways Joint Committee on July 1st, 1904.

Traction System: Steam, until July 26th, 1899, and then Overhead Electric.

Gauge: 3ft 6in.

Description: Originally a 2TS tram shed with one through road it was lengthened at the rear at the time of electrification.

Closed: December 31st, 1929. The site was latterly utilized as an omnibus lay-by.

Tipton Road

Location: At SO95129085 on the east side of Tipton Road, north of Birmingham Road.

Opened: 1885 by the South Staffordshire & Birmingham District Steam Tramways Co. Ltd (Renamed as the South Staffordshire Tramways Company in 1889), taken over by the South Staffordshire Tramways (Lessee) Co. Ltd on June 23rd, 1900 and taken over again, by the Birmingham & Midland Tramways Joint Committee on July 1st, 1904.

Traction System: Steam, until June 15th, 1904, and then Overhead Electric.

Gauge: 3ft 6in.

Description: A corrugated iron built 1TS dead ended shed for locos and cars adjoined by a 1TS dead ended workshop.

Closed: June 15th, 1904 and re-opened as a temporary depot for overhead electric working on November 24th, 1904. It eventually closed sometime in 1905/6 following the opening of Tividale Depot in Oldbury. It was subsequently demolished and the site later incorporated into a playing field.

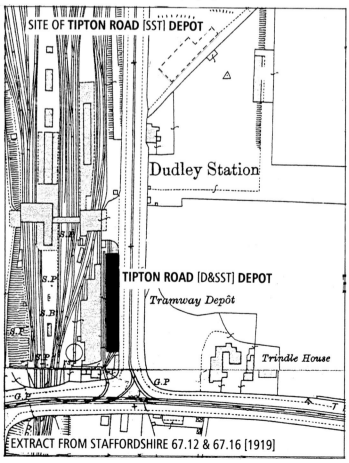

EXTRACT FROM STAFFORDSHIRE 67.12 & 67.16 [1919]

Harts Hill

Location: At SO92198808 on the east side of Dudley Roa south of Canal Street.

Opened: July 26th, 1899 by the Dudley, Stourbridge & Distri Electric Traction Co. Ltd and taken over by the Birmingham Midland Tramways Joint Committee on July 1st, 1904.

Traction System: Overhead Electric.

Gauge: 3ft 6in.

Description: A brick built 9TS dead ended tram shed access via three turntables.

Closed: February 28th, 1925 and subsequently utilized as a omnibus depot.

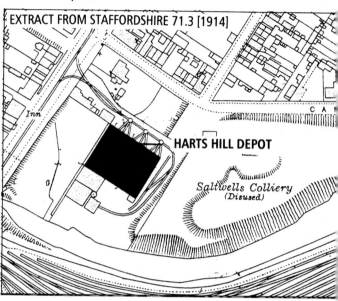

EXTRACT FROM STAFFORDSHIRE 71.3 [1914]

OLDBURY

Tividale Depot

Location: At SO96379869 on the south side of Dudley Road.

Opened: 1905/6 by the Birmingham & Midland Tramways Joir Committee.

Traction System: Overhead Electric.

Gauge: 3ft 6in.

Description: A corrugated iron built 6TS dead ended tram she adjoined, along the north side, by a 3TS dead ended tram she and a 6TS dead ended works which were opened on Januar 1st, 1907. The works were involved with the construction c new tram cars from 1913.

Closed: September 30th, 1930 and utilized for car scrapping.

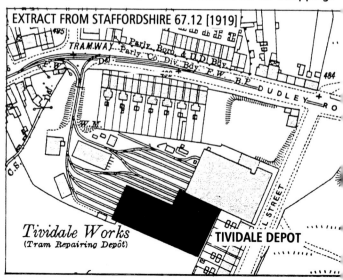

EXTRACT FROM STAFFORDSHIRE 67.12 [1919]

SEDGLEY

Dudley Road

Location: On the east side of Dudley Road, south of Sedgley.
Opened: May 7th, 1883 by Dudley, Sedgley & Wolverhampton Tramways Co. Ltd and taken over by the Midland Tramways Co. Ltd (reformed in 1893 as Dudley & Wolverhampton Tramways Co. Ltd) on October 18th, 1889. Purchased by the British Electric Traction Co. Ltd on April 22nd, 1899 and operated, firstly, by the Dudley, Stourbridge & District Electric Traction Co. Ltd until 1901 and then by Wolverhampton & District Electric Tramways Ltd. It became part of the Birmingham & Midland Tramways Joint Committee on July 1st, 1904 and, finally, it was taken over by Wolverhampton Corporation on August 15th, 1925.

DEPOT No.1

Opened: May 7th, 1883.
Traction System: Horse, until November 8th, 1885, and then steam.
Gauge: 4ft 8.5in.
Description: Originally a 2TS dead ended horse car shed located at SO92109279, it was lengthened in 1885 and converted to a steam loco and car shed, re-opening on January 16th, 1886.
Closed: 1899 and demolished to make way for storage sidings.

DEPOT No.2

Opened: October 3rd, 1900.
Traction System: Overhead Electric.
Gauge: 3ft 6in.
Description: A temporary 2TS dead ended tram shed located at SO92089277.
Closed: 1901 and demolished.

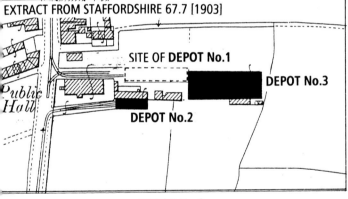

EXTRACT FROM STAFFORDSHIRE 67.7 [1903]

DEPOT No.3

Opened: 1901.
Traction System: Overhead Electric.
Gauge: 3ft 6in.
Description: A corrugated iron built 6TS dead ended tram shed located at SO92159278 and incorporating workshops at the rear.
Closed: November 7th, 1926 and re-opened as a trolleybus depot in 1930.

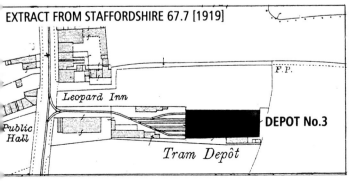

EXTRACT FROM STAFFORDSHIRE 67.7 [1919]

SMETHWICK

West Smethwick Depot

Location: On the south side of Oldbury Road, West Smethwick.
Opened: August 1885 by Birmingham & Midland Tramways Ltd, taken over by the Birmingham & District Tramways Joint Committee on July 1st, 1904 and taken over again on April 1st, 1928 by Birmingham Corporation.
Traction System: Steam, until March 9th, 1904, and then Overhead Electric.
Gauge: 3ft 6in.

DEPOT No.1

Description: Originally a brick built 9TS dead ended car shed, located at SP00258934, it was converted to an 11TS dead ended tram car shed and workshops for electrification.

DEPOT No.2

Description: Originally a 6TS dead ended loco shed, located at SP00358936, it was reduced to four roads in 1902 and rebuilt as a machine shop for electrification.

Closed: September 30th, 1939 and used for storage and scrapping of cars until June 1940. Both buildings still stood, in commercial use, in 1959.

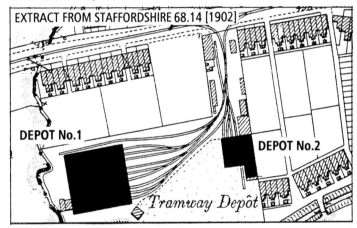

EXTRACT FROM STAFFORDSHIRE 68.14 [1902]

BILSTON

Mount Pleasant

Location: At SD95089677 on the north west side of Mount Pleasant, Bilston.
Opened: 1902 by Wolverhampton District Electric Tramways Ltd, taken over by the Birmingham & Midland Tramways Joint Committee on July 1st, 1904 and taken over again on September 1st, 1928 by Wolverhampton Corporation.
Traction System: Overhead Electric.
Gauge: 3ft 6in.
Description: A brick built 5TS dead ended tram shed.
Closed: November 30th, 1928 and further utilized as a trolley bus and omnibus depot.

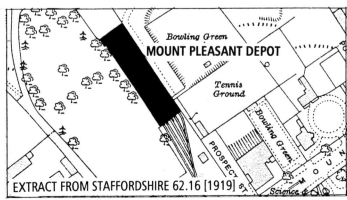

EXTRACT FROM STAFFORDSHIRE 62.16 [1919]

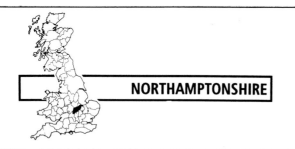

NORTHAMPTONSHIRE

NORTHAMPTON

Abington Street

Location: At SP75786061, on the south side of Abington Street, at the rear of No.72.

Opened: June 4th, 1881 by Northampton Street Tramways and taken over, on October 21st, 1901, by Northampton Corporation.

Traction System: Horse.

Gauge: 3ft 6in.

Description: A 2TS tram shed, later extended at the rear.

Closed: August 18th, 1904. The site was later re-developed and a Carnegie Library erected on it.

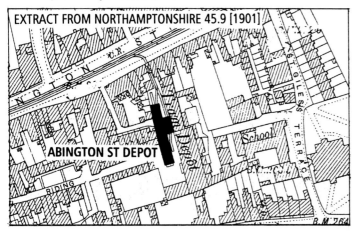

EXTRACT FROM NORTHAMPTONSHIRE 45.9 [1901]

ABINGTON ST DEPOT

St James's Road

Location: At SP74256049, on the west side of St James's Road in St James.

Opened: July 21st, 1904 by Northampton Corporation.

Traction System: Overhead Electric.

Gauge: 3ft 6in.

Description: A brick built 6TS dead ended tram shed.

Closed: December 15th, 1934 and subsequently utilized as an omnibus workshop. The building was still in use as an omnibus depot in 1999.

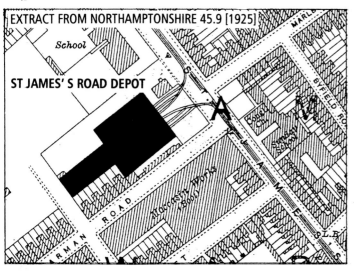

EXTRACT FROM NORTHAMPTONSHIRE 45.9 [1925]

School

ST JAMES'S ROAD DEPOT

PETERBOROUGH

Lincoln Road

Location: At TF18840043, on the north side of Lincoln Road in Millfield.

Opened: January 24th, 1903 by Peterborough Electric Traction Co. Ltd.

Traction System: Overhead Electric.

Gauge: 3ft 6in.

Description: A brick built 5TS dead ended tram shed.

Closed: November 15th, 1930. Subsequently utilized as part of an omnibus depot.

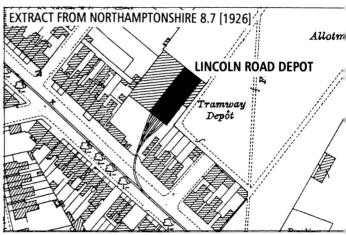

EXTRACT FROM NORTHAMPTONSHIRE 8.7 [1926]

Allotm

LINCOLN ROAD DEPOT

Tramway Depôt

Car No.26 of 1900/1 passing **Bedminster Depot**, Bristol.
Courtesy Peter Davey Photograph Collection (See Page 4

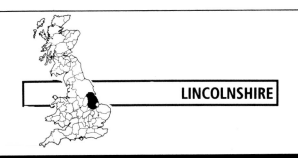

LINCOLNSHIRE

LINCOLN

Bracebridge

Location: At SK96876852, on the east side of High Street.
Opened: September 8th, 1882 by the Lincoln Tramway Co. and taken over by Lincoln Corporation in July 1904.
Traction System: Horse until July 22nd, 1905. Stud Electric from November 23rd, 1905 until conversion to Overhead Electric in 1919/20.
Gauge: 3ft 6in until July 22nd, 1905 and then 4ft 8.5in.
Description: A brick built 4TS dead ended shed and stables, it was adapted for electric working in 1905 and a 1TS lean-to added on the north side of the building in 1919 to accommodate trailer cars. This extension and track were removed in 1924.
Closed: March 4th, 1929. In 1970 it was in use as a car showroom and by 2000 was up for sale.

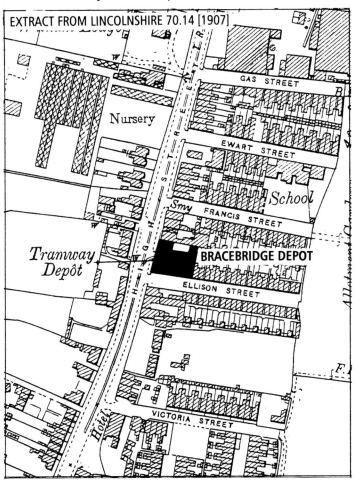

EXTRACT FROM LINCOLNSHIRE 70.14 [1907]

SKEGNESS

Promenade

A short horse tramway is believed to have operated from c1880 to c1882 from the site of the present Clock Tower on the sea front, across the Promenade and beach down to the sea. Existence of a car shed is unconfirmed.

ALFORD

Station Road

Location: At TF44557562, on the north west side of the A1104 (Station Road) opposite the Railway Station.
Opened: April 2nd, 1884 by the Alford & Sutton Tramway Co. and taken over in 1888 by the Great Northern, Lincoln & East Coast Railway Ltd. (Great Northern Tramways Co. Ltd from January 31st, 1889).
Traction System: Steam.
Gauge: 2ft 6in.
Description: A brick built 2TS dead ended loco and tramcar shed*.
Closed: December 1889 and subsequently utilized as an omnibus depot. In 1984 it was part of the premises of a coach hire company.

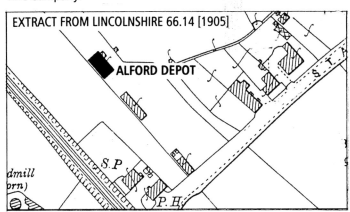

EXTRACT FROM LINCOLNSHIRE 66.14 [1905]

ALFORD DEPOT

*This depot is listed in "The Directory of British Engine Sheds" as TF4475.1/1A.

SUTTON

High Street

Location: At TF51948178, on the south east side of the A111 (High Street).
Opened: April 2nd, 1884 by the Alford & Sutton Tramway Co. and taken over in 1888 by the Great Northern, Lincoln & East Coast Railway Ltd. (Great Northern Tramways Co. Ltd from January 31st, 1889).
Traction System: Steam.
Gauge: 2ft 6in.
Description: A brick built 1TS dead ended loco and tramcar shed*.
Closed: December 1889. In 1946 it was in use as a garage work-shop.

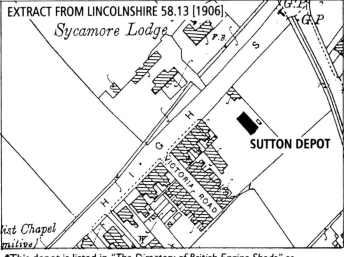

EXTRACT FROM LINCOLNSHIRE 58.13 [1906]

SUTTON DEPOT

*This depot is listed in "The Directory of British Engine Sheds" as TF5181.1/1A.

GRIMSBY

Carr Lane

Location: At TA28721007, on the west side of the corner of Carr Lane (re-named Park St) and Hamilton Street.
Opened: June 4th, 1881 by Great Grimsby Street Tramways Co.
Traction System: Horse.
Gauge: 4ft 8.5in.
Description: A brick built 3TS dead ended shed and stables for cars and horse buses.
Closed: December 6th, 1901 and sold in 1904 to become a piano factory. It was later utilized as a skating rink and cinema before being destroyed by bombing during 1944.

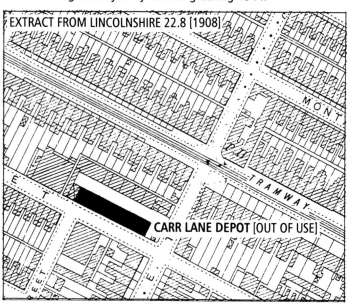

EXTRACT FROM LINCOLNSHIRE 22.8 [1908]

CARR LANE DEPOT [OUT OF USE]

Victoria Street

Location: At TA27120971, on the west side of Victoria Street.
Opened: October 1926, for trolleybuses and January 2nd, 1927 for trams, by Grimsby Corporation.
Traction System: Overhead Electric.
Gauge: 4ft 8.5in.
Description: A 9TS dead ended tram depot with two access tracks. It was converted from a redundant seaplane hangar which had been re-erected and reinforced with concrete walls.
Closed: March 31st, 1937.

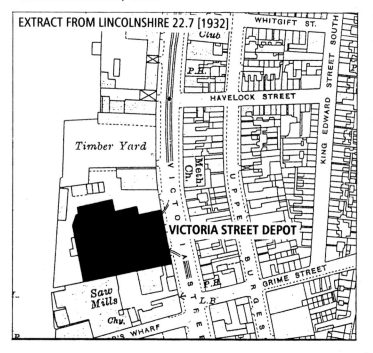

EXTRACT FROM LINCOLNSHIRE 22.7 [1932]

VICTORIA STREET DEPOT

Pyewipe

Location: At TA25521096 on the south side of the railway line, west of Gilbey Road.
Opened: May 15th, 1912 by the Grimsby & Immingham Electric Railway and taken over by the LNER on January 1st, 1923. Became part of BR on January 1st, 1948.
Traction System: Overhead Electric.
Gauge: 4ft 8.5in.
Description: A corrugated iron built 2TS dead ended workshop and paint shop, the trams stabling on adjacent sidings.
Closed: July 1st, 1961 and utilized for industrial purposes. Still standing, disused, in 1992.

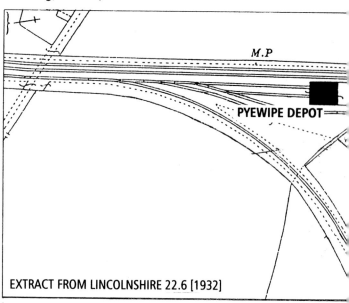

M.P

PYEWIPE DEPOT

EXTRACT FROM LINCOLNSHIRE 22.6 [1932]

CLEETHORPES

Pelham Road

Location: At TA30200943, on the east side of Pelham Road.
Opened: December 7th, 1901 by Great Grimsby Street Tramways Co. and taken over by Cleethorpes Urban District Council on July 15th, 1936.
Traction System: Overhead Electric.
Gauge: 4ft 8.5in.
Description: A brick built 8TS dead ended tram shed and workshops with a corrugated iron frontage. An omnibus garage was added on the west side in 1909.
Closed: July 17th, 1937 and subsequently utilized as a trolley bus garage. It was closed in May 1957 and taken over by a commercial concern.

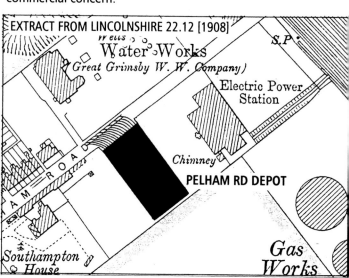

EXTRACT FROM LINCOLNSHIRE 22.12 [1908]

Wells

Water Works
(Great Grimsby W. W. Company)

S.P.

Electric Power Station

Chimney

PELHAM RD DEPOT

Southampton House

Gas Works

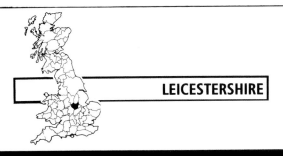

LEICESTERSHIRE

LEICESTER

Humberstone Gate

Location: At SK58860469, on the north side of Humberstone Gate, east of Belgrave Gate and behind the Bell Hotel.
Opened: December 24th, 1874 by the Leicester Tramways Co. Ltd and taken over by Leicester Corporation on July 1st, 1901.
Traction System: Horse, until October 31st, 1904, and then Overhead Electric from November 1st, 1904.
Gauge: 4ft 8.5in.
Description: Originally a 2TS horse tram shed, possibly just a covered yard, with one through road into Belgrave Gate and a stables. It was converted for electric working in 1901 with removal of the Belgrave Gate exit and, in 1922, a 5TS dead ended tram shed was constructed at the rear of the shed. The site was also re-named as Central Depot.
Closed: With the tramway on November 9th, 1949 and subsequently utilized as an omnibus garage. The site is now occupied by a shopping centre.

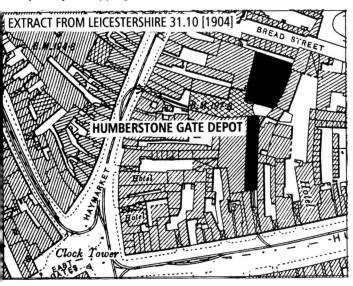

Thurcaston Road

Location: At SK59250727, on the north side of Thurcaston Road, opposite the Talbot Inn.
Opened: 1888 by the Leicester Tramways Co. Ltd and taken over by Leicester Corporation on July 1st, 1901.
Traction System: Horse.
Gauge: 4ft 8.5in.
Description: A 2TS dead ended tram shed converted from a former horse bus depot.
Closed: 1904.

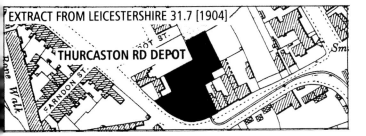

Abbey Park Road

Location: At SK59010591, on the north side of Abbey Park Rd.
Opened: May 18th, 1904 by Leicester Corporation.
Traction System: Overhead Electric.
Gauge: 4ft 8.5in.
Description: Originally an 18TS dead ended tram shed with adjacent paintshop and workshops, it was extended in 1915.
Closed: November 9th, 1949 and subsequently utilized for scrapping trams.

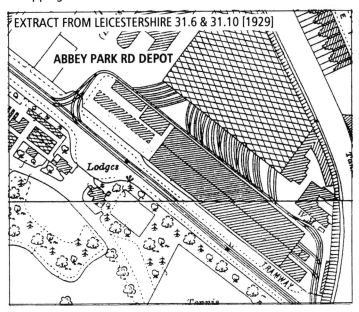

London Road

Location: At SK61330142, on the south west side of London Rd.
Opened: May 18th, 1904 by Leicester Corporation.
Traction System: Overhead Electric.
Gauge: 4ft 8.5in.
Description: A 2TS dead ended tram shed.
Closed: 1922.

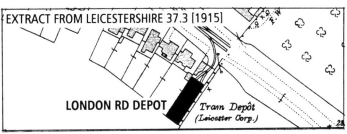

Narborough Road

Location: At SK57380313 on the east side of Narborough Road
Opened: July 17th, 1904 by Leicester Corporation.
Traction System: Overhead Electric.
Gauge: 4ft 8.5in.
Description: A 2TS dead ended tram shed.
Closed: 1922.

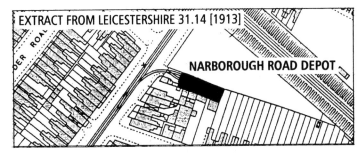

CHESHIRE

BIRKENHEAD

Canning Street

Location: At SJ32648928 in Robert Main's Yard, 26 Canning St, on the north side of the road and east side of Argyle St.

Opened: August 30th, 1860 by the Birkenhead Street Railway Co. Ltd.

Traction System: Horse.

Gauge: 5ft 2in.

Description: A temporary horse and tramcar depot established in the coachbuilder's yard.

Closed: 1861, upon the opening of Palm Grove Depot.

Pacific Road

Location: At SJ32748935, on the corner of Pacific Rd and Shore Rd and adjacent to the former Morpeth Dock.

Opened: April 14th, 1995 by the Wirral Metropolitan Borough Council for the Wirral Tramway and operated by Blackpool Transport Services.

Traction System: Overhead Electric.

Gauge: 4ft 8.5in.

Description: A brick and sandstone built 2TS dead ended tram shed utilizing the Shore Road end of the former 1850 China Steam Navigation Co's transit shed.

Still operational during 2001 with the remainder of the building in use as a store for preserved transport vehicles.

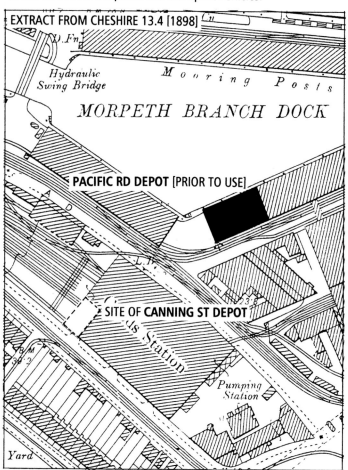

EXTRACT FROM CHESHIRE 13.4 [1898]

Borough Road

Location: At SJ31426763 on the corner of Borough Road and Elmswood Road, Higher Tranmere.

Opened: August 1st, 1878 by the Birkenhead Tramways Co and taken over on August 15th, 1890 by the Birkenhead United Tramway, Omnibus & Carriage Co. Ltd.

Traction System: Horse.

Gauge: 4ft 8.5in.

Description: A 2TS dead ended horse car sned and stables.

Closed: September 27th, 1901 and demolished in 1902.

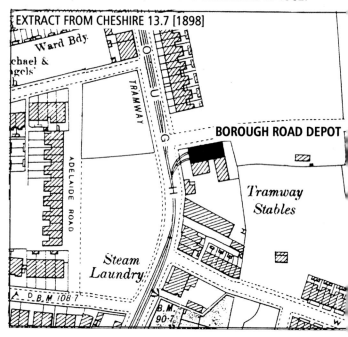

EXTRACT FROM CHESHIRE 13.7 [1898]

Birkenhead Docks Station

Location: On the north side of Birkenhead Docks Station.

Opened: September 6th, 1873 by the Hoylake & Birkenhead Rail & Tramway Co and purchased by the Birkenhead Tramways Co. on October 12th, 1879.

Traction System: Horse.

Gauge: 4ft 8.5in.

Description: The railway/tramway interchange shed located at SJ29589058 was utilized as a 2TS car shed and stables. A 1TS dead ended shed, located at SJ29679056, was added later.

Closed: 1888. The site was later utilized for Birkenhead North Engine Shed* and is the only known example of a tram shed and engine shed sharing the same site.

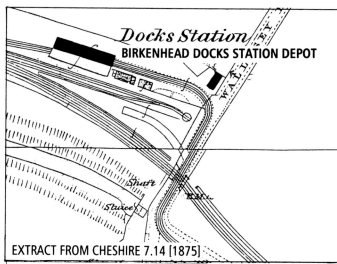

EXTRACT FROM CHESHIRE 7.14 [1875]

*This depot is listed in "The Directory of British Engine Sheds" as SJ2990.1/1A

Laird Street (North End Depot)

Location: At SJ30388976, on the north side of Laird Street.
Opened: March 2nd, 1902 by Birkenhead Corporation.
Traction System: Overhead Electric.
Gauge: 4ft 8.5in.
Description: Originally a 7TS dead ended tram shed and works, a 3TS extension was added on the west side and, in 1925, the front was lengthened. It was further extended in 1928 to allow for the accommodation of omnibuses.
Closed: To trams on July 17th, 1937 and further utilized as an omnibus garage.

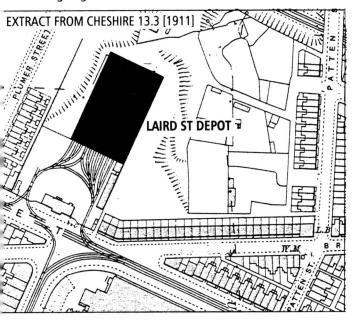

EXTRACT FROM CHESHIRE 13.3 [1911]

New Ferry (South End Depot)

Location: At SJ33718545, on the east side of New Chester Rd, New Ferry.
Opened: July 1877 by the Wirral Tramway Co. Ltd and taken over by Birkenhead Corporation on December 31st, 1899.
Traction System: Horse, until January 22nd, 1901, and then Overhead Electric.
Gauge: 4ft 8.5in.
Description: Formerly a horse car depot and stables with a 3-road covered yard linked to another three roads by a single track. Upon electrification it was rebuilt in brick as two 3TS tram sheds connected by a single track. From 1919 it was also utilized to accommodate omnibuses.
Closed: December 28th, 1931 and subsequently demolished. A new omnibus garage was constructed on the site.

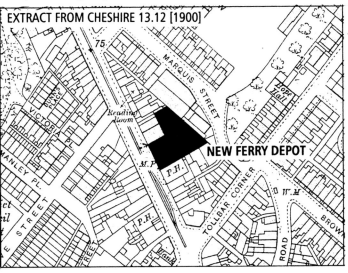

EXTRACT FROM CHESHIRE 13.12 [1900]

Palm Grove

Location: At SJ30726802 on the east side of Palm Grove, Oxton.
Opened: August 1861 by the Birkenhead Street Railway Co. Ltd, taken over by the Birkenhead Tramways Co. in 1877 and taken over again on August 15th, 1890 by the Birkenhead United Tramway, Omnibus & Carriage Co. Ltd.
Traction System: Horse.
Gauge: 5ft 2in (until 1864), 4ft 8.5in.
Description: A 2TS dead ended horse car shed and stables. The depot was rebuilt in 1879.
Closed: November 8th, 1901. The building still stood in 1987.

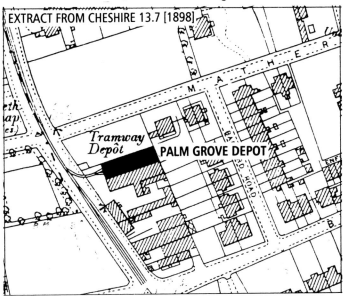

EXTRACT FROM CHESHIRE 13.7 [1898]

HYDE

Mottram Road

Location: At SD97210251, on the north side of Mottram Road.
Opened: 1905 by the Stalybridge, Hyde, Mossley & Dukinfield Tramways & Electricity Board.
Traction System: Overhead Electric.
Gauge: 4ft 8.5in.
Description: A 3TS dead ended tram shed.
Closed: May 12th, 1945.

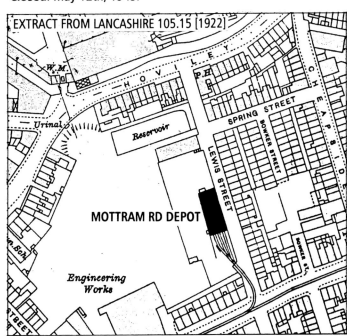

EXTRACT FROM LANCASHIRE 105.15 [1922]

STOCKPORT

Mersey Square

Location: At SJ89359045, on the east side of Mersey Square.
Opened: August 26th, 1901 by Stockport Corporation.
Traction System: Overhead Electric.
Gauge: 4ft 8.5in.
Description: Originally an 11TS dead ended tram shed & works built in brick and gritstone with six access tracks, a 6TS dead ended extension was constructed on the east side in 1929. It was also utilized to accommodate trolleybuses between March 10th, 1913 and September 11th, 1920.
Closed: August 25th, 1951 and utilized for scrapping tramcars prior to further use as an omnibus garage.

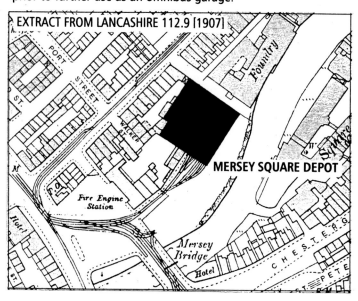

EXTRACT FROM LANCASHIRE 112.9 [1907]

MERSEY SQUARE DEPOT

Heaton Lane

Location: At SJ89099041, on the north side of Heaton Lane and west side of Wellington Road.
Opened: January 31st, 1924 by Stockport Corporation.
Traction System: Overhead Electric.
Gauge: 4ft 8.5in.
Description: A brick built 5TS dead ended tram shed, it suffered air raid damage in 1940.
Closed: March 10th, 1951. The yard was then utilized for the scrapping of tramcars with the building finding further use as an omnibus garage.

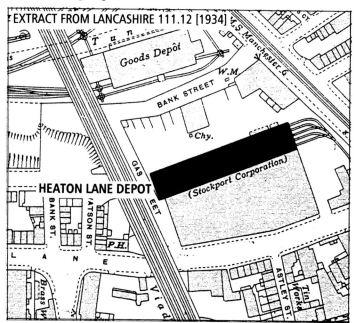

EXTRACT FROM LANCASHIRE 111.12 [1934]

HEATON LANE DEPOT (Stockport Corporation)

Dialstone Lane

Location: At SJ91248779, behind Crown Inn in Dialstone Lane.
Opened: April 4th, 1890 by Stockport & Hazel Grove Carriage Tramway Co. Ltd and taken over by Stockport Corporation on January 24th, 1905.
Traction System: Horse.
Gauge: 4ft 8.5in.
Description: A brick built 2TS horse car shed and stables.
Closed: June 1905.

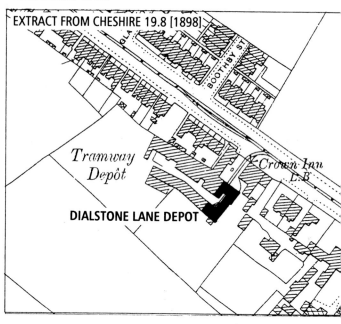

EXTRACT FROM CHESHIRE 19.8 [1898]

Tramway Depot

DIALSTONE LANE DEPOT

STALYBRIDGE

Tame Valley Depot

Location: At SJ95319808, on the south side of Park Road.
Opened: May 22nd, 1904 by the Stalybridge, Hyde, Mossley & Dukinfield Tramways & Electricity Board. (NB. Services had begun on October 15th, 1903 using cars borrowed from Ashton under Lyne).
Traction System: Overhead Electric.
Gauge: 4ft 8.5in.
Description: An 8TS dead ended tram shed and works.
Closed: April 30th, 1938 as a running shed and may have been utilized as workshops until 1945.

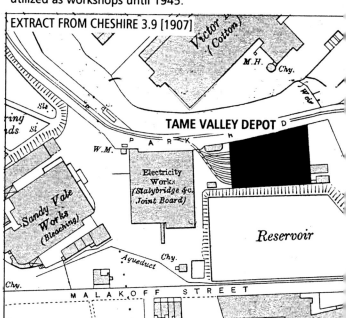

EXTRACT FROM CHESHIRE 3.9 [1907]

TAME VALLEY DEPOT

Electricity Works (Stalybridge &c. Joint Board)

Reservoir

WALLASEY

Field Road

Location: At SJ30659349, on the north side of Field Rd, New Brighton.

Opened: June 28th, 1879 by the Wallasey Tramways Co. and on May 8th, 1891 became part of the Wallasey United Tramway & Omnibus Co. Ltd. Taken over on April 1st, 1901 by Wallasey UDC.

Traction System: Horse.

Gauge: 4ft 8.5in.

Description: Originally a brick built 2TS dead ended car shed with a turntable at the rear, a timber open-sided horse omnibus shed was added on the east side in 1884. The extension was demolished and replaced with a timber shed, again for omnibus use, in 1891.

Closed: March 19th, 1902 and sold to a funeral director.

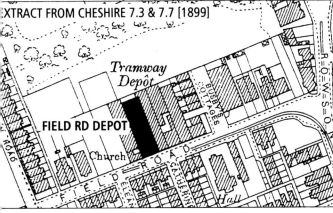

EXTRACT FROM CHESHIRE 7.3 & 7.7 [1899]

Seaview Road

Location: At SJ30309249, on the west side of Seaview Road.

Opened: March 17th, 1902 by Wallasey Corporation.

Traction System: Overhead Electric.

Gauge: 4ft 8.5in.

Description: Originally a brick built 9TS dead ended tram shed and works with a 1TS dead ended paint shop along the north eastern side. In December 1907 the front end was extended with a 10th road added on the south west side, and in 1914-16 a new 7TS works building was constructed on the east side of the site. In 1928 a 2TS paint shop and an omnibus garage were built and the tram depot started to accommodate omnibuses.

Closed: To trams on November 30th, 1933 and finally closed on October 26th, 1986.

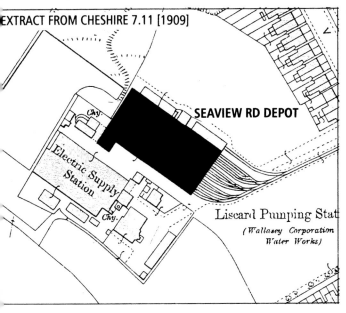

EXTRACT FROM CHESHIRE 7.11 [1909]

MOSSLEY

Stamford Road

Location: At SD97210251, on the south side of Stamford Rd.

Opened: 1905 by the Stalybridge, Hyde, Mossley & Dukinfield Tramways & Electricity Board.

Traction System: Overhead Electric.

Gauge: 4ft 8.5in.

Description: A 4TS dead ended tram shed.

Closed: 1931.

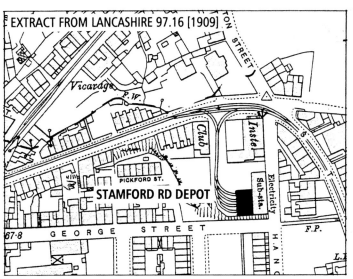

EXTRACT FROM LANCASHIRE 97.16 [1909]

CHESTER

Station Road

Location: At SJ41206692, on the west side of Station Road adjacent to Chester General Station.

Opened: June 10th, 1879 by the Chester Tramways Company and purchased by Chester Corporation on January 1st, 1902.

Traction System: Horse, until 1902, and then Overhead Electric.

Gauge: 4ft 8.5in (until 1902), 3ft 6in.

Description: Originally a brick built 3TS tram shed with one through road and access from either end. Upon electrification it was rebuilt with an additional 1TS dead ended workshop and a 4th shed road was added later.

Closed: November 1902 with the cars being temporarily stabled in Cable Street, Saltney, until December 27th, 1902 when horse working ceased. Re-opened on April 6th, 1903 and closed on February 15th, 1930. Further utilized as an omnibus depot.

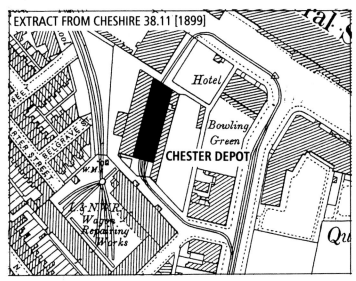

EXTRACT FROM CHESHIRE 38.11 [1899]

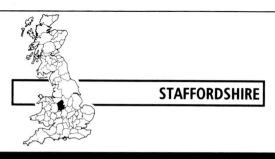

STAFFORDSHIRE

STOKE ON TRENT

Bowstead Street

Location: At SJ87994497, on the east side of Bowstead Street, south of Church Street , Stoke on Trent.
Opened: 1881by the North Staffordshire Tramways Co. Ltd and taken over on June 28th, 1898 by the British Electric Traction Co. Ltd for operation by the Potteries Electric Traction Co. Ltd.
Traction System: Horse until 1884. Steam until 1898 and then Overhead Electric.
Gauge: 4ft.
Description: Originally a 6TS dead ended tram and loco shed with 2TS and 1TS dead ended sheds (possibly works and horse car sheds) accessed via a turntable, it was, upon electrification, converted to a brick built 6TS dead ended tram shed with 3TS and 2TS works buildings.
Closed: July 11th, 1928.

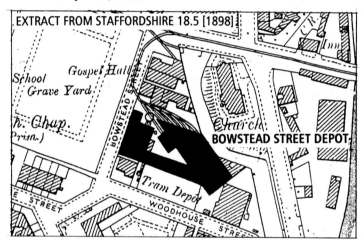

Foundry Street

Location: At SJ88184769, on the west side of Foundry St, Hanley.
Opened: January 11th, 1862 by Staffordshire Potteries Street Railway Co. Ltd and taken over on November 8th, 1879 by the North Staffordshire Tramways Co. Ltd.
Traction System: Horse.
Gauge: 4ft 8.5in.
Description: A 1TS dead ended tram shed.
Closed: 1882.

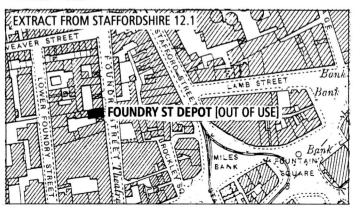

Fenton Depot

Location: At SJ90194416, on the north west side of Baron and south west side of King St, Fenton.
Opened: 1899 by the Potteries Electric Traction Co. Ltd.
Traction System: Overhead Electric.
Gauge: 4ft.
Description: A 4TS tram shed with one through road.
Closed: July 11th, 1928.

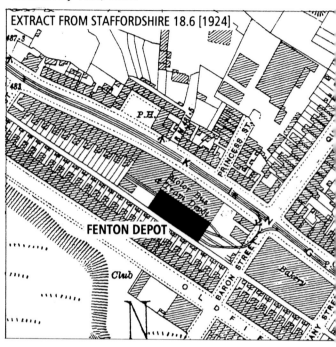

Goldenhill Depot

Location: At SJ85185345, on the north side of Williamson S Goldenhill, Tunstall.
Opened: May 16th, 1899 by the Potteries Electric Traction C Ltd.
Traction System: Overhead Electric.
Gauge: 4ft.
Description: A 5TS dead ended tram shed.
Closed: 1927.

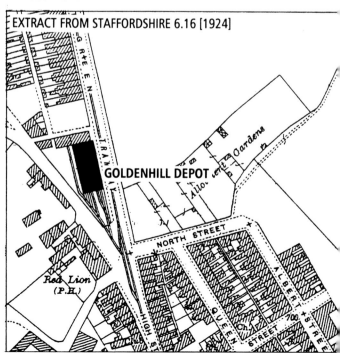

Horninglow Street

Location: At SK25012343, on the north side of Horninglow St.
Opened: August 3rd, 1903 by Burton upon Trent Corporation.
Traction System: Overhead Electric.
Gauge: 3ft 6in.
Description: A 5TS tram shed with 3 through roads accessing a works at the rear. Omnibuses also utilized the depot from May 1st, 1924 and an omnibus garage was added on the east side in 1925.
Closed: To trams on December 31st, 1929 and totally in 1984.

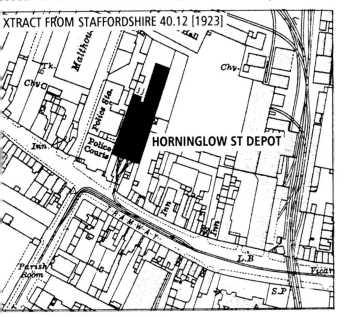

EXTRACT FROM STAFFORDSHIRE 40.12 [1923]

HORNINGLOW ST DEPOT

May Bank Depot

Location: At SJ85304768, on the south side of Lunt Street, off Alexandra Road, May Bank, Wolstanton.
Opened: March 17th, 1900 by the Potteries Electric Traction Co. Ltd.
Traction System: Overhead Electric.
Gauge: 4ft.
Description: An 8TS dead ended tram shed.
Closed: July 11th, 1928.

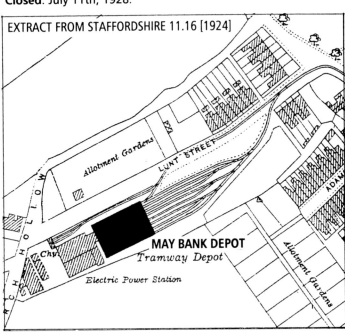

EXTRACT FROM STAFFORDSHIRE 11.16 [1924]

MAY BANK DEPOT
Tramway Depot
Electric Power Station

Finding space for depots could be difficult in built-up areas; often they had to be shoe-horned into small side streets, as was the case with Bristol Tramways' **St George's Depot** here partially visible immediately beyond the tram.
Courtesy Peter Davey Photograph Collection
(See Page 46)

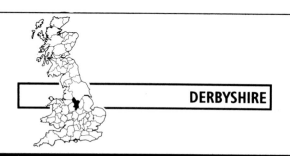

DERBYSHIRE

DERBY

Friargate

Location: At SK34713647, on the north east side of Friargate, immediately west of the GNR bridge.
Opened: 1881 by the Derby Tramways Co. Ltd and taken over by Derby Corporation on November 1st, 1899.
Traction System: Horse.
Gauge: 4ft.
Description: Originally a 2TS roofed yard with stables and work-shops accommodated in the railway arches, a 3rd road was added later. The depot was also utilized for horse buses.
Closed: June 1st, 1907 and vacated by the Corporation on March 25th, 1908. The yard was still in existence in 1999.

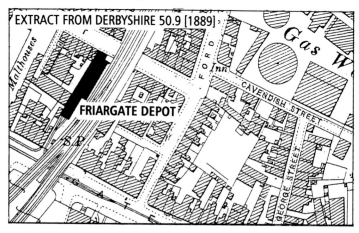

EXTRACT FROM DERBYSHIRE 50.9 [1889]

FRIARGATE DEPOT

Nottingham Road

Location: At SK36033655, on the north side of Nottingham Road, west of Stores Road.
Opened: February 1st, 1909 by Derby Corporation.
Traction System: Overhead Electric.
Gauge: 4ft.
Description: Originally a brick built 4TS dead ended shed, a 5TS extension was added on the north side in 1926.
Closed: March 1931 and subsequently utilized as a trolleybus depot. *(Upon closure the trams were transferred for temporary storage in the Corporation omnibus garage on the west side of Osmaston Road, immediately south of the MR bridge.)*

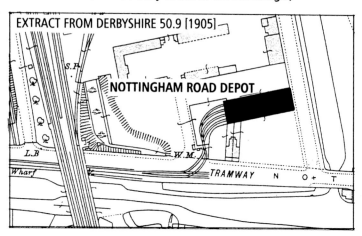

EXTRACT FROM DERBYSHIRE 50.9 [1905]

NOTTINGHAM ROAD DEPOT

Osmaston Road

Location: At SK36323408 on the south side of Abingdon Str and west side of Osmaston Road.
Opened: July 27th, 1904 by Derby Corporation.
Traction System: Overhead Electric.
Gauge: 4ft.
Description: A 9TS dead ended tram shed.
Closed: July 2nd, 1934 and subsequently utilized as a trolley works.

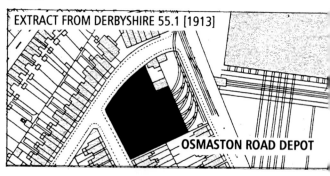

EXTRACT FROM DERBYSHIRE 55.1 [1913]

OSMASTON ROAD DEPOT

Station Street

Location: At SK36043544 on the west side of Lou Carrington Street and south side of Station Street. (la Midland Road).
Opened: March 6th, 1880 by the Derby Tramways Co. Ltd.
Traction System: Horse.
Gauge: 4ft.
Description: A tram shed and stables.
Closed: 1881. The site is now occupied by a Royal M building.

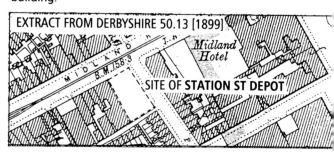

EXTRACT FROM DERBYSHIRE 50.13 [1899]

SITE OF STATION ST DEPOT

GLOSSOP

High Street West

Location: At SK02409430, on the north side of High Str West, west of Glossop town centre.
Opened: August 21st, 1903 by the Urban Electric Supply Ltd trading as Glossop Tramways.
Traction System: Overhead Electric.
Gauge: 4ft 8.5in.
Description: A brick built 4TS dead ended tram shed.
Closed: December 24th, 1927.

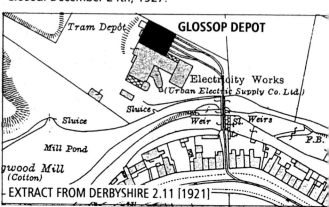

GLOSSOP DEPOT

EXTRACT FROM DERBYSHIRE 2.11 [1921]

CHESTERFIELD

Chatsworth Road

Location: At SK37327100, on the south side of Chatsworth Road, west of Chesterfield town centre.

Opened: November 8th, 1882 by the Chesterfield & District Tramways Co. The company went into liquidation in 1896 and was succeeded by the Chesterfield Tramways Co. Taken over by Chesterfield Corporation on November 22nd, 1897.

Traction System: Horse (until late 1904) and then Overhead Electric from December 20th, 1904.

Gauge: 4ft 8.5in.

Description: Originally a small dead ended depot with one access track, it was rebuilt in brick as a 4TS dead ended tram shed. A 1TS extension was added on the west side in 1914.

Closed: May 23rd, 1927.

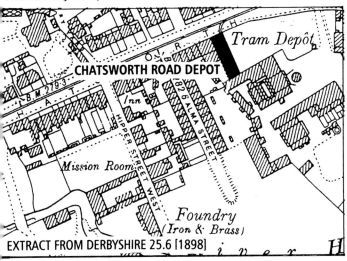

EXTRACT FROM DERBYSHIRE 25.6 [1898]

MATLOCK

Wellington Street

Location: At SK30216085 on the corner of Wellington Street and Rutland Street.

Opened: March 28th, 1893 by the Matlock Cable Tramway Co. Ltd and donated to Matlock UDC on June 28th, 1898.

Traction System: Cable.

Gauge: 3ft 6in.

Description: A stone built 3TS dead ended tram shed and winding house accessed by a single track and traverser.

Closed: September 30th, 1927. It was still standing, in commercial use, in 1999.

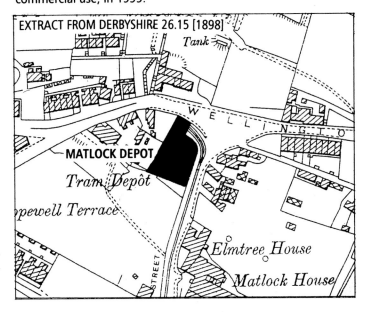

EXTRACT FROM DERBYSHIRE 26.15 [1898]

ILKESTON

Park Road

Location: At SK46754147, on the north side of Park Road.

Opened: May 16th, 1903 by Ilkeston Corporation and taken over in 1916 by the Nottinghamshire & Derbyshire Tramways Co.

Traction System: Overhead Electric.

Gauge: 3ft 6in.

Description: A 5TS dead ended tram shed.

Closed: January 15th, 1931 and subsequently utilized as a trolleybus depot.

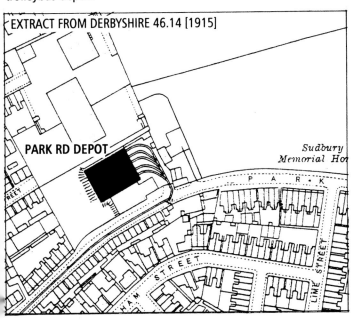

EXTRACT FROM DERBYSHIRE 46.14 [1915]

SWADLINCOTE

Swadlincote Depot

Location: At SK30051997, on the east side of the road opposite Swadlincote Railway Station.

Opened: June 13th, 1906 by the Midland Railway for its Burton & Ashby Light Railways and taken over by the LMS on January 1st, 1923.

Traction System: Overhead Electric.

Gauge: 3ft 6in.

Description: A brick built 8TS dead ended tram shed.

Closed: February 19th, 1927 and still standing, in commercial use, in 1992.

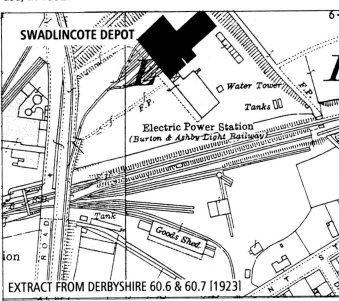

EXTRACT FROM DERBYSHIRE 60.6 & 60.7 [1923]

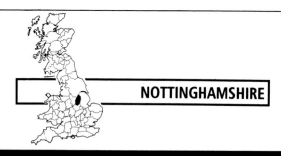

NOTTINGHAMSHIRE

NOTTINGHAM

Sherwood Depot

Location: At SK57394300, on the north west side of Mansfield Road, Sherwood.
Opened: January 1st, 1901 by Nottingham Corporation.
Traction System: Overhead Electric.
Gauge: 4ft 8.5in.
Description: A brick built 8TS dead ended tram shed accessed by two tracks.
Closed: February 2nd, 1936 and subsequently utilized as an omnibus depot.

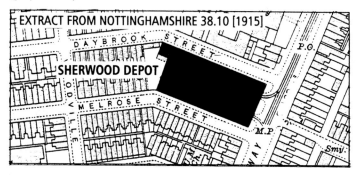

Carter Gate

Location: At SK58013983, on the corner of Carter Gate and Stanhope Street.
Opened: December 2nd, 1928 by Nottingham Corporation.
Traction System: Overhead Electric.
Gauge: 4ft 8.5in.
Description: An 8TS dead ended tram shed. The depot also housed omnibuses and trolley buses.
Closed: To trams from September 5th, 1936 and trolley buses from 1966.

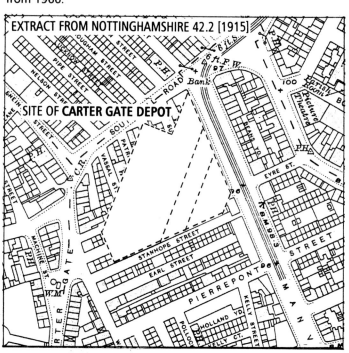

Carrington Depot

Location: At SK57164239, on the west side of Mansfield Road south of Watcombe Road.
Opened: August 11th, 1879 by the Nottingham & District Tramways Co. Ltd and taken over by Nottingham Corporation on October 16th, 1897.
Traction System: Horse.
Gauge: 4ft 8.5in.
Description: A tram shed and stables accessed by one track.
Closed: 1900. The site was subsequently utilized for an open air swimming pool.

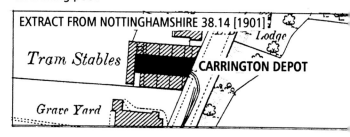

Basford Depot

Location: At SK55644258, on the south side of Isandula Road Basford.
Opened: June 5th, 1881 by the Nottingham & District Tramways Co. Ltd and taken over by Nottingham Corporation on October 16th, 1897.
Traction System: Horse. A steam tram loco was also housed between 1885 & 1889.
Gauge: 4ft 8.5in.
Description: A tram shed and stables accessed by one track.
Closed: July 22nd, 1901 and later utilized for commercial premises.

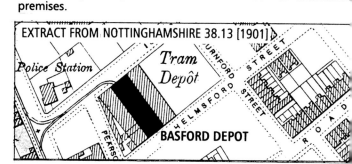

Bulwell Depot

Location: At SK54554456, on the north side of Piccadilly, east of Highbury Road.
Opened: July 23rd, 1901 by Nottingham Corporation.
Traction System: Overhead Electric.
Gauge: 4ft 8.5in.
Description: A brick built 6TS dead ended tram shed.
Closed: May 12th, 1934 and subsequently utilized for trolley buses until 1965, and omnibuses from 1937.

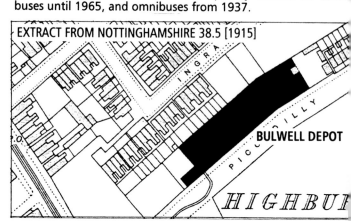

Muskham Street

Location: At SK57783849, on the north side of Muskham Street, west of Arkwright Street.
Opened: September 17th, 1878 by the Nottingham & District Tramways Co. Ltd and taken over by Nottingham Corporation Tramways on October 16th, 1897.
Traction System: Horse.
Gauge: 4ft 8.5in.
Description: A tram shed and stables accessed by one track.
Closed: April 30th, 1902 and subsequently let out as a horse bus depot.

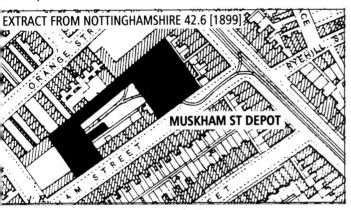

EXTRACT FROM NOTTINGHAMSHIRE 42.6 [1899]
MUSKHAM ST DEPOT

Trent Bridge [1st] Depot

Location: At SK57793817, on the south side of Turney Street, west of Bunbury Street.
Opened: October 21st, 1901 by Nottingham Corporation.
Traction System: Overhead Electric.
Gauge: 4ft 8.5in.
Description: A brick built 11TS dead ended tram shed with a traverser at the rear of the building.
Closed: 1920 and subsequently utilized as a works.

Trent Bridge [2nd] Depot

Location: At SK57783822, on the north side of Turney Street, west of Bunbury Street.
Opened: 1920 by Nottingham Corporation.
Traction System: Overhead Electric.
Gauge: 4ft 8.5in.
Description: A 5TS dead ended tram shed. It also housed omnibuses and, between 1927 & 1928, trolley buses.
Closed: To trams in 1928. Still in use as an omnibus depot in 1999.

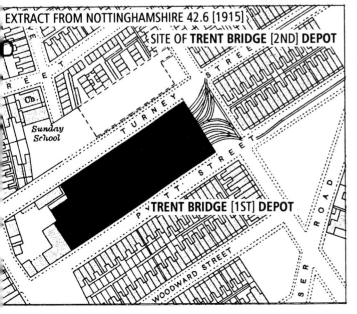

EXTRACT FROM NOTTINGHAMSHIRE 42.6 [1915]
SITE OF **TRENT BRIDGE [2ND] DEPOT**
Sunday School
TRENT BRIDGE [1ST] DEPOT

MANSFIELD

Sutton Road

Location: At SK53056080, on the north side of Sutton Road, west of Spencer Street.
Opened: July 12th, 1905 by the Mansfield & District Light Railway Co.
Traction System: Overhead Electric.
Gauge: 4ft 8.5in.
Description: A brick built 6TS dead ended tram shed adjoined by a 1TS paint shop on the north side.
Closed: October 9th, 1932.

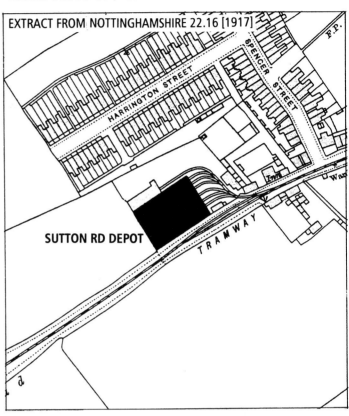

EXTRACT FROM NOTTINGHAMSHIRE 22.16 [1917]
SUTTON RD DEPOT
TRAMWAY

LANGLEY MILL

Langley Mill Depot

Location: At SK44394693, on the south side of Mansfield Road, at Langley Mill.
Opened: July 4th, 1913 by the Nottinghamshire & Derbyshire Tramways Co.
Traction System: Overhead Electric.
Gauge: 4ft 8.5in.
Description: A 6TS dead ended tram shed.
Closed: October 5th, 1932 and subsequently used as a trolley bus depot.

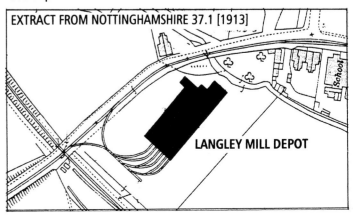

EXTRACT FROM NOTTINGHAMSHIRE 37.1 [1913]
LANGLEY MILL DEPOT

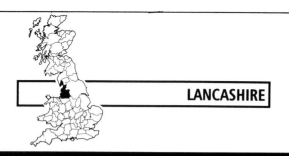

LANCASHIRE

ACCRINGTON

Ellison Street

Location: At SD75012865 at the north end of Ellison Street.
Opened: April 5th, 1886 by the Accrington Steam Tramways Co and taken over by Accrington Corporation on September 20th, 1907.
Traction System: Steam, until 1907, and then Overhead Electric from August 2nd, 1907.
Gauge: 4ft.
Description: Originally a 5TS dead ended tram shed with one access road, a 6TS dead ended brick built extension was added to the east side in 1907 to accommodate electric working. Work shops were constructed and the yard at the front of the shed covered over between 1908 and 1921.
Closed: With the system on January 6th, 1932.

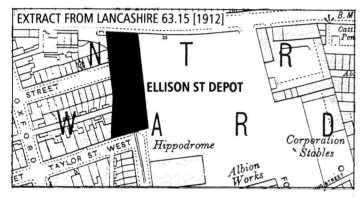

EXTRACT FROM LANCASHIRE 63.15 [1912]

ELLISON ST DEPOT

FARNWORTH

Albert Road

Location: At SD73670552, on the east side of Albert Road.
Opened: January 9th, 1902 by Farnworth UDC and operated by Lancashire United Tramways Ltd from April 1st, 1906.
Traction System: Overhead Electric.
Gauge: 4ft 8.5in.
Description: A 5TS dead ended tram shed accessed by a traverser.
Closed: September 27th, 1906 and subsequently utilized as a trolley bus depot until final closure on November 12th, 1944.

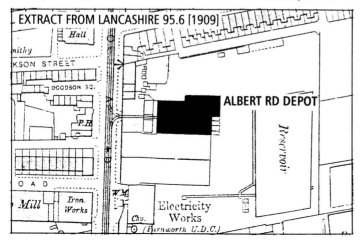

EXTRACT FROM LANCASHIRE 95.6 [1909]

ALBERT RD DEPOT

ASHTON UNDER LYNE

Ashton [No.1] Depot

Location: At SJ94159948, on the corner of Westbury St. an Cowhill Rd.
Opened: June 4th, 1881 by the Manchester Carriage Tramways Co.
Traction System: Horse.
Gauge: 4ft 8.5in.
Description: A 6TS dead ended tram shed, with a traverser a the front, and stables.
Closed: March 31st, 1903 upon the expiry of the lease. It ma have been further utilized by Manchester Corporation for temporary horse tram service which operated from April 17t 1903 until October 14th, 1903 pending the completion c electrification along the route.

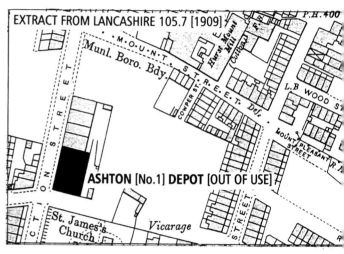

EXTRACT FROM LANCASHIRE 105.7 [1909]

ASHTON [No.1] DEPOT [OUT OF USE]

Ashton [No.2] Depot

Location: At SJ94679939, on the south side of Mossley Rd east of Whiteacre Rd.
Opened: August 16th, 1902 by Ashton under Lyne Corporation
Traction System: Overhead Electric.
Gauge: 4ft 8.5in.
Description: Originally a brick built 6TS dead ended tram shec with a 2TS workshop, an 8TS dead ended extension was addec on the west side in 1921. Trolley buses were also housed from August 26th, 1925 and, at about this time, three roads were removed from the original tram shed building.
Closed: To trams, on the closure of the system, on March 1st 1938. Continued in use as a trolley bus depot until 1966 and still stood in 1996.

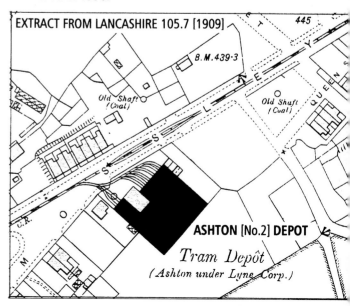

EXTRACT FROM LANCASHIRE 105.7 [1909]

ASHTON [No.2] DEPOT

Tram Depôt
(Ashton under Lyne Corp.)

BLACKBURN

Intack Depot

Location: At SD70772812, on the north side of Accrington Rd, Intack.

Opened: May 28th, 1887 by the Blackburn Corporation Tramways Co. Ltd and taken over by Blackburn Corporation on August 24th, 1898.

Traction System: Steam, until August 9th, 1901, and Overhead Electric from 1900.

Gauge: 4ft.

Description: Originally a brick built 6TS dead ended tram shed, a brick built 9TS dead ended extension was added on the eastern side to accommodate electric working and the original depot converted to a works. Omnibuses were also housed from November 1st, 1929 and an omnibus garage was added on the west side in c1936.

Closed: With the system on September 3rd, 1949 and subsequently utilized as an omnibus depot.

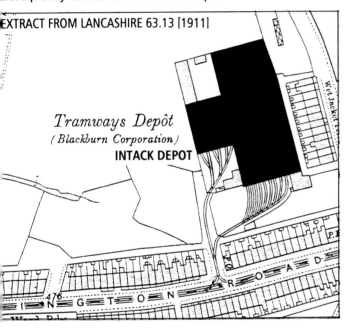

EXTRACT FROM LANCASHIRE 63.13 [1911]

Tramways Depôt
(Blackburn Corporation)
INTACK DEPOT

Simmons Street

Location: At SD67942838, on the north side of Simmons St.

Opened: August 28th, 1888 by the Blackburn Corporation Tramways Co. Ltd and taken over by Blackburn Corporation on August 24th, 1898.

Traction System: Horse, until 1899, and then Overhead Electric from March 24th, 1899.

Gauge: 4ft.

Description: A 4TS dead ended tram shed and stables.

Closed: At some time prior to 1902.

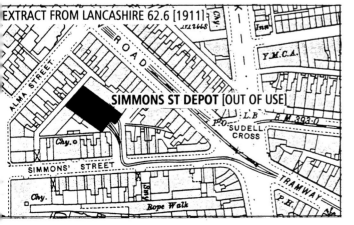

EXTRACT FROM LANCASHIRE 62.6 [1911]

SIMMONS ST DEPOT [OUT OF USE]

DARWEN

Lorne Street

Location: At SD68652303, on the north side of Lorne St., Over Darwen.

Opened: April 16th, 1881 by the Blackburn & Over Darwen Tramways Co. Ltd and jointly taken over by Blackburn and Darwen Corporations.

Traction System: Steam, until October 16th, 1900, and then Overhead Electric.

Gauge: 4ft.

Description: Originally a brick built 6TS dead ended tram shed, it was rebuilt in 1900 as a 5TS dead ended tram shed for electric working and a 3TS extension was added on the west side at some time after 1910.

Closed: October 5th, 1946 upon the closure of the Darwen section.

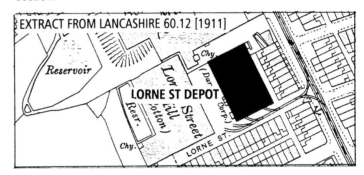

EXTRACT FROM LANCASHIRE 60.12 [1911]

Reservoir

LORNE ST DEPOT

BURNLEY

Queens Gate Depot

Location: At SD84573470, on the north side of Disraeli St., west of Colne Rd.

Opened: September 17th, 1881 by the Burnley & District Tramways Co. and taken over by Burnley Corporation on March 1st, 1900.

Traction System: Steam, until February 28th, 1882. Horse from March 1st, 1882 until March 1883 and then Steam again until November 17th, 1901. Overhead Electric from December 16th, 1901.

Gauge: 4ft 8.5in (Steam & Horse). 4ft (Electric).

Description: Originally a 5TS dead ended tram shed, with the two northernmost roads utilized for steam locos, it was rebuilt in 1901/2 as a 5TS through road tram shed with an 8TS works on the western end and an 8TS, later extended to 18TS, dead ended tram shed on the north side of the works.

Closed: With the tramway on May 7th, 1935.

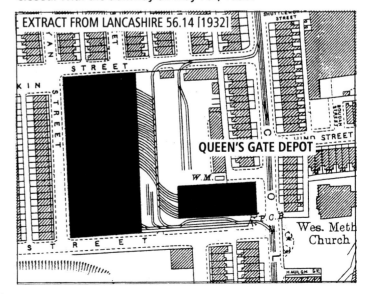

EXTRACT FROM LANCASHIRE 56.14 [1932]

QUEEN'S GATE DEPOT

Bradshawgate Depot & Works

Location: At SD71900893, on the north side of Shiffnall St and west side of Carlton St.

Opened: September 1st, 1880 by Bolton Corporation and other local boards with the operation leased to E Holden & Co. until taken over by Bolton Corporation in June 1899.

Traction System: Horse, until January 2nd, 1900 and then Overhead Electric.

Gauge: 4ft 8.5in.

Description: Originally a horse depot and stables, for electrification it was reconstructed as two brick built 8TS dead ended tram sheds back to back and on different levels with one entrance in Shiffnall St and another in Breightmet St. A 5TS dead ended works adjoined Shiffnall St and a new works, adjacent and on the east side of Carlton St opened on February 5th, 1913.

Closed: With the tramway on March 29th, 1947

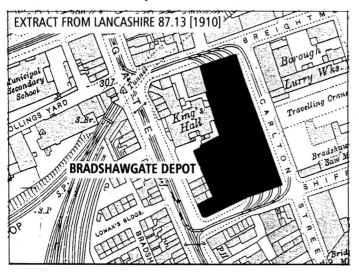

EXTRACT FROM LANCASHIRE 87.13 [1910]

BRADSHAWGATE DEPOT

Tonge Moor

Location: At SD73061161, on the east side of Tonge Moor Rd, south of Scope Hole Lane.

Opened: December 9th, 1899 by Bolton Corporation.

Traction System: Overhead Electric.

Gauge: 4ft 8.5in.

Description: A 4TS dead ended tram shed.

Closed: 1911 and sold for use as a cinema. It was burnt down in 1930 and the site subsequently cleared.

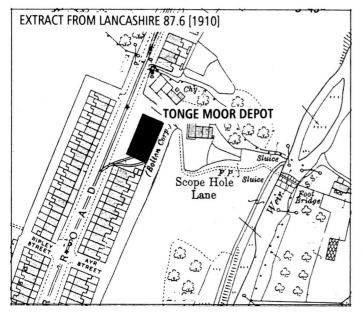

EXTRACT FROM LANCASHIRE 87.6 [1910]

TONGE MOOR DEPOT

Bridgeman Street

Location: At SD71590826, on the corner of Bridgeman St and Nile Street.

Opened: 1909 by Bolton Corporation.

Traction System: Overhead Electric.

Gauge: 4ft 8.5in.

Description: Originally a 7TS dead ended tram shed, it was later extended over the entrance fan and two yard roads added.

Closed: August 17th, 1936.

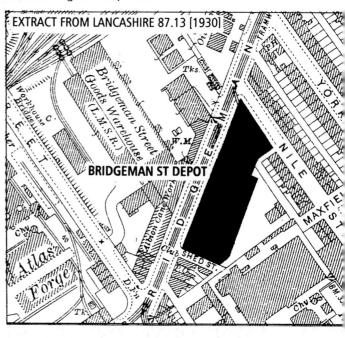

EXTRACT FROM LANCASHIRE 87.13 [1930]

BRIDGEMAN ST DEPOT

Daubhill Depot

Location: At SD69340683, on the corner of St Helens Rd and Hulton Lane, Daubhill.

Opened: January 2nd, 1900 by Bolton Corporation.

Traction System: Overhead Electric.

Gauge: 4ft 8.5in.

Description: A 4TS dead ended tram shed.

Closed: March 28th, 1936 and sold for use as a garage.

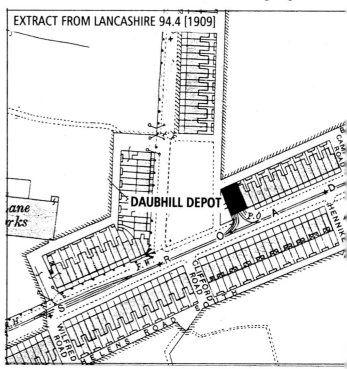

EXTRACT FROM LANCASHIRE 94.4 [1909]

DAUBHILL DEPOT

Rochdale Road

Location: At SD80931076, on the south side of Rochdale Rd, between George St. and Foundry St.
Opened: June 3rd. 1903 by Bury Corporation.
Traction System: Overhead Electric.
Gauge: 4ft 8.5in.
Description: A 15TS tram shed with 12 through roads.
Closed: With the tramway on February 13th, 1949.

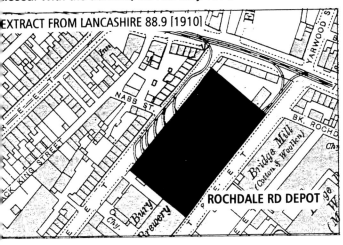

EXTRACT FROM LANCASHIRE 88.9 [1910]

ROCHDALE RD DEPOT

Bury Depot

Location: At SD80361092, on the north side of Castle St.
Opened: 1883 by the Manchester, Bury, Rochdale & Oldham Steam Tramways Co., taken over by the Bury, Rochdale & Oldham Tramway Co. Ltd in October 1888 and taken over by Bury Corporation on August 1st, 1903.
Traction System: Steam, until May 16th, 1904 and Horse from March 20th, 1883 to 1886.
Gauge: 4ft 8.5in until May 16th, 1904 and 3ft 6in from March 1884 until April 8th, 1904.
Description: A complex consisting of, from west to east; a 2TS standard gauge tram shed, a 4TS standard gauge engine shed, a 4TS narrow gauge engine shed, a 3TS narrow gauge tram shed, all dead ended, and four workshop roads and stables.
Closed: May 16th, 1904. (A special was later run on July 10th, 1904) and sold in 1905. It was subsequently demolished to make way for the construction of an army drill hall.

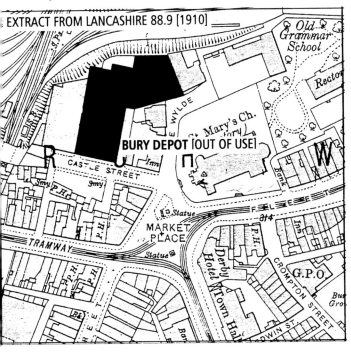

EXTRACT FROM LANCASHIRE 88.9 [1910]

BURY DEPOT [OUT OF USE]

Heifer Lane

Location: At SD90234033, on the south side of Keighley Rd and east side of Cotton Tree Lane.
Opened: November 28th, 1903 by the Colne & Trawden Light Railway Co. Taken over by Colne Corporation on March 25th, 1914 and operated by the Burnley, Colne & Nelson Joint Transport Committee from April 1st, 1933.
Traction System: Overhead Electric.
Gauge: 4ft.
Description: A stone built 4TS dead ended tram shed. From 1919 it was also utilized by omnibuses.
Closed: To trams, along with the system, on January 6th, 1934 and subsequently utilized as an omnibus garage.

Standroyd Depot

Location: At SD90314031, on the south side of Keighley Rd and east side of Standroyd Rd.
Opened: November 1919 by Colne Corporation and operated by the Burnley, Colne & Nelson Joint Transport Committee from April 1st, 1933.
Traction System: Overhead Electric.
Gauge: 4ft.
Description: A brick built 6TS dead ended tram shed.
Closed: To trams, along with the system, on January 6th, 1934 and subsequently utilized as an omnibus garage.

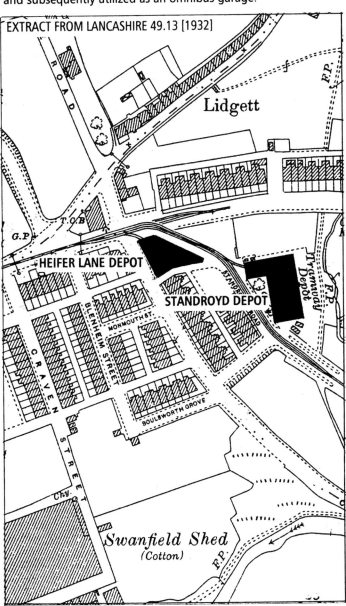

EXTRACT FROM LANCASHIRE 49.13 [1932]

HEIFER LANE DEPOT

STANDROYD DEPOT

Copse Road

Location: At SD33164715, on the east side of Copse Road.
Opened: July 14th, 1898 by the Blackpool & Fleetwood Tramroad Company and taken over by Blackpool Corporation on January 1st, 1920.
Traction System: Overhead Electric.
Gauge: 4ft 8.5in.
Description: Originally a 6TS dead ended tram shed it was later rebuilt in brick as a 4TS dead ended tram shed.
Closed: October 27th, 1963 and sold for commercial use. Still Standing in 1988.

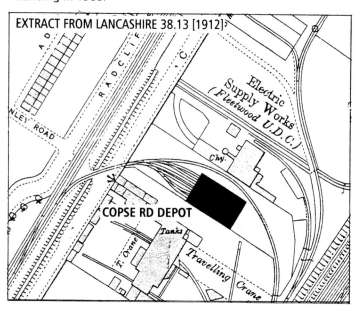

EXTRACT FROM LANCASHIRE 38.13 [1912]

COPSE RD DEPOT

Bold Street

Location: At SD33824840, on the north side of Bold Street.
Opened: 1899 by the Blackpool & Fleetwood Tramroad Company and taken over by Blackpool Corporation on January 1st, 1920.
Traction System: Overhead Electric.
Gauge: 4ft 8.5in.
Description: A brick built 2TS dead ended tram shed.
Closed: 1920 and demolished by 1973.

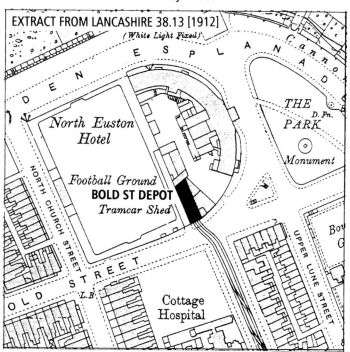

EXTRACT FROM LANCASHIRE 38.13 [1912]

BOLD ST DEPOT

Bispham Depot

Location: At SD31073973, on the south side of Red Bank R Bispham.
Opened: July 14th, 1898 by the Blackpool & Fleetwo Tramroad Co. and taken over on January 1st, 1920 by Blackpo Corporation.
Traction System: Overhead Electric.
Gauge: 4ft 8.5in.
Description: Originally a brick built 6TS dead ended tram sh and works, it was extended rearwards in 1902 and in 1914.
Closed: October 27th, 1963 and subsequently utilized as store until January 1966. Demolished in 1983.

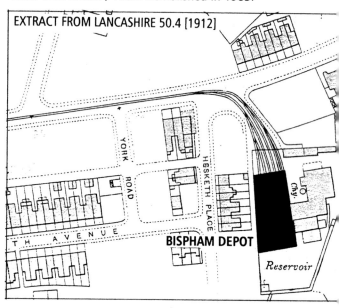

EXTRACT FROM LANCASHIRE 50.4 [1912]

BISPHAM DEPOT

Denton Depot

Location: At SJ92359626, on the corner of Ashton Rd an Denton Rd.
Opened: June 12th, 1899 by the Oldham, Ashton & Hy Electric Tramways Co. Ltd and taken over on July 2nd, 1921 Denton UDC for operation by Manchester Corporation.
Traction System: Overhead Electric.
Gauge: 4ft 8.5in.
Description: A brick built 13TS dead ended tram shed wi access via a traverser.
Closed: Upon the takeover in 1921.

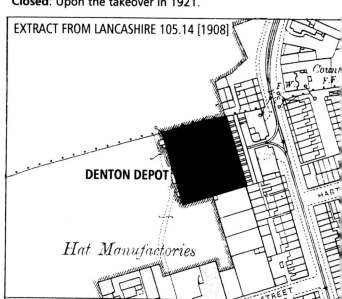

EXTRACT FROM LANCASHIRE 105.14 [1908]

DENTON DEPOT

Hat Manufactories

LANCASTER

Dalton Square

Location: At SD47906153, on the south side of Nelson St. and corner of Dalton Square.
Opened: January 14th, 1903 by Lancaster Corporation.
Traction System: Overhead Electric.
Gauge: 4ft 8.5in.
Description: A 3TS dead ended tram shed constructed in corrugated iron.
Closed: Dismantled in 1905 and removed to Thurnham St. to make way for a new Town Hall.

Thurnham Street

Location: At SD47786137, on the west side of Thurnham St., south of Marton St.
Opened: 1905 by Lancaster Corporation.
Traction System: Overhead Electric.
Gauge: 4ft 8.5in.
Description: A 3TS dead ended tram shed constructed in brick and corrugated iron.
Closed: With the tramway on April 4th, 1930. Still standing, in use as a garage and with an altered frontage, in 2000.

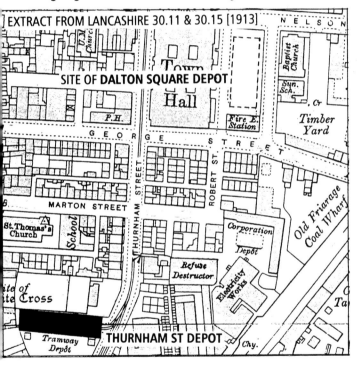

Chapel Street

Location: At SD47746190, on the west side of Chapel St.
Opened: 1890 by Lancaster & District Tramways Co. Ltd.
Traction System: Horse.
Gauge: 4ft 8.5in.
Description: The stables here were utilized from time to time to house a tramcar.
Closed: 1921.

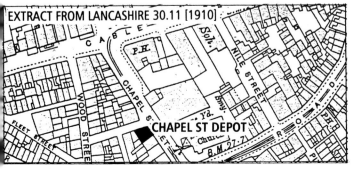

HEYWOOD

York Street

Location: At SD85701075, on the south side of York Street.
Opened: December 10th, 1904 by Heywood Corporation.
Traction System: Steam.
Gauge: 3ft 6in.
Description: A temporary 4 or 5TS corrugated iron dead ended shed.
Closed: September 20th, 1905 and subsequently utilized for scrapping locos and trailers. Since dismantled.

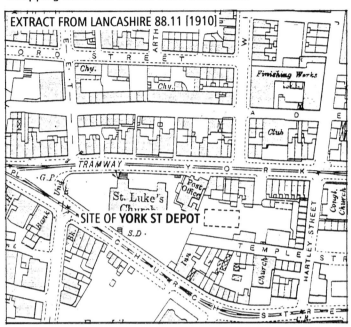

NELSON

Nelson Depot

Location: At SD86003853, on the north side of Charles St.
Opened: February 23rd, 1903 by Nelson Corporation and, from April 1st, 1933, operated by the Burnley, Colne & Nelson Joint Transport Committee.
Traction System: Overhead Electric.
Gauge: 4ft.
Description: Originally a 4TS dead ended tram shed, a small extension was later added at the rear. The depot was demolished in c1914 and a new 6TS dead ended tram shed constructed immediately to the west.
Closed: With the tramway on January 6th, 1934 and retained as a corporation depot. It was still in use in 1994.

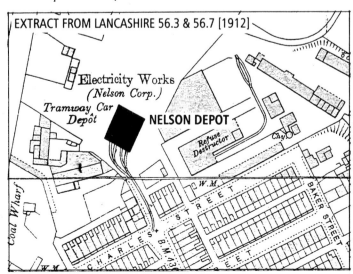

Henry Street

Location: At SD36472713, on the north side of Henry Street.
Opened: February 21st, 1897 by the Blackpool, St.Anne's & Lytham Tramway Company and taken over in October 1898 by the Blackpool, St.Anne's & Lytham Tramway Co. Ltd.
Traction System: Gas.
Gauge: 4ft 8.5in.
Description: A 2TS dead ended tram shed converted from a roller skating rink.
Closed: February 26th, 1903 and utilized as a cinema and, later, commercial premises prior to demolition in 1986.

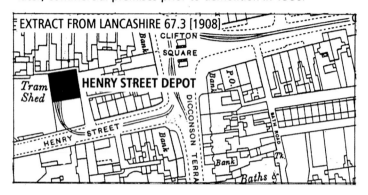

EXTRACT FROM LANCASHIRE 67.3 [1908]
HENRY STREET DEPOT

Squires Gate Lane

Location: At SD31053176, on the south side of Squires Gate Lane (Formerly Fold Lane), west of Westgate Road, Stoney Hill.
Opened: July 11th, 1896 by the Blackpool, St.Anne's & Lytham Tramway Co., taken over in October 1898 by the Blackpool, St.Anne's & Lytham Tramway Co. Ltd and taken over again by St.Anne's UDC (Lytham St.Anne's Corporation from 1922) on October 28th, 1920.
Traction System: Gas, until 1900, Horse from 1900 to 1902 and then Overhead Electric.
Gauge: 4ft 8.5in.
Description: Originally a small tram car shed and stables, it was rebuilt as an 8TS dead ended tram shed for overhead electric working. In 1910 all the roads were extended into a works at the rear of the building and a 4TS dead ended extension was added on the east side in March 1924. The depot was also used to accommodate omnibuses from August 6th, 1923.
Closed: 1902 and re-opened for electric traction in June 1903. Finally to trams, along with the system, on April 28th, 1937. Still in use as an omnibus depot.

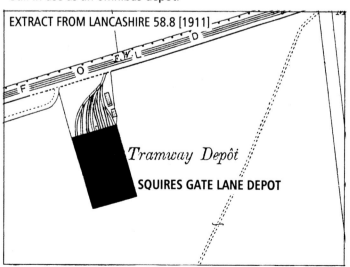

EXTRACT FROM LANCASHIRE 58.8 [1911]
Tramway Depôt
SQUIRES GATE LANE DEPOT

NB. Electric working began on May 30th, 1903 and tram cars were temporarily stored in Fold Lane and on the site of Lytham Road Depot.

Heysham Road

DEPOT No.1

Location: At SD42156350, on the east side of Heysham R south of Bold St., Heysham.
Opened: June 3rd, 1887 by the Morecambe Tramways Co.
Traction System: Horse.
Gauge: 4ft 8.5in.
Description: A 2TS tram shed, with one through road, an stables.
Closed: Dismantled in 1897 and re-erected as No.2 Depot.

DEPOT No.2

Location: At SD42046330, on the east side of Heysham Rd o the former Sandylands Gardens.
Opened: 1897 by the Morecambe Tramways Co. and take over, along with the northern section of the system, on Ju 26th, 1909 by Morecambe Corporation.
Traction System: Horse.
Gauge: 4ft 8.5in.
Description: Re-erected as a 3TS dead ended tram shed.
Closed: October 26th, 1926.

DEPOT No.3

Location: At SD41996327, on the east side of Heysham Rd o the former Sandylands Gardens.
Opened: 1909 by the Morecambe Tramways Co. following th takeover of part of the northern section of the system on Ju 26th, 1909 by Morecambe Corporation.
Traction System: Horse, until January 15th, 1912, and then Petrol. (The petrol trams were converted to gas working for th WWI years).
Gauge: 4ft 8.5in.
Description: A timber 3TS dead ended tram shed converte from a former omnibus shed.
Closed: October 24th, 1924.

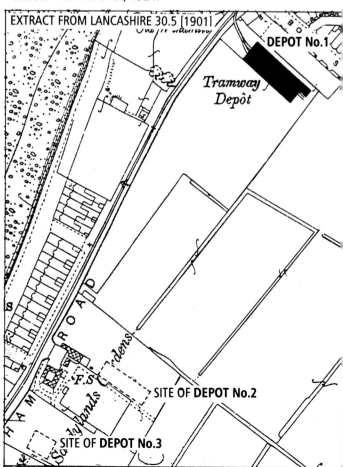

EXTRACT FROM LANCASHIRE 30.5 [1901]
DEPOT No.1
Tramway Depôt
SITE OF DEPOT No.2
SITE OF DEPOT No.3

Morecambe Depot

Location: At SD44336408, on the north side of Lancaster Rd.
Opened: August 2nd, 1890 by Lancaster & District Tramways Co. Ltd.
Traction System: Horse.
Gauge: 4ft 8.5in.
Description: Originally a 2TS dead ended tram shed and stables, by 1911 an extension had been added on the north side.
Closed: December 31st, 1921 and subsequently utilized as an omnibus depot.

EXTRACT FROM LANCASHIRE 30.6 [1889]

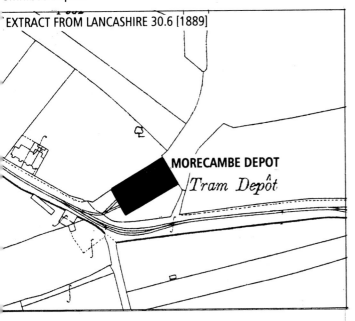

MORECAMBE DEPOT
Tram Depôt

Blackburn Road

Location: At SD78542335, on the east side of Blackburn Road, north of Deardengate.
Opened: August 27th, 1887 by the Accrington Steam Tramways Co., taken over by Haslingden Corporation on January 1st, 1908 and operated by Accrington Corporation from September 28th, 1908.
Traction System: Steam, until September 5th, 1908, and then Overhead Electric from September 28th, 1908.
Gauge: 4ft.
Description: A 4TS dead ended tram shed.
Closed: July 20th, 1916 and subsequently utilized as a garage. (It was also used for the emergency accommodation of tram cars until the route closed on April 30th, 1930.) It was later used as a road haulage depot and was destroyed by a fire in 1977.

EXTRACT FROM LANCASHIRE 71.12 [1911]

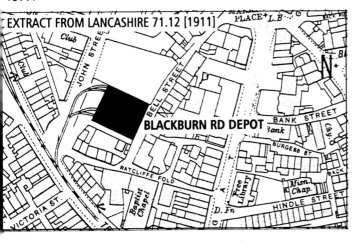

BLACKBURN RD DEPOT

Leigh Road

Location: At SD66260205, on the west side of Leigh Rd, Howe Bridge.
Opened: October 20th, 1902 by the South Lancashire Electric Traction & Power Co. Ltd and taken over by the Lancashire United Tramways Ltd on January 2nd, 1906. (Name changed to South Lancashire Transport in 1929.)
Traction System: Overhead Electric.
Gauge: 4ft 8.5in.
Description: Originally a brick built 8TS dead ended tram shed, it was extended by 1936 to an 8TS through road building with a 2TS extension on the west side. It was also utilized by trolley buses from August 19th, 1931.
Closed: To trams on December 16th, 1933 and to trolley buses from August 31st, 1958. It was subsequently used as omnibus workshops.

EXTRACT FROM LANCASHIRE 94.5 [1908]

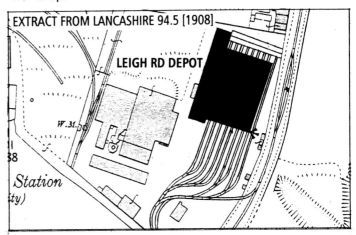

LEIGH RD DEPOT

Hilton Fold Lane

Location: At SD88010613, on the east side of Hilton Fold Lane and north side of Norman Street.
Opened: March 27th, 1902 by the Middleton Electric Tramway Co. Ltd and taken over by Manchester Corporation on June 16th, 1925.
Traction System: Overhead Electric.
Gauge: 4ft 8.5in.
Description: A brick built 8TS dead ended tram shed. It was also used for charabancs from May 1920 and omnibuses from March 25th, 1921.
Closed: June 16th, 1925 and sold to Middleton Corporation for use as a swimming baths.

EXTRACT FROM LANCASHIRE 96.8 [1909]

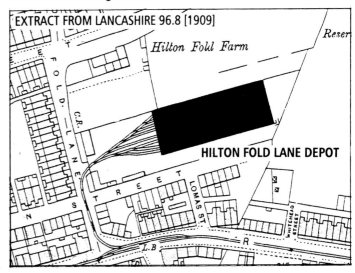

Hilton Fold Farm
HILTON FOLD LANE DEPOT

Bradford Depot

Location: At SJ87129830, on the south side of Ashton New Rd, east side of Butterworth St., Bradford

Opened: June 4th, 1881 by the Manchester Carriage & Tramways Co.

Traction System: Horse.

Gauge: 4ft 8.5in.

Description: A 4TS dead ended tram shed, accessed via a traverser, and stables.

Closed: 1903.

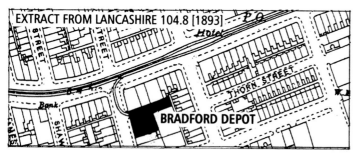

EXTRACT FROM LANCASHIRE 104.8 [1893]

BRADFORD DEPOT

Hyde Road Depot & Works

Location: At SJ85859703, on the north side of Hyde Rd and east side of Devonshire St., Ardwick.

Opened: December 1st, 1902 by Manchester Corporation.

Traction System: Overhead Electric.

Gauge: 4ft 8.5in.

Description: Originally a brick built 57TS tram shed with two through tracks accessing the works which officially opened on October 4th, 1905. The depot was rebuilt in the 1920s and trolley buses were accommodated from March 1st, 1938, and omnibuses from c1940.

Closed: As a running shed for trams on May 17th, 1948 and then utilized for the scrapping of tram cars. The depot continued in use as an omnibus garage until demolition in the 1960s to make way for redevelopment.

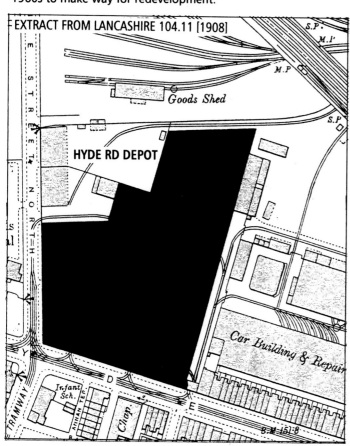

EXTRACT FROM LANCASHIRE 104.11 [1908]

Goods Shed

HYDE RD DEPOT

Car Building & Repair

Grey Street

Location: At SD86149660, on the corner of Grey St. and South St., Longsight.

Opened: May 7th, 1880 by the Manchester Carriage Co. Ltd (Became the Manchester Carriage & Tramways Co. on August 2nd, 1880).

Traction System: Horse.

Gauge: 4ft 8.5in.

Description: A 4TS dead ended shed, accessed via a traverser and stables.

Closed: 1901.

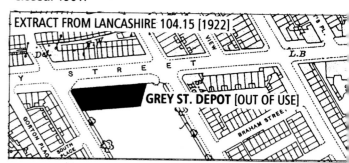

EXTRACT FROM LANCASHIRE 104.15 [1922]

GREY ST. DEPOT [OUT OF USE]

All Saints Depot

Location: At SJ84239716, on the north side of Devonshire St., All Saints.

Opened: November 1st, 1880 by the Manchester Carriage & Tramways Co.

Traction System: Horse.

Gauge: 4ft 8.5in.

Description: A 6TS dead ended tram shed, accessed via a traverser, and stables.

Closed: 1902.

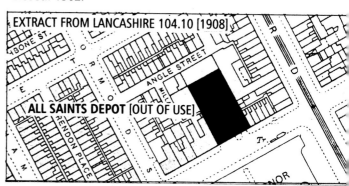

EXTRACT FROM LANCASHIRE 104.10 [1908]

ALL SAINTS DEPOT [OUT OF USE]

Queen's Park Depot

Location: At SD85750086, on the north side of Turkey Lane, east side of Cardiff St., Harpurhey.

Opened: July 23rd, 1881 by the Manchester Carriage & Tramways Co.

Traction System: Horse.

Gauge: 4ft 8.5in.

Description: A 2TS dead ended tram shed and stables.

Closed: 1901.

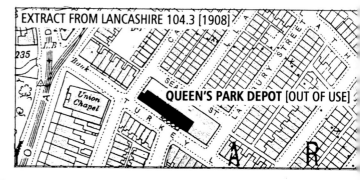

EXTRACT FROM LANCASHIRE 104.3 [1908]

Union Chapel

QUEEN'S PARK DEPOT [OUT OF USE]

Queen's Road

Location: At SD84610056, on the north side of Queen's Rd and east side of Boyle Street, High Town.
Opened: Officially on June 6th, 1901 by Manchester Corporation and for public service on June 7th, 1901.
Traction System: Overhead Electric.
Gauge: 4ft 8.5in.
Description: A brick built 52TS dead ended tram shed.
Closed: February 1938 and subsequently utilized as an omnibus garage.

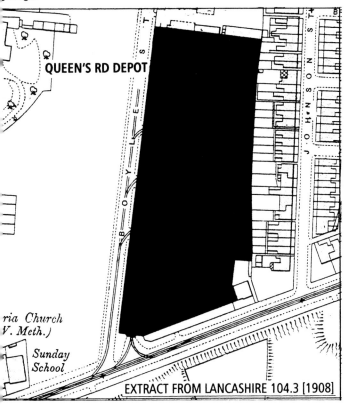

NB. Prior to the opening of Queen's Road Depot, trams were housed in a temporary shed in Grey Street to facilitate crew training.

Chorlton Road

Location: At SJ82909625, on the west side of Chorlton Rd.
Opened: 1897 by the Manchester Carriage & Tramways Co.
Traction System: Horse.
Gauge: 4ft 8.5in.
Description: A 6TS dead ended tram shed, possibly with a traverser. The depot also accommodated omnibuses.
Closed: 1902.

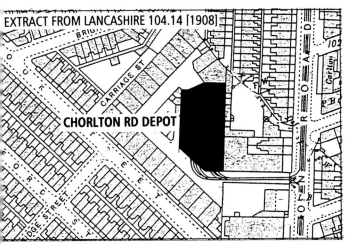

Stretford Depot

Location: At SJ79289382, on the west side of Chester Rd, at the Cock Inn, Stretford.
Opened: November 1st, 1880 by the Manchester Carriage & Tramways Co.
Traction System: Horse.
Gauge: 4ft 8.5in.
Description: A 3TS dead ended tram shed, accessed via a traverser, and stables.
Closed: 1903.

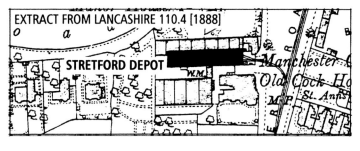

Harpurhey Depot

Location: At SD86030203, on the corner of Rochdale Road and Shepherd Street, Barnes Green.
Opened: July 23rd, 1881 by the Manchester Carriage & Tramways Co.
Traction System: Horse.
Gauge: 4ft 8.5in.
Description: A 4TS dead ended tram shed, accessed via a traverser, and stables.
Closed: 1901.

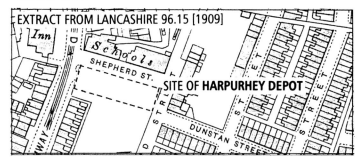

Newton Heath Depot

Location: At SD87880056, off the south side of Oldham Rd, Newton Heath.
Opened: March 28th, 1881 by the Manchester Carriage & Tramways Co.
Traction System: Horse.
Gauge: 4ft 8.5in.
Description: Two 3TS dead ended tram sheds and stables.
Closed: At the end of horse working on March 31st, 1903.

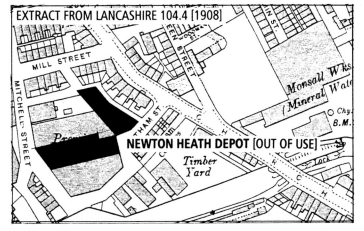

Crumpsall Depot

Location: At SD83940186, on the south side of Thomas St., west of Fountain St., Crumpsall.
Opened: July 27th, 1882 by the Manchester Carriage & Tramways Co.
Traction System: Horse.
Gauge: 4ft 8.5in.
Description: A 9TS dead ended tram shed, accessed via a traverser, and stables. The depot also housed omnibuses.
Closed: 1900.

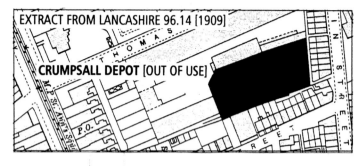

EXTRACT FROM LANCASHIRE 96.14 [1909]

CRUMPSALL DEPOT [OUT OF USE]

Birchfields Road

Location: At SJ86509405, on the corner of Birchfields Rd and Moseley Rd.
Opened: Officially on July 24th, 1928 by Manchester Corporation.
Traction System: Overhead Electric.
Gauge: 4ft 8.5in.
Description: A brick built 43TS dead ended tram shed, It was also utilized by omnibuses from 1947.
Closed: To trams, with the tramway on January 10th, 1949 and subsequently utilized as an omnibus garage.

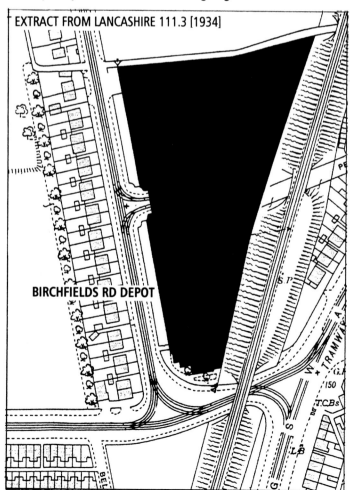

EXTRACT FROM LANCASHIRE 111.3 [1934]

BIRCHFIELDS RD DEPOT

Withington Road

Location: At SJ83029512, on the corner of Withington Rd and Range Rd, Rusholme.
Opened: December 1880 by the Manchester Carriage & Tramways Co.
Traction System: Horse.
Gauge: 4ft 8.5in.
Description: A 7TS dead ended tram shed and stables.
Closed: 1902.

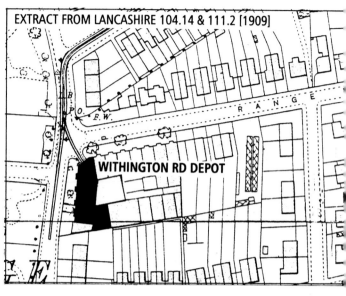

EXTRACT FROM LANCASHIRE 104.14 & 111.2 [1909]

WITHINGTON RD DEPOT

Princess Road

Location: At SJ84009500, on the east side of Princess Rd and south side of Bowes St., Moss Side.
Opened: July 10th, 1909 by Manchester Corporation.
Traction System: Overhead Electric.
Gauge: 4ft 8.5in.
Description: A dead ended tram shed.
Closed: February 12th, 1939 and subsequently utilized as an omnibus garage.

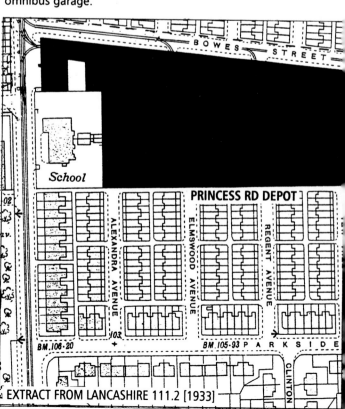

PRINCESS RD DEPOT

School

EXTRACT FROM LANCASHIRE 111.2 [1933]

Rusholme Depot

Location: At SJ85009563, on the west side of Wilmslow Rd, Rusholme.
Opened: November 1st, 1880 by the Manchester Carriage & Tramways Co.
Traction System: Horse.
Gauge: 4ft 8.5in.
Description: An 11TS dead ended tram shed, accessed via a traverser, a 5TS dead ended tram shed, and stables. Omnibuses were also accommodated.
Closed: 1902.

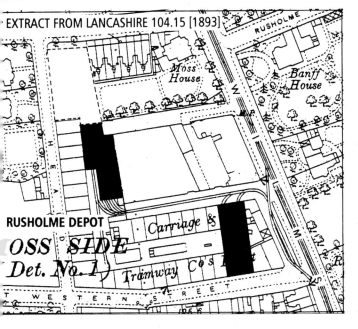

Stockport Road

Location: At SJ86269626, between the east side of Stockport Rd and South St., Longsight.
Opened: May 7th, 1880 by the Manchester Carriage Co. Ltd. (Became the Manchester Carriage & Tramways Co. on August 2nd, 1880).
Traction System: Horse.
Gauge: 4ft 8.5in.
Description: A 6TS dead ended shed, accessed via a traverser, and stables.
Closed: 1901.

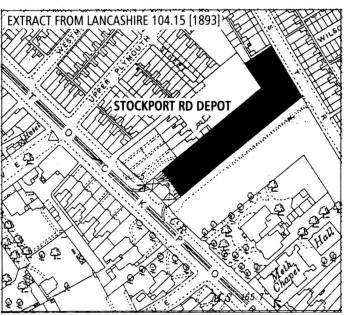

Broughton Depot

Location: At SD82681016, on the north side of Knoll St., west off Bury New Rd, Higher Broughton.
Opened: July 30th, 1877 by the Manchester Carriage Co. Ltd. (Became the Manchester Carriage & Tramways Co. on August 2nd, 1880).
Traction System: Horse.
Gauge: 4ft 8.5in.
Description: A brick built 4TS dead ended tram shed and stables. It was also utilized to accommodate omnibuses.
Closed: 1901.

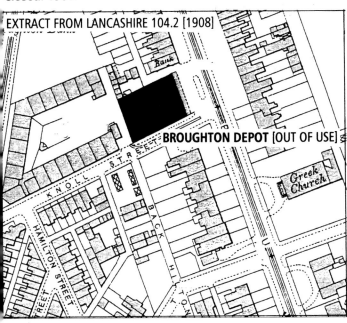

Openshaw Depot

Location: At SJ88739742, on the corner of Ashton Old Rd and Louisa St., Openshaw.
Opened: March 28th, 1881 by the Manchester Carriage & Tramways Co.
Traction System: Horse.
Gauge: 4ft 8.5in.
Description: A 4TS dead ended tram shed, accessed via a traverser, and stables.
Closed: At the end of horse working on March 31st, 1903.

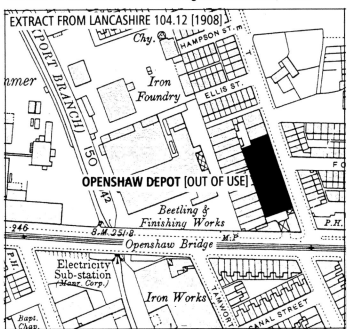

Barton Depot

Location: At SJ76829736, at the entrance to Trafford Park, south of the Ship Canal and Bridgewater Canal junction.
Opened: July 23rd, 1897 by the British Gas Traction Co. Ltd and taken over by Trafford Park Estates Ltd at the end of 1899.
Traction System: Gas.
Gauge: 4ft 8.5in.
Description: A timber built 2TS dead ended tram shed.
Closed: May 1st, 1908 when gas working ceased and the tramway was converted into a railway. The building was sold by auction in June 1908 and dismantled and the site was subsequently occupied by a power station.

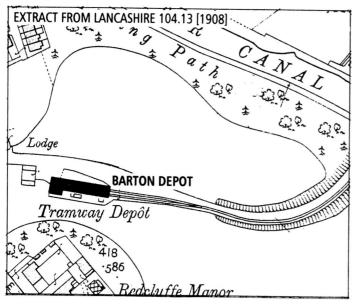

EXTRACT FROM LANCASHIRE 104.13 [1908]

Trafford Park Depot

Location: At SJ79779626, north of the junction of 3rd Ave and Westinghouse Rd, Trafford Park.
Opened: July 14th, 1903 by Trafford Park Estates Ltd. The operation was taken over by Salford Corporation on October 31st, 1905 and worked jointly with Manchester Corporation.
Traction System: Overhead Electric.
Gauge: 4ft 8.5in.
Description: A 3TS tram shed with one through road.
Closed: November 12th, 1905 following the take over by Salford Corporation.

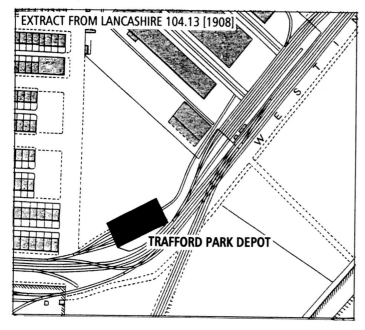

EXTRACT FROM LANCASHIRE 104.13 [1908]

BLACKPOOL

Blundell Street/Rigby Road

Location: At SD30773516, on the east side of Blundell Street.
Opened: September 12th, 1885 by the Blackpool Electric Tramways Co. and taken over on September 10th, 1892 by Blackpool Corporation.
Traction System: Horse, until September 29th, 1885, Conduit Electric until 1899 and then Overhead Electric.
Gauge: 4ft 8.5in.
Description: A brick built 5TS dead ended tram shed. It was rebuilt in 1898 and utilized as a works for trams and omnibuses until 1920 when a works was constructed on the south side of Rigby Road. A 19TS dead ended tram shed and omnibus garage was added on the south side of the works in 1934. As the original Blundell St building fell into disuse, the depot became known as Rigby Road. Still operational in 2000.

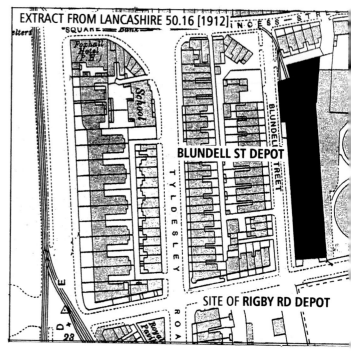

EXTRACT FROM LANCASHIRE 50.16 [1912]

Marton Depot

Location: At SD32373495, on the north east side of Whitegate Drive, north of Preston Old Rd, Marton.
Opened: 1901 by Blackpool Corporation.
Traction System: Overhead Electric.
Gauge: 4ft 8.5in.
Description: Originally a brick built 8TS dead ended tram shed, it was extended to the rear in 1912.
Closed: October 28th, 1962 and utilized for scrapping tram cars. Later sold and site now occupied by a filling station.

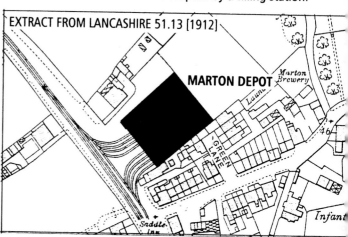

EXTRACT FROM LANCASHIRE 51.13 [1912]

Lytham Road

Location: At SD31253189, on the east side of Lytham Rd, north of Squires Gate Lane.
Opened: 1900 by the Blackpool, St Anne's & Lytham Tramways Co. Ltd.
Traction System: Gas.
Gauge: 4ft 8.5in.
Description: A small brick built dead ended tram shed.
Closed: With the end of gas working on February 26th, 1903. The depot was partially demolished by gales on the following morning and was then utilized as a temporary store for electric trams until the opening of Squires Gate Lane Depot. Site now occupied by housing.

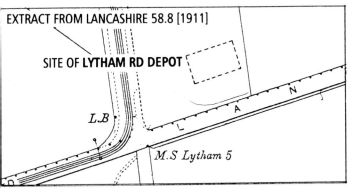

EXTRACT FROM LANCASHIRE 58.8 [1911]

SITE OF **LYTHAM RD DEPOT**

L.B

M.S Lytham 5

The Hull Street Tramways former horsecar **Holderness Road** [No.1] **Depot**, with an uncertain future today. Note the Jesmond Street entrance nearest the camera: unusually, the internal tracks ran parallel with the roadway and across the other three bays.
RJ Buckley (See Page 110)

BARROW IN FURNESS
Salthouse Road

Location: On the south side of Salthouse Road.
Gauge: 4ft.

DEPOT No.1

Opened: July 11th, 1885 by the Barrow in Furness Tramways Co Ltd and taken over by the British Electric Traction Co. Ltd on December 23rd, 1899. It was purchased by Barrow in Furness Corporation on January 1st, 1920.
Traction System: Steam, until July 13th, 1903 and then Overhead Electric from February 6th, 1904.
Description: Originally a 4TS dead ended tram shed, located at SD20756882, and destroyed by a fire on June 27th, 1902. It was reconstructed as a brick built 6TS dead ended depot on the same site and utilized for overhead electric working.
Closed: April 5th, 1932.

DEPOT No.2

Opened: 1921 by Barrow in Furness Corporation.
Traction System: Overhead Electric.
Description: A 4TS dead ended shed located at SD20796876.
Closed: April 5th, 1932.

Both depot buildings, from December 1932, were subsequently utilized as an omnibus garage and in December 1936 it became a Corporation Electricity Depot. Still in use, for the North Western Electricity Board, in 1960.

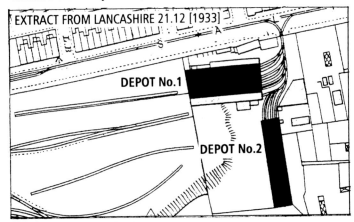

EXTRACT FROM LANCASHIRE 21.12 [1933]

DEPOT No.1

DEPOT No.2

BACUP
Rochdale Road

Location: At SD87562199, on the north east side of Rochdale Rd, Bacup by Sheephouse Reservoir.
Opened: July 27th, 1911 by Rochdale Corporation.
Traction System: Overhead Electric.
Gauge: 4ft 8.5in.
Description: A 2TS dead ended tram shed.
Closed: May 14th, 1932.

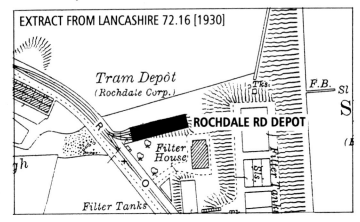

EXTRACT FROM LANCASHIRE 72.16 [1930]

Tram Depot (Rochdale Corp.)

F.B.

ROCHDALE RD DEPOT

Filter House

Filter Tanks

Copster Hill Road

Location: At SD92490375, on the east side of Copster Hill Rd, opposite Eyre St.
Opened: July 18th, 1901 by Oldham Corporation.
Traction System: Overhead Electric.
Gauge: 4ft 8.5in.
Description: A 1TS dead ended tram shed probably constructed in timber.
Closed: Probably in 1902 and utilized for sand drying prior to opening as an omnibus garage on May 12th, 1913. It was also utilized by trolley buses between August 26th, 1925 and September 5th, 1926.

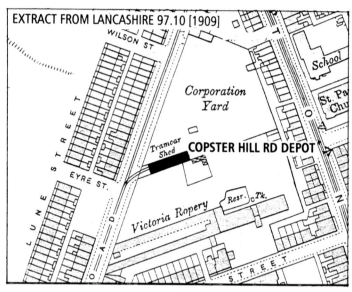

Wallshaw Street

Location: At SD93300520, on the north side of Wallshaw Place, Mumps.
Opened: May 17th, 1902 by Oldham Corporation.
Traction System: Overhead Electric.
Gauge: 4ft 8.5in.
Description: A brick built 8TS dead ended tram shed. In 1936 half of the accommodation was given over to omnibuses and an omnibus garage was added at the rear in 1938.
Closed: With the system on August 3rd, 1946.

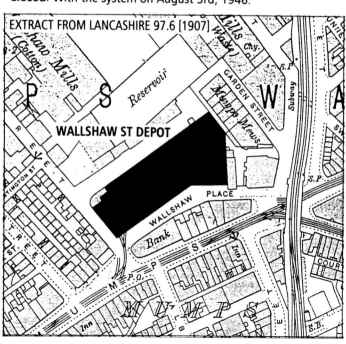

Hudson St [Hollinwood No.1] Depot

Location: At SD90470255, on the corner of Hudson St. and Stables St., Hollinwood.
Opened: November 1st, 1880 by the Manchester Carriage & Tramways Co.
Traction System: Horse.
Gauge: 4ft 8.5in.
Description: A 5TS dead ended tram shed and stables.
Closed: October 31st, 1901. It still stood in 1954.

Manchester Rd [Hollinwood No.2] Depot

Location: At SD90380245, on the north west side of Manchester Road, Hollinwood.
Opened: August 18th, 1910 by Oldham Corporation.
Traction System: Overhead Electric.
Gauge: 4ft 8.5in.
Description: Originally a brick built 6TS dead ended tram shed with a 2TS paint shop and 3TS workshop, it was extended in 1915.
Closed: August 7th, 1937 and sold to Ferranti Ltd for utilization as an armaments factory.

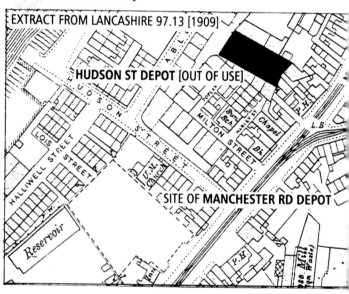

Neville Street

Location: At SD91330523, on the east side of Neville Street and north side of Denton Road, Westwood.
Opened: December 15th, 1900 by Oldham Corporation.
Traction System: Overhead Electric.
Gauge: 4ft 8.5in.
Description: A timber built 2TS dead ended tram shed.
Closed: Although originally built as a temporary depot it lasted until 1910. The land and shed building were sold separately in 1911.

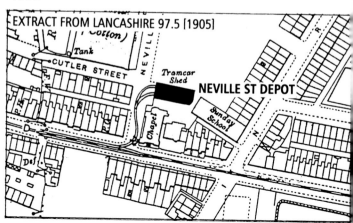

Gargrave Street

Location: At SD93780470, on the north side of Gargrave St.
Opened: June 15th, 1901 by Oldham Corporation.
Traction System: Overhead Electric.
Gauge: 4ft 8.5in.
Description: A timber built 2TS dead ended tram shed.
Closed: Although originally built as a temporary depot it lasted until 1910 when it was then utilized for sand drying.

EXTRACT FROM LANCASHIRE 97.6 [1909] S

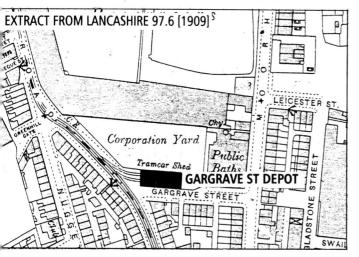

RAWTENSTALL

Bacup Road [No.1] Depot

Location: At SD81302269, on the north side of Bacup Road.
Opened: January 31st, 1889 by the Rossendale Valley Tramways Co. and taken over by Rawtenstall Corporation on October 1st, 1908.
Traction System: Steam, until July 22nd, 1909, and then Overhead Electric from May 15th, 1909.
Gauge: 4ft.
Description: Originally a 4TS dead ended tram shed, it was later enlarged to 5TS and works. In 1909 it was converted for electric working and extended at the front in 1911/2.
Closed: As a running shed upon the opening of No.2 Depot in 1921. It was subsequently utilized as a store and also housed omnibuses from 1924 onwards.

Bacup Road [No.2] Depot

Location: At SD81282278, on the south side of Bacup Road.
Opened: 1921 by Rawtenstall Corporation.
Traction System: Overhead Electric.
Gauge: 4ft.
Description: Originally a brick built 4TS dead ended tram shed, with a dead ended yard road and pw siding, it was extended at the rear in 1925.
Closed: With the tramway on March 31st, 1932. It was then utilized as an omnibus garage with temporary tracks being laid outside of the building to facilitate tram car scrapping.

ROYTON

Dogford Road

Location: At SD91800823, between Dogford Rd and Schofield St., off the east side of Rochdale Rd.
Opened: March 1st, 1885 by the Manchester, Bury, Rochdale & Oldham Steam Tramways Company and taken over by the Bury, Rochdale & Oldham Tramway Co. Ltd in October 1888.
Traction System: Steam.
Gauge: 3ft 6in (& 4ft 8.5in).
Description: Originally a brick built 2TS engine shed adjoined by a 4TS tram car shed, a similar 2TS engine shed and 4TS tram car shed was added (probably in July 1885) to accommodate the locos and cars working the 4ft 8.5in gauge section of the tramway.
Closed: May 30th, 1904. Part of the depot was then utilized as an omnibus garage until 1926, whilst the other part was sold in January 1905 for use as a wrestling booth and, subsequently, as a cinema. The buildings were later utilized by a steel stockholder and still stood in 1978.

EXTRACT FROM LANCASHIRE 89.14 [1909]

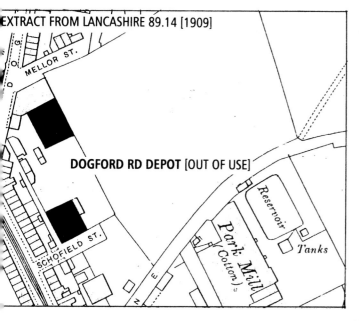

EXTRACT FROM LANCASHIRE 72.9 [1911]

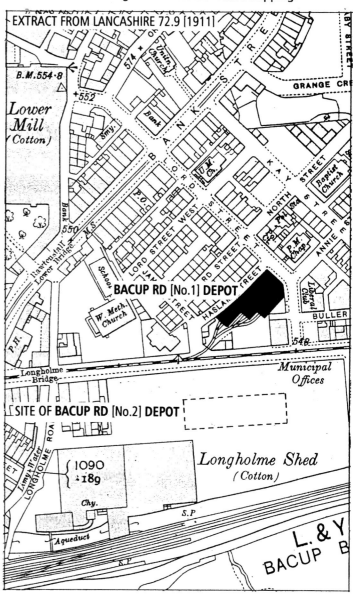

Fishergate

Location: At SD35432926, on the corner of Fishergate and Pitt Street.
Opened: April 14th, 1882 by Preston Corporation and worked by the local horse bus operator W. Harding & Co. Ltd.
Traction System: Horse.
Gauge: 3ft 6in.
Description: A 3TS dead ended tram shed.
Closed: 1895 and demolished to make way for the construction of the County Hall.

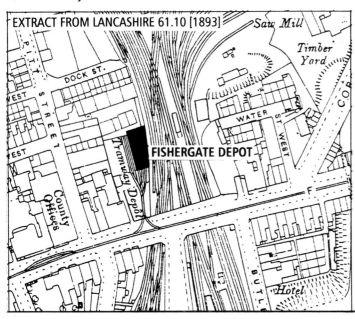

EXTRACT FROM LANCASHIRE 61.10 [1893]

FISHERGATE DEPOT

Fulwood

Location: Approximately at SD54753159, on the south side of Watling St. Rd, west of Deepdale Rd, Fulwood.
Opened: March 20th, 1879 by the Preston Tramways Co., taken over by Preston Corporation in 1886 and leased by the local horse bus operator W. Harding & Co. Ltd.
Traction System: Horse.
Gauge: 3ft 6in.
Description: A small horse tram depot.
Closed: Not known, but either on, or prior to, the cessation of horse working on December 31st, 1903.

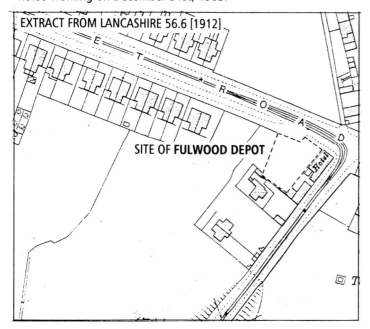

EXTRACT FROM LANCASHIRE 56.6 [1912]

SITE OF **FULWOOD DEPOT**

Deepdale Road

Location: At SD53943044, on the corner of Holmbrook Road and Deepdale Road.
Opened: June 7th, 1904 by Preston Corporation.
Traction System: Overhead Electric.
Gauge: 4ft 8.5in.
Description: Originally a brick built 6TS dead ended tram shed and works with an entrance in Holmbrook Road, a temporary extension was added in 1912. In 1915 the temporary building was removed, the entrance to the shed re-aligned to Deepdale Road and a new 4TS shed, with entrance in Holmbrook Road, constructed to the rear. Omnibuses were also accommodated from January 23rd, 1922 and an omnibus garage extension was added in 1931. In 1933 half of the tram depot was given over to omnibuses.
Closed: To trams, along with the system, on December 15th, 1935.

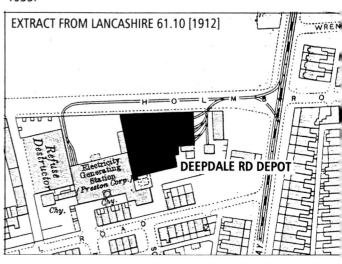

EXTRACT FROM LANCASHIRE 61.10 [1912]

DEEPDALE RD DEPOT

Old Vicarage Depot

Location: At SD54072968, on the north side of Old Vicarage, east off Lancaster Rd.
Opened: 1895 by W. Harding & Co. Ltd for Preston Corporation.
Traction System: Horse.
Gauge: 3ft 6in.
Description: A brick built 2TS dead ended tram shed.
Closed: Not known, but probably on the cessation of horse working on December 31st, 1903. It was subsequently utilized as a furniture store. Demolished in 1970.

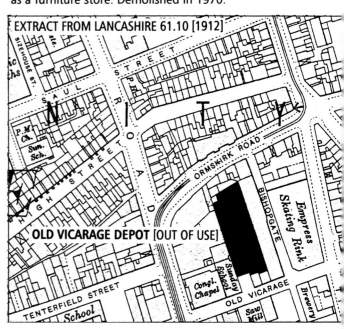

EXTRACT FROM LANCASHIRE 61.10 [1912]

OLD VICARAGE DEPOT [OUT OF USE]

Crowlands Depot

Location: At SD36161682, on the east side of Crowlands Rd.
Opened: July 18th, 1900 by Southport Corporation.
Traction System: Overhead Electric.
Gauge: 4ft 8.5in.
Description: Originally a dead ended tram shed, probably 3TS, it was enlarged in 1920.
Closed: With the tramway on December 31st, 1934 and subsequently utilized as an omnibus garage.

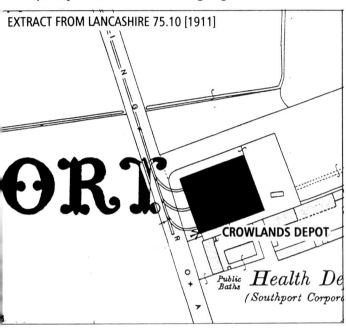

EXTRACT FROM LANCASHIRE 75.10 [1911]

CROWLANDS DEPOT

Boundary Street

Location: At SD33621596, on the south west side of Boundary St., opposite Sefton St.
Opened: May 12th, 1883 by the Birkdale & Southport Tramways Co. and taken over by Southport Corporation on January 1st, 1900.
Traction System: Horse.
Gauge: 4ft 8.5in.
Description: A tram depot and stables. No further details are known other than it may not have had rail access.
Closed: Probably on December 13th, 1902 when horse working ceased.

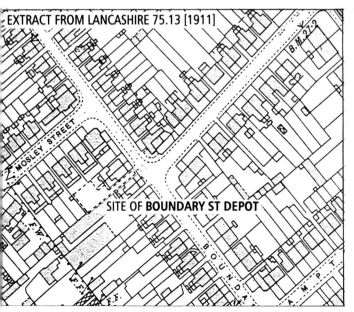

EXTRACT FROM LANCASHIRE 75.13 [1911]

SITE OF **BOUNDARY ST DEPOT**

Churchtown Depot

Location: At SD36371858, on the east side of Manor Rd.
Opened: May 31st, 1873 by the Southport Tramways Co. and taken over on January 1st, 1918 by Southport Corporation.
Traction System: Horse, until December 13th, 1902, and then Overhead Electric from August 11th, 1901.
Gauge: 4ft 8.5in.
Description: A 4TS tram shed with one through road.
Closed: 1918 and sold for commercial use in 1919.

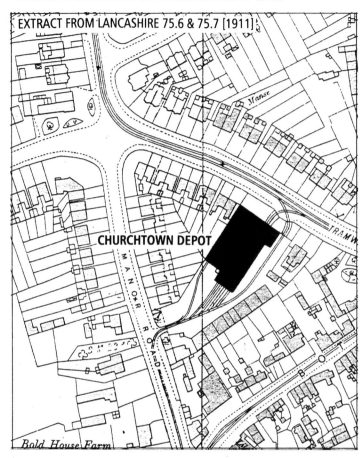

EXTRACT FROM LANCASHIRE 75.6 & 75.7 [1911]

CHURCHTOWN DEPOT

Bold House Farm

Partington Lane

Location: At SD77490117, on the east side of Partington Lane.
Opened: September 27th, 1906 by Lancashire United Tramways Ltd. (Name changed to South Lancashire Transport in 1926).
Traction System: Overhead Electric.
Gauge: 4ft 8.5in.
Description: A 7TS dead ended tram shed. An omnibus garage extension was later added on the north side.
Closed: To trams on August 18th, 1931 and utilized as a trolley bus depot from the following day. Finally closed on August 31st, 1958.

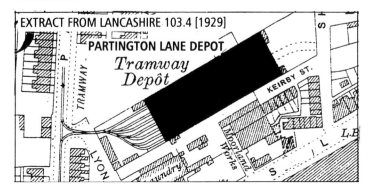

EXTRACT FROM LANCASHIRE 103.4 [1929]

PARTINGTON LANE DEPOT

Tramway Depôt

ROCHDALE

Entwistle Road

Location: At SD90251348, on the south side of Entwistle Rd.

Opened: May 7th, 1883 by the Manchester, Bury, Rochdale & Oldham Steam Tramways Co., taken over in October 1888 by the Bury, Rochdale & Oldham Tramway Co. Ltd and taken over on July 10th, 1904 by Rochdale Corporation.

Traction System: Steam.

Gauge: 3ft 6in.

Description: A 4TS dead ended tram shed, 3TS dead ended loco shed and workshops.

Closed: At the end of steam working on May 11th, 1905 and subsequently demolished. Site later utilized for a public baths.

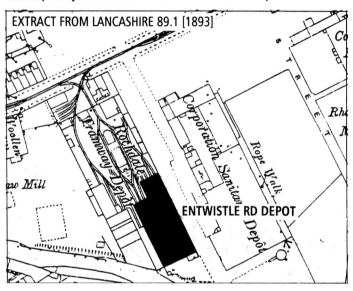

EXTRACT FROM LANCASHIRE 89.1 [1893]

ENTWISTLE RD DEPOT

Mellor Street

Location: At SD88661363, on the east side of Mellor St, on the bank of the River Spodden.

Opened: May 22nd, 1902 by Rochdale Corporation.

Traction System: Overhead Electric.

Gauge: 4ft 8.5in.

Description: A brick built 8TS through road shed.

Closed: With the tramway on November 12th, 1932. It was subsequently utilized as an omnibus garage.

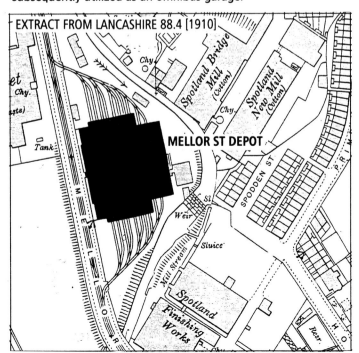

EXTRACT FROM LANCASHIRE 88.4 [1910]

MELLOR ST DEPOT

ST HELENS

Hall Street

Location: At SJ51519551, on the corner of Parade Street and Hall Street.

Opened: November 5th, 1881 by the St Helens & District Tramways Co., taken over on January 1st, 1892 by the St Helens & District Tramways Co. Ltd (Name changed to the New St Helens & District Tramways Co. Ltd on November 4th, 1898 and taken over by St Helens Corporation on October 1st, 1919.

Traction System: Horse, until May 11th, 1890, Steam, between April 4th, 1890 and April 6th, 1900 and Overhead Electric from July 20th, 1899.

Gauge: 4ft 8.5in.

Description: Originally a brick built 6TS dead ended tram shed, it was extended on the north side to an 8TS building for electric working. It was also utilized to house cars of the Liverpool and Prescot Light Railway between June 24th, 1902 and September 30th, 1919, and trolley buses from July 1st, 1907.

Closed: To trams, along with the tramway, on March 31st, 1936.

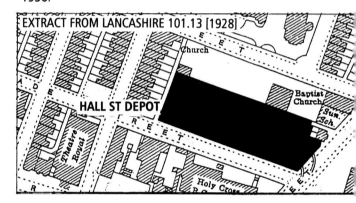

EXTRACT FROM LANCASHIRE 101.13 [1928]

HALL ST DEPOT

WARRINGTON

Mersey Street

Location: At SD60888802, on the corner of Mersey Street and Lower Bank Street.

Opened: April 21st, 1902 by Warrington Corporation.

Traction System: Overhead Electric.

Gauge: 4ft 8.5in.

Description: A brick built 5TS dead ended tram shed adjoined by a 3TS dead ended tram shed. An omnibus garage was added on the north western part of the site in 1928 and the yard was roofed over in 1934.

Closed: August 28th, 1935 and subsequently utilized as an omnibus depot.

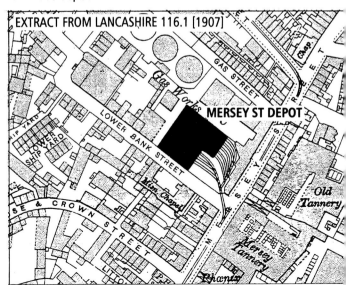

EXTRACT FROM LANCASHIRE 116.1 [1907]

MERSEY ST DEPOT

WIGAN

Central Depot

Location: At SD57410508, on the east side of Melverley St., Newtown.
Opened: July 26th, 1904 by Wigan Corporation.
Traction System: Overhead Electric.
Gauge: 4ft 8.5in.
Description: Originally a brick built 9TS dead ended tram shed, it was extended frontwards and a 2TS workshop added on the south side in 1921. Omnibuses were also accommodated from June 9th, 1919 and trolley buses from May 7th, 1925.
Closed: To trams from March 28th, 1931 and trolley buses from September 30th, 1931.

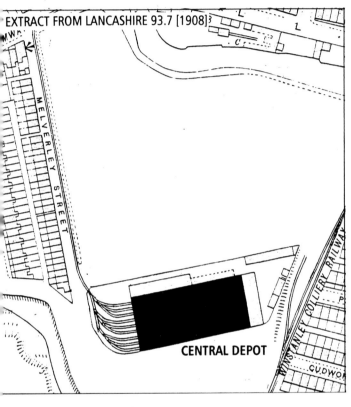

EXTRACT FROM LANCASHIRE 93.7 [1908]

CENTRAL DEPOT

Martland Mill Depot

Location: At SD56650651, on the south west side of Woodhouse Lane, Martland Mill.
Opened: January 25th, 1901 by Wigan Corporation.
Traction System: Overhead Electric.
Gauge: 3ft 6in.
Description: A brick built 6TS dead ended tram shed.
Closed: May 7th, 1925 and sold. Demolished in 1926.

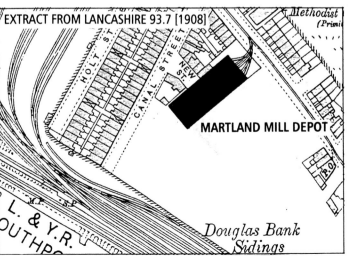

EXTRACT FROM LANCASHIRE 93.7 [1908]

MARTLAND MILL DEPOT

Douglas Bank Sidings

Pemberton Depot

Location: At SD55290439, on the south side of Smethurst St., Pemberton.
Opened: August 2nd, 1880 by the Wigan Tramways Co. Ltd, taken over by the Wigan & District Tramways Co. Ltd in 1893 and taken over again by Pemberton UDC in May 1902.
Traction System: Horse, until March/April 1885, and Steam from February 8th, 1882 until February 10th, 1884 and then from August 23rd, 1884.
Gauge: 3ft 6in.
Description: A brick built 2TS tram shed and stables.
Closed: To trams on April 10th, 1904 and utilized as a paint shop from 1908 until 1921 by Wigan Corporation after the system was converted to electric working. Most of the depot was rented by Massey Brothers, tramcar builders, from May 1920.

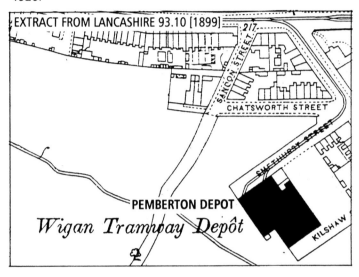

EXTRACT FROM LANCASHIRE 93.10 [1899]

CHATSWORTH STREET

PEMBERTON DEPOT

Wigan Tramway Depôt

KILSHAW

HINDLEY

Albert Street

Location: At SD61630440, on the south west side of Albert St., off Market St., Hindley.
Opened: January 13th, 1883 by the Wigan Tramways Co. Ltd, taken over by the Wigan & District Tramways Co. Ltd in 1893 and taken over again by Hindley UDC in 1903.
Traction System: Horse, until November 1883, and then Steam.
Gauge: 3ft 6in.
Description: A brick built 4TS dead ended tram shed.
Closed: September 26th, 1904 and subsequently let out for commercial use.

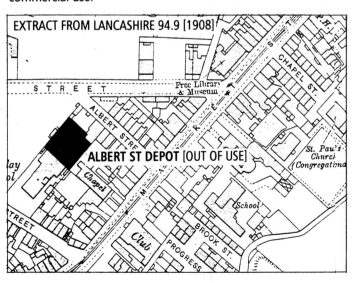

EXTRACT FROM LANCASHIRE 94.9 [1908]

ALBERT ST DEPOT [OUT OF USE]

Church Street

Location: At SJ81119942, on the east side of Church St, Pendleton.

Opened: May 18th, 1877 by the Manchester Carriage Co. Ltd (became the Manchester Carriage & Tramways Co. in 1880) and taken over by Salford Corporation on May 1st, 1901.

Traction System: Horse.

Gauge: 4ft 8.5in.

Description: A 12TS dead ended tram shed, probably built in brick, and stables. The depot also housed omnibuses and other vehicles.

Closed: At the end of horse working on March 24th, 1903.

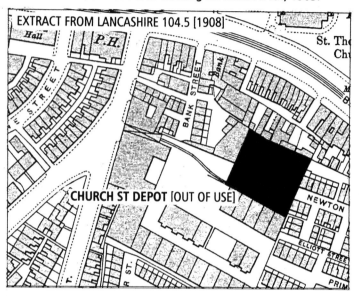

EXTRACT FROM LANCASHIRE 104.5 [1908]

CHURCH ST DEPOT [OUT OF USE]

Frederick Road

Location: At SJ82109980, at the junction of Frederick Rd and Seaford Rd, Pendleton.

Opened: October 4th, 1901 by Salford Corporation.

Traction System: Overhead Electric.

Gauge: 4ft 8.5in.

Description: Originally a brick built 20TS dead ended tram shed with a traverser for the northern ten tracks serving workshops, in 1907 it was extended on the north side with another three roads accessing the traverser. The workshops were extended in 1915/16 and an omnibus depot was later added at the rear. The building was damaged during World War II.

Closed: With the tramway on March 31st, 1947 and then used as an omnibus garage.

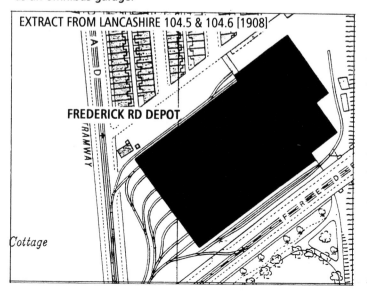

EXTRACT FROM LANCASHIRE 104.5 & 104.6 [1908]

FREDERICK RD DEPOT

Cottage

Weaste Depot [No.1]

Location: At SJ80809839, on the east corner of Derby Rd and Eccles New Rd, Weaste.

Opened: June 1st, 1878 by the Manchester Carriage Co. Ltd (became the Manchester Carriage & Tramways Co. in 1880) and taken over by Salford Corporation on May 1st, 1901.

Traction System: Horse.

Gauge: 4ft 8.5in.

Description: Originally, probably a 4TS dead ended tram shed and stables, it was extended in 1891 with another four dead ended roads and four dead ended roads in a covered yard. It was probably built in brick, with additional stables, and was accessed from Heyworth St.

Closed: April 4th, 1902.

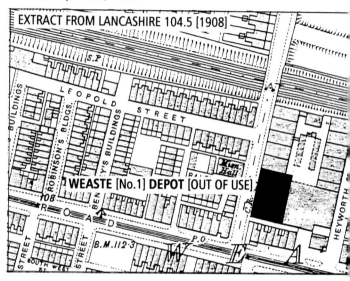

EXTRACT FROM LANCASHIRE 104.5 [1908]

WEASTE [No.1] DEPOT [OUT OF USE]

Weaste Depot [No.2]

Location: At SJ79619841, on the south side of Eccles New Rd, Weaste

Opened: October 29th, 1929 by Salford Corporation.

Traction System: Overhead Electric.

Gauge: 4ft 8.5in.

Description: A brick built omnibus depot with 9 roads and a traverser, with access to Hessel St, installed at the western end. The building was damaged during World War II.

Closed: To trams on March 2nd, 1947 and subsequently utilized as an omnibus garage. In 2000 it was in industrial use.

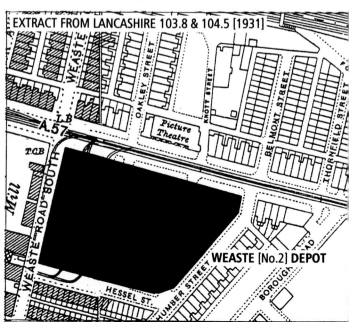

EXTRACT FROM LANCASHIRE 103.8 & 104.5 [1931]

WEASTE [No.2] DEPOT

Lower Broughton Depot

Location: At SJ82499958, on the south side of Lower Broughton Rd, Lower Broughton.

Opened: 1891 by the Manchester Carriage & Tramways Co. and taken over by Salford Corporation on May 1st, 1901.

Traction System: Horse.

Gauge: 4ft 8.5in.

Description: A 5TS dead ended tram shed and stables probably built in brick.

Closed: May 2nd, 1902.

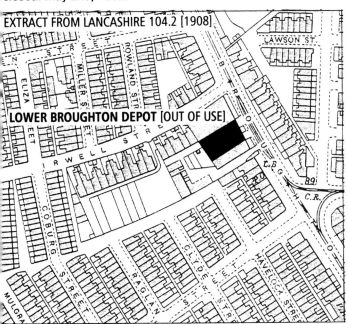

PLATT BRIDGE

Capps Street

Location: At SD60740328, off the south side of Liverpool Rd (formerly Stony Lane), Platt Bridge.

Opened: March 30th, 1903 by the South Lancashire Electric Traction & Power Co. Ltd and taken over by Lancashire United Tramways Ltd on January 2nd, 1906. (Name changed to South Lancashire Transport in 1929.)

Traction System: Overhead Electric.

Gauge: 4ft 8.5in.

Description: A 5TS dead ended tram shed.

Closed: At some time prior to 1927 when the depot was converted for omnibus use. It was also utilized for trolley buses from August 3rd, 1930 until November 11th, 1956.

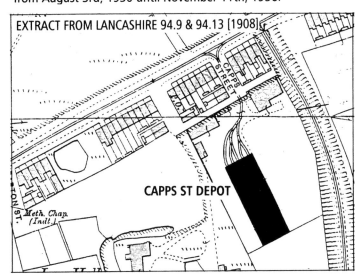

WATERLOO

Seaforth Sands

Location: At SD33019632 adjacent to Seaforth Sands (Liverpool Overhead Railway) Station.

Opened: June 19th, 1900, jointly, by the Waterloo-with-Seaforth and Great Crosby UDCs and operated by the Liverpool Overhead Railway.

Traction System: Overhead Electric.

Gauge: 4ft 8.5in.

Description: Originally a 2TS dead ended tram shed built under the railway viaduct, the station was replaced by a carriage shed and works in 1925 and a new station opened on the south east side.

Closed: December 31st, 1925 and let out as an omnibus garage until 1935. It was dismantled in 1957.

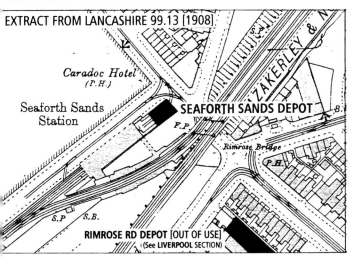

Tram Street

Location: At SD60370246, on the north west side of Tram St., Platt Bridge.

Opened: September 2nd, 1896 by the Wigan & District Tramways Co. Ltd and taken over by Wigan Corporation on September 30th, 1902.

Traction System: Steam, until March/April 1903, and then Overhead Electric from May 29th, 1903.

Gauge: 3ft 6in, until cJune 1904, and 4ft 8.5in from September 2nd, 1904.

Description: A brick built dead ended tram shed.

Closed: 1904/5 and let out for commercial use in 1907.

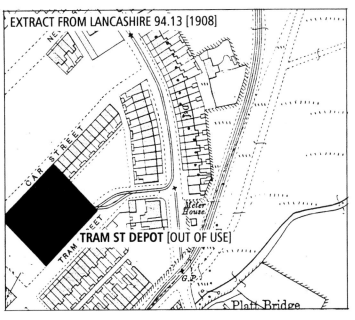

Old Swan [No.1] Depot

Location: At SJ39389106, behind the Old Swan Hotel on the south side of the junction of Prescot Rd and Broad Green Rd.
Opened: July 2nd, 1861 by the Liverpool Road & Rail Omnibus Co.
Traction System: Horse.
Gauge: 4ft 8.5in (Nominal).
Description: Existing horse bus stables were utilized as the tram depot.
Closed: Probably in May 1862. It continued in use as a horse bus depot and stables and, later, stables for Old Swan No.2 Depot until c1900 when it was abandoned and part of the site sold in 1906 for the construction of a Technical College. The remainder of the site was utilized as a Corporation motor car and omnibus depot until the 1930s when it was absorbed by the expansion of the college.

Old Swan [No.2] Depot

Location: At SJ39409117, on the north side of the junction of Prescot Rd and Broad Green Rd.
Opened: August 11th, 1881 by the Liverpool United Tramways & Omnibus Co. and taken over by Liverpool Corporation on January 1st, 1897.
Traction System: Horse, until 1900, and then Overhead Electric from August 5th, 1900.
Gauge: 4ft 8.5in.
Description: Originally a 3TS dead ended tram shed constructed in corrugated iron and utilizing the stables of the former Old Swan No.1 Depot, it was converted to electric working in 1900 and two dead ended roads were added in the field on the east side of the depot.
Closed: 1903/4. The building was subsequently dismantled and the site later used for road widening.

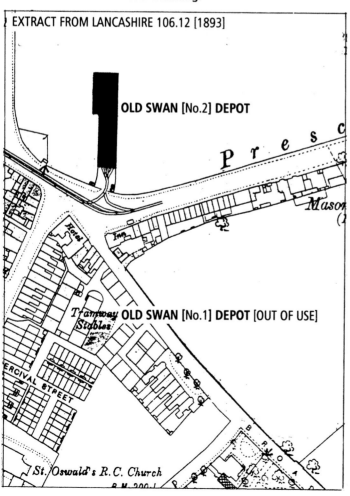

EXTRACT FROM LANCASHIRE 106.12 [1893]

OLD SWAN [No.2] DEPOT

P r e s c

OLD SWAN [No.1] DEPOT [OUT OF USE]

Stanley Road

Location: At SJ34449465, on the east side of Stanley Rd, Boot
Opened: 1882 by the Liverpool United Tramways & Omnibu Co. and taken over by Liverpool Corporation on January 1s 1897.
Traction System: Horse.
Gauge: 4ft 8.5in.
Description: A 2TS through road shed and stables.
Closed: c1897 and demolished in 1900. The site was late cleared and incorporated within Stanley Gardens.

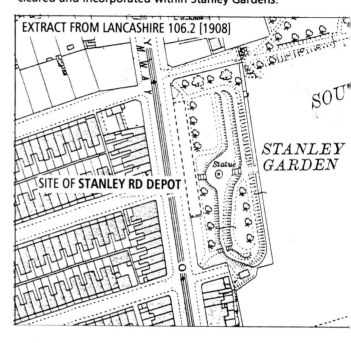

EXTRACT FROM LANCASHIRE 106.2 [1908]

SITE OF **STANLEY RD DEPOT**

SOU

STANLEY GARDEN

Beaumont Street

Location: At SJ36858930, on the south side of Beaumont St. east of Priest St.
Opened: c1884 by the Liverpool United Tramways & Omnibus Co. and taken over by Liverpool Corporation on January 1st 1897.
Traction System: Horse.
Gauge: 4ft 8.5in.
Description: Originally a horse omnibus depot and stables, a tramway access track was added in 1884. Part of the yard was later roofed over for use as an omnibus shed and it is not known if it was also utilized by trams.
Closed: 1901 and subsequently rented as commercial premises.

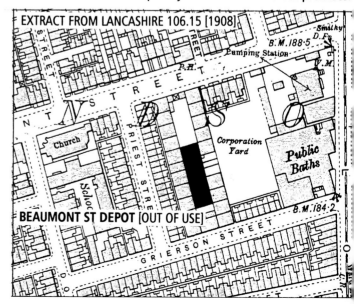

EXTRACT FROM LANCASHIRE 106.15 [1908]

Corporation Yard

Public Baths

BEAUMONT ST DEPOT [OUT OF USE]

Park Place

Location: At SJ35518873, on the east side of Park Place, north of Upper Warwick Rd.
Opened: 1882 by the Liverpool United Tramways & Omnibus Co and taken over by Liverpool Corporation on January 1st, 1897.
Traction System: Horse.
Gauge: 4ft 8.5in.
Description: A roofed-over yard, utilized as a tram shed and stables and possibly adapted from an earlier horse bus depot.
Closed: Not known but prior to electrification of the line on January 15th, 1899. The site was later utilized for council flats.

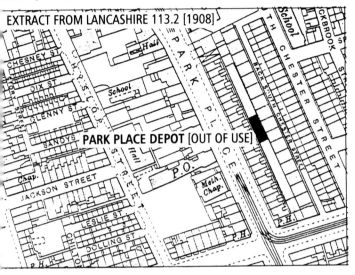

EXTRACT FROM LANCASHIRE 113.2 [1908]
PARK PLACE DEPOT [OUT OF USE]

Lambeth Road Carriage Works

Location: At SJ34909305, on the west side of Smith St. between Lambeth Rd and Leison St.
Opened: 1927 by Liverpool Corporation.
Traction System: Overhead Electric.
Gauge: 4ft 8.5in.
Description: Originally a brick built horse depot and stables, it was converted into a tramway and horse bus carriage works in 1893 by the Liverpool United Tramways & Omnibus Co. It was taken over by Liverpool Corporation on January 1st, 1897 and exetnded in 1900 to become a construction and maintenance works for electric tramcars and, later, omnibuses with 8 through and 3 dead ended roads. After the works facility was removed in 1927 it was partially utilized as a running shed for trams and omnibuses.
Closed: August 12th, 1935 and sold in 1936 with the site later being used for a school.

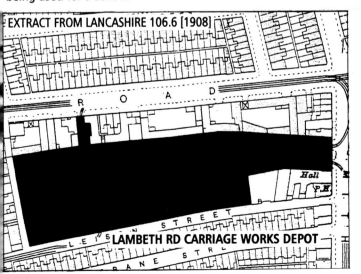

EXTRACT FROM LANCASHIRE 106.6 [1908]
LAMBETH RD CARRIAGE WORKS DEPOT

Commercial Road

Location: At SJ34599305, on the east side of Commercial Rd, between Lambeth Rd and Aspinall St.
Opened: 1882/3 by the Liverpool United Tramways & Omnibus Co.
Traction System: Horse.
Gauge: 4ft 8.5in.
Description: A 2TS dead ended tram shed, possibly just a roofed-in yard, and stables.
Closed: Probably by 1890 and subsequently utilized as commercial premises. The site was cleared in 1970.

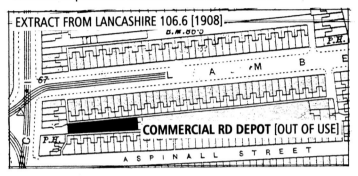

EXTRACT FROM LANCASHIRE 106.6 [1908]
COMMERCIAL RD DEPOT [OUT OF USE]

Kirkdale Depot

Location: At SJ35099295, on the south east corner of Smith St. and Whittle St.
Opened: c1882 by the Liverpool United Tramways & Omnibus Co. and taken over by Liverpool Corporation on January 1st, 1897.
Traction System: Horse.
Gauge: 4ft 8.5in.
Description: A roofed yard and stables, possibly originating as a horse bus depot, with 1 or 2 through roads.
Closed: c1901 and subsequently utilized by the Building Dept. The site was cleared in 1966 for redevelopment.

EXTRACT FROM LANCASHIRE 106.6 [1908]
WHITTLE STREET
KIRKDALE DEPOT [OUT OF USE]

Warbreck Moor

Location: At SJ36629715, on the north west side of Warbreck Moor, opposite Hall Lane, Aintree.
Opened: c1881 by the Liverpool United Tramways & Omnibus Co. and taken over by Liverpool Corporation on January 1st, 1897.
Traction System: Horse.
Gauge: 4ft 8.5in.
Description: A dead ended tram shed and stables. It was also known as Aintree Depot.
Closed: Upon electrification in 1901/2 and demolished to make way for a public park.

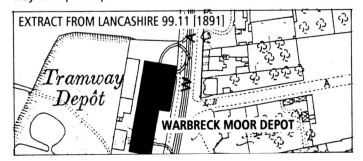

EXTRACT FROM LANCASHIRE 99.11 [1891]
Tramway Depôt
WARBRECK MOOR DEPOT

Smithdown Rd [Penny Lane] Depot

Location: At SJ39118848, on the north side of the corner of Kenyon Rd and Smithdown Rd, Penny Lane.
Opened: July 9th, 1899 by Liverpool Corporation.
Traction System: Overhead Electric.
Gauge: 4ft 8.5in.
Description: Originally a brick built 5TS dead ended tram shed, another 5TS dead ended building was added on the south side in 1902. The north shed was converted for omnibus use in 1927 and the south shed in 1930, with trams only utilizing the depot intermittently from this time.
Closed: To trams in 1936.

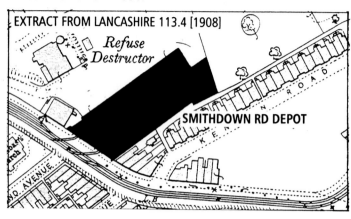

Prince Alfred Road Depot

Location: At SJ39158855, on the south west side of Prince Alfred Rd, west off Church Rd.
Opened: Early 1928 by Liverpool Corporation.
Traction System: Overhead Electric.
Gauge: 4ft 8.5in.
Description: A concrete built 14TS through road shed with 4 dead ended yard roads. Following the closure of the adjacent Smithdown Rd Depot to trams in 1936 the yard was also utilized by omnibuses.
Closed: December 12th, 1949 and subsequently utilized as an omnibus garage.

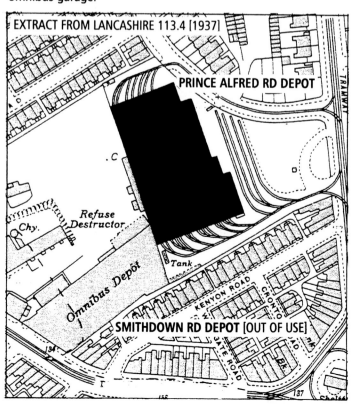

Edge Lane Depot & Works

Location: At SJ37949063, on the south side of Edge Lane.
Opened: 1921 by Liverpool Corporation.
Traction System: Overhead Electric.
Gauge: 4ft 8.5in.
Description: Originally a 9TS dead ended tram shed utilizing the Tournament Hall built for the 1913 Liverpool Exhibition, it was replaced in 1926 with a 9TS tram shed and in 1928 with a multi-road works both constructed in brick, stone and concrete. An omnibus garage was constructed on the site in 1926.
Closed: To trams, along with the tramway, on September 14th, 1957 and subsequently utilized as an omnibus garage.

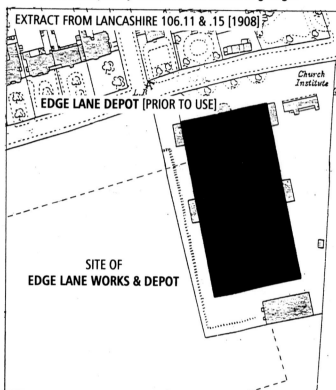

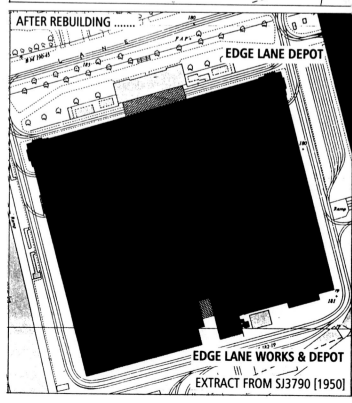

Tramway Road Depot & Works

Location: At SJ37048690, at the end of Tramway Rd, south off Aigburth Rd.

Opened: November 1st, 1869 by the Liverpool Tramways Co. Became part of the Liverpool United Tramways & Omnibus Co. in February 1876.

Traction System: Horse.

Gauge: 4ft 8.5in.

Description: Consisting of a tram shed, stables and works, it was also used for building trams and omnibuses.

Closed: As a running shed in the 1870s and as a works in 1893, with the stables remaining in use as part of an Engineers Department Yard. It was subsequently utilized by the Territorial Army and the remaining buildings were demolished in the 1960s.

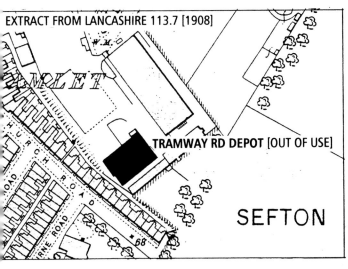

EXTRACT FROM LANCASHIRE 113.7 [1908]

TRAMWAY RD DEPOT [OUT OF USE]

Wavertree Depot

Location: At SJ38968944, west off Prince Alfred Rd and south off High St, Wavertree.

Opened: August 11th, 1881 by the Liverpool United Tramways & Omnibus Co. and taken over by Liverpool Corporation on January 1st, 1897.

Traction System: Horse.

Gauge: 4ft 8.5in.

Description: A 2TS or 3TS through road tram shed and stables.

Closed: Upon electrification in 1900 and used as a cinema from 1911 to 1918 before being requisitioned by the military. In 1920/21 it was refurbished for works use, for the electric trams, as a paint shop and sand drier with a car wash opening on June 9th, 1921. The paint shop closed in 1928, following the opening of Edge Lane Works, and the car wash in 1931. The buildings were demolished in 1935 and council flats later built on the site.

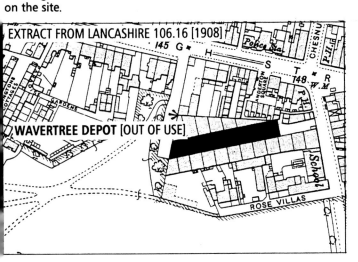

EXTRACT FROM LANCASHIRE 106.16 [1908]

WAVERTREE DEPOT [OUT OF USE]

Walton Depot

Location: At SJ35469403, on the west side of Carisbrooke Rd, south of Harlech St, Walton.

Opened: September 1st, 1870 by the Liverpool Tramways Co. Became part of the Liverpool United Tramways & Omnibus Co. in February 1876 and was taken over by Liverpool Corporation on January 1st, 1897.

Traction System: Horse, until c1900, and Overhead Electric from January 1900.

Gauge: 4ft 8.5in.

Description: Originally a brick built 4TS tram shed with one through road, a 2TS dead ended repair shop accessed via a turntable, and stables. The tram shed was converted to a 4TS dead ended building for electric working and in 1901 a new brick built 15TS dead ended tram shed was constructed on the site of the former stables. The depot was also utilized by omnibuses after World War II.

Closed: To trams on November 4th, 1956 and subsequently utilized as an omnibus garage. In 1962-4 the former horse car shed was demolished and replaced by a garage and offices.

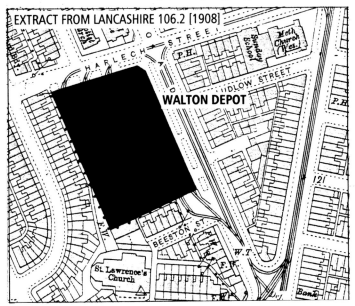

EXTRACT FROM LANCASHIRE 106.2 [1908]

WALTON DEPOT

Strand Road Depot

Location: At SJ33759538, on the north side of Strand Rd, off Derby Rd, Bootle.

Opened: c1890 by the Liverpool United Tramways & Omnibus Co. and taken over by Liverpool Corporation on January 1st, 1897.

Traction System: Horse.

Gauge: 4ft 8.5in.

Description: Probably a 4TS tram shed and stables with turntable access to a repair shop. The site may have previously been used as a horse bus depot and stables.

Closed: Upon electrification of the route in 1900. It was sold for commercial premises in 1903 and later demolished.

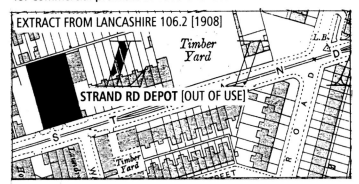

EXTRACT FROM LANCASHIRE 106.2 [1908]

Timber Yard

STRAND RD DEPOT [OUT OF USE]

Litherland Depot

Location: At SJ33789700, on the east side of Linacre Rd.

Opened: c1894 by the Liverpool United Tramways & Omnibus Co. and taken over by Liverpool Corporation on January 1st, 1897.

Traction System: Horse, until the end of horse working on August 25th, 1903, and then Overhead Electric from 1904.

Gauge: 4ft 8.5in.

Description: Originally a brick built 3TS dead ended tram shed and stables, it was converted for electric working in 1903 and a 5TS dead ended extension added on the north side. In 1938 the existing eight roads were lengthened and an 8TS extension, which officially opened on June 29th, built on the north side. The depot was also known as Linacre Road Depot and it housed omnibuses as well after World War II.

Closed: To trams on December 30th, 1950 and subsequently utilized as an omnibus garage.

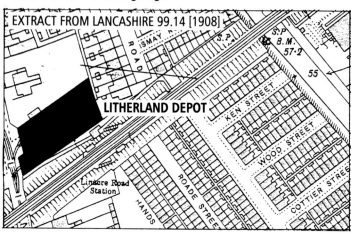

EXTRACT FROM LANCASHIRE 99.14 [1908]

LITHERLAND DEPOT

West Derby Depot

Location: At SJ39639325, on the south west corner of Derby Rd and Almond's Garden, West Derby.

Opened: February 2nd, 1882 by the Liverpool United Tramways & Omnibus Co. and taken over by Liverpool Corporation on January 1st, 1897.

Traction System: Horse.

Gauge: 4ft 8.5in.

Description: A brick built tram shed with stables on the first floor.

Closed: Upon the electrification of the route in 1900 and then utilized as a tramway office and, later, as commercial premises.

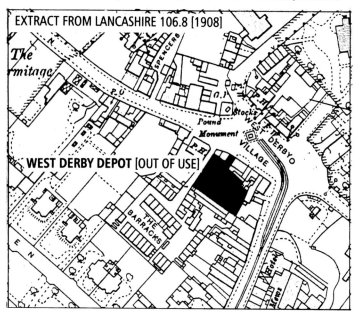

EXTRACT FROM LANCASHIRE 106.8 [1908]

WEST DERBY DEPOT [OUT OF USE]

Dingle Depot

Location: At SJ36438763, on the north side of the junction of Park Rd, Aigburth Rd and Ullet Rd, Dingle.

Opened: November 16th, 1898 by Liverpool Corporation.

Traction System: Overhead Electric.

Gauge: 4ft 8.5in.

Description: Originally constructed as a brick built 10TS dead ended tram shed with three dead ended yard roads and a traverser at the rear, in 1909 the traverser pit was filled in and the roads lengthened. The depot was enlarged in 1936/7 when a 12TS dead ended tram shed, officially opened on January 12th, 1938, was built on the east side of the yard with access through the original shed. The depot also housed omnibuses after World War II.

Closed: To trams in September 1951 and subsequently utilized as an omnibus garage. Demolished in the early 1990s.

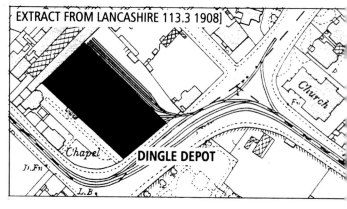

EXTRACT FROM LANCASHIRE 113.3 1908]

DINGLE DEPOT

Green Lane Depot

Location: At SJ39009150, on the east side of the junction of Prescot Rd and Green Lane.

Opened: Late 1881 by the Liverpool United Tramways & Omnibus Co. and taken over by Liverpool Corporation on January 1st, 1897.

Traction System: Horse, until 1900, and then Overhead Electric from 1901.

Gauge: 4ft 8.5in.

Description: Originally a through road tram shed and stables, it was demolished and replaced by a brick built 10TS dead ended tram shed in 1900/01. It also accommodated omnibuses after World War II and tramcars only used it infrequently following a fire on November 7th, 1947 which caused severe damage to the building.

Closed: To trams on April 4th, 1954 and subsequently utilized as an omnibus garage.

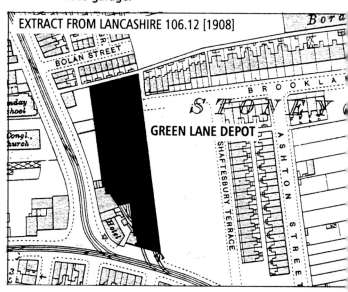

EXTRACT FROM LANCASHIRE 106.12 [1908]

GREEN LANE DEPOT

Rimrose Road Depot

Location: At SJ33099622, on the south corner of Rimrose Rd nd Regent Rd, Seaforth.

Opened: c1883 by the Liverpool United Tramways & Omnibus Co. and taken over by Liverpool Corporation on January 1st, 897.

Traction System: Horse.

Gauge: 4ft 8.5in.

Description: A brick built 3TS through road shed and stables.

Closed: As a running shed in c1901. The offices continued in ramway use for a while before being utilized as commercial premises.

EXTRACT FROM LANCASHIRE 99.13 [1893]

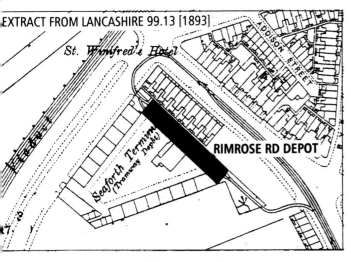

Speke Road [Garston] Depot

Location: At SJ40588450, on the north side of Speke Rd, east of Church Rd, Garston.

Opened: March 21st, 1910 by Liverpool Corporation.

Traction System: Overhead Electric.

Gauge: 4ft 8.5in.

Description: Originally a brick built 5TS dead ended tram shed, it was extended at the front in 1940 and an omnibus garage, which opened on June 4th, 1940, was added on the east side with three sidings in it used by trams from May 28th, 1940.

Closed: To trams on June 7th, 1953 and subsequently utilized as an omnibus garage.

EXTRACT FROM LANCASHIRE 113.12 [1927]

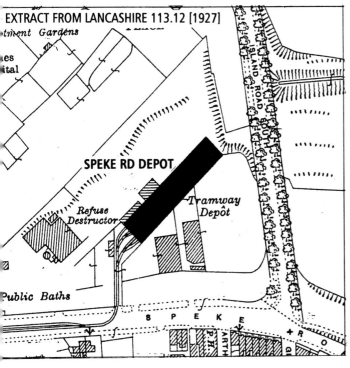

Franklin Place

Location: At SJ36689218, at the end of Franklin Place, north off Whitefield Rd, Anfield.

Opened: 1895 by the Liverpool United Tramways & Omnibus Co and taken over by Liverpool Corporation on January 1st, 1897.

Traction System: Horse.

Gauge: 4ft 8.5in.

Description: Originally horse bus stables, a 2TS or 3TS through road tram shed was added in 1895 in the centre of the yard. It was latterly known as the Whitefield Road Depot.

Closed: Upon electrification of the system in 1900 and later utilized as a sweet factory.

EXTRACT FROM LANCASHIRE 106.11 [1908]

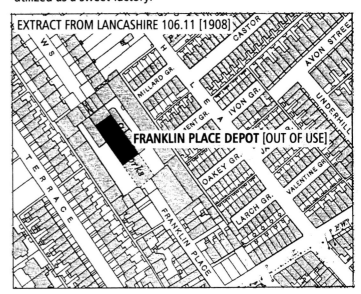

HORWICH

Horwich Depot

Location: At SD63591160, on the corner of Chorlton New Rd and Beatrice St.

Opened: May 19th, 1900 by Bolton Corporation.

Traction System: Overhead Electric.

Gauge: 4ft 8.5in.

Description: A 4TS dead ended tram shed.

Closed: October 6th, 1946.

EXTRACT FROM LANCASHIRE 86.6 [1908]

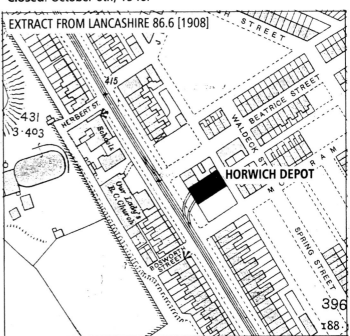

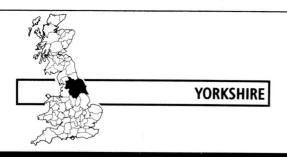

BRADFORD

Bankfoot

Location: At SE15703035, on the south side of Rathmell St, west of Manchester Rd.

Opened: September 8th, 1884 by Bradford & Shelf Tramway Co. Ltd and taken over by Bradford Corporation on February 1st, 1902.

Traction System: Steam, until September 1st, 1903, and then Overhead Electric.

Gauge: 4ft.

Description: Originally a timber built 4TS dead ended tram shed, it was enlarged in 1902 on the north and west sides with timber extensions for storing redundant steam stock and, in 1903, was reconstructed as a brick built 11TS dead ended tram shed. It was also utilized for trolley buses between October 1927 and 1940, and, from 1949, for omnibuses.

Closed: May 6th, 1950 and utilized for scrapping tram cars prior to conversion to an omnibus garage. It closed in 1978 and was let as commercial premises.

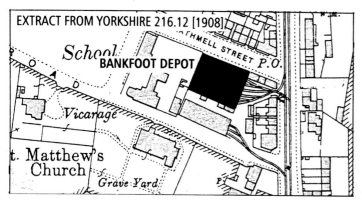

EXTRACT FROM YORKSHIRE 216.12 [1908]

Necropolis Rd [Lidget Green] Depot

Location: At SE13913234, on the south side of Scholemoor Rd, west of Cemetery Road.

Opened: August 31st, 1900 by Bradford Corporation.

Traction System: Overhead Electric.

Gauge: 4ft.

Description: A timber built 1TS dead ended tram shed.

Closed: 1931 and subsequently demolished. Site now occupied by housing.

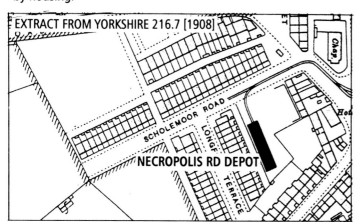

EXTRACT FROM YORKSHIRE 216.7 [1908]

Bowling Depot

Location: At SE17663196, on the south side of Foundry Lan east of Wakefield Road.

Opened: 1905 by Bradford Corporation.

Traction System: Overhead Electric.

Gauge: 4ft.

Description: A stone built 7TS dead ended tram shed.

Closed: July 6th, 1938 and subsequently utilized for the storin of redundant tram cars. It was requisitioned during World W II and again used as a tram store after the war with tram ca being scrapped in the adjacent permanent way yard after th system closed in 1950. The yard was then utilized as a trolle bus training depot and an omnibus garage, with the latte moving out in 1978 prior to occupation by a road haulier. Th whole site was cleared and re-developed in the mid 1980s.

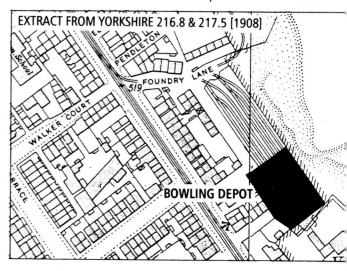

EXTRACT FROM YORKSHIRE 216.8 & 217.5 [1908]

Horton Bank Top

Location: At SE12563074, on the north side of the junction o Great Horton Road and Beacon Road.

Opened: August 27th, 1898 by Bradford Corporation.

Traction System: Overhead Electric.

Gauge: 4ft.

Description: Reckoned to be Britain's highest tram shed a 940ft, it was 4TS, dead ended, and constructed in corrugate iron.

Closed: November 5th, 1949 and subsequently utilized as a omnibus garage until 1978 when it was demolished.

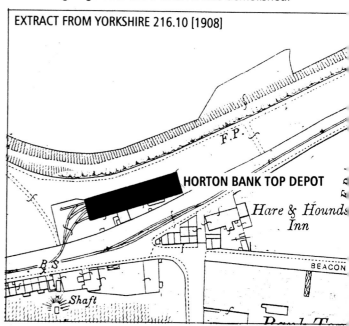

EXTRACT FROM YORKSHIRE 216.10 [1908]

Bolton Junction

Location: At SE17583564, on the north side of Bolton Road, west of Idle Road.
Opened: July 30th, 1898 by Bradford Corporation.
Traction System: Overhead Electric.
Gauge: 4ft.
Description: The tram cars stood in the open until the 4TS dead ended tram shed, constructed in corrugated iron, was finally completed in late 1898 or early 1899. It was rebuilt in brick in 1922 and trolley buses were then also accommodated from March 30th, 1930.
Closed: May 30th, 1934 and subsequently utilized as a trolley bus and, later, omnibus depot. It finally closed in 1958 and was sold to a haulage contractor in 1960. Demolished in 1969, the site is now occupied by a filling station.

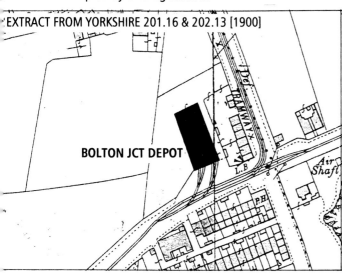

EXTRACT FROM YORKSHIRE 201.16 & 202.13 [1900]

Oak Lane

Location: At SE15073379, on the north side of Oak Lane, west of St.Mary's Road.
Opened: February 1st, 1882 by Bradford Tramways & Omnibus Co. Ltd and taken over by Bradford Corporation on February 1st, 1902.
Traction System: Horse.
Gauge: 4ft.
Description: A 1TS or 2TS dead ended tram shed.
Closed: May 17th, 1902 and subsequently demolished. Site now occupied by a supermarket.

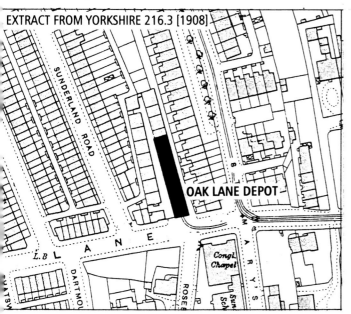

EXTRACT FROM YORKSHIRE 216.3 [1908]

Duckworth Lane

Location: At SE14003447, on the north side of Duckworth Lane, west of Toller Lane.
Opened: November 2nd, 1900 by Bradford Corporation.
Traction System: Overhead Electric.
Gauge: 4ft.
Description: A timber built 4TS dead ended tram shed. In 1902 this was removed and utilized as an extension at the Bank Foot Depot (*qv*), with a stone built 8TS dead ended replacement tram shed being erected on the site.
Closed: August 2nd, 1935 and utilized as a trolley bus depot until April 1972 and for omnibuses from 1971. It totally closed in 1978 and was subsequently demolished, the site now being occupied by a supermarket and car park.

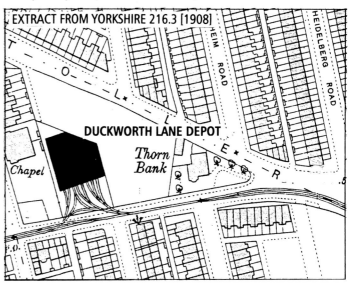

EXTRACT FROM YORKSHIRE 216.3 [1908]

Fairweather Green

Location: At SE13063330, on the south side of Thornton Rd, west of Green Top St.
Opened: December 18th, 1900 by Bradford Corporation.
Traction System: Overhead Electric.
Gauge: 4ft.
Description: A brick built 2TS dead ended tram shed.
Closed: March 1932 and sold for industrial use.

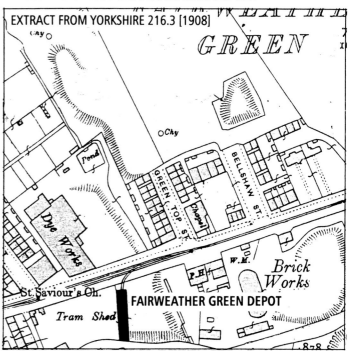

EXTRACT FROM YORKSHIRE 216.3 [1908]

Thornbury

Location: *At SE19193354, on the east side of Leeds Rd, north of Lower Rushton Rd.*

Opened: 1882 by Bradford Tramways & Omnibus Co. Ltd and taken over by Bradford Corporation in 1900.

Traction System: Steam, until February 27th, 1902, and then Overhead Electric.

Gauge: 4ft.

Description: The original layout is not known, but by 1900 it was probably a 6TS dead ended shed. Upon conversion to Overhead Electric traction it was reconstructed as a brick built 14TS dead ended tram shed and works. It was further extended westwards, by 3TS and 5TS in 1903 and a further 4TS in 1909. The yard was also utilized by trolley buses from 1911 and a trolley bus shed was added to the site in 1914/15 and a large works was built behind the depot in 1915-22. From 1930 trolley buses started to occupy part of the tram shed.

Closed: May 6th, 1950 and subsequently used by trolley buses until 1972 and then omnibuses.

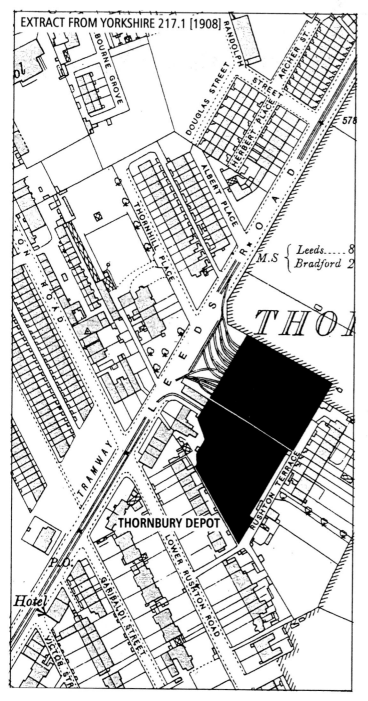

EXTRACT FROM YORKSHIRE 217.1 [1908]

THORNBURY DEPOT

Sheffield Road

Location: *At SE35300513, on the east side of Upper Barnsley Road.*

Opened: October 31st, 1902, by the Barnsley & District Electric Traction Co. Ltd (Name changed to Barnsley & District Traction Co. in 1910).

Traction System: Overhead Electric.

Gauge: 4ft 8.5in.

Description: A 4TS dead ended tram shed & works constructed in galvanized iron sheeting. Omnibus garages were later added on the site from 1913 onwards.

Closed: September 3rd, 1930 and later demolished to facilitate the construction of a new omnibus depot.

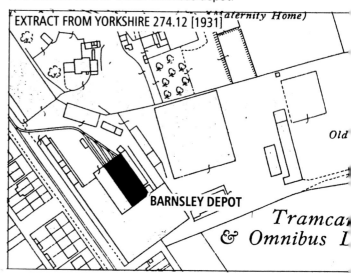

EXTRACT FROM YORKSHIRE 274.12 [1931]

BARNSLEY DEPOT

RAWMARSH

Dale Road

Location: *At SE44009670, on the east side of Dale Rd, south of Kilnhurst Road, Rawmarsh.*

Opened: February 6th, 1907 by the Mexborough & Swinton Tramways Company.

Traction System: Stud, until 1908, and then Overhead Electric.

Gauge: 4ft 8.5in.

Description: An 8TS dead ended tram shed and works constructed in corrugated iron sheeting.

Closed: With the system on March 9th, 1929 and subsequently utilized for scrapping tram cars, prior to its use as a trolley bus depot. It was later demolished and replaced by a new omnibus garage.

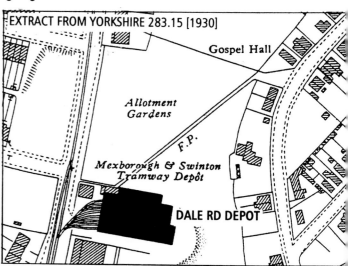

EXTRACT FROM YORKSHIRE 283.15 [1930]

DALE RD DEPOT

Terry Street

Location: Approximately at TA08933017, on the corner of Beverley Road and Terry Street.
Opened: 1877 by the Hull Street Tramways Co. Ltd.
Traction System: Horse.
Gauge: 4ft 8.5in.
Description: A timber built 1TS or 2TS dead ended tram shed and stables.
Closed: 1882.

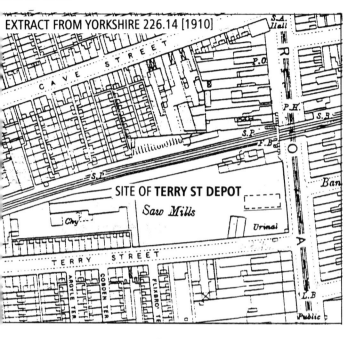

Temple Street

Location: At TA09103033, on the north side of Temple Street, east of Beverley Road.
Opened: 1882 by the Hull Street Tramways Co. Ltd and taken over by Hull Corporation on October 15th, 1896.
Traction System: Horse.
Gauge: 4ft 8.5in.
Description: A brick built 3TS dead ended tram shed and stables.
Closed: September 30th, 1899 and later let for commercial use, including a period as a dogs' home. Since demolished.

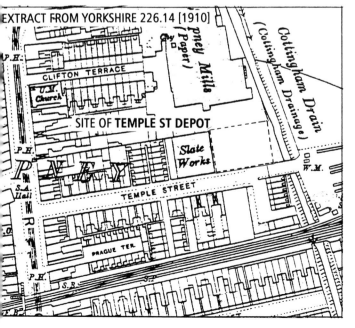

Hotham Street

Location: At TA11822937, on the west side of Hotham Street, north of Hedon Road.
Opened: May 21st, 1889 by the Drypool and Marfleet Steam Tramway Co. Ltd and purchased on January 31st, 1900 by Hull Corporation.
Traction System: Steam.
Gauge: 4ft 8.5in.
Description: A brick built 2TS dead ended tram shed and a brick built 3TS dead ended tram shed and works.
Closed: January 13th, 1901 and utilized for scrapping tram cars prior to letting out for commercial use.

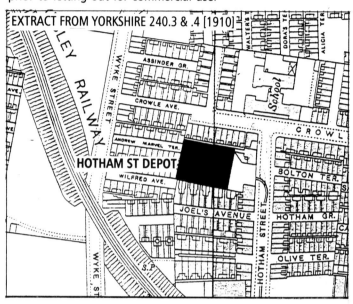

Hessle Rd

Location: At TA08552804, on the corner of Hessle Road and Regent Street.
Opened: 1877 by the Hull Street Tramways (the system had been opened on January 9th, 1875 by the Continental & General Tramway Co. Ltd and taken over on November 1st, 1876) and taken over by Hull Corporation on October 15th, 1896.
Traction System: Horse.
Gauge: 4ft 8.5in.
Description: Originally a horse depot, probably two timber built 2TS dead ended sheds and stables, it was extended over the front of the yard in 1879 and extended at the rear and along the side to give a 5th road in 1882. In December 1887 it was burnt down and rebuilt, by 1888, as a 4TS dead ended tram shed, stables and works.
Closed: May 1898.

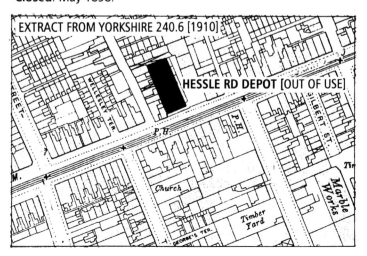

Witham

Location: *Approximately at TA10702928, on the south side of Witham.*
Opened: May 7th, 1877 by the Hull Street Tramways Co. Ltd.
Traction System: Horse.
Gauge: 4ft 8.5in.
Description: Originally a temporary horse depot, possibly a timber built 2TS tram shed and stables, it was rebuilt in brick in 1880. There was no track connection to the main line until the summer of 1880, prior to which the trams were hauled across the footpath.
Closed: 1882.

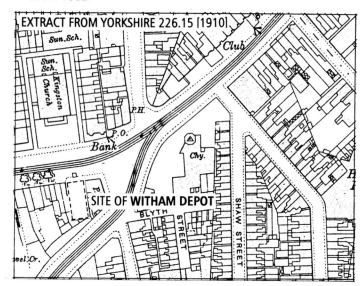

Hedon Road

Location: *At TA12952936, on the north side of Hedon Road.*
Opened: December 17th, 1903 by Hull Corporation.
Traction System: Overhead Electric.
Gauge: 4ft 8.5in.
Description: A brick built 4TS tram shed with one through road.
Closed: December 31st, 1937. In commercial use in 2000.

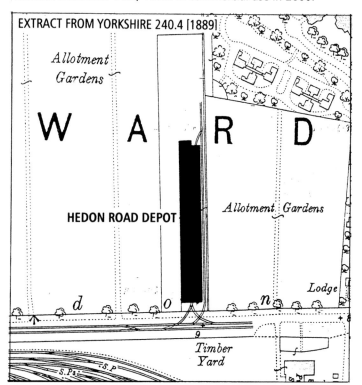

Holderness Rd [No.1] Depot

Location: *At TA11613020, on the south side of Holderness Road, opposite Jalland Street.*
Opened: 1882 by the Hull Street Tramways Co. Ltd and taken over by Hull Corporation on October 15th, 1896.
Traction System: Horse.
Gauge: 4ft 8.5in.
Description: A brick built 2TS dead ended tram shed and stables.
Closed: June 1899. Still standing in January 2000.

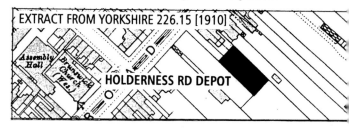

Holderness Rd [No.2] Depot

Location: *At TA12643110, on the south side of Holderness Rd, west of Aberdeen St.*
Opened: March 27th, 1903 by Hull Corporation.
Traction System: Overhead Electric.
Gauge: 4ft 8.5in.
Description: Originally a 4TS tram shed with two through roads, a 3TS shed with one through road was later added on the southern side.
Closed: February 17th, 1940 and subsequently demolished. The site is now occupied by a supermarket.

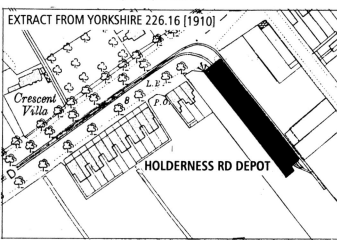

Holderness Rd [Temp] Depot

Location: *Approximately at TA11783050, on the corner of Summergangs Road and Holderness Road, by East Park.*
Opened: April 10th, 1900 by Hull Corporation.
Traction System: Overhead Electric.
Gauge: 4ft 8.5in.
Description: A temporary timber built tram shed.
Closed: 1903.

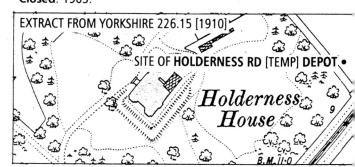

Wheeler Street

Location: At TA06592855, between Wheeler Street and the railway line, south of Anlaby Road.
Opened: July 5th, 1899 by Hull Corporation.
Traction System: Overhead Electric.
Gauge: 4ft 8.5in.
Description: Originally a medium sized brick built dead ended tram shed, by 1928 it had been extended to a 9TS depot with one through road.
Closed: September 5th, 1942 and subsequently utilized as a trolley bus depot. It was in commercial use in 2000.

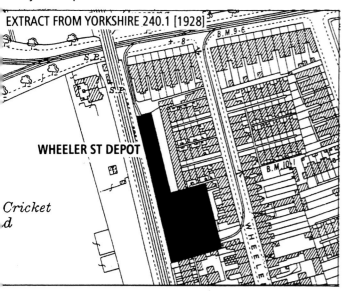

Liverpool Street

Location: At TA07272750, on the east side of Liverpool Street, south of Hessle Road.
Opened: July 5th, 1899 by Hull Corporation.
Traction System: Overhead Electric.
Gauge: 4ft 8.5in.
Description: A brick built tram shed and works with a 10TS dead ended section and a 6TS section accessed via a traverser, one track of which was connected to one of the dead ended roads by turntables.
Closed: June 30th, 1945 and subsequently utilized as an omnibus garage. Subsequently demolished, the site was unused in 2000 with the trackwork still *in situ*.

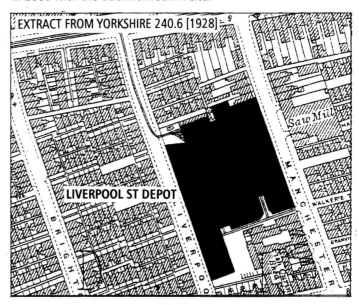

Cottingham Road

Location: At TA08393159, on the north side of Cottingham Rd west of Beverley Rd.
Opened: March 13th, 1909 by Hull Corporation.
Traction System: Overhead Electric.
Gauge: 4ft 8.5in.
Description: An 8TS dead ended tram shed. An omnibus garage, which was also utilized for trolley buses from 1937, was added on the east side in 1934.
Closed: September 3rd, 1938 and all but the office at the shed entrance was later demolished and replaced by housing.

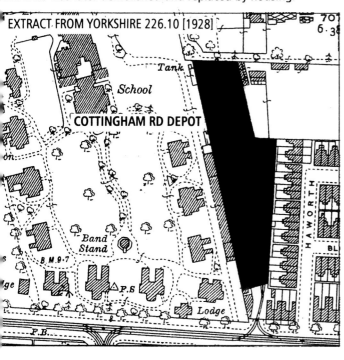

Stepney Lane

Location: At TA09263040, on the south side of Stepney Lane, east of Beverley Road.
Opened: December 8th, 1900 by Hull Corporation.
Traction System: Overhead Electric.
Gauge: 4ft 8.5in.
Description: A 3TS dead ended tram shed.
Closed: It was considered as too small and closed in 1909, later being utilized as a permanent way yard.

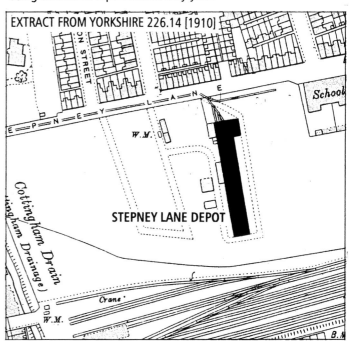

LEEDS

Hunslet Car Yard

Location: *Approximately at SE30603270, on the north west corner of Hunslet Rd and Black Bull St, by the Black Bull Inn.*
Opened: April 19th, 1874 by the Leeds Tramways Co.
Traction System: Horse.
Gauge: 4ft 8.5in.
Description: A temporary facility utilizing a yard and stables.
Closed: 1875.

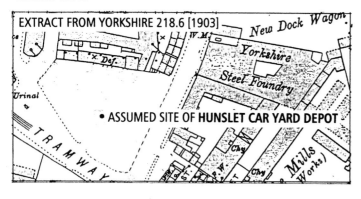

Harrison Street

Location: *At SE30353382, on the north side of Harrison Street, west of Vicar Lane.*
Opened: 1874 by the Leeds Tramways Co.
Traction System: Horse.
Gauge: 4ft 8.5in.
Description: A tram shed and stables utilized as a temporary depot.
Closed: August 1876 and subsequently demolished. The Grand Theatre was erected on the site in 1878.

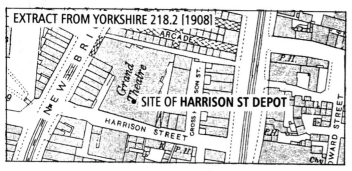

Hyde Park Stables

Location: *Approximately at SE28923553, on the north side of Hyde Park Corner.*
Opened: September 16th, 1871 by William and Daniel Busby and taken over by the Leeds Tramways Co. between March and August 1873.
Traction System: Horse.
Gauge: 4ft 8.5in.
Description: A temporary facility utilizing a yard and stables. It may also have been used as a works.
Closed: 1874.

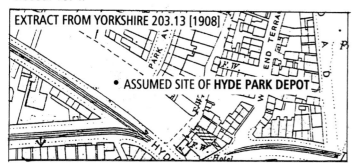

Chapeltown Depot

Location: *At SE30763665, on the west side of Harrogate Rd, north of Potternewton Lane.*
Opened: August 14th, 1876 by the Leeds Tramways Co. and taken over by Leeds Corporation on February 2nd, 1894.
Traction System: Horse, until January 2nd, 1900 and then Overhead Electric.
Gauge: 4ft 8.5in.
Description: Originally a brick built 3TS dead ended tram shed and stables, it was converted for electric working in 1899 and closed on September 9th, 1907 for rebuilding as a 7TS dead ended tram shed. This was brought into use on March 20th, 1908 and there was also a 1TS dead ended shed at the north corner capable of holding one car.
Closed: April 23rd, 1955 and subsequently utilized as a store for withdrawn tram cars prior to use by the Corporation's Central Purchasing Department.

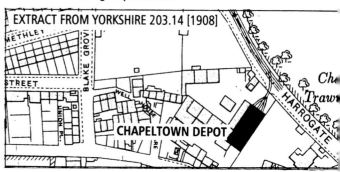

Torre Road Depot

Location: *On the south side of Torre Rd, west side of Lupton Avenue.*
Opened: Officially on April 8th, 1937 by Leeds Corporation.
Traction System: Overhead Electric.
Gauge: 4ft 8.5in.
Description: A depot complex consisting of a brick built "main shed", located at SE32353378 and accommodating omnibuses at the west end and trams at the east with eight through roads and two terminal stubs, and a 5TS dead ended "top shed" tram depot sited to the south of the main building at SE33253368.
Closed: To trams on November 19th, 1955 and subsequently used as an omnibus depot until 1996. The tram section of the "main shed" was demolished in 1996 and the "top shed" demolished in 1998.

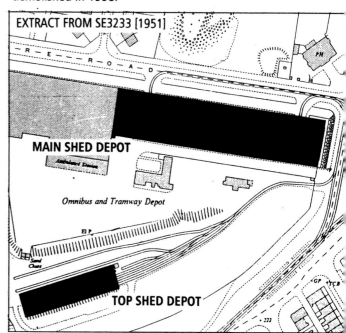

Kirkstall Road Depot & Works

Location: At SE28603374, on the south side of Kirkstall Rd.
Opened: Officially on July 29th, 1897 and for service on August 2nd, 1897 by Leeds Corporation.
Traction System: Steam, until February 6th, 1898, and Overhead Electric.
Gauge: 4ft 8.5in.
Description: A brick built 20TS dead ended tram shed, 3TS dead ended paint shop, 3TS engine shed and a 3TS repair shop linked with a traverser at the rear. After the end of steam working the engine shed became a truck repair shop and in 1905 an omnibus and motor vehicle garage was added by the entrance. This closed in 1923, with the vehicles transferring to Swinegate, and the workshops were gradually extended with major alterations undertaken in 1920 and 1931/2 resulting in the reduction in capacity of the running shed.
Closed: As a running shed on September 15th, 1931. The works closed on November 8th, 1957 and the depot was subsequently utilized as a central omnibus repair depot.

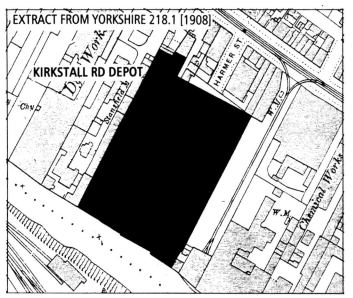

Kirkstall Depot

Location: At SE26273564, on the west side of Abbey Rd, north of Bridge Rd.
Opened: Probably November 4th, 1876 by the Leeds Tramways Co. and taken over by Leeds Corporation on February 2nd, 1894.
Traction System: Horse, until March 10th, 1892, and then Steam from April/May 1894.
Gauge: 4ft 8.5in.
Description: Originally a brick built 2TS dead ended tram shed and stables it was refurbished in 1894 for use as a temporary steam tram depot.
Closed: 1897 and subsequently demolished. The site was later utilized for a commercial yard.

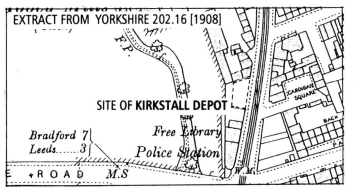

Swinegate

Location: At SE30143317, on the corner of Swinegate and Sovereign St.
Opened: October 13th, 1914 by Leeds Corporation.
Traction System: Overhead Electric.
Gauge: 4ft 8.5in.
Description: A brick built 15TS dead ended tram shed with additional storage sidings sited beneath the arches of the NER/L&NWR New Station. The depot was requisitioned by the Army on November 30th, 1914 and re-instated as a tram depot on September 26th, 1919. A corrugated iron Army hut at the rear of the site was converted into an omnibus garage in 1922 and this was demolished during 1927-31 when the tracks were extended rearwards out of the tram depot and a new 15TS dead ended shed constructed on the site of the garage and former Gas Department Works. A pw yard was added on the opposite side of Sovereign St. and the depot took over the repair work when Kirkstall Road Works closed in November 1957.
Closed: With the tramway on November 7th, 1959.

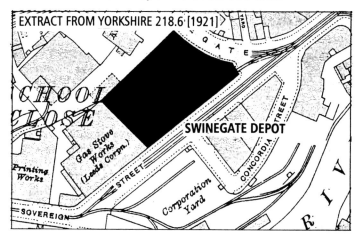

Beckett Street

Location: At SE32033480, on the north side of Stanley Rd, east of Beckett St.
Opened: November 11th, 1891 by the Thomson-Houston Co. (USA) and taken over by Leeds Corporation on August 1st, 1896.
Traction System: Overhead Electric until July 31st, 1896 and then Horse from April 25th, 1898 until just shortly before June 2nd, 1900 when the route was electrified. Overhead Electric from 1902.
Gauge: 4ft 8.5in.
Description: Originally a brick built 4TS dead ended tram shed sited adjacently to a corrugated iron temporary generating station, it was left empty after electric working ceased in 1896 until conversion to stables in 1897/8. It was rebuilt in 1902 for electric working with the car shed extended at the rear. Two further roads were later installed and, in 1913/14, three more dead ended roads added on the east side. It was later known as Stanley Road Depot.
Closed: June 13th, 1939 and utilized by the ARP during WWII and subsequently as a corporation depot. Still standing in 2000.

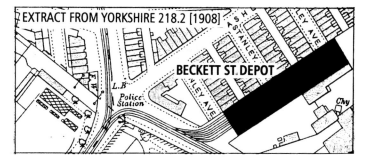

Bramley Depot

Location: At SE25033436, on the south east side of the junction of Stanningley Rd and Lower Town St.
Opened: July 9th, 1906 by Leeds Corporation.
Traction System: Overhead Electric.
Gauge: 4ft 8.5in.
Description: A brick built 7TS dead ended tram shed.
Closed: January 30th, 1949 and subsequently utilized as an omnibus garage, opening on December 4th, 1949.

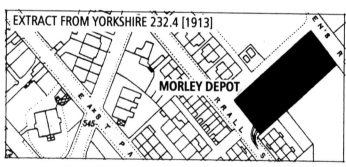

Morley Depot

Location: At SE25812735, on the east side of Worrall St, north off Fountain St, Morley.
Opened: February 19th, 1920 by Leeds Corporation.
Traction System: Overhead Electric.
Gauge: 4ft 8.5in.
Description: A 2TS dead ended tram shed, it was originally built in 1915 but utilized as a Drill Hall during World War I.
Closed: January 22nd, 1935 and later let out for commercial use.

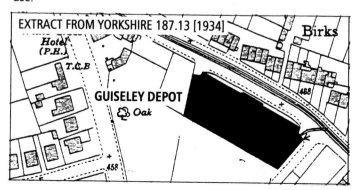

Guiseley Depot

Location: At SE18264240, on the south west side of Otley Rd, east of Bradford Rd, Guiseley.
Opened: March 9th, 1915 by Leeds Corporation.
Traction System: Overhead Electric.
Gauge: 4ft 8.5in.
Description: A stone-faced 4TS dead ended tram shed.
Closed: October 16th, 1934 and later let out for commercial use.

Headingley Depot

Location: At SE27523700, on the corner of Hollin Rd and Otley Rd.
Opened: May 25th, 1874 by the Leeds Tramways Co. and taken over by Leeds Corporation on February 2nd, 1894.
Traction System: Horse until cMay 1886. Steam from early 1884 until March 10th, 1892 and horse again from mid-1892 until cJanuary 1900. Overhead Electric from cAugust 1900.
Gauge: 4ft 8.5in.
Description: Originally a brick built 3TS dead ended tram shed and stables with a 1TS fitting shop, it was also used to house a horse bus. In 1883/4 one road was extended into a 2TS dead ended steam engine shed and, in 1886, the stables were converted to a 3TS dead ended steam car shed and the original depot altered to a 3TS dead ended steam engine shed. Temporary stables were added in 1892 and the depot utilized as the main steam loco workshops until Kirkstall Rd Works opened.
It was converted to electric working, with a modified track layout, in 1900/2 and closed on September 19th, 1934 and demolished. A new depot, with an omnibus garage alongside, was erected and opened as a running shed on June 30th, 1935.
Closed: April 3rd, 1954 and absorbed into the omnibus garage.

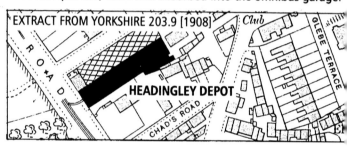

Hunslet Depot

Location: At SE31983113, on the west side of Wakefield Rd, east of Spring Grove St.
Opened: October 12th, 1875 by the Leeds Tramways Co. and taken over by Leeds Corporation on February 2nd, 1894.
Traction System: Horse, until August 23rd, 1900 and then Overhead Electric from September 1901.
Gauge: 4ft 8.5in.
Description: Originally a brick built 3TS dead ended tram shed and stables, a 2TS fitting shop was added at the rear in 1876. The depot also housed a horse bus. Upon electric working two extra roads were added on the west side and one yard road was installed in 1914 following the demolition of the stables.
Closed: December 15th, 1931 and utilized as a store until re-opening as an omnibus garage on November 7th, 1935. In 2000 it was in use as commercial premises.

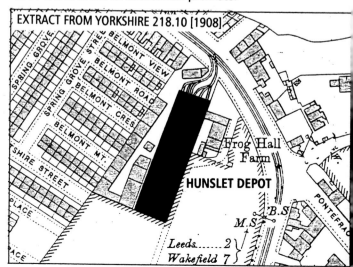

Wellington Bridge

Location: At SE28963346, on the corner of Wellington Rd and Wellington St.
Opened: March/April 1883 by the Leeds Tramways Co. and taken over by Leeds Corporation on February 2nd, 1894.
Traction System: Steam.
Gauge: 4ft 8.5in.
Description: Originally a brick built 4TS dead ended tram car and engine shed with a single yard siding, the depot was extended at the northern end with a 2TS corrugated iron roof supported on cast iron columns. Three dead ended yard roads were added on the south east side in 1894.
Closed: As a running shed in the latter half of 1898, and from the summer of 1902 it was utilized as a pw depot until the expiry of the lease on December 31st, 1908.

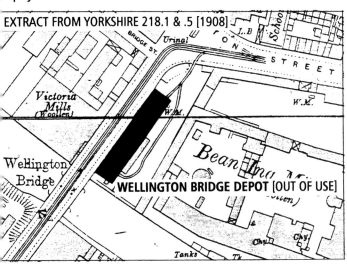
EXTRACT FROM YORKSHIRE 218.1 & .5 [1908]
WELLINGTON BRIDGE DEPOT [OUT OF USE]

North Street

Location: At SE30523388, on the south side of Sheepshanks Yard, east of Vicar Lane.
Opened: Early 1888 by the Leeds Tramways Co.
Traction System: Horse.
Gauge: 4ft 8.5in.
Description: Originally a horse bus depot and stables it was acquired in 1882. An access track, two dead ended yard roads and a 2TS dead ended covered workshop area were installed in 1888.
Closed: With the end of horse working on October 13th, 1901. Upon the expiry of the lease on May 31st, 1902 it was utilized as horse trading premises. Demolished in 1967 to make way for a new road scheme.

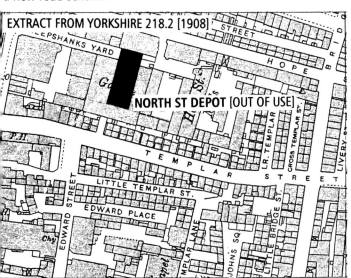
EXTRACT FROM YORKSHIRE 218.2 [1908]
NORTH ST DEPOT [OUT OF USE]

MIDDLESBROUGH

Newport Road

Location: At NZ48321979, on the south side of Newport Rd, east of Parliament Rd.
Opened: November/December 1874 by the Middlesbrough & Stockton Tramways Co., taken over by the Imperial Tramways Co. Ltd in August 1878 and converted to electric working as Middlesbrough, Stockton & Thornaby Electric Tramways. Taken over by Middlesbrough Corporation on April 3rd, 1921.
Traction System: Horse, until December 24th, 1897, and then Overhead Electric from May 21st, 1898.
Gauge: 4ft 8.5in (until 1898), 3ft 7in.
Description: Originally a 3TS dead ended tram shed, it was enlarged to a 6TS dead ended tram shed upon electrification.
Closed: 1922. The site was later utilized as a coal yard.

Parliament Road

Location: At NZ48441970, on the north side of Parliament Rd, east of Newport Rd.
Opened: April 1922 by Middlesbrough Corporation.
Traction System: Overhead Electric.
Gauge: 3ft 7in.
Description: A 7TS dead ended tram shed and works.
Closed: With the system on June 9th, 1934.

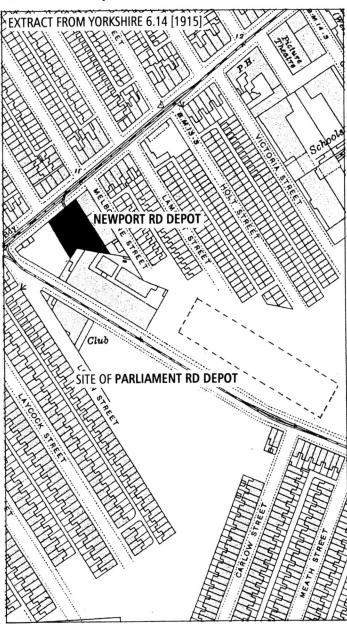
EXTRACT FROM YORKSHIRE 6.14 [1915]
NEWPORT RD DEPOT
SITE OF PARLIAMENT RD DEPOT

Brightside

Location: At SK38529050, in the yard of The Bridge Inn, on the corner of Brightside Lane and Weedon St.
Opened: 1885 by the Sheffield Tramways Co. and taken over by Sheffield Corporation on July 11th, 1896.
Traction System: Horse.
Gauge: 4ft 8.5in.
Description: A depot probably consisting of two tracks utilizing a railway arch and covered yard.
Closed: 1900. The site is now used as the car park for the Bridge Inn and the railway arches are still *in situ*.

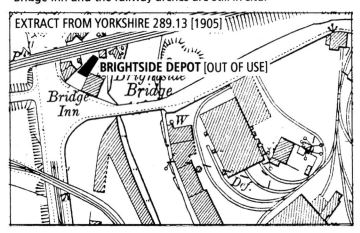

Tinsley

Location: At SK39128029, on the corner of Weedon St. and Sheffield Rd, Tinsley.
Opened: October 6th, 1873 by the Sheffield Tramways Co. as a stables and opened as a running shed on May 7th, 1874. Taken over by Sheffield Corporation on July 11th, 1896.
Traction System: Horse, until 1899, and then Overhead Electric from September 6th, 1899.
Gauge: 4ft 8.5in.
Description: Originally a brick built tram shed, stables and workshops, to facilitate electric working it was converted and enlarged to a 13TS dead ended tram shed, with part of it utilized as a paint shop, and a 3TS body shop.
Closed: The body shop was damaged by fire on August 12th, 1910, with the work moving to Nether Edge Depot, and the paint shop closed in 1929 and moved to Queen's Road Depot. It closed as a running shed on October 3rd, 1959 and was then utilized as a store for tram cars awaiting scrapping until the system closed on October 8th, 1960. It was subsequently let out for a variety of uses, including as the premises of the *Sheffield Bus Museum*.

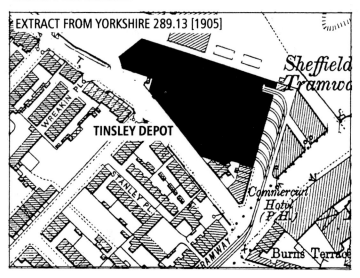

Nether Edge

Location: At SK34148480, on the south side of Machon Bank Rd, west of Nether Edge Rd.
Opened: December 24th, 1877 by the Sheffield Tramways Co. and taken over by Sheffield Corporation on July 11th, 1896.
Traction System: Horse, until 1910, and then Overhead Electric.
Gauge: 4ft 8.5in.
Description: A brick built 2TS dead ended tram shed.
Closed: As a running shed for horse working by the summer of 1910. Following the fire at Tinsley Depot it was converted and used for the assembly of electric tramcars until Shoreham St Depot opened in 1911. At the same time the body shop moved to Queen's Road and the depot continued in use, as a works until final closure in 1915. It was subsequently demolished.

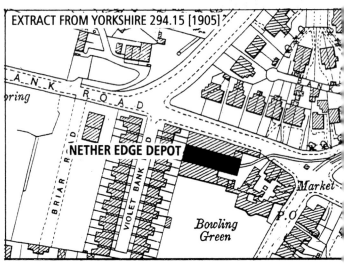

Heeley

Location: At SK35068472, on the south side of Albert Rd, east of London Rd South, Heeley.
Opened: October 29th, 1877 by the Sheffield Tramways Co. and taken over by Sheffield Corporation on July 11th, 1896.
Traction System: Horse.
Gauge: 4ft 8.5in.
Description: A 2TS dead ended tram shed, it also housed omnibuses.
Closed: 1901 and let out for commercial use. By 2000 it was in use as a car repair garage.

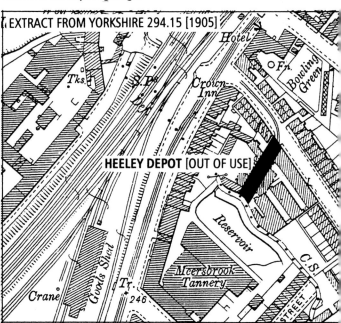

Hillsborough

Location: At SK33088960, on the north side of Holme Lane, west of Middlewood Road, Hillsborough.
Opened: May 19th, 1877 by the Sheffield Tramways Co. and taken over by Sheffield Corporation on July 11th, 1896.
Traction System: Horse, until November 11th, 1902 and then Overhead Electric from May 30th, 1903.
Gauge: 4ft 8.5in.
Description: Originally a 3TS dead ended tram shed and stables, following the cessation of horse working it was utilized as an electric tramcar store until it was reconstructed in brick and re-opened as an 8TS shed for electric working on March 30th, 1914.
Closed: April 1954 and subsequently demolished although the entrance portico was retained for access to the Tramways Medical Centre which now occupies the site.

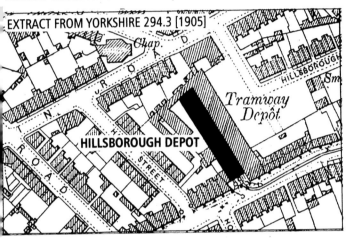
EXTRACT FROM YORKSHIRE 294.3 [1905]
HILLSBOROUGH DEPOT

Shoreham Street

Location: At SE35648671, on the corner of Leadmill Rd and Shoreham St.
Opened: February 21st, 1911 by Sheffield Corporation.
Traction System: Overhead Electric.
Gauge: 4ft 8.5in.
Description: A brick built 12TS tram shed with two access roads at the north end of the building. Between February 8th, 1913 and the summer of 1919, omnibuses were housed in a covered yard alongside the depot and a new omnibus depot was added at the rear in 1940.
Closed: February 28th, 1959. It was adapted in 1963 to form part of the Leadmill Omnibus Garage and by 2000 it had been vacated to allow for redevelopment.

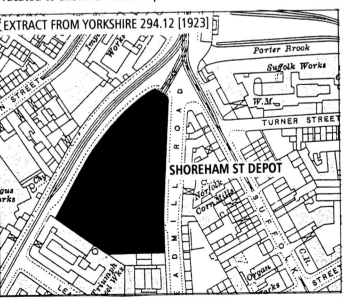
EXTRACT FROM YORKSHIRE 294.12 [1923]
SHOREHAM ST DEPOT

Queen's Road

Location: At SE35708581, on the corner of Queen's Rd and Charlotte Rd.
Opened: July 18th, 1900 by Sheffield Corporation.
Traction System: Overhead Electric.
Gauge: 4ft 8.5in.
Description: Originally only a temporary shed, in 1901 it was reconstructed as a brick built 7TS dead ended tram shed and works.
Closed: 1929 as a running shed. The tram shed was converted to a paint shop and the depot utilized for car building and as a repair works until closure of the system on October 8th, 1960. It then saw use as an omnibus works until demolition. The site is now occupied by a retail park.

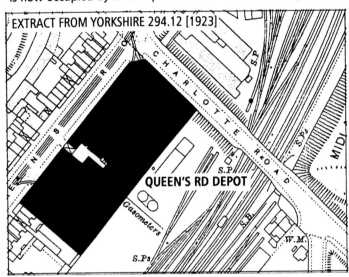
EXTRACT FROM YORKSHIRE 294.12 [1923]
QUEEN'S RD DEPOT

Tenter Street

Location: At SK35208755, on the south side of the corner of Tenter St and Silver St.
Opened: September 20th, 1929 by Sheffield Corporation.
Traction System: Overhead Electric.
Gauge: 4ft 8.5in.
Description: A two storey building consisting of a brick built 22TS dead ended tram shed with an omnibus garage above.
Closed: With the tramway on October 8th, 1960 and converted to an omnibus garage. It was subsequently demolished.

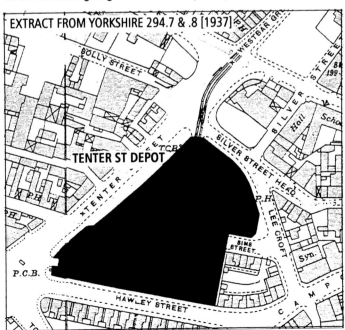
EXTRACT FROM YORKSHIRE 294.7 & .8 [1937]
TENTER ST DEPOT

Crookes

Location: At SK32938756, on the corner of Pickmere Rd and Fitzgerald Rd, Crookes.
Opened: In stages during 1922 by Sheffield Corporation.
Traction System: Overhead Electric.
Gauge: 4ft 8.5in.
Description: By completion it was a brick built 11TS dead ended tram shed.
Closed: June 1st, 1957 and subsequently demolished.

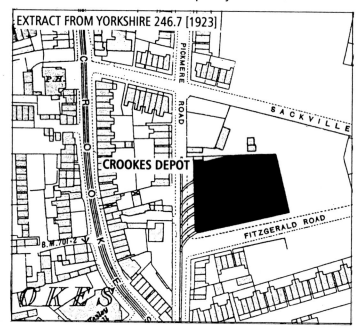

The City of Hull Tramways **Wheeler Street Depot** in existence in 2000 and w... a good example of the system's uncommon centre-grooved rail *in situ*.

RJ Buckley (See Page 11

Golden Ball Depot

Location: At SK38138905, at the rear of the Golden Ball, on the corner of Attercliffe Road and Old Hall Road.
Opened: Officially on October 6th, 1873 by the Sheffield Tramways Co. prior to public running on the following day.
Traction System: Horse.
Gauge: 4ft 8.5in.
Description: A temporary depot. No details are known.
Closed: Probably 1874 upon the opening of Tinsley Depot.

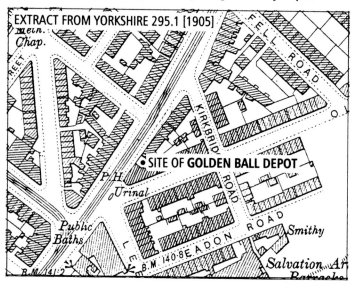

ROTHERHAM

Rawmarsh Road

Location: At SK43359397, on the east side of Rawmarsh Road.
Opened: January 31st, 1903 by Rotherham Corporation.
Traction System: Overhead Electric.
Gauge: 4ft 8.5in.
Description: Originally a 5TS dead ended tram shed, it was enlarged in 1903 and in 1938 to an 11TS depot and works. It also housed trolley buses from October 1912 and omnibuses from 1915.
Closed: To trams, along with the system, on November 13th, 1949. It was later demolished and the site is partially occupied by a canal wharf.

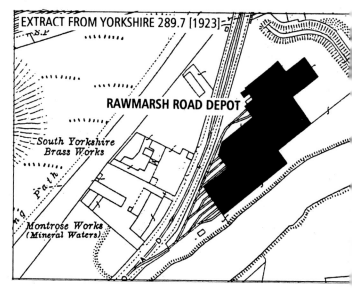

NB. The South Yorkshire Supertram 4ft 8.5in gauge overhead electric system, which opened on March 21st, 1994, has a depot at Nunnery on the west side of Woodburn Road but this is not a running shed and consists of a 3TS workshop and stabling sidings. (See *Appendix*, P.160)

Highroad Well

Location: At SE07222502, on the corner of Spring Hall Lane and Gibraltar Rd.
Opened: June 29th 1898 by Halifax Corporation.
Traction System: Overhead Electric.
Gauge: 3ft 6in.
Description: A brick built 6TS dead ended tram shed.
Closed: August 1902 and subsequently utilized as a works until commandeered by the Army in WW1. From 1920 it was in use as a motor garage until 1924 when it was taken over by the Corporation Electricity Department

EXTRACT FROM YORKSHIRE 230.12 [1907]

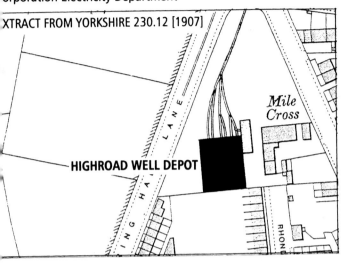

Skircoat Road

Location: At SE09402422, on the corner of Skircoat Rd and Shaw Hill.
Opened: August 1902 by Halifax Corporation.
Traction System: Overhead Electric.
Gauge: 3ft 6in.
Description: Originally a brick built 12TS through road tram shed and works a 6TS dead ended shed was added on the north part of the site in 1928. Omnibuses were also accommodated from October 17th, 1912 until 1927 when an adjacent garage opened and trolley buses were also housed from July 21st, 1921 until October 24th, 1926.
Closed: To trams on the closure of the system on February 14th, 1939 and subsequently utilized as an omnibus garage.

EXTRACT FROM YORKSHIRE 231.9 [1907]

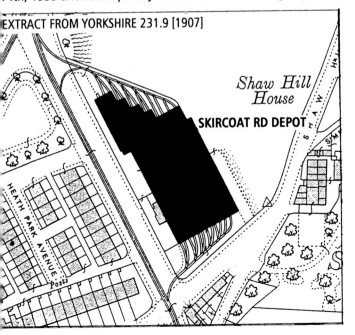

Greyfriars Road

Location: In Greyfriars Rd, on the east side of French Gate.
Traction System: Overhead Electric.
Gauge: 4ft 8.5in.

SOUTH DEPOT

Opened: June 2nd, 1902 by Doncaster Corporation.
Description: Originally a brick built 5TS dead ended tram shed, located at SE57270358, a 2TS dead ended extension was added in 1916.

NORTH DEPOT

Opened: 1920 by Doncaster Corporation.
Description: A brick built 3TS dead ended tram shed located at SE57160359.

Closed: Both depots closed, along with the tramway, on June 8th, 1935, with the South Depot being further utilized as a trolley bus depot until the system closed on December 14th, 1963. Demolished in 1983, the site is now occupied by a supermarket.

EXTRACT FROM YORKSHIRE 277.13 [1930]

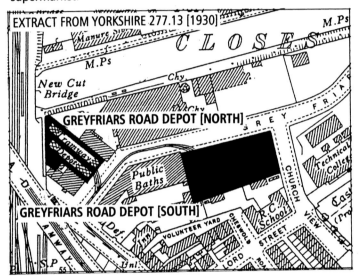

Marsh Gate

Location: Approximately at SE56850380, on the north side of Marsh Gate.
Opened: October 27th, 1902 by Doncaster Corporation.
Traction System: Overhead Electric.
Gauge: 4ft 8.5in.
Description: A 2TS dead ended tram shed converted from a barn to serve as a temporary depot whilst the new North Bridge was being constructed over the GNR main line. It was blown down and re-erected in 1904.
Closed: Prior to the opening of the North Bridge on May 12th, 1910 when it was demolished to make way for a new approach road to the bridge.

EXTRACT FROM YORKSHIRE 277.13 [1906]

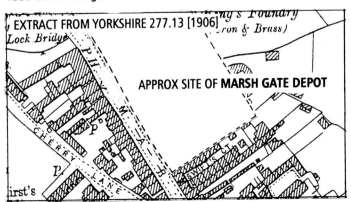

HUDDERSFIELD

Northumberland Street

Location: At SE1458169 over the track in the middle of Lord St, south of Northumberland Street.
Opened: January 11th, 1883 by Huddersfield Corporation.
Traction System: Steam.
Gauge: 4ft 7.75in.
Description: A temporary timber built depot.
Closed: It was blown down in a gale on January 26th, 1883, re-assembled and finally closed later in the year.

Northumberland Street

Location: At SE14561693, on the south west corner of Lord St and Northumberland St.
Opened: 1883 by Huddersfield Corporation.
Traction System: Steam, Horse from May 9th, 1895.
Gauge: 4ft 7.75in.
Description: An ex-circus building utilized as a timber built tram shed.
Closed: 1887 and subsequently demolished.

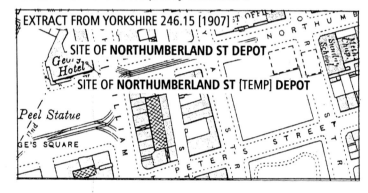

Longroyd Bridge

Location: At SE13651608, on the north side of St Thomas's Rd east of Thornton Road.
Opened: February 14th, 1901 by Huddersfield Corporation.
Traction System: Overhead Electric.
Gauge: 4ft 7.75in.
Description: An 8TS dead ended tram shed constructed in steel sheeting and a concrete built 13TS dead ended tram shed which opened on July 21st, 1921 and was also utilized by trolley buses from December 4th, 1933.
Closed: The 8TS building closed in 1909 and was used as a store. The depot closed to trams on November 5th, 1938 and was utilized as a trolley bus garage.

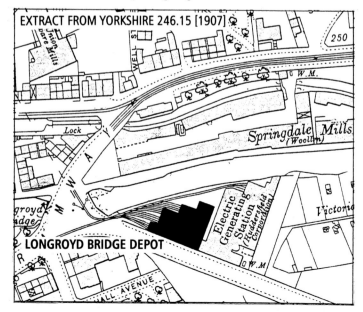

Great Northern Street

Location: At SE14721737, on the east side of Great Northern Street, north of Beaumont Street.
Opened: July 20th, 1887 by Huddersfield Corporation.
Traction System: Horse, until August 9th, 1888, Steam until June 21st, 1902 and then Overhead Electric.
Gauge: 4ft 7.75in.
Description: Originally a brick built 12TS dead ended tram shed with a stone facade, it was rebuilt in 1908 as an 11TS dead ended tram shed and extended at the rear in 1912.
Closed: 1908, re-opened on January 11th, 1909 and closed as a running shed in 1921, after which it was utilized as the main workshops. Re-opened as a tram shed on November 5th, 1938 when Longroyd Bridge closed, and finally closed on June 29th, 1940. Still standing in 1983.

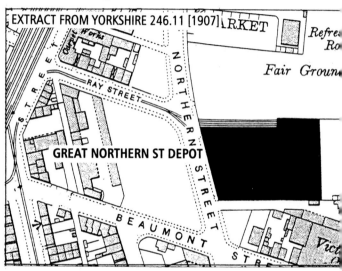

KEIGHLEY

South Street

Location: At SE05934040, on the corner of Queen's Road and South Street.
Opened: May 8th, 1889 by the Keighley Tramways Co. Ltd and taken over by Keighley Corporation on January 15th, 1901.
Traction System: Horse (until May 28th, 1904) and then Overhead Electric.
Gauge: 4ft.
Description: Originally a 2TS dead ended tram shed, upon electrification it was extended on the south side to a 4TS dead ended building. In 1909 a trolley bus depot was built at the rear with a separate entrance in Acacia Street.
Closed: December 17th, 1924 and utilized as an omnibus and trolley bus depot until the end of Corporation services in 1932. Prior to use as commmercial premises withdrawn omnibuses were stored in the building until 1935.

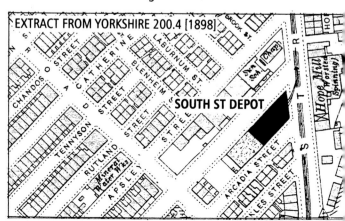

Moorhead Lane

Location: At SE13653766, on the south east corner of Bingley Road and Moorhead Lane.

Opened: August 1882 by Joseph Speight, taken over in 1884 by Maurice Jones and taken over again in 1885 by Bradford Steam Tramways Ltd. It was taken over in March 1888 by Bradford & District Tramways Ltd and then purchased by Shipley Council in 1893 which leased it to the Bradford Tramways & Omnibus Co. On April 30th, 1904 it was finally taken over by Bradford Corporation.

Traction System: Horse (until 1893), Steam (until April 29th, 1902) and then Overhead Electric.

Gauge: 4ft.

Description: Originally a 2TS dead ended tram shed it was converted to a 2TS brick built dead ended tram shed for steam working.

Closed: Temporarily in May 1883 and October 9th, 1891, and then permanently in August 1904 at which point it was sold for commercial use. It still stood in 1984, in use as a warehouse.

Hirst Lane [Saltaire] Depot

Location: At SE13573774, on the north east corner of Hirst Lane and Bingley Road.

Opened: August 1904 by Bradford Corporation.

Traction System: Overhead Electric.

Gauge: 4ft.

Description: A brick built 6TS dead ended tram shed

Closed: May 6th, 1939 and utilized as a trolley bus depot until August 20th, 1963.

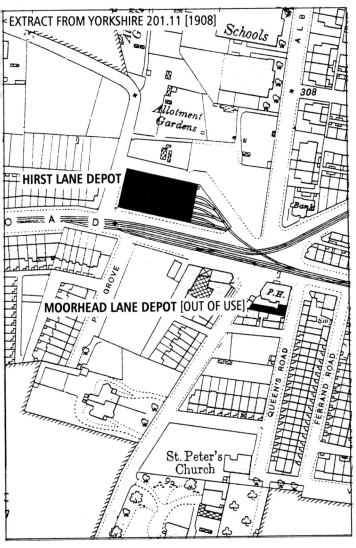

EXTRACT FROM YORKSHIRE 201.11 [1908]

Exhibition Road

Location: At SE14003780, on the north east corner of Saltaire Road and Exhibition Road.

Opened: July 23rd, 1903 by the Mid-Yorkshire Tramways Company and taken over by Bradford Corporation on April 30th, 1904.

Traction System: Overhead Electric.

Gauge: 4ft.

Description: A 5TS dead ended tram shed. The depot was built whilst the site was being used for tram servicing and stabling.

Closed: August 1904 and demolished in the same year. In 1984 the site was occupied by a car park.

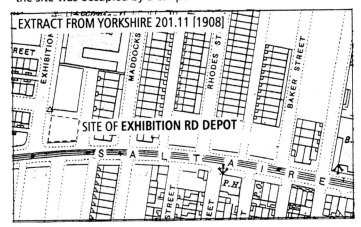

EXTRACT FROM YORKSHIRE 201.11 [1908]

SITE OF EXHIBITION RD DEPOT

Carlinghow

Location: At SE23742488, on the north side of Bradford Road, east of Carlinghow..

Opened: July 25th, 1874 by the Dewsbury, Batley & Birstal Tramway Company, taken over by the British Electric Traction Co. Ltd in January 1902 and worked by the Yorkshire (Woollen District) Electric Tramways Ltd from November 23rd, 1905.

Traction System: Horse (until 1881), Steam (from April 10th, 1880 until September 1905) and then Overhead Electric.

Gauge: 4ft 8.5in.

Description: Originally a stone built 5TS dead ended tram shed and stables accessed by one track and three turntables, a 3TS dead ended extension was added on the east side in c1886.

Closed: April 3rd, 1932 and still stood in 1980, in commercial use.

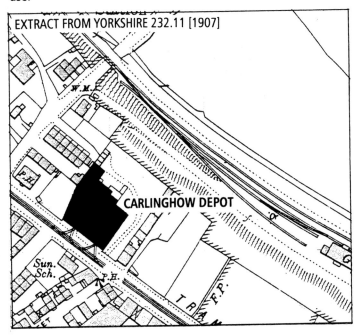

EXTRACT FROM YORKSHIRE 232.11 [1907]

CARLINGHOW DEPOT

LIVERSEDGE
Frost Hill

Location: At SE20992377, on the north east corner of Frost Hill and Vernon Road.
Opened: April 24th, 1903 by the Yorkshire (Woollen District) Electric Tramways Ltd.
Traction System: Overhead Electric.
Gauge: 4ft 8.5in.
Description: A brick built 11TS dead ended tram shed. A 2TS paint and repair shed was added in 1904.
Closed: October 31st, 1934 and subsequently utilized as an omnibus depot.

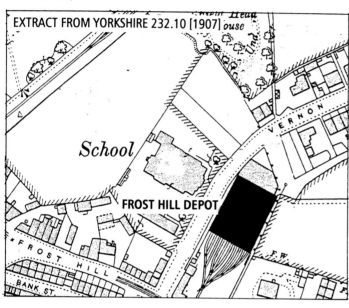

EXTRACT FROM YORKSHIRE 232.10 [1907]

FROST HILL DEPOT

OSSETT
Church Street

Location: At SE27732104, on the east side of Church St, south of Springstone Avenue.
Opened: November 11th, 1908 by the National Electric Construction Co. Ltd as the Dewsbury, Ossett & Soothill Nether Tramways.
Traction System: Overhead Electric.
Gauge: 4ft 8.5in.
Description: A brick built 4TS dead ended tram shed.
Closed: October 19th, 1933. By 1980 it was in use as an electricity board depot.

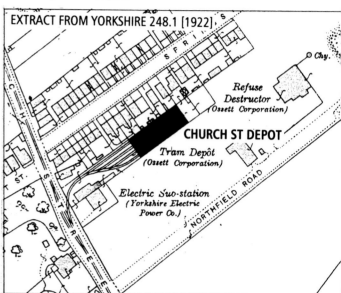

EXTRACT FROM YORKSHIRE 248.1 [1922]

CHURCH ST DEPOT

DEWSBURY
Savile Town

Location: At SE24632121, on the north side of Mill Street, east of Savile Road.
Opened: February 18th, 1903 by the Yorkshire (Woollen District) Electric Tramways Ltd.
Traction System: Overhead Electric.
Gauge: 4ft 8.5in.
Description: A brick built 4TS dead ended tram shed.
Closed: April 3rd, 1932 and subsequently utilized as an omnibus depot.

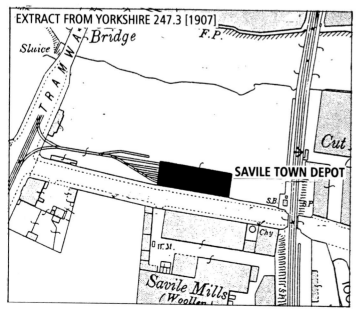

EXTRACT FROM YORKSHIRE 247.3 [1907]

SAVILE TOWN DEPOT

CASTLEFORD
Wheldon Lane

Location: At SE43242608, on the south side of Wheldon Lane.
Opened: October 29th, 1906 by the Yorkshire (West Riding) Electric Tramways Co. Ltd.
Traction System: Overhead Electric.
Gauge: 4ft 8.5in
Description: A brick built 4TS dead ended tram shed.
Closed: November 1st, 1925 and subsequently utilized as an omnibus depot.

EXTRACT FROM YORKSHIRE 234.7 [1908]

WHELDON LANE DEPOT

Belle Isle Depot

Location: At SE33741956, on the west side of Barnsley Road, north of Porto Bello Road.

Opened: August 15th, 1904 by the Wakefield & District Light Railway Co. Ltd and taken over by the Yorkshire (West Riding) Electric Tramways Co. Ltd in 1905.

Traction System: Overhead Electric.

Gauge: 4ft 8.5in.

Description: A brick built 5TS dead ended tram shed and works. An omnibus garage was added in 1922.

Closed: July 25th, 1932 and subsequently utilized as an omnibus garage.

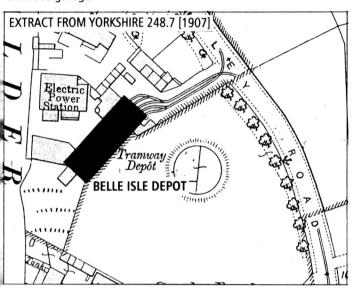

Rothwell Haigh

Location: At SE32792924, on the north east corner of Wood Lane and Wakefield Road.

Opened: August 15th, 1904 by the Wakefield & District Light Railway Co. Ltd and taken over by the Yorkshire (West Riding) Electric Tramways Co. Ltd in 1905.

Traction System: Overhead Electric.

Gauge: 4ft 8.5in.

Description: A 3TS dead ended tram shed.

Closed: May 31st, 1932 and sold for commercial use in 1933. By 1980 it was being utilized by a motor engineering firm.

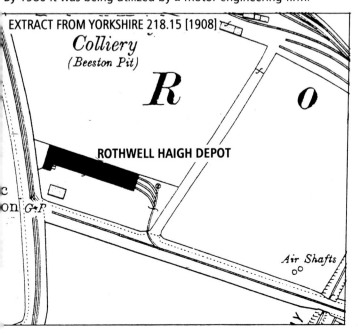

Sowood Lane

Location: At SE28471910, on the west side of Sowood Lane, South Ossett.

Opened: August 15th, 1904 by the Wakefield & District Light Railway Co. Ltd and taken over by the Yorkshire (West Riding) Electric Tramways Co. Ltd in 1905.

Traction System: Overhead Electric.

Gauge: 4ft 8.5in.

Description: A 3TS dead ended tram shed.

Closed: July 25th, 1932 and sold for commercial use in 1933. By 1980 it was being utilized as a county council highways depot.

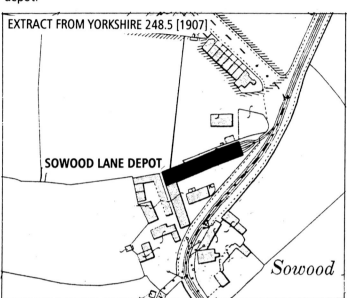

Car Barns

Location: At SE40920232, on the west side of Brampton Road, south of Wath Road.

Opened: July 14th, 1924 by the four local UDCs and operated as the Dearne District Light Railways.

Traction System: Overhead Electric.

Gauge: 4ft 8.5in.

Description: A brick built 6TS dead ended tram shed.

Closed: September 30th, 1933 and subsequently utilized as an omnibus depot. It was completely rebuilt after World War II.

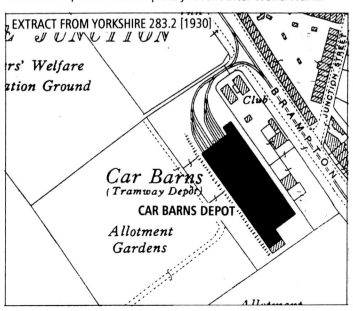

YORK

Plough Inn Depot

Location: At SE61034907, by The Plough Inn, on the west side of Fulford Road, Fulford.
Opened: October 27th, 1880 by the York Imperial Tramways Co.
Traction System: Steam, until December 7th, 1880, and Horse.
Gauge: 4ft.
Description: A temporary depot and stables.
Closed: 1882.

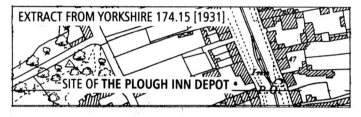

EXTRACT FROM YORKSHIRE 174.15 [1931]

SITE OF **THE PLOUGH INN DEPOT** •

Fulford Rd [Fulford Cross] Depot

Location: At SE60825014, on the west side of Fulford Road, Fulford Cross.
Opened: 1882 by the York Imperial Tramways Co., taken over by the City of York Tramways Co. on January 1st, 1886 and taken over by York Corporation on February 2nd, 1909.
Traction System: Horse, until September 7th, 1909, and, from January 20th, 1910, Overhead Electric.
Gauge: 4ft (until September 7th, 1909), 3ft 6in (from January 20th, 1910).
Description: Originally a brick built 3TS tram shed and stables, it was lengthened and converted for electric working in 1909/10 with 2 workshop roads added on the north side. An extension containing a 4th dead ended road was added on the south side in 1912 and it was enlarged again in 1928/9. An omnibus and trolley bus garage was added on the south side in 1931.
Closed: With the system on November 16th, 1935. It was later demolished in 1995 to make way for a supermarket.

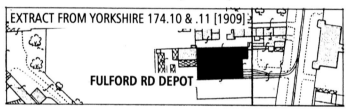

EXTRACT FROM YORKSHIRE 174.10 & .11 [1909]

FULFORD RD DEPOT

Acomb

Location: At SE57885146, on the south side of Acomb Rd.
Opened: June 9th, 1910 by York Corporation.
Traction System: Overhead Electric.
Gauge: 3ft 6in.
Description: A temporary timber built 1TS dead ended tram shed to serve the Acomb extension whilst Holgate Bridge was being rebuilt.
Closed: As a tram shed on August 1st, 1911 and subsequently utilized for housing a water-car and sand-car until 1921 when the building was removed.

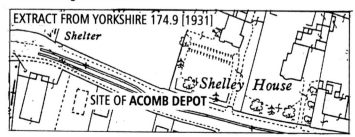

EXTRACT FROM YORKSHIRE 174.9 [1931]

Shelter

Shelley House

SITE OF **ACOMB DEPOT**

NB. A temporary horse tram shed and/or stables may have been located at The Mount in the latter years of horse working.

MEXBOROUGH

Denaby

Location: At SK48809999, on the south side of Doncaster Road at Old Toll Bar, Denaby Main.
Opened: August 31st, 1915 by the Mexborough & Swinton Tramways Company.
Traction System: Overhead Electric.
Gauge: 4ft 8.5in.
Description: A combined 1TS dead ended tram shed and trolley bus depot.
Closed: To trams on March 19th, 1928 and subsequently utilized exclusively as a trolley bus depot.

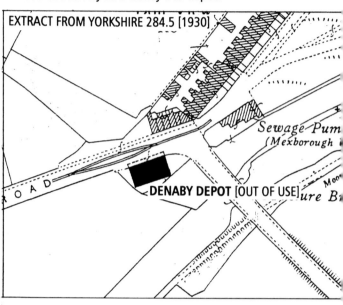

EXTRACT FROM YORKSHIRE 284.5 [1930]

Sewage Pum
(Mexborough

DENABY DEPOT [OUT OF USE]

SCARBOROUGH

Scalby Road

Location: At TA03088720, on the east side of Scalby Road and north side of Hampton Road.
Opened: May 6th, 1904 by the Scarborough Tramways Co.
Traction System: Overhead Electric.
Gauge: 3ft 6in.
Description: A 6TS dead ended tram shed.
Closed: September 30th, 1931.

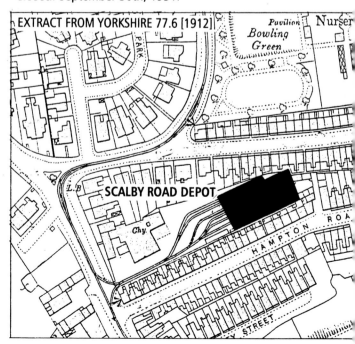

EXTRACT FROM YORKSHIRE 77.6 [1912]

Pavilion Nurser
Bowling
Green

SCALBY ROAD DEPOT

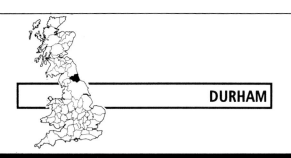

DURHAM

HARTLEPOOL

Hart Road

Location: At NZ51593443, on the north side of Cleveland Rd and corner of Hart Road.

Opened: August 2nd, 1884 by the Hartlepools Steam Tramways Co. Ltd.

Traction System: Steam.

Gauge: 3ft 6in.

Description: A dead ended tram shed, probably 4TS and constructed in brick, wood and corrugated iron.

Closed: February 21st, 1891and subsequently demolished. The site was partially utilized for housing.

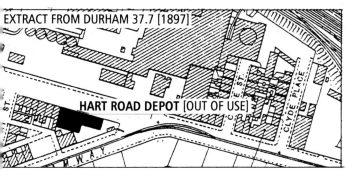

EXTRACT FROM DURHAM 37.7 [1897]

HART ROAD DEPOT [OUT OF USE]

Cleveland Road

Location: At NZ50903412, on the north side of Cleveland Road, east of the railway bridge.

Opened: May 19th, 1896 by the General Electric Tramways Co. Ltd and taken over the the British Electric Traction Co. Ltd in January 1899. The line was operated by the Hartlepool Electric Tramways Co. Ltd and was taken over on August 31st, 1912 by West Hartlepool Corporation.

Traction System: Overhead Electric.

Gauge: 3ft 6in.

Description: Originally a brick built 2TS dead ended tram shed with an internal traverser connecting to the workshop on the east side of the building, the traverser was later removed and the workshop converted to a 2TS tram shed. In 1915 the shed was extended rearwards and a new workshop added. The depot was also utilized for trolleybuses from February 28th, 1924.

Closed: To trams from March 25th, 1927. It was also utilized to accommodate omnibuses from mid-1927 for which a new shed was added, until 1982 when it was demolished.

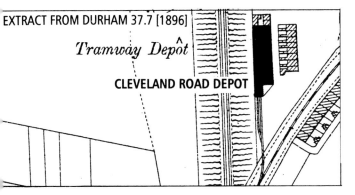

EXTRACT FROM DURHAM 37.7 [1896]

Tramway Depôt

CLEVELAND ROAD DEPOT

SUNDERLAND

Hylton Road

Location: At NZ38985725, on the north side of the junction of Hylton Road and Silksworth Row.

Opened: September 30th, 1903 by Sunderland Corporation.

Traction System: Overhead Electric.

Gauge: 4ft 8.5in.

Description: A brick built 5TS dead ended tram shed and works In March 1943 it sustained air raid damage.

Closed: January 3rd, 1954 and converted to an omnibus depot.

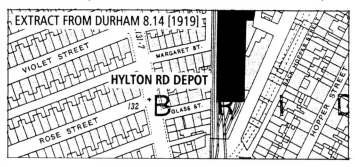

EXTRACT FROM DURHAM 8.14 [1919]

HYLTON RD DEPOT

Wheat Sheaf Depot

Location: At NZ39735787, on the east side of North Bridge St.

Opened: April 28th, 1879 by the Sunderland Tramways Co. and taken over by Sunderland Corporation on March 26th, 1900.

Traction System: Horse until February 19th, 1901. Overhead Electric working commenced on August 15th, 1900.

Gauge: 4ft 8.5in.

Description: Details of the original building are not known, but by 1897 it was a 5TS dead ended tram shed and by 1932 it had been extended on the south side to an 11TS dead ended tram shed with access to the enlarged depot via four tracks.

Closed: October 1st, 1954 and converted to an omnibus depot.

EXTRACT FROM DURHAM 8.10 [1897]

WHEAT SHEAF DEPOT

PHILADELPHIA

Philadelphia Lane

Location: At NZ33465210 on the east side of Philadelphia Lane, Philadelphia.

Opened: June 10th, 1905 by the Sunderland District Electric Tramways Ltd.

Traction System: Overhead Electric.

Gauge: 4ft 8.5in.

Description: A 6TS dead ended shed and works constructed in corrugated sheeting on a steel frame. It was extended in 1920.

Closed: July 12th, 1925 and subsequently utilized as an omnibus depot. By 1964 the depot had been enlarged and was still in use.

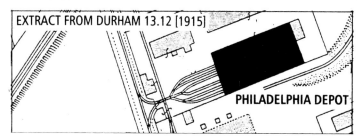

EXTRACT FROM DURHAM 13.12 [1915]

PHILADELPHIA DEPOT

Darlington Street Railroad Co. Ltd

A one mile long tramway was opened on January 1st 1862 and closed on January 8th, 1865. The existence of a horse car shed is unconfirmed.

Woodland Road

Location: *At NZ28551476, on the south side of Woodland Rd.*
Opened: October 10th, 1880 by the Stockton & Darlington Steam Tramway Co. Ltd and taken over in 1893 by the Stockton & District Tramways Company. It was taken over again in 1896 by the Imperial Tramways Co. Ltd and purchased by Darlington Corporation on January 24th, 1902.
Traction System: Horse.
Gauge: 3ft.
Description: A 2TS dead ended tram shed.
Closed: August 18th, 1903 and still in use, as a garage, in 1953.

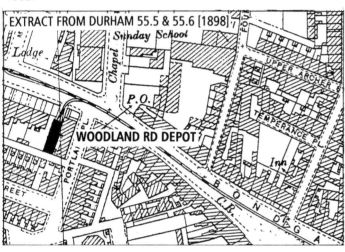

Freemans Place

Location: *At NZ29471486 on the east side of the junction of Freemans Place and Borough Road.*
Opened: June 1st, 1904 by Darlington Corporation.
Traction System: Overhead Electric.
Gauge: 3ft 6in.
Description: An 8TS dead ended tram shed.
Closed: Officially on April 10th, 1926 but it is believed that a limited service was provided for a short while until trolleybuses were able to totally take over the route.

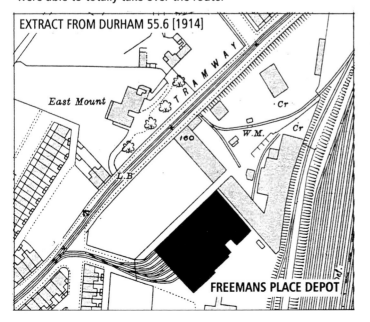

Sunderland Road

Location: *At NZ26026280, on the north side of Sunderland Rd.*
Opened: October 22nd, 1883 by the Gateshead & District Tramways Company and taken over by British Electric Traction Co. Ltd on November 12th, 1897.
Traction System: Steam, until May 8th, 1901, and then Overhead Electric.
Gauge: 4ft 8.5in.
Description: Originally a 7TS steam loco and car shed with two through roads, upon electrification it was converted to a 5TS dead ended tram shed and a 6TS dead ended shed was built on the eastern side. In 1910 the former steam shed was extended at the rear to make a long running shed and works.
Closed: August 4th, 1951. The yard was then utilized for the scrapping of tram cars.

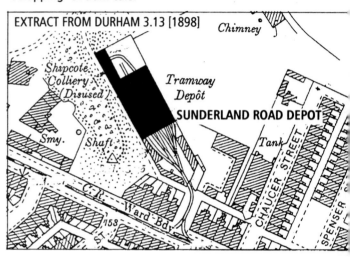

Swinburne Street

Location: *At NZ34266485, on the south side of Swinburne St, East Jarrow.*
Opened: November 29th, 1906 by the Jarrow & District Electric Traction Co. Ltd.
Traction System: Overhead Electric.
Gauge: 4ft 8.5in.
Description: A 5TS dead ended shed and works constructed in iron sheeting on a steel frame.
Closed: June 30th, 1929 and further utilized as an omnibus depot. It was demolished in 1946 and the site used for a trading estate.

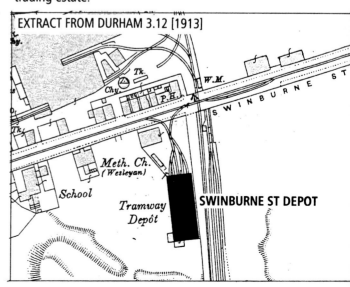

Victoria Road

Location: At NZ36426632 on the south side of Victoria Road.

Opened: August 1st, 1883 by the South Shields Tramways Co., taken over by the South Shields Tramways & Carriage Co. Ltd on March 28th, 1887 and taken over again by the British Electric Traction Company in July 1899.

Traction System: Horse.

Gauge: 3ft 6in.

Description: A medium sized dead ended tram shed with one access track.

Closed: April 30th, 1886, re-opened on March 28th, 1887 and finally closed on January 31st, 1906.

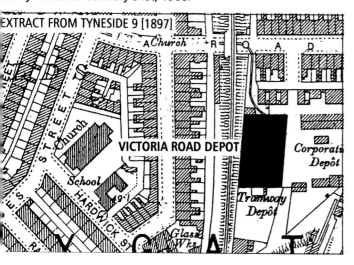

EXTRACT FROM TYNESIDE 9 [1897]

Dean Road

Location: On the south east side of Dean Road, just west of the railway bridge.

Opened: March 30th, 1906 by South Shields Corporation.

Traction System: Overhead Electric.

Gauge: 4ft 8.5in.

Description: A brick built 6TS dead ended tram shed with a 2TS works attached, located at NZ36396577. In November 1925 an additional 6TS shed and works, located at NZ36326571, was constructed to the west of the original building. From May 3rd, 1937 the buildings also accommodated trolleybuses.

Closed: The original shed was believed to be out of use by mid-1945 and the depot closed to trams on March 31st, 1946. It was then utilized for trolleybuses and then omnibuses. The buildings, although up for sale, still stood in 1999.

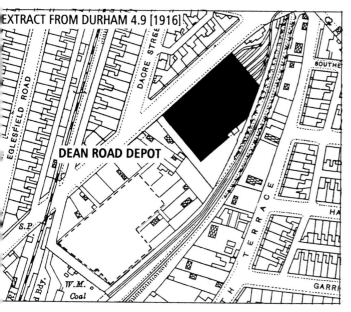

EXTRACT FROM DURHAM 4.9 [1916]

Bridge Road

Location: At NZ44781827, on the south side of Bridge Road, west of Victoria Bridge.

Opened: November 1881 by the Stockton & Darlington Steam Tramways Co. Ltd and taken over by the Stockton & District Steam Tramways Co in 1893. It was taken over again in 1896 by the Imperial Tramways Co. Ltd and finally taken over on April 3rd, 1921 by Stockton Corporation.

Traction System: Steam, until November 1897, and then Overhead Electric.

Gauge: 4ft (until 1897), 3ft 7in.

Description: Originally a 7TS dead ended steam loco and car shed, upon electrification it was re-gauged to 3ft 7in and converted to a tram shed and works.

Closed: November 1897 and re-opened upon electrification on July 13th, 1898. It was finally closed on December 31st, 1931 and further utilized as an omnibus depot.

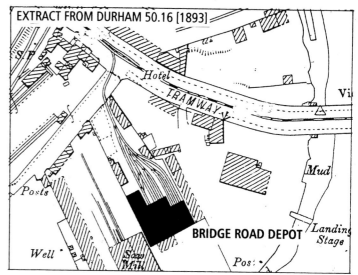

EXTRACT FROM DURHAM 50.16 [1893]

Norton

Location: At NZ44632190, on the east side of High St, just south of Billingham Road, Norton.

Opened: July 13th, 1898 by the Imperial Tramways Co. Ltd and taken over by Stockton Corporation on April 3rd, 1921.

Traction System: Overhead Electric.

Gauge: 3ft 7in.

Description: A 4TS dead ended tram shed.

Closed: December 31st, 1931 and initially utilized for scrapping tramcars before being taken over by the Highways Department.

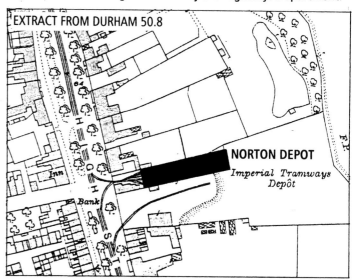

EXTRACT FROM DURHAM 50.8

Gosforth Depot

Location: At NZ24386801, on the corner of Ivy Road and High Street, Gosforth.

Opened: 1878 by Newcastle & Gosforth Tramways & Carriage Company Ltd and taken over by Newcastle Corporation in 1899.

Traction System: Horse, until April 13th, 1901 (Steam also used between 1879 & 1882), and Overhead Electric from September 29th, 1902.

Gauge: 4ft 8.5in.

Description: A 4TS dead ended tram shed.

Closed: July 1908 and then utilized for commercial use. Still standing in 1999.

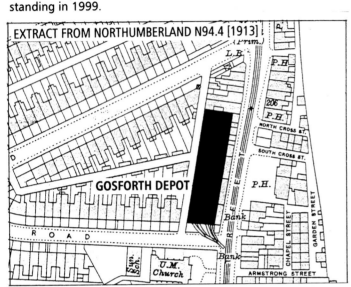

Haymarket

Location: At NZ24686487, in George Place on the west side of Haymarket.

Opened: 1878 by Newcastle & Gosforth Tramways & Carriage Company Ltd and taken over by Newcastle Corporation in 1899.

Traction System: Horse, until April 13th, 1901 and then Overhead Electric.

Gauge: 4ft 8.5in.

Description: Originally a horse tram depot it re-opened for overhead electric on December 16th, 1901 as a 6TS dead ended tram shed with one access road.

Closed: April 17th, 1948 and was subsequently utilized as an omnibus depot. It was demolished in 1958.

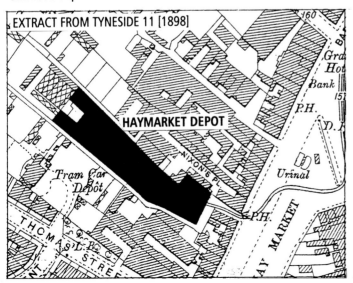

Wingrove Depot

Location: At NZ22586460, on the north side of Westgate Road, west of Wingrove Road.

Opened: 1903 by Newcastle Corporation.

Traction System: Overhead Electric.

Gauge: 4ft 8.5in.

Description: A 6TS dead ended tram shed with two access roads.

Closed: June 3rd, 1944 and subsequently utilized as a trolley bus and omnibus depot. It still stood, in commercial use, in 1999.

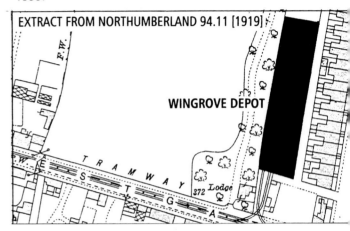

Byker Depot

Location: At NZ27526512, on the south side of Shields Road, Byker.

Opened: December 16th, 1901 by Newcastle Corporation.

Traction System: Overhead Electric.

Gauge: 4ft 8.5in.

Description: Originally a concrete built 10TS tram depot and works with eight through roads, a corrugated iron clad body shop was later added to the western side. Part of the body shop was subsequently utilized to accommodate omnibuses.

Closed: March 4th, 1950 and later used for scrapping tramcars. The site was in use, by Stagecoach Busways, in 1999.

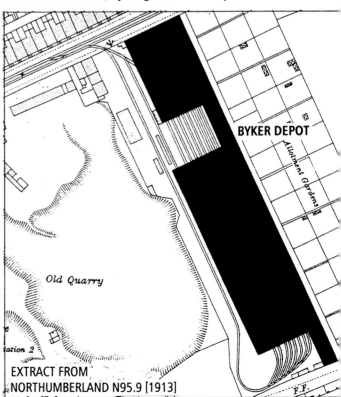

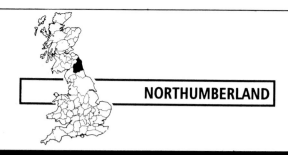

NORTHUMBERLAND

TYNEMOUTH

Suez Street

Location: At NZ35806837, in Suez Street.

Opened: 1883 by the Tynemouth & District Tramways Ltd and sold in 1884 to the North Shields & District Tramways Co. Ltd. It was sold again in 1890 to the North Shields & Tynemouth District Tramways Ltd and taken over in 1897 by the British Electric Traction Co. Ltd. The company name was changed in 1899 to the Tynemouth & District Electric Traction Co. Ltd.

Traction System: Horse, until 1884, Steam until 1900 and then Overhead Electric from March 18th, 1901.

Gauge: 3ft until 1900 and then 3ft 6in.

Description: A 2TS dead ended tram shed.

Closed: August 4th, 1931 and then used as an ambulance garage until demolition in 1959.

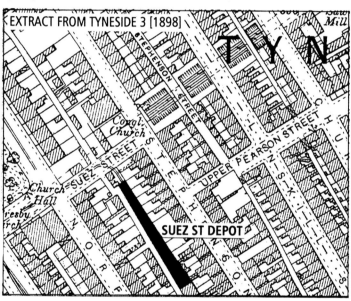

John Street

Location: At NZ36167150, on the west side of John Street, Cullercoats.

Opened: 1902 by the Tynemouth & District Electric Traction Co. Ltd.

Traction System: Overhead Electric.

Gauge: 3ft 6in.

Description: A 6TS dead ended tram shed accessed via two tracks and a traverser.

Closed: August 4th, 1931 and subsequently utilized as a paint shop for omnibuses. Still in use in 1961.

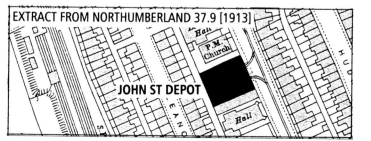

WALLSEND

Neptune Bank

Location: At NZ29806570, on the east side of Neptune Road, north of Maurice Road.

Opened: September 4th, 1902 by the Tyneside Tramways & Tramroad Company.

Traction System: Overhead Electric.

Gauge: 4ft 8.5in.

Description: A 6TS dead ended tram shed.

Closed: April 6th, 1930. Still Standing in 1961.

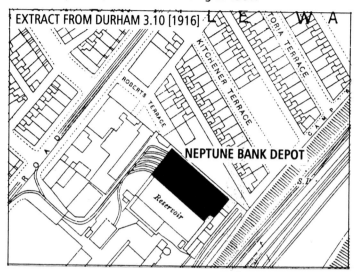

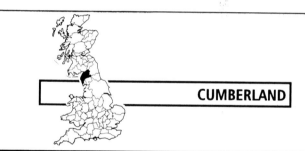

CUMBERLAND

CARLISLE

London Road

Location: At NY41015500 on the north east side of London Road.

Opened: June 30th, 1900 by the City of Carlisle Electric Tramways Co. Ltd and sold to Balfour, Beatty & Co. Ltd in November 1911.

Traction System: Overhead Electric.

Gauge: 3ft 6in.

Description: A curved brick built 4TS dead ended tram shed with two access roads.

Closed: November 21st, 1931. In 1962 it was in use as a Post Office garage.

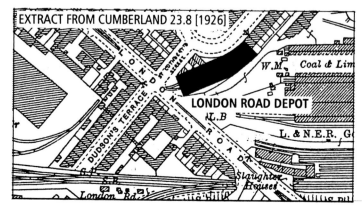

THE DIRECTORY OF
BRITISH TRAM DEPOTS

PART TWO
WALES

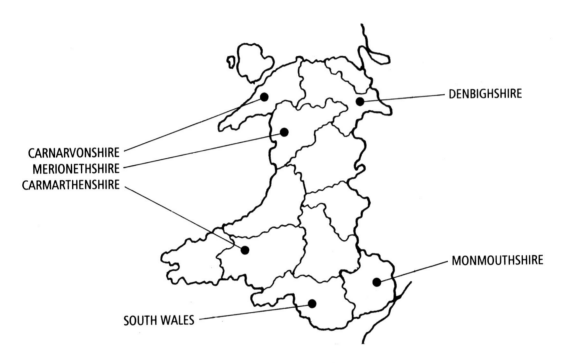

DENBIGHSHIRE

CARNARVONSHIRE
MERIONETHSHIRE
CARMARTHENSHIRE

MONMOUTHSHIRE

SOUTH WALES

ALL OTHER COUNTIES: NO DEPOTS

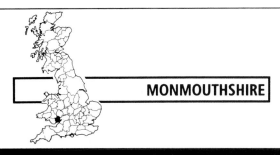

MONMOUTHSHIRE

Friars' Fields

Location: At ST31218796, on the south side of Union Road (Later Friars St), east of Commercial Street.
Opened: February 1st, 1875 by the Newport Tramways Co. Ltd.
Traction System: Horse.
Gauge: 4ft 8.5in.
Description: A 2TS dead ended tram shed.
Closed: 1886.

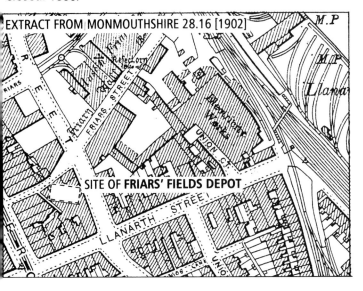

Mountjoy Street

Location: At ST31398731, on the south side of Mountjoy St, west of Commercial St.
Opened: 1886 by the Newport Tramways Co. Ltd and taken over by Newport Corporation on July 30th, 1894.
Traction System: Horse.
Gauge: 4ft 8.5in.
Description: A 3TS dead ended tram shed with one access road.
Closed: 1903 and sold.

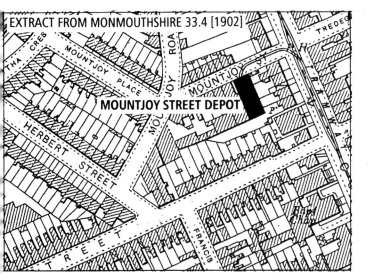

Clarence Place

Location: At ST31468857, on the north side of Clarence Place, at the east end of Newport Bridge.
Opened: 1894 by the Newport Tramways Co. Ltd and taken over by Newport Corporation on July 30th, 1894.
Traction System: Horse.
Gauge: 4ft 8.5in.
Description: A 6TS dead ended tram shed with one access road.
Closed: November 3rd, 1903.

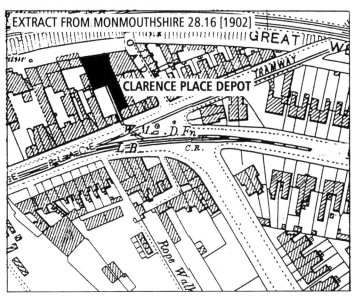

Corporation Road

Location: At ST31868792 on the south side of Corporation Rd.
Opened: April 9th, 1903 by Newport Corporation.
Traction System: Overhead Electric.
Gauge: 4ft 8.5in.
Description: A brick built 9TS dead ended tram shed adjoined by a 3TS dead ended works on the western side.
Closed: September 5th, 1937.

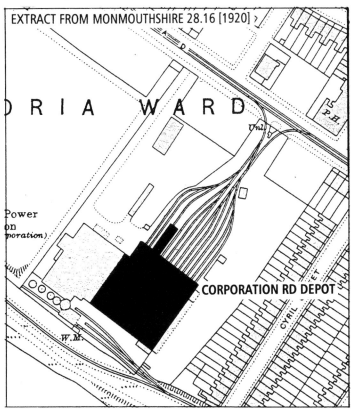

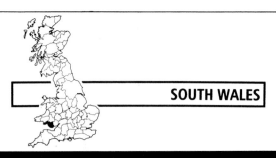

CARDIFF

Wood Street

Location: *At ST18307599, on the west side of Great Western Lane, south of Wood Street.*

Opened: July 12th, 1872 by the Cardiff Tramways Co. Ltd and taken over by Cardiff Corporation on January 1st, 1902.

Traction System: Horse (until October 17th, 1902) and then Overhead Electric.

Gauge: 4ft 8.5in.

Description: A 3TS dead ended tram shed.

Closed: October 17th, 1902 and re-opened on March 31st, 1904 for electric working. It finally closed in c1938 and was demolished as part of an urban development scheme.

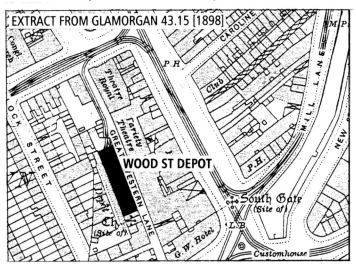

EXTRACT FROM GLAMORGAN 43.15 [1898]

WOOD ST DEPOT

Severn Road

Location: *At ST16767665, on the corner of Severn Road and Cowbridge Road, Canton.*

Opened: April 1879 by the Cardiff Tramways Co. Ltd and taken over by Cardiff Corporation on January 1st, 1902.

Traction System: Horse.

Gauge: 4ft 8.5in.

Description: A 3TS through road tram shed.

Closed: October 17th, 1902.

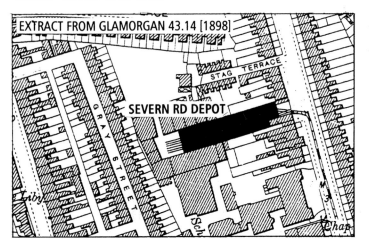

EXTRACT FROM GLAMORGAN 43.14 [1898]

SEVERN RD DEPOT

Harbour Road

Location: *At ST17707431, on the south side of York Place Grangetown.*

Opened: November 28th, 1881 by the Cardiff District & Penarth Harbour Tramways Co. Ltd and taken over by Cardiff Corporation on February 10th, 1903.

Traction System: Horse.

Gauge: 4ft 8.5in.

Description: A tram shed and stables.

Closed: February 10th, 1903 and still stood in 1976, in use as commercial premises.

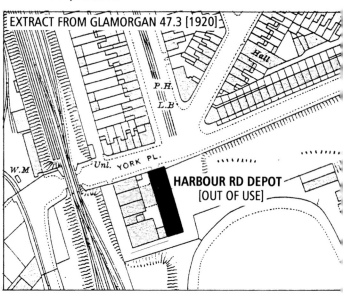

EXTRACT FROM GLAMORGAN 47.3 [1920]

HARBOUR RD DEPOT
[OUT OF USE]

Clare Road

Location: *At ST17747581, on the east side of Clare Road.*

Opened: 1902 by Cardiff Corporation.

Traction System: Overhead Electric.

Gauge: 4ft 8.5in.

Description: A brick built 9TS dead ended tram shed, it also housed trolleybuses from 1942.

Closed: August 25th, 1946 and utilized as a trolleybus depot until 1953. Later utilized as a council vehicle depot.

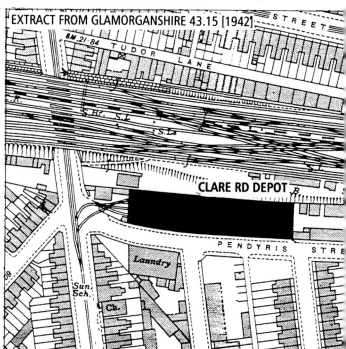

EXTRACT FROM GLAMORGANSHIRE 43.15 [1942]

CLARE RD DEPOT

Lucas Street

Location: At ST18507769, at the east end of Lucas St, Cathays.
Opened: December 1886 by the Cardiff Tramways Co. Ltd and taken over by Cardiff Corporation on January 1st, 1902.
Traction System: Horse.
Gauge: 4ft 8.5in.
Description: A 1TS dead ended tram shed.
Closed: October 17th, 1902.

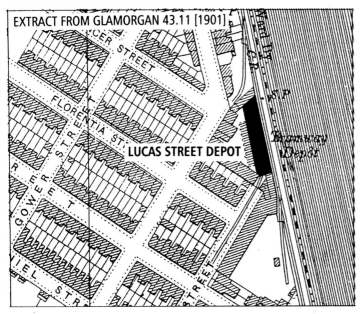

EXTRACT FROM GLAMORGAN 43.11 [1901]

Roath Depot

Location: At ST20557786, on the north side of Newport Road, Roath.
Opened: September 18th, 1902 by Cardiff Corporation.
Traction System: Overhead Electric.
Gauge: 4ft 8.5in.
Description: A brick built 12TS dead ended tram shed and works, it also housed trolleybuses from 1948.
Closed: February 19th, 1950 and subsequently utilized for trolleybuses and omnibuses. Finally closed in 1986.

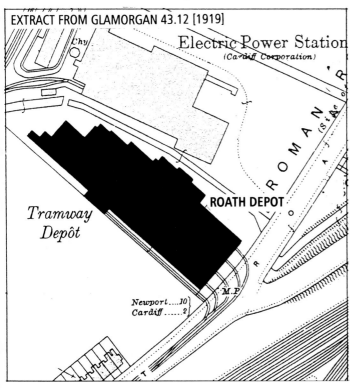

EXTRACT FROM GLAMORGAN 43.12 [1919]

ABERDARE

Gadlys

Location: At SO00140295, in Depot Rd on the north east side of Gadlys Road.
Opened: October 9th, 1913 by the Aberdare UDC.
Traction System: Overhead Electric.
Gauge: 3ft 6in.
Description: Originally a brick built 4TS dead ended tram shed Between January 15th, 1914 and July 23rd, 1925 it also accommodated trolley buses and, from September 10th, 1920, omnibuses. The facilities included paint and repair shops and the depot was enlarged in 1921.
Closed: April 1st, 1935 and subsequently utilized as an omnibus depot.

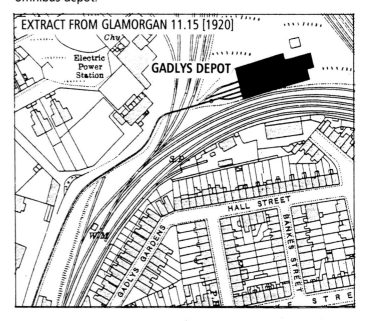

EXTRACT FROM GLAMORGAN 11.15 [1920]

MERTHYR

Penydarren Depot

Location: At SO05580692, at the east end of Trevethick St.
Opened: April 6th, 1901 by the Merthyr Electric Traction & Lighting Co. Ltd.
Traction System: Overhead Electric.
Gauge: 3ft 6in.
Description: A 4TS dead ended tram shed.
Closed: August 23rd, 1939 and subsequently utilized as an omnibus depot.

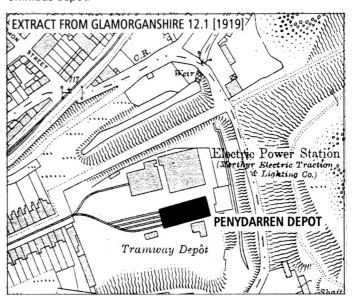

EXTRACT FROM GLAMORGANSHIRE 12.1 [1919]

Rutland Street [1st] Depot

Location: At SS65719276, on the north side of Rayner's Place.
Opened: July 27th, 1860 by the Swansea & Mumbles Railway.
Traction System: Horse (until August 17th, 1877) and then Steam.
Gauge: 4ft 8.5in.
Description: Originally a 3TS dead ended tram and loco shed, it was reduced to 2TS by 1897.*
Closed: March 1st, 1929.

Replaced by ...

Rutland Street [2nd] Depot

Location: At SS65669272, on the south side of Rayner's Place.
Opened: March 2nd, 1929 by the South Wales Transport Co. Ltd.
Traction System: Overhead Electric.
Gauge: 4ft 8.5in.
Description: A 4TS dead ended tram shed constructed in steel sheeting.
Closed: January 5th, 1960 and demolished to make way for road improvements.

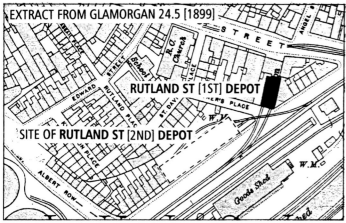

*This depot is listed in "The Directory of British Engine Sheds" as SS6592.4/1A.

Argyle Street

Location: At SS65019239, on the south side of the corner of Argyle St and Oystermouth Rd.
Opened: c1878 by the Swansea & Mumbles Railway Co. Ltd (re-incorporated in 1893 as the Swansea & Mumbles Railways Ltd), leased initially by the Swansea Improvements & Tramways Co. Ltd from July 1st, 1899 and then by the South Wales Transport Co. Ltd from January 1st, 1927.
Traction System: Steam.
Gauge: 4ft 8.5in.
Description: A 2TS dead ended carriage shed, it also probably housed the two battery electric cars experimented with in 1902.
Closed: March 1st, 1929.

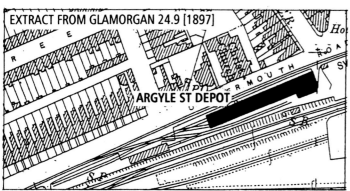

St Helens Road

Location: At SS64559242, on the east side of St Helens Rd.
Opened: April 12th, 1878 by the Swansea Improvements and Tramways Co. Ltd.
Traction System: Horse (until June 30th, 1900) and then Overhead Electric.
Gauge: 4ft 8.5in.
Description: Originally a 4TS dead ended tram shed accessed via a traverser, upon electrification it was rebuilt as an 8TS dead ended tram shed.
Closed: June 29th, 1937 and later demolished.

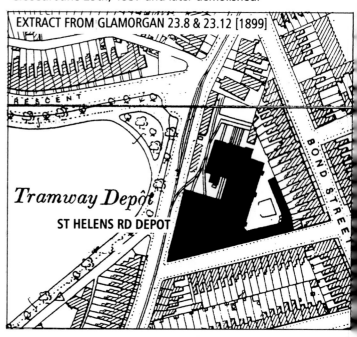

Cwmbwrla

Location: At SS64959470, on the west side of Carmarthen Rd.
Opened: 1882 by the Swansea Improvements and Tramways Co. Ltd.
Traction System: Steam (until 1884) and then Horse.
Gauge: 4ft 8.5in.
Description: A 2TS dead ended tram shed.
Closed: June 30th, 1900.

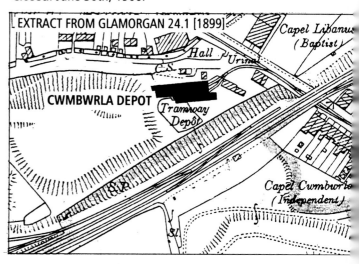

Oystermouth Tramroad

A c4ft gauge horse-drawn passenger service operated between Swansea and Oystermouth from March 25th, 1807 until c1827. The existence of a tram shed is unconfirmed. The line was relaid and re-opened in 1855 for coal traffic as the Swansea & Mumbles Railway.

Glyntaff Depot

Location: At ST08538919, in Gas Works Road, Treforest.
Opened: March 5th, 1905 by Pontypridd UDC.
Traction System: Overhead Electric.
Gauge: 3ft 6in.
Description: A brick built 4TS dead ended tram shed, it was extended at the rear in 1920, utilizing the redundant building from Trehafod Depot *(qv)*. It also accommodated trolleybuses from September 18th, 1930.
Closed: August 30th, 1931 and subsequently utilized as a depot for trolleybuses and omnibuses.

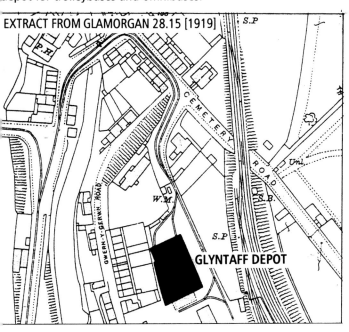

EXTRACT FROM GLAMORGAN 28.15 [1919]

GLYNTAFF DEPOT

Trehafod Depot

Location: At ST04919097, on the south side of Trehafod Road, west of Gyfeillon.
Opened: April 4th, 1907 by Pontypridd UDC.
Traction System: Overhead Electric.
Gauge: 3ft 6in.
Description: A 2TS dead ended tram shed constructed in galvanized iron.
Closed: July 14th, 1919, dismantled in 1920 and re-erected at Glyntaff Depot as an extension to the tram shed.

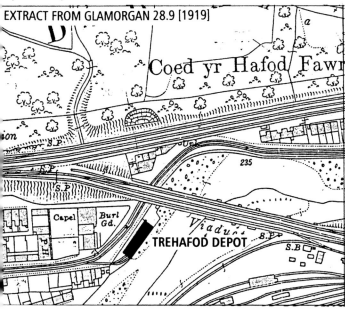

EXTRACT FROM GLAMORGAN 28.9 [1919]

Coed yr Hafod Fawr

TREHAFOD DEPOT

Eirw Road

Location: Approximately at ST03199095, on the south side of Eirw Rd, opposite Edmund St.
Opened: March 1888 by the Pontypridd & Rhondda Valley Tramway Co. and taken over in 1891 by the South Wales Property, Machinery and Carriage Co. Ltd.
Traction System: Horse.
Gauge: 3ft 6in.
Description: A small tram shed accessed through an archway.
Closed: February 1902.

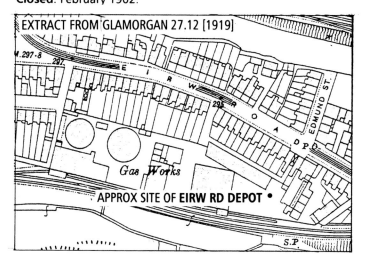

EXTRACT FROM GLAMORGAN 27.12 [1919]

Gas Works

APPROX SITE OF **EIRW RD DEPOT** •

Troedyrhiw Road

Location: At ST02399186, on the north side of Troedyrhiw Rd, Porth.
Opened: July 11th, 1908 by the Rhondda Tramways Co. Ltd.
Traction System: Overhead Electric.
Gauge: 3ft 6in.
Description: An 8TS dead ended tram shed.
Closed: February 1st, 1934 and subsequently utilized as an omnibus depot.

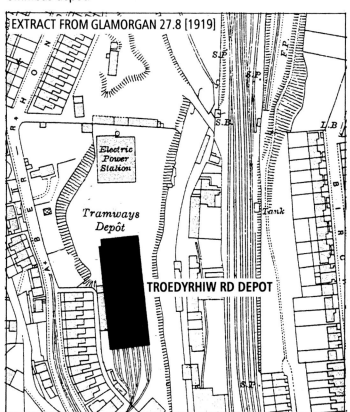

EXTRACT FROM GLAMORGAN 27.8 [1919]

Electric Power Station

Tramways Depôt

TROEDYRHIW RD DEPOT

NEATH

Creswell Road

Location: At SS75259730, on the corner of Creswell Road and London Road.

Opened: 1875 by the Neath & District Tramways Co. and taken over by Neath Corporation in 1897. Leased to the British Gas Traction Co. Ltd in April 1898 and leased again in 1902 to the Neath Gas Traction Co. Ltd (name changed to the Provincial Gas Traction Co. Ltd in the same year). From 1916 it was operated by Neath Corporation.

Traction System: Horse (until August 31st, 1899) and then Gas.

Gauge: 4ft 8.5in.

Description: A brick built 3TS dead ended tram shed.

Closed: August 8th, 1920 and subsequently demolished.

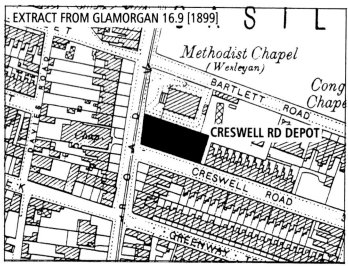

The loco shed at **Chirk GVT Station** some time after the line was abandoned in 1935.   *Courtesy RA Griffiths (See Page 137)*

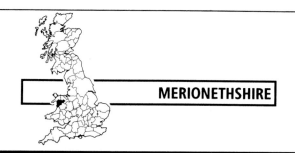

MERIONETHSHIRE

FAIRBOURNE

Station Road

Location: At SH61801316, in the Brickworks in Station Road, immediately north of the Cambrian Railways Station.

Opened: 1895 by Arthur McDougall for use as a construction line transporting bricks from the works to the housing plots and for passengers in c1898. The estate was sold to the Fairbourne Estate Co. in 1914.

Traction System: Horse.

Gauge: 2ft.

Description: There was no building. Tram cars were housed on the spur line.

Closed: c1914 and re-opened in 1916 after being rebuilt as a 15in gauge miniature railway.

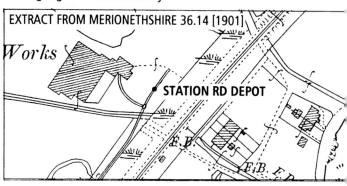

BARMOUTH

Barmouth Junction

Location: At SH63161460, on the east side of the stables, north of Barmouth Junction Station.

Opened: 1899 by Barmouth Junction & Arthog Tramways.

Traction System: Horse.

Gauge: 3ft.

Description: There was no building. Tram cars were probably stored on the line alongside the stables.

Closed: 1903.

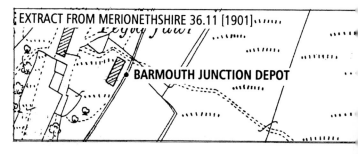

HARLECH

Harlech

From c1880 to c1882 a 600 yard long horse tramway was operated by Samuel Holland from the Cambrian Railways Station in Harlech across the sand dunes to the seashore. The gauge was possibly 2ft and the existence of a tramcar shed is unconfirmed.

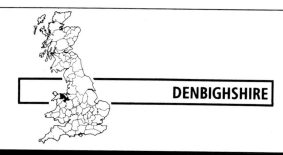

DENBIGHSHIRE

CHIRK

GVT Station

Location: On the west side of the line, at the north end of Chirk GVT Station.
Traction System: Steam.
Gauge: 2ft 4.5in.

CARRIAGE SHED No.1/LOCO SHED*
Opened: March 15th, 1891 by the Glyn Valley Tramway Co.
Description: A brick built 1TS through road shed located at SJ28413791 and although probably constructed to serve as the loco shed it was, instead, utilized to house carriages.
Closed: April 6th, 1933 when passenger services ceased.

LOCO SHED**
Opened: July 1888 by the Glyn Valley Tramway Co.
Description: A brick and timber built 1TS through road loco shed located at SJ28353807.
Closed: July 6th, 1935.

CARRIAGE SHED No.2
Opened: 1891 by the Glyn Valley Tramway Co.
Description: A brick built 1TS dead ended carriage shed located at SJ28363829.
Closed: April 6th, 1933 when passenger services ceased.

*This depot is listed in *"The Directory of British Engine Sheds"* as SJ2837.1/1A
**This depot is listed in *"The Directory of British Engine Sheds"* as SJ2838.1/1A

GLYNCEIRIOG

GVT Station

Location: At SJ20293782, on the north side of Glynceiriog GVT Station.
Opened: June 1888 by the Glyn Valley Tramway for goods and on March 15th, 1891 for passenger services.
Traction System: Steam.
Gauge: 2ft 4.5in.
Description: A brick built 1TS dead ended loco shed*.
Closed: April 1st, 1933, for passenger services and totally on July 6th, 1935. The building still stood in 1999, in use as a council depot.

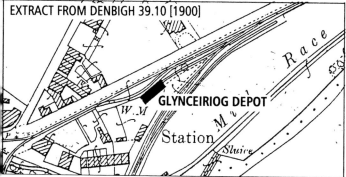

EXTRACT FROM DENBIGH 39.10 [1900]

GLYNCEIRIOG DEPOT

*This depot is listed in *"The Directory of British Engine Sheds"* as SJ2037.1/1A.

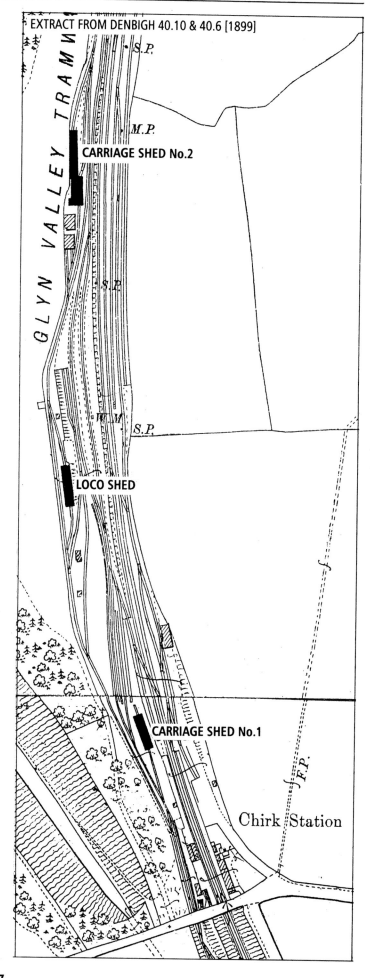

EXTRACT FROM DENBIGH 40.10 & 40.6 [1899]

CARRIAGE SHED No.2

LOCO SHED

CARRIAGE SHED No.1

Chirk Station

WREXHAM

Johnstown Depot

Location: At SJ30034633, on the south side of Maelor Road on the corner with Offa Street, Johnstown.

Opened: November 1st, 1876 by the Wrexham District Tramways Co. (renamed as Wrexham Tramways Ltd from 1879) and taken over by the Wrexham & District Electric Tramways Co. Ltd in 1901. The name was changed in 1914 to the Wrexham & District Transport Co. Ltd.

Traction System: Horse (until 1901) and then Overhead Electric.

Gauge: 3ft (until 1901), 3ft 6in.

Description: Originally a timber built 3ft gauge 2TS dead ended tram shed, it was demolished and rebuilt, re-opening on April 4th, 1903 as a 3ft 6in gauge brick built 5TS dead ended tram shed.

Closed: March 31st, 1927 and subsequently utilized as an omnibus depot. By 1997 it still stood, in a derelict condition.

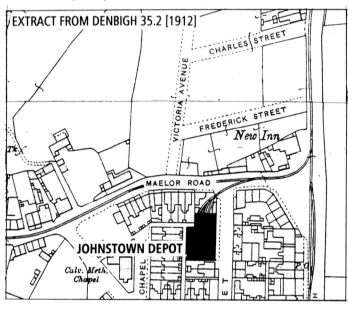

Maesgwyn Road

Location: At SJ32835078, between Maesgwyn Road and the railway line, on the south side of Regent Street.

Opened: 1920 by the Wrexham & District Electric Tramways Co. Ltd.

Traction System: Overhead Electric.

Gauge: 3ft 6in.

Description: A 2TS dead ended tram shed.

Closed: 1925 and subsequently utilized as an omnibus depot. Still standing in 1984.

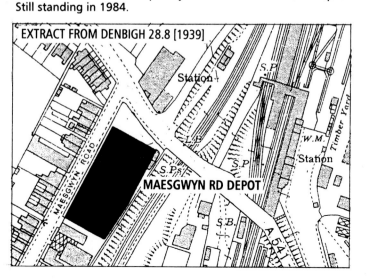

COLWYN BAY

Tramway Avenue

Location: At SH83538101, on the south west side of Penrhyn Avenue (formerly Tramway Avenue), north west of Church Rd, Rhos on Sea.

Opened: October 19th, 1907 by the Llandudno & District Electric Traction Co. Ltd. The name was changed in 1909 to the Llandudno & Colwyn Bay Electric Railway Ltd.

Traction System: Overhead Electric.

Gauge: 3ft 6in.

Description: An 8TS dead ended tram shed constructed in timber on a steel frame.

Closed: March 24th, 1956 and utilized as an omnibus depot until 1961. Subsequently used for commercial premises.

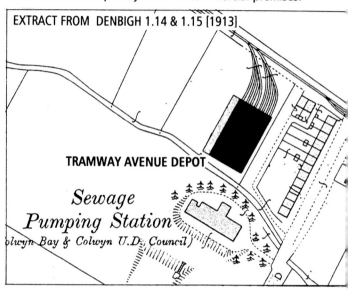

PONTFAEN

Pontfaen

Location: At SJ27953701, 0.5 miles south west of Chirk Station and south of the River Ceiriog.

Opened: April 1873 by the Glyn Valley Tramway for goods and on April 1st, 1874 for a passenger service between Pontfaen and Glynceiriog.

Traction System: Horse.

Gauge: 2ft 4.25in.

Description: There was no shed building. Tram cars stabled in the siding alongside the stables.

Closed: March 31st, 1886.

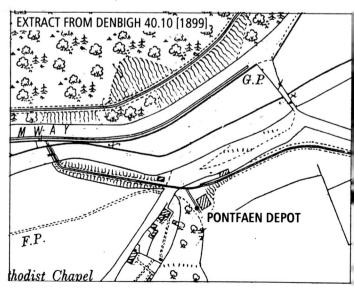

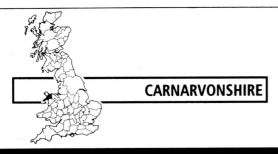

CARNARVONSHIRE

PWLLHELI

Pen y Cob

Traction System: Horse.
Gauge: 2ft 6in.

DEPOT No.1

Location: At SH37453503, at the north end of the line, east of Mitre Terrace.
Opened: July 24th, 1899 by Pwllheli Corporation.
Description: Originally a timber built 1TS dead ended tram shed, a 1TS lean-to extension was added on the east side in 1901.
Closed: 1908 to accommodate the re-siting of the Cambrian Railways Station.

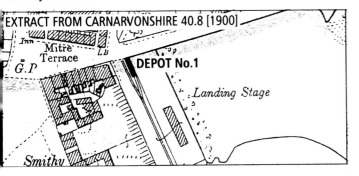

DEPOT No.2

Location: On the east side of Pen y Cob, south of the Cambrian Railways Station.
Opened: 1908 by Pwllheli Corporation.
Description: The original depot, and extension, were re-sited at the new terminus at SH37483496 and, in 1909, were again re-sited, this time at 90° to the track, at SH37493496, with access via two turntables.
Closed: September 1919.

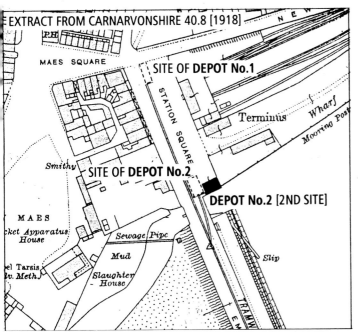

Cardiff Road

Location: At SH36963435, off the west side of Cardiff Road, north of the West End Promenade.
Opened: 1894 by the Pwllheli & Llanbedrog Tramways.
Traction System: Horse.
Gauge: 3ft.
Description: A 2TS dead ended tram shed & works converted from redundant farm buildings.
Closed: As a running shed in 1898, but continued in use as a works and stores until the tramway closed in 1928. The site was redeveloped for housing in 1964.

West End Promenade

Location: At SH37133420, at the east end of the West End Promenade.
Opened: 1898 by the Pwllheli & Llanbedrog Tramways.
Traction System: Horse.
Gauge: 3ft.
Description: Originally a brick built 1TS dead ended tram shed and stables accessed by a turntable, by 1905 it had been rebuilt as a 2TS dead ended shed with conventional access. By the time it closed it had been enlarged to a 4TS building.
Closed: 1928. In 1995 it was in use as a garage and omnibus depot.

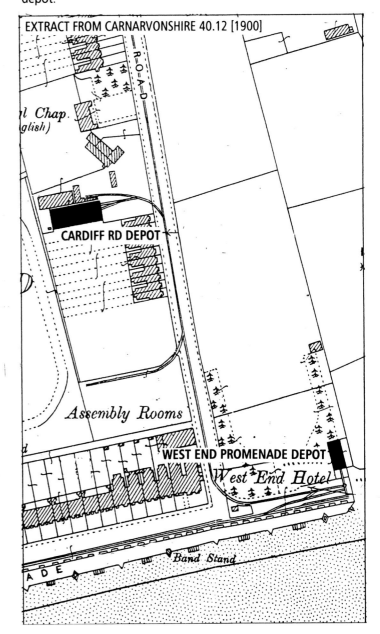

LLANDUDNO
Great Orme

Opened: 1904 by the Great Orme Tramways Co, taken over by the Great Orme Railway Ltd in 1935 and taken over again by Llandudno UDC in 1949. It passed to Aberconwy District Council in 1974 and was re-named as the Great Orme Tramway in 1977 before becoming the responsibility of Conwy County Borough Council in 1996.

Traction System: Cable.

Gauge: 3ft 6in.

The depots were still operational in 2000.

VICTORIA STATION

Location: At SH77858272, on the north side of Church Walks at the corner of Old Road.

Description: An iron-framed dead ended tram shed.

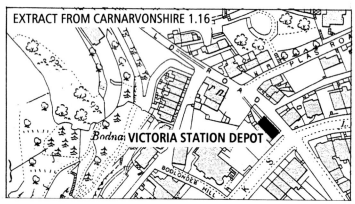

HALFWAY STATION (LOWER SECTION)

Location: At SH77338410, at the south end of Halfway Station.

Description: A stone built 1TS through road tram shed.

HALFWAY STATION (UPPER SECTION)

Location: At SH77278412, at the north end of Halfway Station.

Description: A stone built 1TS dead ended tram shed.

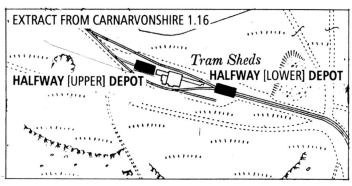

SUMMIT STATION

Location: At SH76598330, at the Summit Station.

Description: A stone built 1TS dead ended tram shed.

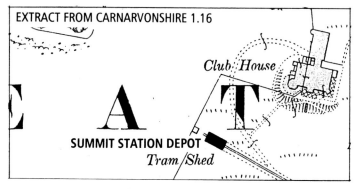

NB. Prior to the opening of the tram sheds all the cars were kept in the open at the termini from July 31st, 1902 (Lower Section) and July 8th, 1903 (Upper Section). Prior to the opening of Victoria Station, the southern terminus was in the yard of the Victoria Hotel in Old Road (at SH77828273) immediately to the north of the station site.

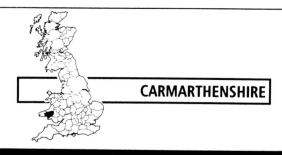

CARMARTHENSHIRE

LLANELLY
Robinson Street

Location: At SS50629998 on the north side of Robinson S... east of Station Rd.

Opened: September 28th, 1882 by the Llanelly Tramways Co Ltd and taken over in 1905 by the Llanelly & District Electric Lighting & Traction Co. Ltd, a subsidiary of the British Power Co Ltd. The name was changed in 1924 to the Llanelly & District Electric Supply Co. Ltd.

Traction System: Horse (until 1911) and then Overhead Electric.

Gauge: 3ft (until April 1908), 4ft 8.5in.

Description: Originally a 1TS or 2TS dead ended tram shed probably constructed in stone and with one access track, it was re-gauged in April 1908 and rebuilt in brick and corrugated sheeting as a 4TS dead ended tram shed for overhead electric working which commenced on June 12th, 1911. It also housed trolley buses from December 26th, 1932.

Closed: February 16th, 1932 and utilized as a trolley bus depot until November 8th, 1952 and subsequently as an omnibus depot.

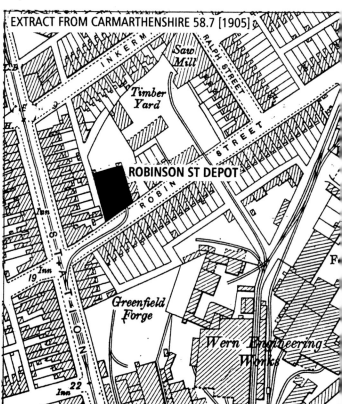

THE DIRECTORY OF
BRITISH TRAM DEPOTS

PART THREE
SCOTLAND

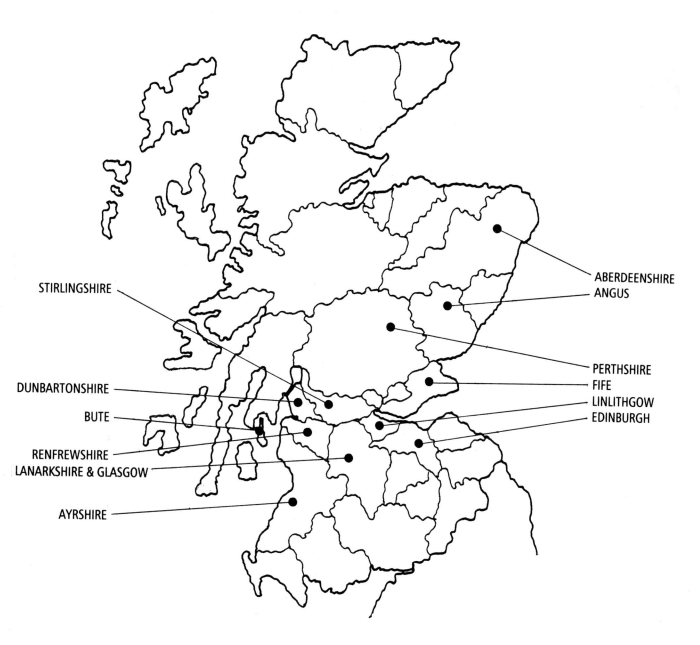

ALL OTHER COUNTIES: NO DEPOTS

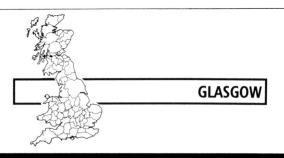

GLASGOW

Kelvinhaugh Depot

Location: At NS56886592, on the north side of Kelvinhaugh St. between Lymburn St. and Overnewton Place, Kelvinhaugh.
Opened: July 1st, 1894 by Glasgow Corporation.
Traction System: Horse.
Gauge: 4ft 7.75in.
Description: A dead ended, probably 2TS, tram shed.
Closed: 1901 and remained in tramway use. Site later cleared.

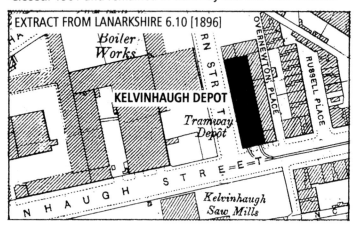

Dennistoun Depot

Location: At NS61756511, on the east side of Paton St. north off Duke St., Dennistoun.
Opened: July 1st, 1894 by Glasgow Corporation.
Traction System: Horse, until 1901, and then Overhead Electric from 1903.
Gauge: 4ft 7.75in.
Description: Originally a horse tram shed and stables, it was reconstructed as a brick built 8TS dead ended shed for electric working. It was also used to house trolleybuses from June 1958.
Closed: Totally on November 5th, 1960 and retained for further corporation use.

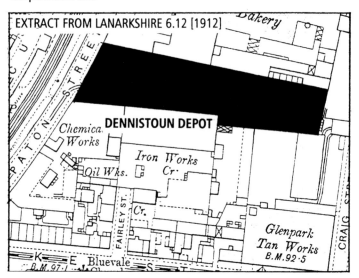

Dalmarnock Depot

Location: At NS61086370, on the corner of Baltic St. and Rub̶ St.
Opened: July 1st, 1894 by Glasgow Corporation.
Traction System: Horse, until 1901, and then Overhead Electri̶ from 1903.
Gauge: 4ft 7.75in.
Description: Originally a horse tram shed and stables, it wa̶ reconstructed as a brick built 27TS dead ended shed for electri̶ working. The two central roads were later replaced by office̶ and the depot was left roofless following a fire on March 22n̶ 1961.
Closed: With the tramway on September 4th, 1962 an̶ subsequently demolished.

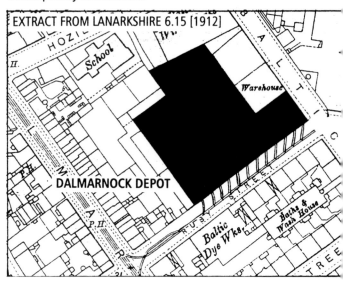

Whitevale Depot

Location: At NS61286450, on the east side of Rowchester St̶ Whitevale.
Opened: July 1st, 1894 by Glasgow Corporation.
Traction System: Horse, until April 14th, 1902, and the̶ Overhead Electric from 1902.
Gauge: 4ft 7.75in.
Description: Originally a horse tram shed and stables, it wa̶ rebuilt as an 18TS dead ended shed for electric working.
Closed: 1924, upon the opening of Parkhead Depot, an̶ continued in use as a sub-station. Part of the depot was late̶ utilized by the Housing & Works Dept.

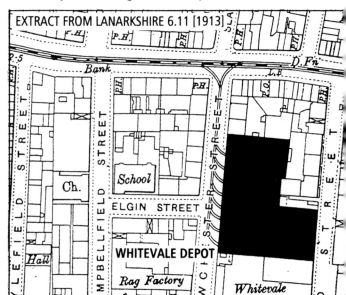

Langside Depot

Location: At NS58466130, on the south side of Battlefield Rd.
Opened: 1901 by Glasgow Corporation.
Traction System: Overhead Electric.
Gauge: 4ft 7.75in.
Description: A 22TS dead ended tram shed.
Closed: September 29th, 1956 and subsequently utilized as an omnibus garage.

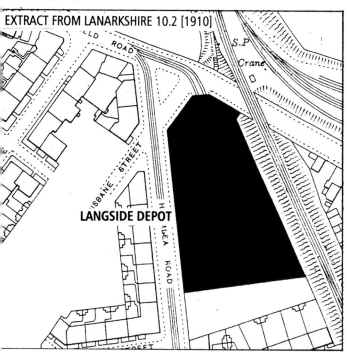

EXTRACT FROM LANARKSHIRE 10.2 [1910]

LANGSIDE DEPOT

Maryhill Depot

Location: At NS56236950, on north side of Celtic St., west off Main St., Maryhill.
Opened: July 1st, 1894 by Glasgow Corporation.
Traction System: Horse, until 1901, and then Overhead Electric from 1902.
Gauge: 4ft 7.75in.
Description: Originally a horse tram shed and stables, it was reconstructed as a brick built 23TS dead ended shed for electric working.
Closed: October 21st, 1961 and subsequently utilized as an omnibus garage.

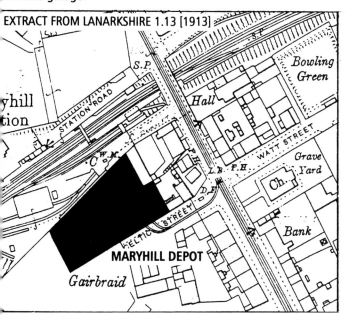

EXTRACT FROM LANARKSHIRE 1.13 [1913]

MARYHILL DEPOT

Newlands Depot

Location: At NS56626120, at the west end of Newlandsfield Rd west off Kilmarnock Rd, Newlands.
Opened: 1910 by Glasgow Corporation.
Traction System: Overhead Electric.
Gauge: 4ft 7.75in.
Description: An 18TS dead ended tram shed, it was damaged by a fire on April 11th, 1948.
Closed: June 4th, 1960 and subsequently utilized as an omnibus garage.

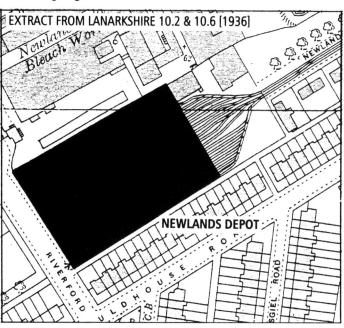

EXTRACT FROM LANARKSHIRE 10.2 & 10.6 [1936]

NEWLANDS DEPOT

Kinning Park Depot

Location: At NS57476434, on the east side of Great Wellington St., south off Paisley Rd West.
Opened: July 1st, 1894 by Glasgow Corporation.
Traction System: Horse, until 1901, and then Overhead Electric from 1902.
Gauge: 4ft 7.75in.
Description: Originally a horse tram shed and stables, it was reconstructed as a brick built 8TS dead ended shed for electric working.
Closed: 1915, upon the opening of Govan No.2 Depot, and continued in use as a sub-station. Part of the depot was utilized as a clothing store and sand drier and, later, as commercial premises. The whole site was subsequently cleared to accommodate construction of the M8.

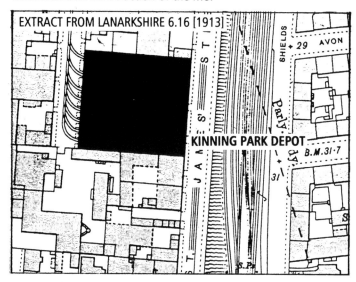

EXTRACT FROM LANARKSHIRE 6.16 [1913]

KINNING PARK DEPOT

Partick [No.1] Depot

Location: At NS56366640, on the south east corner of Queen St. (now Thurso St.) and Newton St. (now Dunaskin St.).
Opened: Post-1877 by the Glasgow Tramway & Omnibus Co.
Traction System: Horse.
Gauge: 4ft 7.75in.
Description: A dead ended tram shed and stables.
Closed: Probably on June 30th, 1894 upon the takeover of the system by Glasgow Corporation.

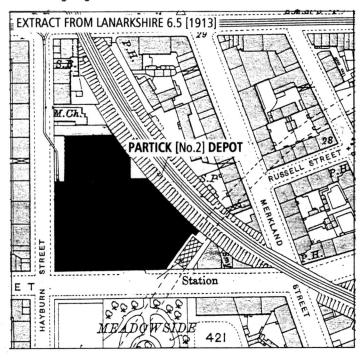

Partick [No.2] Depot

Location: At NS55556647, on the east side of Hayburn St.
Opened: July 1st, 1894 by Glasgow Corporation.
Traction System: Horse, until 1901, and then Overhead Electric from 1902.
Gauge: 4ft 7.75in.
Description: Originally a horse tram shed and stables, it was reconstructed as a 21TS dead ended shed, with stone facings, for electric working.
Closed: June 2nd, 1962 and subsequently utilized as an omnibus garage.

Govan [No.1] Depot

Location: At NS55436566, on the south side of Govan Rd, jus[t] west of Govan Station.
Opened: January 1st, 1873 by the Vale of Clyde Tramways Co[.] and operated by the Glasgow Tramway & Omnibus Co. unti[l] June 30th, 1874. Taken over by the Govan Polic[e] Commissioners on June 30th, 1893 and operated again by th[e] Glasgow Tramway & Omnibus Co. until November 11th, 189[6] when it was taken over by Glasgow Corporation.
Traction System: Horse, until 1877, and then Steam. Horse again from July 10th, 1893.
Gauge: 4ft 7.75in.
Description: A tram depot and stables. It may also have been utilized by the Glasgow & Ibrox Tramway Co. between July 18th, 1879 and May 25th, 1891 to house its horse cars.
Closed: Probably in 1896 upon the takeover by Glasgow Corporation, and may have been utilized as a temporary electric overhead depot. It was later retained for tramway use.

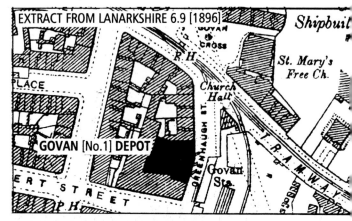

Govan [No.2] Depot

Location: At NS56686457, on the south side of Brand St., wes[t] off Harvie St., Govan.
Opened: August 11th, 1915 by Glasgow Corporation.
Traction System: Overhead Electric.
Gauge: 4ft 7.75in.
Description: A brick built 14TS dead ended tram shed, it als[o] housed the conductors' training school and accommodate[d] trolley buses from April 1958.
Closed: To trams on November 15th, 1958 and continued i[n] use as a trolley bus depot. It was also utilized until February 28th, 1959 to store tram cars awaiting scrapping. The whol[e] site was later occupied by a church.

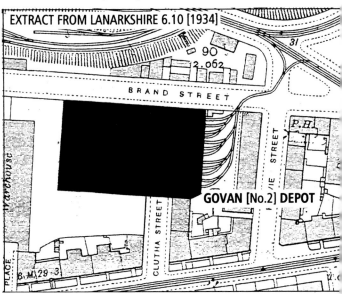

Springburn [No.1] Depot

Location: At NS60436734, at the end of Mollinsburn St, east of Springburn Rd.

Opened: Probably on December 8th, 1886 by the Glasgow Tramway & Omnibus Co.

Traction System: Horse.

Gauge: 4ft 7.75in.

Description: A dead ended, possibly 2TS, tram shed and stables.

Closed: Probably on June 30th, 1894 upon the takeover of the system by Glasgow Corporation.

Springburn [No.2] Depot

Location: At NS60396743, on the south side of Keppochhill Rd, west of Springburn Rd, Springburn.

Opened: July 1st, 1894 by Glasgow Corporation.

Traction System: Horse, until 1898, and then Overhead Electric from October 13th, 1898.

Gauge: 4ft 7.75in.

Description: Originally a horse tram shed and stables, it was converted to electric working in 1898 utilizing generating equipment for Glasgow's first experimental electric tramway service.

Closed: To trams, probably on April 24th, 1901 when Pinkston Power Station opened at Port Dundas, with the depot continuing in use as a sub-station. The tram shed was later used as a Drill Hall , and then as commercial premises.

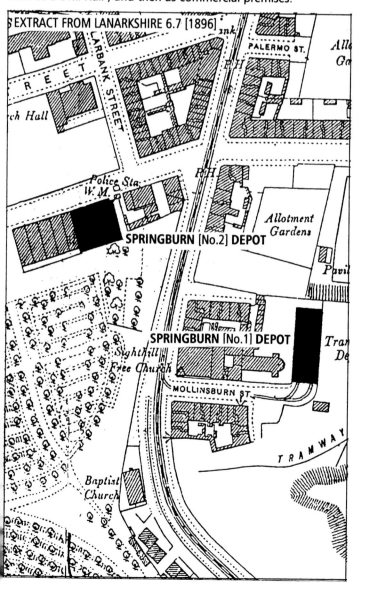

Cambridge Street

Location: At NS58636596, on the west side of Cambridge St, north of Renfrew St.

Opened: August 19th, 1872 by the Glasgow Tramway & Omnibus Co.

Traction System: Horse.

Gauge: 4ft 7.75in.

Description: A dead ended tram shed and stables, probably consisting of a 2TS covered yard.

Closed: Probably on June 30th, 1894 upon the takeover of the system by Glasgow Corporation.

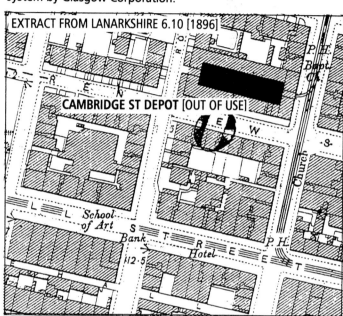

Pollokshaws Depot

Location: At NS56546143, on the south side of Pleasance St.

Opened: Possibly on September 15th, 1882 by the Glasgow Tramway & Omnibus Co. and taken over on November 11th, 1896 by Glasgow Corporation

Traction System: Horse, until 1901, and then Overhead Electric.

Gauge: 4ft 7.75in

Description: Originally a horse tram shed and stables, it was rebuilt as a dead ended shed for electric working.

Closed: 1910 and replaced by Newlands Depot. It was subsequently let for commercial use.

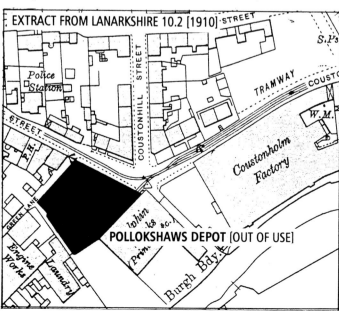

Parkhead Depot

Location: At NS62806390, on the west side of Canmore St., off Tollcross Rd, Parkhead.
Opened: 1924 by Glasgow Corporation.
Traction System: Overhead Electric.
Gauge: 4ft 7.75in.
Description: A 9TS dead ended tram shed with one dead ended yard road. An omnibus depot was sited along the south side of the depot.
Closed: March 12th, 1960 and subsequently utilized as an omnibus garage.

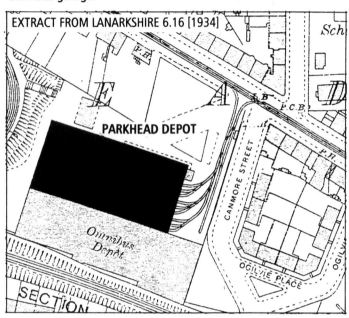

Possilpark Depot

Location: At NS59456818, on the corner of Hawthorn St. and Ashfield St.
Opened: 1901 by Glasgow Corporation.
Traction System: Overhead Electric.
Gauge: 4ft 7.75in.
Description: Originally a 19TS dead ended shed, with two dead end yard roads, the seven southern roads were later extended.
Closed: June 7th, 1959 and subsequently utilized as an omnibus garage.

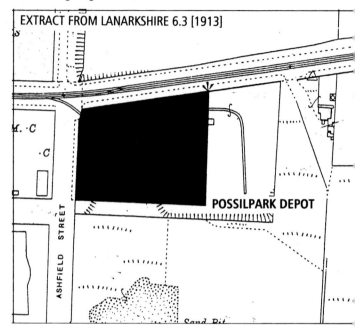

North Street

Location: At NS58056549, on the east side of North St. opposite Union Place.
Opened: Probably on December 27th, 1872 by the Glasgow Tramway & Omnibus Co.
Traction System: Horse.
Gauge: 4ft 7.75in.
Description: Originally a 2TS dead ended tram shed and stables occupying three floors, the depot was rebuilt after it was destroyed by a fire on May 31st, 1884.
Closed: Probably on June 30th, 1894 upon the takeover of the system by Glasgow Corporation.

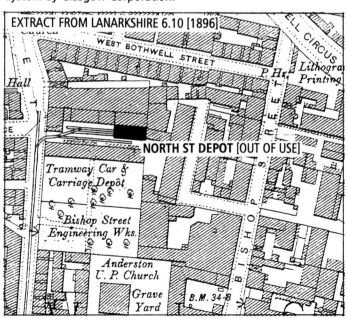

Dalhousie Depot

Location: At NS58516634, on the west side of Dalhousie St., north of West Graham St.
Opened: July 1st, 1894 by Glasgow Corporation.
Traction System: Horse.
Gauge: 4ft 7.75in.
Description: A dead ended, probably 2TS, tram shed.
Closed: 1901 at the end of horse working and retained for use as an electricity sub-station and, possibly, as a temporary tram depot for overhead working.

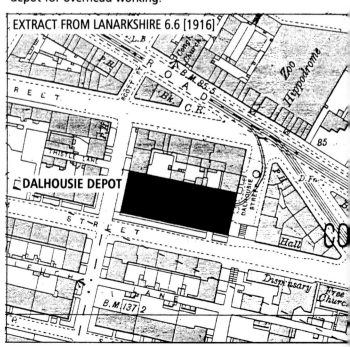

Crownpoint Depot

Location: At NS61376448, south off Gallowgate, between Crownpoint Rd and David St.

Opened: Probably on December 19th, 1873 by the Glasgow Tramway & Omnibus Co.

Traction System: Horse.

Gauge: 4ft 7.75in

Description: Originally a tram shed and stables, a car works was added alongside in 1877, and the depot was completely rebuilt following a fire on November 30th, 1885. It possibly replaced a temporary depot which was located in Bluevale St, just to the north. In 1890 the works was turned over to omnibus construction.

Closed: Probably on June 30th, 1894 upon the takeover of the system by Glasgow Corporation.

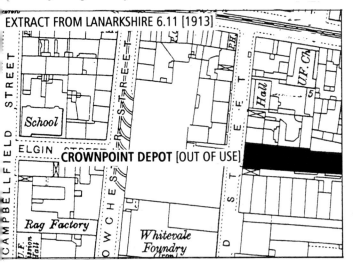

EXTRACT FROM LANARKSHIRE 6.11 [1913]

CROWNPOINT DEPOT [OUT OF USE]

Tobago Street Depot

Location: At NS60456432, on the east side of Tobago St, north off Great Hamilton St.

Opened: Probably on December 1st, 1873 by the Glasgow Tramway & Omnibus Co.

Traction System: Horse.

Gauge: 4ft 7.75in.

Description: Originally a tram shed and stables, it was rebuilt after being destroyed by a fire on March 11th, 1893. It was also known as Blackfaulds Depot.

Closed: Probably on June 30th, 1894 upon the takeover of the system by Glasgow Corporation.

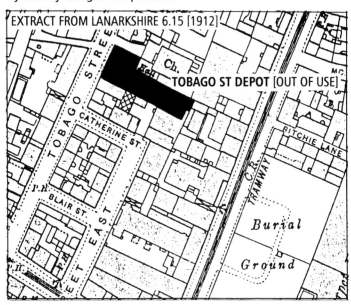

EXTRACT FROM LANARKSHIRE 6.15 [1912]

TOBAGO ST DEPOT [OUT OF USE]

Nelson Street

Location: At NS58356451, south off Nelson St.

Opened: Probably on December 16th, 1872 by the Glasgow Tramway & Omnibus Co.

Traction System: Horse.

Gauge: 4ft 7.75in.

Description: A tram shed and stables.

Closed: Probably on June 30th, 1894 upon the takeover of the system by Glasgow Corporation.

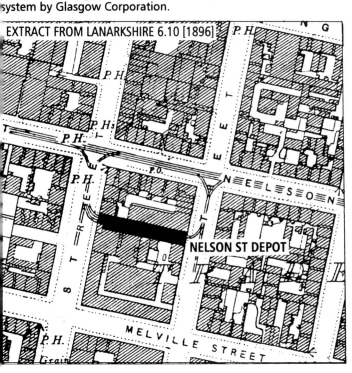

EXTRACT FROM LANARKSHIRE 6.10 [1896]

NELSON ST DEPOT

Whiteinch Depot

Location: At NS54426676, south off Dumbarton Rd.

Opened: Probably on December 27th, 1872 by the Glasgow Tramway & Omnibus Co.

Traction System: Horse.

Gauge: 4ft 7.75in.

Description: A tram shed and stables.

Closed: Probably on June 30th, 1894 upon the takeover of the system by Glasgow Corporation.

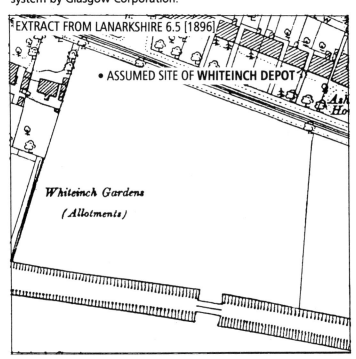

EXTRACT FROM LANARKSHIRE 6.5 [1896]

• ASSUMED SITE OF **WHITEINCH DEPOT**

Whiteinch Gardens (Allotments)

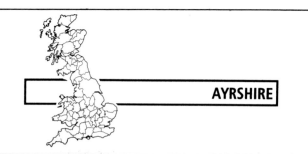

AYRSHIRE

AYR

Prestwick Road

Location: At *NS34412349, on the east side of Prestwick Rd.*
Opened: September 26th, 1901 by Ayr Corporation.
Traction System: Overhead Electric.
Gauge: 4ft 8.5in.
Description: Originally a brick built 3TS dead ended tram shed it was extended on the south side to a 6TS building in 1902.
Closed: December 31st, 1931 and subsequently utilized as an omnibus garage.

Bellesleyhill Road

Location: At *NS34432354, on the east side of Prestwick Rd, north of Bellesleyhill Road.*
Opened: 1923 by Ayr Corporation.
Traction System: Overhead Electric.
Gauge: 4ft 8.5in.
Description: A brick built 4TS dead ended tram shed.
Closed: December 31st, 1931 and subsequently utilized for scrapping tramcars.

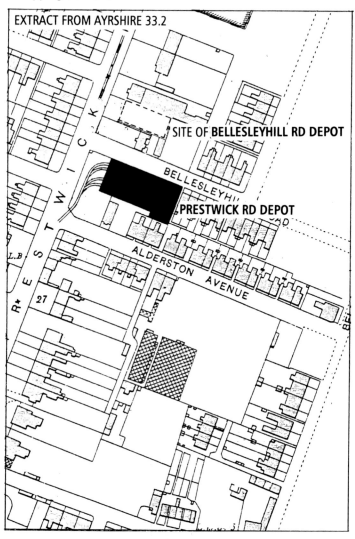

KILMARNOCK

Greenholm Street

Location: At *NS42683661, on the south side of Greenholm S̶ west of Campbell Street.*
Opened: December 10th, 1904 by Kilmarnock Corporation.
Traction System: Overhead Electric.
Gauge: 4ft 8.5in.
Description: A brick built 3TS dead ended tram shed with a r̶ sandstone and white brick frontage.
Closed: May 3rd, 1926 and utilized as an omnibus garage fro̶ November 1927 to December 31st, 1931. Later demolished.

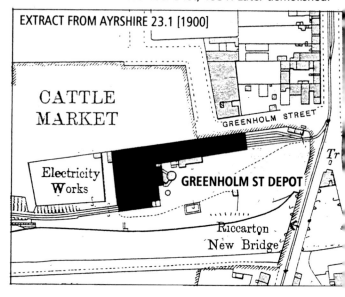

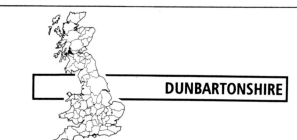

DUNBARTONSHIRE

DUMBARTON

Bonhill Road

Location: At *NS40127559, on the corner of Bonhill Road an̶ Hartfield Gardens.*
Opened: February 20th, 1907 by the Electric Supp̶ Corporation Ltd and transferred to the Dumbarton Burgh ̶ County Tramways Co. Ltd on December 20th, 1907.
Traction System: Overhead Electric.
Gauge: 4ft 7.75in.
Description: A brick and corrugated iron clad 11TS dead ende̶ tram shed.
Closed: March 3rd, 1928. It still stood in 1985.

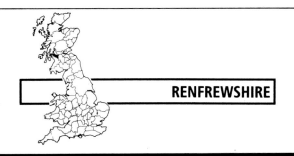

RENFREWSHIRE

Chapel Street

Location: At NS24557727, on the south west side of Chapel St.
Opened: July 7th, 1873 by the Vale of Clyde Tramways Co. and taken over by the Greenock & Port Glasgow Tramways Co. on May 15th, 1893.
Traction System: Horse.
Gauge: 4ft 7.75in.
Description: A stone built 2TS dead ended tram shed and stables.
Closed: c1901 when conversion to overhead electric working began. A shop was later built at the front of the premises and it was demolished in 1968.

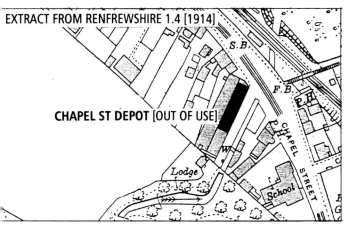

EXTRACT FROM RENFREWSHIRE 1.4 [1914]

CHAPEL ST DEPOT [OUT OF USE]

Shore Street

Location: At NS24257772, on the west side of Shore Street.
Opened: By the Greenock & Port Glasgow Tramways Company at some date prior to World War I.
Traction System: Overhead Electric.
Gauge: 4ft 7.75in.
Description: A 1TS dead ended tram shed.
Closed: At some date after World War I.

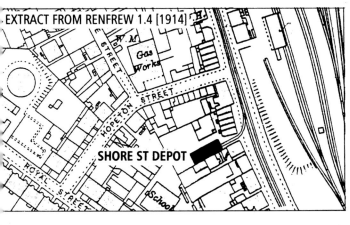

EXTRACT FROM RENFREW 1.4 [1914]

SHORE ST DEPOT

NB. A temporary electric depot was in use at the east end of Cardwell Road from October 3rd, 1901, when overhead electric working began, until the opening of Greenock Ladyburn Depot in July 1902.

Ladyburn

Location: At NS30357518, on the corner of Pottery Street and Glasgow Road.
Opened: July 1902 by the Greenock & Port Glasgow Tramways Co. Ltd.
Traction System: Overhead Electric.
Gauge: 4ft 7.75in.
Description: A brick and timber built 8TS dead ended tram shed and workshops.
Closed: July 15th, 1929 and let out for commercial use. Still standing in 1975.

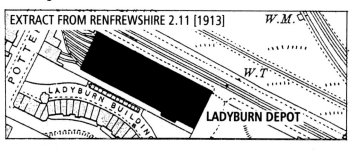

EXTRACT FROM RENFREWSHIRE 2.11 [1913]

LADYBURN DEPOT

Cartsburn Street

Location: Approximately at NS28677569, on the west side of Cartsburn St., south of Main St.
Opened: November 29th, 1889 by the Greenock & Port Glasgow Tramways Company.
Traction System: Horse.
Gauge: 4ft 7.75in.
Description: A tram depot, possibly 2TS dead ended, and stables converted from a sugar store.
Closed: November 7th, 1901.

EXTRACT FROM RENFREW 2.6 [1914]

APPROX SITE OF **CARTSBURN ST DEPOT**

Paisley Road

Location: At NS49916649, on the corner of Newmains Rd and Paisley Rd.
Opened: September 22nd, 1904 by William M Murphy operating as Paisley District Tramways (Co. from 1905) and taken over by Glasgow Corporation on August 1st, 1923.
Traction System: Overhead Electric.
Gauge: 4ft 7.75in.
Description: A brick built 5TS dead ended tram shed.
Closed: October 4th, 1936 and demolished to make way for a housing development.

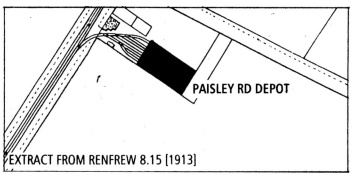

PAISLEY RD DEPOT

EXTRACT FROM RENFREW 8.15 [1913]

PAISLEY

Incle Street

Location: At NS48806420, on the north side of Incle Street.
Opened: December 30th, 1885 by the Paisley Tramways Co. Ltd and taken over by William M Murphy for electrification on September 17th, 1903.
Traction System: Horse, until November 21st, 1903 and then Overhead Electric.
Gauge: 4ft 7.75in.
Description: A 2TS dead ended shed and stables utilizing existing buildings.
Closed: July 12th, 1904 and subsequently demolished.

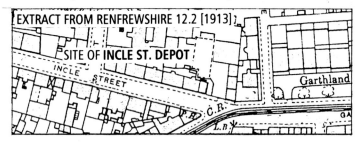

Elderslie Rd

Location: At NS45726340, on the south side of Beith Road.
Opened: July 12th, 1904 by William M Murphy operating as Paisley District Tramways (Co. from 1905) and taken over by Glasgow Corporation on August 1st, 1923.
Traction System: Overhead Electric.
Gauge: 4ft 7.75in.
Description: Originally a brick built 6TS dead ended tram shed and works, an omnibus garage was added on the east side in 1931/2 and a brick built 3TS dead ended tram shed was added to the south side in 1938.
Closed: May 12th, 1957 and sold for use as a road haulage depot. It was damaged by fire in November 1960 and still stood, in a derelict condition, until demolished in 1983.

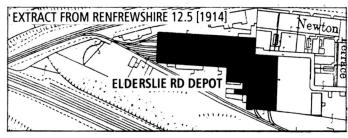

Aurs Road

Location: At NS50725916, on the east side of Aurs Road, Barrhead.
Opened: December 31st, 1910 by the Paisley District Tramways Company and taken over by Glasgow Corporation on August 1st, 1923.
Traction System: Overhead Electric.
Gauge: 4ft 7.75in.
Description: A 2TS dead ended tram shed.
Closed: August 1st, 1923. (The track connection to the system was not removed until 1938.)

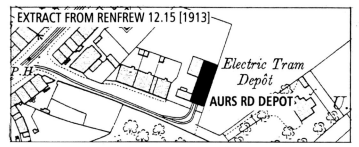

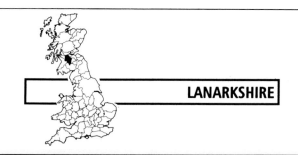

LANARKSHIRE

COATBRIDGE

Jackson Street

Location: At NS73916487, on the north side of Main Street between Jackson Street and Hillcrest Avenue.
Opened: February 8th, 1904 by the Airdrie & Coatbridge Tramways Co., taken over on September 30th, 1920 jointly by Coatbridge and Airdrie Councils and by Glasgow Corporation on January 1st, 1922.
Traction System: Overhead Electric.
Gauge: 4ft 7.75in.
Description: A brick built 5TS dead ended tram shed.
Closed: Temporarily between June 3rd, 1924 and May 23rd, 1925, during work to connect the tramway to the Glasgow system, and finally on November 4th, 1956. It was subsequently sold for use as commercial premises.

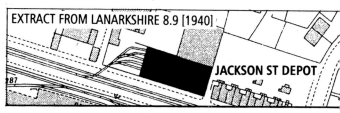

MOTHERWELL

Power House

Location: At NS74325660, on the south side of Clyde Street (Later Hamilton Street).
Opened: July 22nd, 1903 by the Hamilton, Motherwell & Wishaw Tramways Co. (name changed to Lanarkshire Tramways Co. in same year and to the Lanarkshire Traction Co. on October 1st, 1930).
Traction System: Overhead Electric.
Gauge: 4ft 7.75in.
Description: A brick built 8TS dead ended tram shed and 4TS works. A roller skating rink, to the east, was purchased in 1913 and converted to an omnibus garage.
Closed: With the tramway system on February 14th, 1931 and subsequently utilized as an omnibus depot and works (renamed as Traction House). In 1997 the site was reported as likely to be sold for housing.

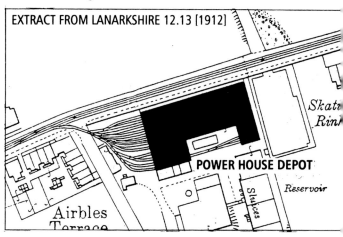

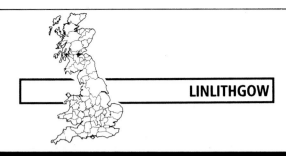

Larbert Road [1st] Depot

Location: At NS86268149, on the south side of Larbert Rd, Carmuirs.

Opened: October 21st, 1905 by the Falkirk Electric Construction Syndicate Ltd as the Falkirk & District Tramways. It was renamed as the Falkirk & District Tramways Co. Ltd in 1914 and taken over by the Fife Tramway Light & Power Co. in 1920.

Traction System: Overhead Electric.

Gauge: 4ft.

Description: A 6TS dead ended tram shed constructed in corrugated iron. An omnibus garage was added on the eastern side in 1909.

Closed: 1931 and subsequently utilized as an omnibus depot.

Larbert Road [2nd] Depot

Location: At NS86148159, on the south side of Larbert Rd, Carmuirs.

Opened: 1931 by the Fife Tramway Light & Power Co.

Traction System: Overhead Electric.

Gauge: 4ft.

Description: A 4TS dead ended tram shed constructed in corrugated iron.

Closed: July 21st, 1936. It still stood in 1975.

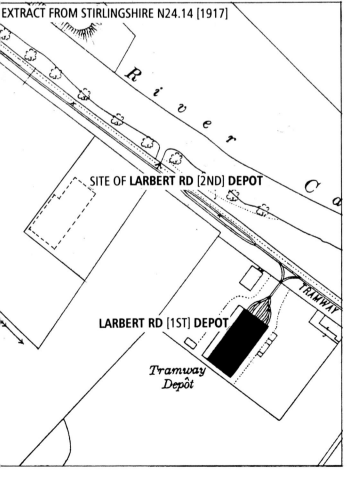

EXTRACT FROM STIRLINGSHIRE N24.14 [1917]

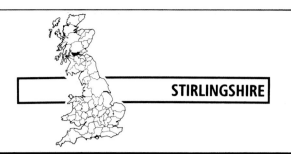

Causewayhead [1st] Depot

Location: At NS80369533, on the east side of Causewayhead Road, just west of the NBR Causewayhead Station.

Opened: July 27th, 1874 by the Stirling & Bridge of Allan Tramways Co. Ltd.

Traction System: Horse. (A steamcar was utilized for one day only on August 3rd, 1878.)

Gauge: 4ft 8.5in.

Description: Originally a timber built 2TS dead ended tram shed and stables, it was enlarged in 1888.

Closed: 1898 and subsequently utilized as a fodder store and harness room. It was blown down in a gale in 1968 and the site was later occupied by a restaurant.

Causewayhead [2nd] Depot

Location: At NS80319537, on the west side of Causewayhead Road, opposite the first depot.

Opened: 1898 by the Stirling & Bridge of Allan Tramways Co. Ltd.

Traction System: Horse until February 5th, 1920 and Petrol from December 9th, 1913.

Gauge: 4ft 8.5in.

Description: A 6TS dead ended tram shed accessed via a traverser. It also housed omnibuses from November 1919.

Closed: May 20th, 1920 to trams. By 1991 it was in use as a motor vehicle store.

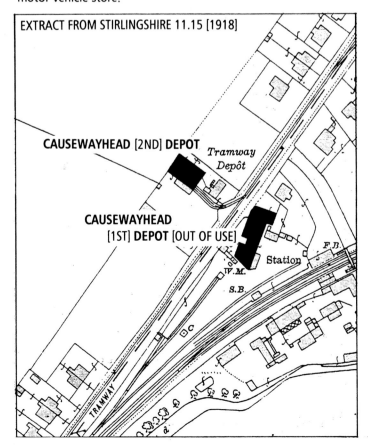

EXTRACT FROM STIRLINGSHIRE 11.15 [1918]

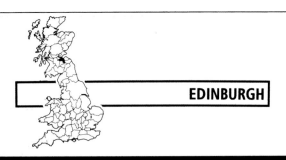

EDINBURGH

EDINBURGH [CITY]

Henderson Row

Location: At NT25007475, on the south side of Henderson Row, west of Pitt Street.

Opened: January 28th, 1888 by Edinburgh Northern Tramways Co., taken over by Edinburgh & District Tramways on January 1st, 1897 and taken over by Edinburgh Corporation on July 1st, 1897.

Traction System: Cable.

Gauge: 4ft 8.5in.

Description: Originally a brick built 9TS dead ended tram shed, accessed via a traverser, and a winding station, it was later enlarged with a 3TS extension.

Closed: December 29th, 1920. The cable power station continued in use until January 24th, 1921 and the building was utilized as an omnibus garage until 1926 and then as a police garage. The façade was later incorporated into the Scottish Life Assurance Building which opened on November 2nd, 1992.

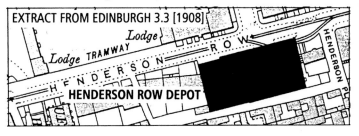

EXTRACT FROM EDINBURGH 3.3 [1908]

HENDERSON ROW DEPOT

Gorgie Depot

Location: At NT22627235, on the north side of Gorgie Rd, between Westfield Rd and Westfield St.

Opened: August 12th, 1925 by Edinburgh Corporation.

Traction System: Overhead Electric.

Gauge: 4ft 8.5in.

Description: A 3TS through road tram shed.

Closed: To trams on May 2nd, 1953 and utilized as an omnibus garage until 1955. Sold in 1957 and by 2000 it was in use as a whisky bonded store.

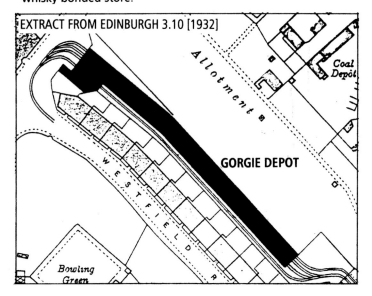

EXTRACT FROM EDINBURGH 3.10 [1932]

GORGIE DEPOT

Shrubhill

Location: At NT26327514, on the west side of Leith Walk.

Opened: November 6th, 1871 by Edinburgh Street Tramways and taken over by Edinburgh Corporation on December 9th, 1893.

Traction System: Horse, until August 24th, 1907, Cable between October 26th, 1899 and October 21st, 1922, and Overhead Electric from 1922.

Gauge: 4ft 8.5in.

Description: Originally a small horse tram depot it was enlarged in 1879/80 and in 1882 to a tram depot of between 2 and 7 tracks in width with stables and a works. In 1899 it was rebuilt in brick as a 31TS shed with a central traverser, works and winding station with the yard also accommodating omnibuses. It was rebuilt, again, for electric working with 2 dead end tracks, 2 through tracks and a 3TS works.

Closed: Along with the system on November 16th, 1956. It was subsequently converted to an omnibus garage with much of the site being demolished and cleared in 1962. In 2000 it was due to be sold for housing development although the former cable house and two other buildings were to be preserved.

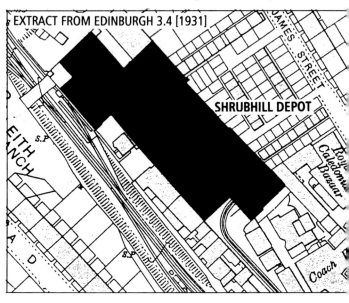

EXTRACT FROM EDINBURGH 3.4 [1931]

SHRUBHILL DEPOT

Tollcross

Location: At NT24837296, on the north side of West Tollcross, between Ponton St. and Dunbar St.

Opened: October 26th, 1899 by the Edinburgh & District Tramways Co. Ltd and taken over by Edinburgh Corporation on July 1st, 1919.

Traction System: Cable, until March 17th, 1923, and Overhead Electric from February 3rd, 1924.

Gauge: 4ft 8.5in.

Description: Originally an 18TS dead ended shed with one track accessing a rear traverser, and a winding station, it was rebuilt for electric working as a 13TS dead ended tram shed.

Closed: With the tramway on November 16th, 1956 and later demolished.

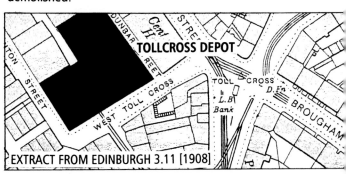

TOLLCROSS DEPOT

EXTRACT FROM EDINBURGH 3.11 [1908]

High Street

Location: At NT30447393, on the south side of High Street, east of Rosefield Avenue, Portobello.

Opened: May 14th, 1875 by the Edinburgh Street Tramways Co. and taken over by Edinburgh Corporation on December 9th, 1893.

Traction System: Horse (also Steam working between April 23rd, 1881 and October 27th, 1882).

Gauge: 4ft 8.5in.

Description: A 2TS dead ended tram shed and stables.

Closed: 1902.

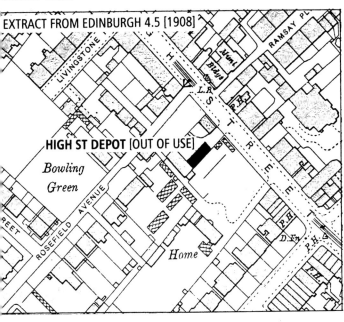

Portobello

Location: At NT36287406, on the south west side of High St.

Opened: May 1st, 1902 by the Edinburgh & District Tramways Co. Ltd and taken over by Edinburgh Corporation on July 1st, 1919.

Traction System: Cable, until June 23rd, 1923, and then Overhead Electric.

Gauge: 4ft 8.5in.

Description: Originally a brick built 6TS dead ended tram shed with a central traverser, it was rebuilt and enlarged for electric working as a 9TS dead ended tram shed.

Closed: To trams on November 13th, 1954 and subsequently sold and demolished.

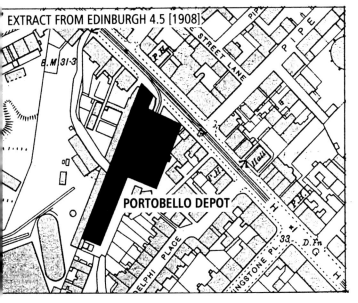

Leith Walk

Location: At NT26947555, on the east side of Leith Walk.

Opened: June 9th, 1894 by the Edinburgh Street Tramways Co., taken over by Leith Corporation on October 23rd, 1904 and taken over by Edinburgh Corporation on November 20th, 1920.

Traction System: Horse, until November 2nd 1905, and then Overhead Electric from August 18th, 1905.

Gauge: 4ft 8.5in.

Description: Originally a dead ended horse tram shed and stables, it was reconstructed for electric working as a brick built 9TS dead ended tram shed and workshops. It was further enlarged in 1937 with 3 roads being added on the south side and the front end being extended.

Closed: May 5th, 1956 and converted to an omnibus garage. By 2000 it was still largely intact and in use as a depot for Social Work Department vehicles.

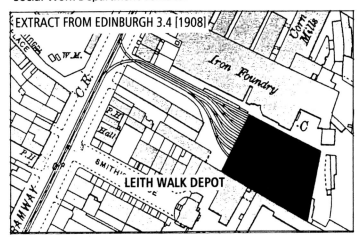

MUSSELBURGH

High Street

Location: At NT34737265, on the south side of the High St.

Opened: December 12th, 1904 by the National Electric Construction Co. Ltd and taken over in August 1905 by the Musselburgh & District Electric Light & Traction Co. Ltd.

Traction System: Overhead Electric.

Gauge: 4ft 8.5in.

Description: A 4TS dead ended tram shed constructed in corrugated iron, and a power station.

Closed: March 31st, 1928. The western half of the system was subsequently worked by Edinburgh Corporation whilst the depot was utilized for scrapping tram cars. Demolished.

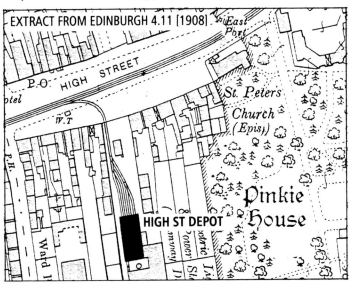

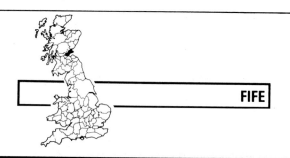

FIFE

COWDENBEATH

Cowdenbeath

Location: At NT15899091, on the north side of Broad Street.

Opened: November 2nd, 1909 by the Dunfermline and District Tramways Co.

Traction System: Overhead Electric.

Gauge: 3ft 6in.

Description: A 7TS dead ended tram shed.

Closed: July 5th, 1937 and subsequently utilized as an omnibus garage.

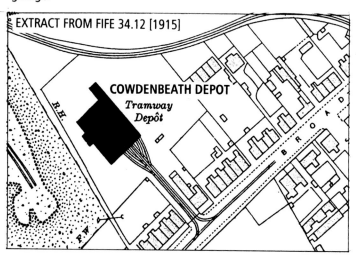

EXTRACT FROM FIFE 34.12 [1915]

COWDENBEATH DEPOT
Tramway Depôt

DUNFERMLINE

St Leonard's

Location: At NT09648656, on the west side of St Leonard's Street.

Opened: May 17th, 1918 by the Dunfermline and District Tramways Co.

Traction System: Overhead Electric.

Gauge: 3ft 6in.

Description: A 4TS dead ended tram shed. An omnibus garage was added on the east side of the site in 1924.

Closed: July 5th, 1937 and subsequently utilized as an omnibus garage.

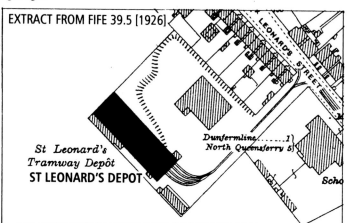

EXTRACT FROM FIFE 39.5 [1926]

St Leonard's Tramway Depôt
ST LEONARD'S DEPOT

Dunfermline......1
North Queensferry 5

KIRKCALDY

Gallatown

Location: At NT29709414, on the corner of Oswald Road and Rosslyn Street.

Opened: February 28th, 1903 by Kirkcaldy Corporation.

Traction System: Overhead Electric.

Gauge: 3ft 6in.

Description: A red sandstone built 11TS dead ended tram shed.

Closed: May 15th, 1931 and subsequently utilized as an omnibus depot. Demolished during the 1980s.

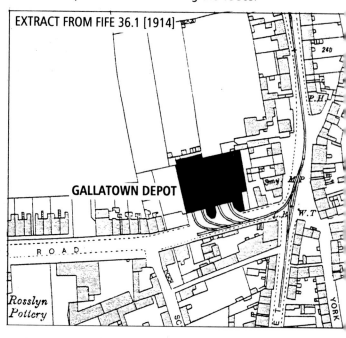

EXTRACT FROM FIFE 36.1 [1914]

GALLATOWN DEPOT

ROAD

Rosslyn Pottery

WEMYSS

Aberhill

Location: At NO37460004, on the west side of Wellesley Road.

Opened: August 25th, 1906 by Wemyss & District Tramways Co. Ltd.

Traction System: Overhead Electric.

Gauge: 3ft 6in.

Description: A 6TS dead ended tram shed. An omnibus garage was added on the east side in 1922.

Closed: January 30th, 1932.

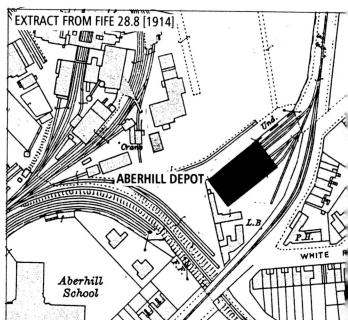

EXTRACT FROM FIFE 28.8 [1914]

ABERHILL DEPOT

Aberhill School

WHITE

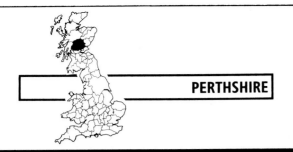

PERTHSHIRE

PERTH

Perth Road

Location: At NO13752612, on the north side of Perth Road, Scone.
Opened: September 17th, 1895 by the Perth & District Tramways Co. Ltd and taken over by Perth Corporation on October 7th, 1903.
Traction System: Horse (until October 31st, 1905) and then Overhead Electric.
Gauge: 3ft 6in.
Description: Originally a 2TS dead ended tram shed and stables, it was extended to a 3TS building in 1898 and rebuilt in brick as a 5TS dead ended tram shed with a 1TS workshop/paint shop in 1905.
Closed: January 19th, 1929.

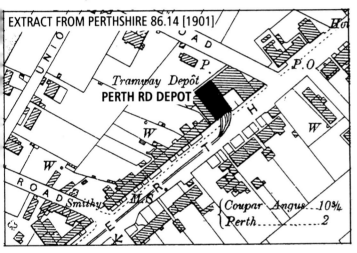

Cuddies Grave

Location: Probably at NO12742480, on the south side of the Coupar Angus Road, east of Pitwarden Rd, Bridgend.
Opened: 1905 by Perth Corporation Tramways.
Traction System: Horse.
Gauge: 3ft 6in.
Description: A temporary tram shed.
Closed: 1905.

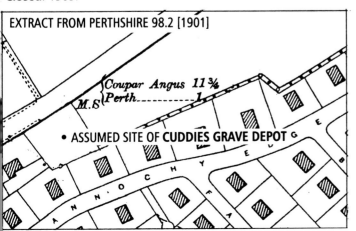

INCHTURE

Crossgates

Location: At NO27692753, on the north side of the Perth to Dundee Road.
Opened: 1849 by the Dundee & Perth Railway and taken over by the Caledonian Railway in 1865.
Traction System: Horse.
Gauge: 4ft 8.5in.
Description: A 1TS dead ended tram shed.
Closed: Probably on December 31st, 1916.

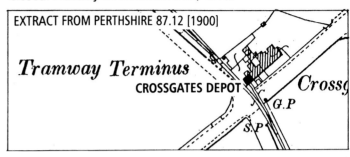

BUTE

ROTHESAY

Pointhouse Depot

Location: At NS08046702, on the west side of Ardbeg Road.
Opened: June 1st, 1882 by the Rothesay Tramways Co. Ltd and taken over by the British Electric Traction Co. Ltd in 1901. It was again taken over on January 1st, 1914 by the Scottish General Transport Co and by the Scottish Motor Traction Group (known from June 1st, 1932 as the Western Scottish Traction Group) in 1931.
Traction System: Horse until August 19th, 1902, and then Overhead Electric.
Gauge: 4ft until May 17th, 1902 and then 3ft 6in.
Description: Originally a 3TS dead ended tram shed and stables it was rebuilt in brick as an 8TS dead ended tram shed in 1902. From December 1930 it also housed omnibuses.
Closed: March 2nd, 1902 for regauging and electrification, re-opened on May 17th, 1902 and finally closed to trams on September 30th, 1936. Still in use as an omnibus garage in 1986.

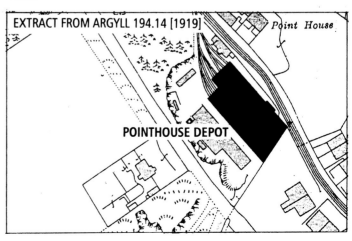

ABERDEENSHIRE

Cruden Bay Hotel

Location: At NK08203603, on the north side of Cruden Bay Hotel, south of Aulton Road.

Opened: 1899 by the Great North of Scotland Railway and taken over by the London & North Eastern Railway in 1923.

Traction System: Overhead Electric.

Gauge: 3ft 6.5in.

Description: Tramcars were initially stored in the open for a short while until the 2TS dead ended tram shed, accessed by a turntable, opened in 1899. The building may have been utilized, from time to time, as accommodation for summer hotel staff, the tramcars being stored in the yard.

Closed: October 31st, 1932 upon the cessation of passenger services, but the tramway remained open for goods traffic until at least 1941. Demolished, along with the hotel buildings, by 1952.

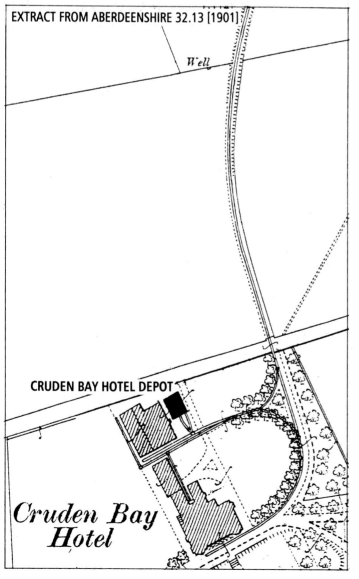

EXTRACT FROM ABERDEENSHIRE 32.13 [1901]

Well

CRUDEN BAY HOTEL DEPOT

Cruden Bay Hotel

Club House

Location: At NJ95450983, on the east side of the line, north of the terminus.

Opened: 1909 by the Seaton Brick & Tile Co. Ltd and taken over by the Murcar Golf Club in 1924.

Traction System: Petrol.

Gauge: 3ft.

Description: A timber built 1TS dead ended railcar shed.

Closed: 1949. (It may have gone out of use in 1932 upon the opening of the Links Road Station shed.)

Links Road Station

Location: At NJ94850976 over the track at the north end of the station site.

Opened: 1932 by the Murcar Golf Club.

Traction System: Petrol.

Gauge: 3ft.

Description: A timber built 1TS through road railcar shed.

Closed: 1949. The whole site was cleared and utilized for housing.

The tramway was horse worked between 1900 and 1909 but there is no evidence of the existence of a tramcar shed in this period. The goods service was steam worked and the shed* for the loco was located at NJ94700968.

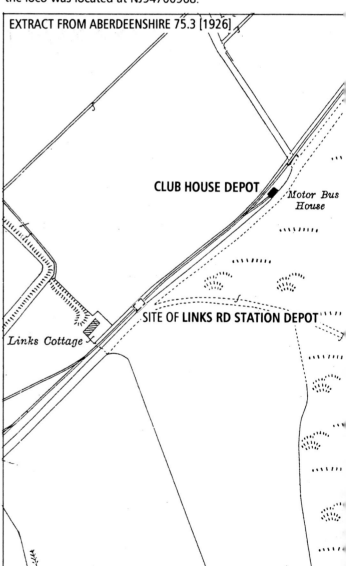

EXTRACT FROM ABERDEENSHIRE 75.3 [1926]

CLUB HOUSE DEPOT

Motor Bus House

SITE OF **LINKS RD STATION DEPOT**

Links Cottage

*This depot is listed in "The Directory of British Engine Sheds" as NJ9409.1/1A

King Street

Location: At NJ94230741, on the south side of St Peter Street, west of King Street.
Opened: 1920 by Aberdeen Corporation.
Traction System: Overhead Electric.
Gauge: 4ft 8.5in.
Description: Originally a granite built 3TS dead ended tram shed, sited within a former barracks, a 3TS dead ended shed was added on the south side in 1932. At some stage an omnibus and tram works was constructed at the west end.
Closed: May 3rd, 1958 and later demolished, the site being utilized as accommodation for Aberdeen University.

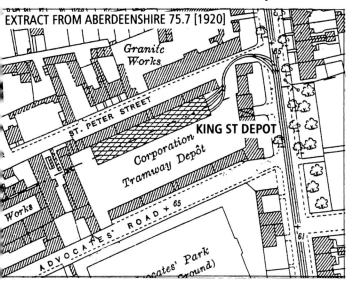

EXTRACT FROM ABERDEENSHIRE 75.7 [1920]

Woodside

Location: At NJ92760866, on the east side of Great Northern Road, opposite Tanfield Walk, Woodside.
Opened: 1881 by the Aberdeen District Tramways Company and taken over by Aberdeen Corporation on August 27th, 1898.
Traction System: Horse, until December 23rd, 1899, and then Overhead Electric.
Gauge: 4ft 8.5in.
Description: Originally a granite built 4TS dead ended tram shed and stables, it was demolished in 1898 and a temporary corrugated iron built shed was erected adjacently until a granite built 5TS dead ended tram shed was ready for overhead electric working in 1899.
Closed: November 26th, 1955 and later demolished for housing.

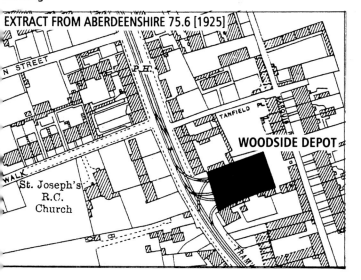

EXTRACT FROM ABERDEENSHIRE 75.6 [1925]

Queens Cross
EAST DEPOT

Location: At NJ92440591, on the east side of Fountainhall Road.
Opened: August 31st, 1874 by the Aberdeen District Tramways Company and taken over by Aberdeen Corporation on August 27th, 1898.
Traction System: Horse.
Gauge: 4ft 8.5in.
Description: Originally a 2TS dead ended tram shed and stables, it was enlarged in 1890.
Closed: 1900 and taken over by the Cleansing Department.

WEST DEPOT

Location: At NJ92350588, on the west side of Fountainhall Road.
Opened: 1892 by the Aberdeen District Tramways Company and taken over by Aberdeen Corporation on August 27th, 1898.
Traction System: Horse, until 1900, and then Overhead Electric.
Gauge: 4ft 8.5in.
Description: Originally a granite built 4TS dead ended tram shed, a 3TS dead ended extension was added in 1951.
Closed: October 7th, 1956 and subsequently demolished.

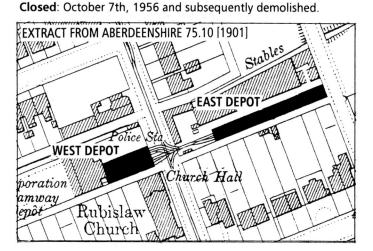

EXTRACT FROM ABERDEENSHIRE 75.10 [1901]

Bankhead

Location: At NJ89231021, on the south west side of Bankhead Road at the junction with Greenburn Road.
Opened: July 8th, 1904 by the Aberdeen Suburban Tramways Company.
Traction System: Overhead Electric.
Gauge: 4ft 8.5in.
Description: A 2TS dead ended tram shed constructed in corrugated iron.
Closed: July 2nd, 1927 and demolished in the 1930s. Site now occupied by a cafe.

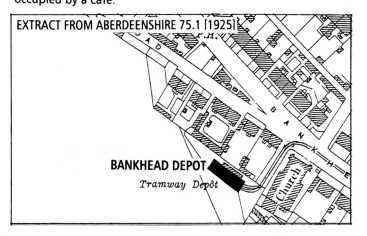

EXTRACT FROM ABERDEENSHIRE 75.1 [1925]

Mannofield [1st] Depot

Location: At NJ91830458, on the south side of Great Western Road between Duthie Terrace and Cranford Road, Mannofield.

Opened: September 1880 by the Aberdeen District Tramways Company and taken over by Aberdeen Corporation on August 27th. 1898.

Traction System: Horse until c1900, and then Overhead Electric.

Gauge: 4ft 8.5in.

Description: Originally a 2TS dead ended tram shed (the tracks were not laid into the building until 1896), it was enlarged with three more dead ended roads on the west side and the two roads in the original building were extended. It was rebuilt in granite in the late 1920s as a 6TS through road shed.

Closed: March 3rd, 1951 and utilized as an omnibus garage. It was later demolished.

Mannofield [2nd] Depot

Location: At NJ91670434, on the south side of Great Western Road, between Cranford Road and Morningside Road.

Opened: June 23rd, 1904 by the Aberdeen Suburban Tramways Company.

Traction System: Overhead Electric.

Gauge: 4ft 8.5in.

Description: A 3TS dead ended tram shed constructed in corrugated iron sheeting with a granite facade. A corrugated iron extension for omnibuses was added later on the north east side.

Closed: Probably on July 9th, 1927 and later utilized as a car garage. It was demolished in 1975 and replaced with a filling station.

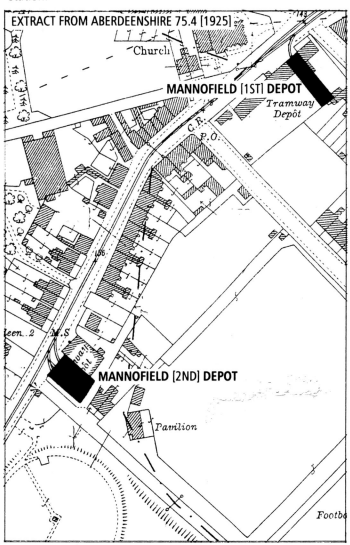

EXTRACT FROM ABERDEENSHIRE 75.4 [1925]

Constitution Street

Location: At NJ94970694, on the north side of Constitution St, opposite Links Road.

Opened: 1921 by Aberdeen Corporation.

Traction System: Overhead Electric.

Gauge: 4ft 8.5in.

Description: A combined omnibus and tram depot, the tram portion of which was a granite built 2TS dead ended shed.

Closed: Probably in 1938 to trams. The tram shed was later utilized as commercial premises before the whole site was taken over for a corporation depot.

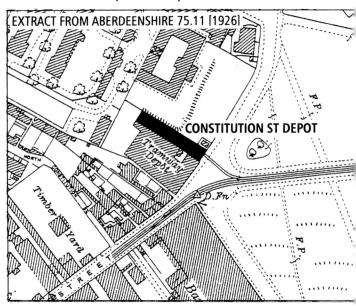

EXTRACT FROM ABERDEENSHIRE 75.11 [1926]

Market Street

Location: At NJ94610556, on the corner of Market Street and North Esplanade West.

Opened: c1903 by Aberdeen Corporation.

Traction System: Overhead Electric.

Gauge: 4ft 8.5in.

Description: A granite built 2TS dead ended tram shed.

Closed: February 28th, 1931. By 2000 it was in use as office premises.

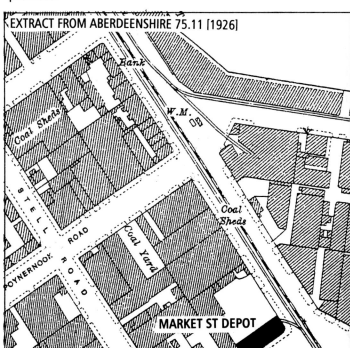

EXTRACT FROM ABERDEENSHIRE 75.11 [1926]

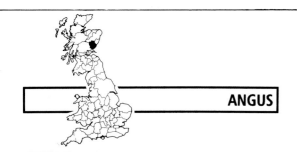

ANGUS

DUNDEE

Perth Road

Location: At NO39352973, on the south side of Perth Rd, west side of Westfield Lane.

Opened: August 30th, 1877 by the Dundee & District Tramway Co. Ltd and taken over by Dundee Corporation on June 1st, 1899.

Traction System: Horse.

Gauge: 4ft 8.5in.

Description: A 2TS dead ended tram shed and works.

Closed: July 12th, 1900.

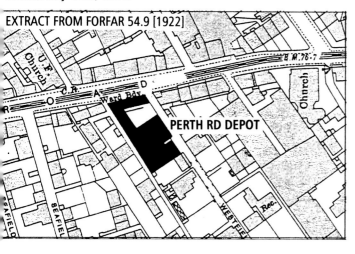

Milton Depot

Location: At NO48723187, on the south side of Dundee Rd, Milton.

Opened: December 27th, 1905 by the Dundee, Broughty Ferry & District Tramways Co. Ltd and taken over by Dundee Corporation on May 15th, 1931.

Traction System: Overhead Electric.

Gauge: 4ft 8.5in.

Description: A brick built 3TS dead ended shed and works.

Closed: May 15th, 1931. By 1965 it was in use as a carpet factory.

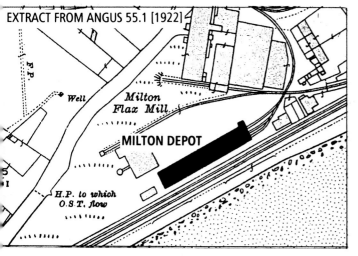

Lochee Depot

Location: At NO37823164, on the west side of High Street.

Opened: December 24th, 1879 by the Dundee & District Tramway Co. Ltd and taken over by Dundee Corporation on June 1st, 1899.

Traction System: Horse, until October 22nd, 1900 and then Overhead Electric. A steam car was utilized between August 6th, 1880 and December 1880, and a steam locomotive from June 20th, 1885 until May 14th, 1902.

Gauge: 4ft 8.5in.

Description: Originally a 2TS dead ended tram shed and works, a steam loco shed was added in 1885 and a new 10TS depot and works constructed on the site in 1888. Following the cessation of steam working it was rebuilt again as a 3TS dead ended tram shed on the northern part of the site.

Closed: October 20th, 1956. In 1965 it was in use as a store.

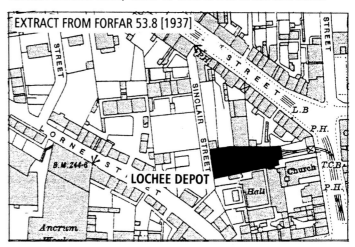

Central Depot

Location: At NO39753056, on the corner of Lochee Road and Dudhope Crescent Road.

Opened: July 1900 by Dundee Corporation.

Traction System: Overhead Electric.

Gauge: 4ft 8.5in.

Description: A brick built 6TS dead ended tram shed and works

Closed: 1921 and subsequently utilized for repair work. The building was refurbished in 1929 as workshops and a new combined tram/omnibus garage was added to the south side as a repair depot. After the tramways closed in 1956 it reverted to an omnibus garage and was still operational in 1965.

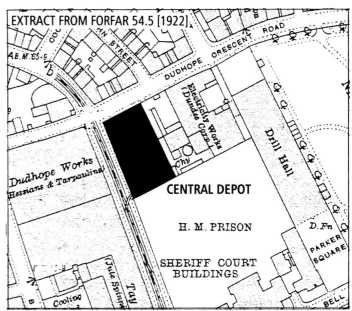

Forfar Road [Maryfield] Depot

Location: At NO41440001, on the corner of Forfar Road and Walrond Street.

Opened: June 1901 by Dundee Corporation. (From March 6th, 1901 and until the opening of this depot the cars were housed temporarily in the Tay Foundry Yard at Stobswell).

Traction System: Overhead Electric.

Gauge: 4ft 8.5in.

Description: Originally a 6TS dead ended tram shed it was extended at the rear before and after World War I.

Closed: October 20th, 1956 and subsequently utilized as an omnibus garage.

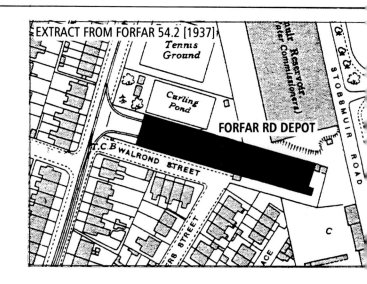

EXTRACT FROM FORFAR 54.2 [1937]

APPENDIX
THE SUPERTRAM DEPOTS

The new generation of "tramlink" or "metro" tramways, built to serve major conurbations in England, do not operate from running sheds as such. Rather their "depots" follow modern railway dmu and emu practice in that tramcars are stabled in storage sidings when not in use, the only covered shelter being provided for workshop use.

To date, four of these "supertrams" - all standard gauge overhead electric systems - have opened. These are listed below with the opening dates and locations of their storage sidings:

Manchester Metrolink (April 6th, 1992)
Queens Road Operations & Maintenance Centre: At SD84900040 between Queens Road and the railway bridge by Cheetham Hill Junction, west of the tramline and just north east of the city centre.

South Yorkshire Supertram (March 21st, 1994)
Nunnery Depot: At SK37208781, on the west side of Woodburn Road, immediately south of the railway bridge and north east of the city centre. This site was formerly occupied by the ex-London & North Western Railway Nunnery engine shed. (Listed in *The Directory of British Engine Sheds* as SK3787.1/1A)

Midland Metro (May 31st, 1999)
Metro Centre: At SO98309455, on the south side of Wednesbury Great Western St. Stop.

Croydon Tramlink (May 10th, 2000)
Therapia Lane Depot: At TQ29906690, on the south side of the tram line, north west of the Therapia Lane Stop.

The shape of things to come? Car No.01 passing the entrance road to the new Midland Metro's storage sidings and workshop (in far distance) as seen from Wednesbury Great Western St. (Parkway) Station on March 3rd, 2001.   *K Turner*

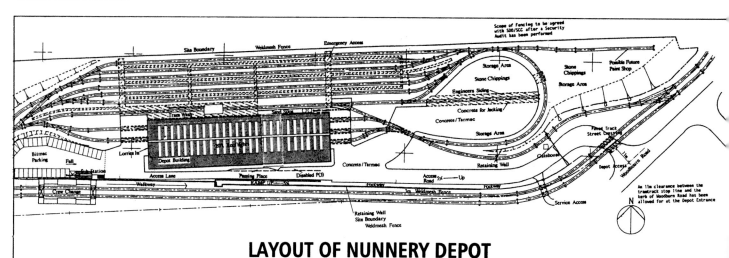

LAYOUT OF NUNNERY DEPOT

Reproduced by Courtesy of South Yorkshire PTE.

INDEX

This Index includes, where known to the authors. the fate and/or current use being made of the depot buildings. Information to fill any gaps, or to record changes of usage, would be welcomed. Dates in brackets for those depots still extant are those of the most recent inspection.

D; Demolished F; Destroyed by fire P; Preserved S; Still Standing.

Depot	Page	Current Site Usage
Fishergate, Preston	94	D. Site occupied by County Hall.
Foleshill Road, Coventry	60	D. Site occupied by housing.
Folkestone Road, Dover	20	S. In use as a Corporation Depot (1992).
Forfar Road, Dundee	160	S. Vacant (2000).
Fosse Way, Bath	9	Demolished in the 1970s.
Foundry Street, Stoke on Trent	72	D. Site redeveloped.
Franklin Place, Liverpool	105	
Fratton Road, Portsmouth	15	D.
Frederick Road, Salford	98	
Freemans Place, Darlington	126	
Friargate, Derby	74	D. Site in use as a car park.
Friars' Field, Newport	131	D.
Frost Hill, Liversedge	122	
Fulford Road, York	124	Demolished in 1995 and site now occupied by a supermarket.
Fulwell, Greater London	24	S. In use as an Omnibus Garage (1998).
Fulwood, Preston	94	D.
Gadlys, Aberdare	133	D.
Gallatown, Kirkcaldy	154	Demolished in the 1980s. Site redeveloped.
Gargrave Street, Oldham	93	
Gladys Avenue, Portsmouth	15	D. Site occupied by housing.
Glyntaff, Pontypridd	135	
Golden Ball, Sheffield	118	D.
Goldenhill, Stoke on Trent	72	
Goldhawk Road Yard, Greater London	26	D.
Gorgie, Edinburgh	152	S. In use as a Whisky Bonded Store (2000).
Gosforth, Newcastle upon Tyne	128	S. In commercial use (1999).
Gosport Road, Gosport	17	
Govan [No.1], Glasgow	144	D. Site occupied by a shopping centre.
Govan [No.2], Glasgow	144	D. Site occupied by a Church.
Great Northern Street, Huddersfield	120	
Great Orme, Llandudno	140	All depots still operational.
Greenholme Street, Kilmarnock	148	D.
Green Lane, Liverpool	104	
Green Lanes, Greater London	42	
Greenwich, Greater London	37	
Greyfriars Road, Doncaster	119	Demolished in 1983. Site occupied by a supermarket.
Grey Street, Manchester	86	
Grove Road, Greater London	42	
Guiseley, Leeds	114	
GVT Station, Chirk	137	D. Sites cleared.
GVT Station, Glynceiriog	137	S. In use as a council depot building (1999).
Hackney, Greater London	41	
Hall Street, St Helens	96	
Hammersmith, Greater London	27	
Hanwell, Greater London	25	
Harbour Road, Cardiff	132	
Harpurhey, Manchester	87	
Harrison Street, Leeds	112	D. Site redeveloped.
Hart Road, Hartlepool	125	D. Site occupied by housing.
Harts Hill, Dudley	62	S. In commercial use (2001).
Haymarket, Newcastle upon Tyne	128	Demolished in 1958.
Headingley, Leeds	114	D.
Heaton Lane, Stockport	70	
Heavitree Road, Exeter	12	D.
Hedon Road, Kingston upon Hull	110	S. In commercial use (2000).
Heeley, Sheffield	116	S. In use as a garage (2000).
Heifer Lane, Colne	81	
Henderson Row, Edinburgh	152	D. Facade incorporated into the Scottish Life Assurance Co. building.
Hendon, Greater London	29	
Henry Street, Lytham St Anne's	84	Demolished c1986 and site now occupied by housing.
Herne Bay Pier, Herne Bay	19	D.
Hessle Road, Kingston upon Hull	109	D.

Depot	Page	Current Site Usage
Tram Street, Platt Bridge	99	
Tramway Avenue, Colwyn Bay	138	S. In commercial use.
Tramway Avenue, Liverpool	103	D.
Trehafod, Pontypridd	135	Demolished in 1920.
Trenmar Gardens, Greater London	28	
Trent Bridge [1st], Nottingham	77	
Trent Bridge [2nd], Nottingham	77	S. In use as an Omnibus Garage (1999).
Troedyrhiw Road, Porth	135	
Tunmarsh Lane, Greater London	45	
Tunnel Avenue, Greater London	44	D.
Victoria, Greater London	28	D.
Victoria Road, Dartford	21	F. Destroyed by a fire in 1917.
Victoria Road, South Shields	127	
Victoria Street, Bristol	47	S. Vacant.
Victoria Street, Grimsby	66	
Walcot Street, Bath	9	S. In use as an Antiques Market (1992).
Wallshaw Street, Oldham	92	
Walnut Tree Road, Erith	20	
Walthamstow, Greater London	43	Demolished in 1995. Site occupied by housing.
Walton, Liverpool	103	Demolished in the 1960s.
Warbreck Moor, Liverpool	101	D. Site now part of park.
Warlter's Road, Greater London	38	
Washwood Heath Road, Birmingham	57	S. In use as an Omnibus Garage (1999).
Wavertree, Liverpool	103	Demolished in 1935. Site occupied by housing.
Weaste [No.1], Salford	98	
Weaste [No.2], Salford	98	S. In use as industrial premises (1999).
Wellington Bridge, Leeds	115	D.
Wellington Street, Matlock	75	S. In commercial use (1999).
West Derby, Liverpool	104	
West End Promenade, Pwllheli	139	S. In use as a garage and Omnibus Depot (1995).
West Ham, Greater London	45	
Westhill Avenue, Torquay	12	Demolished in the 1990s. Site occupied by housing.
West Smethwick, Smethwick	63	D. Site occupied by industrial premises.
Wheat Sheaf, Sunderland	125	
Wheeler Street, Kingston upon Hull	111	S. In commercial use (2000).
Wheldon Lane, Castleford	12	
Whiteinch, Glasgow	147	D.
Whitevale, Glasgow	142	D. Site redeveloped.
Whitson Street, Bristol	46	D. Site occupied by a 'bus station.
Wimborne Road, Bournemouth	14	
Wingrove, Newcastle upon Tyne	128	S. In commercial use (1999).
Wisbech, Cambridgeshire	50	D. Site occupied by bungalows.
Witham, Kingston upon Hull	110	D.
Withington Road, Manchester	88	
Witton Lane, Birmingham	58	P. In use as Aston Manor Transport Museum (2001).
Wolverton Road, Stony Stratford	49	
Wood Green, Greater London	43	S. In use as an Omnibus Garage (2000).
Woodland Road, Darlington	126	
Woodside, Aberdeen	157	D. Site occupied by housing.
Wood Street, Cardiff	132	D. Site redeveloped.
Yardley, Birmingham	58	D. Site occupied by commercial premises.
York Street, Greater London	38	D.
York Street, Heywood	83	D.

BIBLIOGRAPHY

Interest in British tramways is such that virtually no line or system, however small, has not had its history written in some shape or form during the past forty years or so. As writers have become ever more diligent in their researches, so the quality and depth of such histories have steadily improved. This consideration, and constraints of space, means that this *Bibliography* is limited to the more important studies published (unless part of a set) during the past twenty-five years. Older titles are listed in *The Directory of British Tramways* cited below.

GENERAL

COLLINS, Paul. *The Tram Book* (Ian Allan 1995) 0 7110 2268 2

TURNER, Keith. *The Directory of British Tramways* (Patrick Stephens 1996) 1 85260 549 9

Pier Tramways & Tramways of the British Isles Locomotion Papers No.60 (Oakwood Press, 2nd Revised Edition, 1999) 0 85361 541 1

WALLER, Michael H & Peter. *British & Irish Tramway Systems Since 1945* (Ian Allan 1992) 0 7110 1989 4

WHITCOMBE, Dr HA. *History of the Steam Tram* (Adam Gordon, Chetwode, 2000) 1 87442 228 1

ENGLISH TRAMWAYS

ABELL, PH, GARNHAM, JA & McLOUGHLIN I. *The Tramways of Lytham St Annes* Locomotion Papers No.189 (Oakwood Press 1995) 0 85361 475 X

BADDELEY, GE. *The Tramways of Croydon* (The Light Rail Transit Association Revised Edition 1983) 0 900433 90 6

BAKER, T. *Transport in Great Yarmouth Volume 1: Electric Tramways 1902-1918* (Author, Chipping Sodbury 1980) 0 950688 90 8

Transport in Great Yarmouth Volume 2: 1919-1933 Electric Tramways & Petrol Omnibuses (Author, Chipping Sodbury 1983) 0 950688 91 6

BARHAM, Fisher. *Torbay Transport* (Glasney Press, Falmouth 1979) 0 950282 54 5

BROOK, Roy. *Huddersfield Corporation Tramways* (Author, Accrington 1983) 0 950858 91 9

BROWN, Colin. *Luton Trams* (Irwell Press 1999) 1 871608 91 0

CLARK, WD & DIBDIN, HG. *Trams and Buses of the City of Chester* (Manchester Transport Museum Society 1979) 0 900857 16 1

COATES, DM. *Bradford City Tramways 1882-1950* (Wyvern Publications, Skipton 1984) 0 907941 12 5

COLLINS, Paul. *Birmingham Corporation Transport 1904-1939* Ian Allan Transport Library (Ian Allan 1999) 0 7110 2627 0

Birmingham Corporation Transport 1939-1969 Ian Allan Transport Library (Ian Allan 1999) 0 7110 2656 4

CORMACK, Ian L. *Barrow in Furness Transport - A Century on Wheels* (Author, Glasgow 1977)

COURSE, Edwin. *Portsmouth Corporation Tramways 1896-1936* Portsmouth Papers No.45 (Portsmouth City Council 1986) 0 901559 66 0

de COURTAIS, Nicholas. *The Wantage Tramway 1875-1945* (Wild Swan Publications 1981) 0 906867 06 1

DENTON, AS. *D.D.L.R. The Story of the Dearne District Light Railway and Competitors* (The Omnibus Society 1980) 0 901307 35 1

DENTON, AS & GROVES, FP. *Coventry Transport 1884-1940* (The Birmingham Transport Historical Group 1985) 0 905103 05 X

DOW, George. *Alford & Sutton Tramway* (Author 1984)

EDWARDS, Barry. *The Story of Transport in Derby* (Breedon Books, Derby 1993) 1 87362 657 6

FOX, Peter, JACKSON, Paul & BENTON, Roger. *Tram to Supertram* (Platform 5 Publishing Ltd 1995) 1 872524 61 3

GANDY, Kenneth. *Sheffield Corporation Tramways* (Sheffield City Libraries 1985) 0 86321 032 5

GRAY, Edward. *The Manchester Carriage and Tramways Company* (Manchester Transport Museum Society 1977)

Salford's Tramways Part One (Foxline Publishing 1997) 1 870119 47 9

Salford's Tramways Part Two (Foxline Publishing 1999) 1 870119 55 X

GRAY, Ted. *Trafford Park Tramways 1897-1946* (Northern Publishing Services, Manchester Centenary Edition 1996) 1 899181 34 2

GROVES, FP. *Nottingham City Transport* (The Transport Publishing Co. 1978) 0 903839 25 3

HALL, Chas C. *Sheffield Transport* (The Transport Publishing Co. 1977) 0 903839 04 0

Rotherham and District Transport Volume 1: to 1914 (Rotherwood Press 1996) 0 903666 89 2

Rotherham and District Transport Volume 2: to 1939 (Rotherwood Press 1998) 0 903666 92 8

Rotherham and District Transport Volume 3: to 1974 (Rotherwood Press 2000) 0 903666 93 6

HART, Brian. *The Hythe & Sandgate Railway* (Wild Swan Publications 1987) 0 906867 53 3

HAWKINS, Chris & REEVE, George. *The Wisbech & Upwell Tramway* (Wild Swan Publications 1982) 0 906867 09 6

HOLT, David. *Manchester Metrolink* UK Light Rail Systems No.1 (Platform 5 Publishing Ltd 1992) 1 872524 36 2

HORNE, JB & MAUND, TB. *Liverpool Transport Vol 1: 1830-1900* (Senior Publications, Glossop 2nd Revised Edition 1995) 0 86317 200 8

Liverpool Transport Vol 2: 1900-1930 (The Transport Publishing Co./The Light Rail Transit Association 1982) 0 903839 50 4

Liverpool Transport Vol 3: 1931-1939 (The Transport Publishing Co./The Light Rail Transit Association 1987) 0 86317 141 9

Liverpool Transport Vol 4: 1939-1957 (The Transport Publishing Co. 1989) 0 86317 148 6

HYDE, WGS. *A History of Public Transport in Ashton-under-Lyne* (Manchester Transport Museum Society 1980)

The Manchester Bury Rochdale and Oldham Steam Tramway (The Transport Publishing Co. 1979) 0 903839 37 7

JACKSON, HE. *The Tramways of Reading* (Adam Gordon, Chetwode 2nd Edition 1990)

JENSON, Alec G. *Birmingham Transport Volume 1* (The Birmingham Transport Historical Group 1978) 0 905103 00 9

KING, JS. *Bradford Corporation Tramways* (Venture Publications 1999) 1 898432 80 5

KIRBY, AK. *Middleton Tramways* (Manchester Transport Museum Society 1976)

KIRBY, Arthur. *Oldham Corporation Tramways* (Triangle Publishing 1998) 0 9529333 1 4

LANGLEY, Martin & SMALL, Edwina. *The Trams of Plymouth: A 73 Years Story* (Ex Libris Press, Bradford on Avon 1990) 0 948578 25 4

MAGGS, Colin G. *Bath Tramways* Locomotion Papers No.52 (Oakwood Press, 2nd revised Edition 1992) 0 85361 392 3

Seaton Branch and Seaton Tramway Locomotion Papers No.182 (Oakwood Press 1992) 0 85361 425 3

MARSDEN, Barry M. *Tramtracks and Trolleybooms: Chesterfield Trams and Trolleybuses Part 2.* (Headstock Publications, Barnsley 1988) 0 951279 33 5

Glossop Tramways 1903-1927 (Foxline Publishing, Stockport 1991) 1 870119 12 6

MAUND, TB & JENKINS, Martin. *The Tramways of Birkenhead & Wallasey* (The Light Rail Transit Association 1987) 0 948106 03 4

MURRAY, Hugh. *The Horse Tramways of York* (The Light Rail Transit Association 1980) 0 900433 81 7

OAKLEY, ER. *The London County Council Tramways Volume 1: South London* (The London Tramways History Group 1989) 0 951300 10 5

The London County Council Tramways Volume 2: North London (The London Tramways History Group 1991) 0 951300 11 3

OAKLEY, ER & HOLLAND CE. *London Transport Tramways 1933-1953* (The London Tramways History Group 1998) 0 951300 12 1

PALMER, GS & TURNER, BR. *Blackpool by Tram* (The Transport Publishing Co. Revised Edition 1981) 0 903839 55 5

PALMER, Steve. *Blackpool & Fleetwood - 100 Years by Tram* (Platform 5 Publishing Ltd 1998) 1 902336 02 X

PICKLES, W. *The Tramways of Dewsbury and Wakefield* (The Light Rail Transit Association 1980) 0 900433 73 6

PRICE, JH. *The Tramways of Grimsby, Immingham & Cleethorpes* (The Light Rail Transit Association 1991) 0 948106 10 7

PROUDLOCK, Noel. *Leeds: A History of its Tramways*. (JND Proudlock, Leeds 1991) 0 951718 50 9

SAMBOURNE, RC. *Exeter, A Century of Public Transport* (Glasney Press, Falmouth 1976) 0 950282 53 7

SENIOR, John & OGDEN, Eric. *Metrolink* (The Transport Publishing Co. 1992) 0 86317 155 9

SHUTTLEWORTH, S. *The Lancaster and Morecambe Tramways* Locomotion Papers No.95 (Oakwood Press 1976)

SIMPSON, Frank D. *The Wolverton & Stony Stratford Trams* (The Omnibus Society 1981) 0 901307 42 4

SMEETON, CS. *London United Tramways Volume 1: Origins to 1912* (The Light Rail Transit Association/The Tramway & Light Railway Society 1995) 0 948106 13 1

  The London United Tramways Volume 2: 1913 to 1933 (The Light Rail Transit Association/The Tramway & Light Railway Society 2000) 0 948106 24 7

  The Metropolitan Electric Tramways Volume 1: Origins to 1920 (The Light Rail Transit Association 1984) 0 900433 94 9

  The Metropolitan Electric Tramways Volume 2: 1921 to 1933 (The Light Rail Transit Association 1986) 0 948106 00 X

SOPER, J. *Leeds Transport Volume 1: 1830 to 1902* (The Leeds Transport Historical Society 1985) 0 951028 00 6

  Leeds Transport Volume 2: 1902 to 1931 (The Leeds Transport Historical Society 1996) 0 9510280 1 4

STANIER, David, WEST, Keith & STANIER, Linda. *Trams and Buses in Burton 1903-1985* (Carlton Publishing, Derby 1991) 0 951756 90 7

STEWARD, Michael, GENT, John & STANNARD, Colin. *Tramlink Official Handbook* (Capital Transport 2000) 1 85414 222 4

SWINGLE, SL & TURNER, K. *The Kinver Light Railway* Locomotion Papers No.73 (Oakwood Press 2nd Edition 1987) 0 85361 333 8

  The Leamington & Warwick Tramways Locomotion Papers No.112 (Oakwood Press 1978)

TAYLOR, Clifford. *Rochdale's Tramways* (Manchester Transport Museum Society 1987) 0 900857 26 9

TURNER, Brian. *Blackpool to Fleetwood* (The Light Railway Transport League 1977) 0 900433 67 1

WARRINGTON TRANSPORT DEPT. *75 Years of Municipal Transport in Warrington* (Warrington Borough Council 1977)

WATTS, Eric. *Fares Please: The History of Passenger Transport in Portsmouth* (Milestone Publications, Portsmouth 1987) 0 903852 98 5

WEBB JS. *Black Country Tramways Volume 1: 1872-1912* (Author, Bloxwich 1974)

  Black Country Tramways Volume 2 (Author, Bloxwich 1976)

WEBB, Stanley & ADDENBROOKE, Paul. *A History of Wolverhampton Transport Volume 1: 1833-1930* (Birmingham Transport Historical Group/Uralia Press, Wolverhampton) 0 905103 07 6

WHITE, PM & STORER, JW. *Sixpenny Switchback* (JM Pearson & Son, Burton-on-Trent 1983) 0 907864 08 2

WILKINSON, Reg. *The Wantage Tramway* Locomotion Papers No.92 (Oakwood Press 2nd Revised Edition 1995) 0 85361 436 9

YEARSLEY, Ian & GROVES, Philip. *The Manchester Tramways* (The Transport Publishing Co. 1988) 0 86317 144 3

WELSH TRAMWAYS

ANDREWS, John F. *The Pwllheli & Llanbedrog Tramways* (D. Brown & Sons, South Wales 1995) 1 872808 40 9

BENYON, David H. *Swansea's Street Tramways* (Swansea Maritime and Industrial Museum 1994) 1 873524 04 8

BOYD, JIC. *Narrow Gauge Railways in North Caernarvonshire Volume 1: The West* The British Narrow Gauge Railway No.5 (Oakwood Press 1981) 0 85761 273 0

  Narrow Gauge Railways in North Caernarvonshire Volume 3 The British Narrow Gauge Railway No.5 (Oakwood Press 1986) 0 85361 328 1

GITTENS, Rob. *Rock & Roll to Paradise: the History of the Mumbles Railway* (Gower Press 1982) 0 85088 638 4

GOULD, David. *Cardiff's Electric Tramways* Locomotion Papers No.81 (Oakwood Press 2nd Edition 1996) 0 85361 487 3

GRIFFITHS, Geoff. *Llanelly Trolleybuses* (Trolleybooks 1992) 0 904235 15 7

LARGE, R. *Passenger Tramways of Pontypridd* Locomotion Papers No.106 (Oakwood Press 1977)

LEE, Charles E. *The Swansea & Mumbles Railway* Locomotion Papers No.50 (Oakwood Press Revised Edition 1977) 0 85361 381 8

MAGGS, Colin. *Newport Trams* Locomotion Papers No.105 (Oakwood Press 1977)

MILNER, WJ. *Rails Through the Sand* (RailRomances, Chester 1996) 1 900622 00 9

  The Glyn Valley Tramway (Oxford Publishing Co. 1984) 0 86093 286 9

TURNER, Keith. *North Wales Tramways* (David & Charles 1979) 0 7153 7769 8

  The Llandudno & Colwyn Bay Electric Railway Locomotion Papers No.187 (Oakwood Press 1993) 0 85361 450 4

SCOTTISH TRAMWAYS

BRASH, Ronald W. *The Tramways of Ayr* (NB Traction, Dundee 1983) 0 905069 19 6

BROTCHIE, AW & GRIEVES, RL. *Paisley's Trams & Buses: 'Eighties to 'Twenties* (NB Traction, Dundee 1986) 0 905069 25 0

  Paisley's Trams & Buses: 'Twenties to 'Eighties (NB Traction, Dundee 1988) 0 905069 26 9

  Dumbarton's Trams and Buses: (NB Traction, Dundee 1985) 0 905069 24 2

BROTCHIE, Alan W. *The Tramways of Falkirk* Tramways of Fife and The Forth Valley: Part 1 (NB Traction, Dundee 1975)

  The Wemyss and District Tramways Company Ltd Tramways of Fife and The Forth Valley: Part 3 (NB Traction, Dundee 1976)

  The Tramways of Kirkcaldy Tramways of Fife and The Forth Valley: Part 4 (NB Traction, Dundee 1978) 0 905069 00 9

  Stirling's Trams and Buses (NB Traction, Dundee 1991) 0 905069 28 5

  (Editor). *Lanarkshire's Trams* (NB Traction, Dundee 1993) 0 905069 29 3

CORMACK Ian L. *Tramways of Greenock, Gourock and Port Glasgow* (The Scottish Tramway Museum Society 1975)

  The Rothesay Tramways Company 1879-1949 (Scottish Tramway & Transport Society 1986) 0 900648 23 6

DEANS, Brian T. *Green Cars to Hurlford* (The Scottish Tramway Museum Society 1986) 0 900648 22 8

HUNTER, DLG. *Edinburgh's Transport Volume 1: The Early Years* (Mercat Press, Edinburgh 1992) 1 873644 02 7

  Edinburgh's Transport Volume 2: The Corporation Years 1919-1975 (Adam Gordon, Chetwode 1999) 1 874422 23 0

MITCHELL, MJ & SOUTER, IA. *The Aberdeen District Tramways* Public Transport in Aberdeen Volume 1 (NB Traction, Dundee 1983) 0 905069 20 X

  The Aberdeen Suburban Tramways (NB Traction, Dundee 1980) 0 905069 14 5

ROBERTSON, Struan Jno T. *The Glasgow Horse Tramways* (Scottish Tramway & Transport Society 2000) 0 900648 25 2